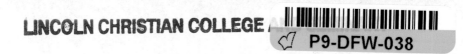

Contact Linguistics

Contact Linguistics

Bilingual Encounters and Grammatical Outcomes

CAROL MYERS-SCOTTON

OXFORD UNIVERSITY PRESS

OXFORD
UNIVERSITY PRESS

Great Clarendon Street, Oxford OX2 6DP

Oxford University Press is a department of the University of Oxford.
It furthers the University's objective of excellence in research, scholarship,
and education by publishing worldwide in

Oxford New York

Auckland Bangkok Buenos Aires Cape Town Chennai
Dar es Salaam Delhi Hong Kong Istanbul Karachi Kolkata
Kuala Lumpur Madrid Melbourne Mexico City Mumbai
Nairobi São Paulo Shanghai Taipei Tokyo Toronto

Oxford is a registered trade mark of Oxford University Press
in the UK and in certain other countries

Published in the United States
By Oxford University Press Inc., New York

First published 2002

British Library Cataloguing in Publication Data
Data available

Library of Congress Cataloging in Publication Data
Data applied for

ISBN 0-19-829952-4
ISBN 0-19-829953-2 (pbk.)

3 5 7 9 10 8 6 4

Typeset in Minion
by SNP Best-set Typesetter Ltd., Hong Kong
Printed in Great Britain
on acid-free paper by
Biddles Ltd., King's Lynn, Norfolk

Contents

Symbols and Abbreviations vii
Preface xi

1. Introduction 1
   - 1.1. Introduction 1
   - 1.2. General premises in the theoretical orientation 8
   - 1.3. The Matrix Language Frame model and its setting 10
   - 1.4. The 4-M model 16
   - 1.5. The Abstract Level model 18
   - 1.6. Implications for a model of language production 23
   - 1.7. How proficiency figures in 25
   - 1.8. Competence and performance 26
   - 1.9. Summary 28
   - 1.10. The coming chapters 28
2. The Roots of Language Contact 30
   - 2.1. Introduction 30
   - 2.2. Factors favoring adding a language 31
   - 2.3. Bilingual competence 33
   - 2.4. The costs and rewards of bilingualism in the international arena 33
   - 2.5. Motivations to become bilingual 36
   - 2.6. Bilingualism and language-use patterns 40
   - 2.7. Language shift 48
   - 2.8. Structural results of bilingualism and language shift 51
3. Explaining the Models and Their Uses 53
   - 3.1. Introduction 53
   - 3.2. Clarifying the MLF model 54
   - 3.3. Content vs. system morphemes 69
   - 3.4. What the 4-M model adds 73
   - 3.5. The MLF model plus the 4-M model: revisiting classic codeswitching 86
   - 3.6. The Abstract Level model further explicated 96
   - 3.7. Codeswitching and convergence 104
   - 3.8. Conclusion 105
4. Considering Problematic Codeswitching Data and Other Approaches 108
   - 4.1. Introduction 108
   - 4.2. Bare forms 113
   - 4.3. Nouns and their determiners when Arabic is the Matrix Language 113
   - 4.4. Another view: Uniform structure 119

4.5. Bare nouns without Bantu noun-class prefixes 127
4.6. Explaining other codeswitching phenomena with the Uniform Structure Principle 131
4.7. Other lexical categories and system morphemes 132
4.8. Another case of bare elements: the 'do' construction 134
4.9. About Embedded Language islands 139
4.10. Borrowing vs. codeswitching 153
4.11. Conclusion 161

5. Convergence and Attrition 164
5.1. Introduction 164
5.2. Convergence areas 173
5.3. Individual attrition: a social and psycholinguistic view 179
5.4. An overview of attrition studies 184
5.5. Supporting my own theoretical assumptions 193
5.6. Conclusion 229

6. Lexical Borrowing, Split (Mixed) Languages, and Creole Formation 233
6.1. Introduction 233
6.2. Lexical borrowing 234
6.3. Mixed languages > split languages 246
6.4. Michif 254
6.5. Mednyj Aleut 258
6.6. Ma'a (Mbugu) 265
6.7. Summary: mixed/split languages 270
6.8. Creole formation 271
6.9. Conclusion: from lexical borrowing to creole formation 293

7. Concluding Remarks: The Out of Sight in Contact Linguistics 295
7.1. Concluding remarks 295
7.2. Hypotheses for further testing 296
7.3. Lexical borrowing and codeswitching 299
7.4. Content morphemes 299
7.5. Early system morphemes 300
7.6. Late system morphemes 301
7.7. Multimorphemic elements 305
7.8. Insufficient congruence 306
7.9. Change in frame requirements 306
7.10. Levels of abstract lexical structure 307
7.11. Split (mixed) languages 307
7.12. Creole formation 308
7.13. Conclusion 309

References 311
Substantive Index 331
Index of Authors 336
Index of Languages 340

Symbols and Abbreviations

Note: some grammatical categories are referred to by two different abbreviations; this duplication occurs because the abbreviations that are in the original source are given.

[ ]	indicates broad phonetic transcription
/ /	indicates phonemic transcriptin
1, 2, 3	1st, 2nd, 3rd person
*	not grammatically well-formed
4-M	four types of morpheme
ABL	ablative
ABS	absolutive
ABSOL	absolute
ACC, ACCUS	accusative case
ADJ	adjective
AdjP	adjective phrase
AE	American English
AFFIRM	affirmative
AFFIX	affix
Agr	agreement
ANT	anterior
AOR	aorist
APPL	applied
ART	article
ASP	aspect
ASSOC	associative
CIA	Central Intelligence Agency
CL	noun class
CLASSIF	classifier
CLI	clitic
COMIT	comitative
Comp	complementizer
CONDIT	conditional
CONJ	conjunction
CONN	connective
CONSEC	consecutive
COP	copula
CP	projection of complementizer
CR	cognitive representation
CVCV	consonant–vowel–consonant–vowel

D, DET	determiner
DAT	dative
DEF	definite article
DEM	demonstrative
DERIV	derivational affix
DNG	definiteness–number–gender
DNP	determiner noun phrase
DP	determiner phrase
EL	embedded language
EMPH	emphatic
Eng	English
ESG	East Sutherland Gaelic
F, FEM	feminine
FI	full interpretation
FOC	focus
FOOT	foot feature
FUT	Future
FV	final vowel
GB	government and binding model
GEN	genitive
GER	gerund
GPSG	generalized phrase structure grammar
HAB	habitual
Head	head feature
HORT	hortative
HPSG	head phrase structure grammar
IFOTT	Institute for Functional Research into Language and Language Use
ILLAT	illative
IMP	imperative, imperfect
IMPER	imperative
IMPERF	imperfective
IMPERS	impersonal
INDEF	indefinite
INDOBJ	indirect object
INF, INFIN	infinitive
Infl	inflection
INSTR	instrumental
INT	interjection
INTRANS	intransitive
IO	indirect object
IP	inflectional phrase
L1	first language

L2	second language
LA	language attriters
LC	language competence
LOC	locative
LOC16	locative noun class 16
M, MASC	masculine
MA	Moroccan Arabic
ML	Matrix Language
MLF	matrix language frame model
MP	masculine plural
MSA	monolingual structure approach
MULT	multiple objects
N-GEN	noun—genitive case
N-POSS	noun—possessive case
NEG	negative
NEUT	neutral gender
NOM	nominative case
NONPST	non-past
NP	noun phrase
O, OBJ	object
OE	Old English
OSV	object–subject–verb
OVS	object–verb–subject
P, PL	plural
PART	participle
PASS	passive
PAST	past
PERF	perfect, perfective
PF	phonetic form
PG	Pennsylvania German
PM	predicate marker
POSS	possessive
POSTPOS	postposition
PP	prepositional phrase
PREP	preposition, prepositional
PRES	present
PREV	preverb
PROG	progressive
PRT	past participle
PREDM	predicate marker
PRET	preterite
PST	past
REFL	reflexive

REL	relative
S	sentence, singular
S-bar	sentence-bar
S(Aux)VO	subject–auxiliary–verb–object
S, SG	singular
SM	singular masculine
SOV	subject–object–verb
SUB	subject
SUBJUNC	subjunctive
SV	stem vowel
T	tense
TA	tense-agreement marker
TAG	Tree Adjoining Grammar
TI	transitive inanimate verb
TL	target language
TMA	tense–mode–aspect particle
TOP	topic, topicalizer
TP	tense phrase
TRANS	transitive
UG	universal grammar
USP	Uniform Structure Principle
V	verb
V2	second verb in clause
VN	verbal noun
VSO	verb–subject–object
VP	verb phrase
XP	any maximal projection

Preface

For me, the amount of intellectual activity (and the controversy, too!) that has emerged in the study of grammatical aspects of language contact in the last decade makes the content of this volume potentially exciting, even galvanizing. But I'm aware this volume won't be everyone's cup of tea. First, it has a theoretical rather than a descriptive bent. Those linguists studying contact who say we need caution and 'more data' before any explanations/conclusions can be attempted may well not be satisfied with my arguments—although I support my arguments with many examples from many languages. Second, structural outcomes with bilingual language are not always simple. Consequently, the arguments are often necessarily very involved and this may well discourage those readers with a new interest in bilingual data—although I try to make the text very accessible in various ways (e.g. I limit abbreviations, repeat premises of the models, etc.). Third, I have no illusions that I'll convince all of even those dedicated readers who persist that I'm 'right' in all my claims. Certainly, they will find some of my claims to be radical, such as the import and scope I claim for my Uniform Structure Principle, or my argument about how the mechanisms of incorporating grammatical forms from one language in another differ from those for lexical borrowing. Fourth, other students of contact will want to anchor any explanations of grammatical outcomes more firmly in the social setting than I have. I readily acknowledge the role of social factors in influencing why these outcomes differ from one type of contact phenomena to another (e.g. why creoles do not just represent lexical borrowing and also are different from split (mixed) languages). But my basic argument is that not just 'anything structural' can happen in contact situations. The general principles and processes at work provide a set of options, but a limited set. All this is in line with my premise that—viewed through the lens of such generalizations—grammatical outcomes in contact situations are not all that surprising and certainly not unique; it is supporting this claim that makes the study of contact phenomena appealing for me.

I hope many readers will agree that this quest is engaging and find this volume worth the read. The main contingent of intended readers includes advanced students, especially of linguistics, and faculty from any of the disciplines concerned with bilingualism and language contact. The volume is also relevant to linguists who study theories of morphology and syntax because I argue that what happens in contact phenomena tells us something about how language (with a big L) is organized. Those psycholinguists who study language production should also find data and arguments to interest them. To repeat what I've written elsewhere, contact phenomena offer an empirical window on how language 'works'. This is an especially transparent window because contact data are readily available for analysis and because when two or more varieties are in contact, their structures are often exposed in a way not obvious when a language is examined through monolingual data alone.

However, if you expect a totally comprehensive volume, you will be disappointed. First, I include only a short chapter about the sociopolitical and psychological factors that promote bilingualism and that therefore—indirectly—promote the use of two or more varieties in the same structure or the influence of one or more of these varieties on the others. As I've indicated, grammatical outcomes of these contacts are my main subject. However, I don't cover *all* grammatical outcomes nor do I offer encyclopedic coverage of those outcomes that are considered. With the coverage I do provide I aim to achieve my main goal: to argue that the same set of principles and processes explains all contact phenomena. Further, these principles and processes are apparent in language in general.

When did I get interested in bilingualism and grammatical outcomes of contact between speakers and their languages? Accidental turns in my life made the difference. First, on something of a lark I spent a year studying French in Paris after my undergraduate days and enjoyed grammatical aspects of the experience as well as the ambience. Then, a few years later, I found myself in Madison, Wisconsin, with the University of Wisconsin down the street. There I discovered that linguistics was a discipline and was successful in receiving a United States government fellowship to study critical languages. I went down the list and selected Swahili, reasoning that linguists should study other than Indo-European languages if possible. Later, that fellowship and a Ford Foundation grant took me to Tanzania for eight months where I did my dissertation research on Swahili verbs and their derivational extensions. The next significant stop was Makerere University in Kampala, Uganda, where I was the first instructor in their new Linguistics and African Languages Department. Now I was truly immersed in language contact, doing research on patterns of language use in a multilingual housing estate, arming myself for the experience by reading up on what sociolinguistics there was then, as well as sociology and anthropology, none of which I had studied before. More than twenty years later I returned to Uganda in the summer of 1995 to do research on codeswitching. In between, I taught at the University of Nairobi for a year and lived in Lagos, Nigeria, before returning to the United States. In the 1980s I made research trips to Malaŵi (I co-authored a textbook on Chicheŵa for the Peace Corps) and Zimbabwe (where I collaborated with Janice Bernsten on English lexical borrowing into Shona), and to South Africa in 1995. I also returned to Kenya on several research trips in the late 1970s and in the 1980s. My two 1993 volumes on codeswitching (*Social Motivations for Codeswitching: Evidence from Africa* and *Duelling Languages: Grammatical Structure in Codeswitching*) rely heavily on 1988 data from Nairobi, Kenya. Among research assistants who gathered data, I am especially indebted to Shem Lusimba Mbira, a Kenyan of the Luyia ethnic group, who began assisting me with research in Kampala in 1970 and continued to work with me for the next twenty years.

My early research and writings largely dealt with the social side of multilingualism: I wrote about patterns of language use and language policy. When I considered codeswitching, I was interested in the social and psychological motivations for switching, not the grammatical structure. Then, in 1988, I discovered that others were studying the grammar of codeswitching, but I found their constraints did not fit my data. I went back to my original training in morphology and syntax and joined the fray. Although I maintain an interest in linguistic choices as carriers of social and psychological messages, I am more absorbed today with the morphosyntactic aspects of contact phenomena. I developed the Matrix Language Frame (MLF) model to explain distributions in my African data, but also claimed that the premises and principles of that model have general applicability beyond my own data to any corpus qualifying as what I now call classic codeswitching. Meeting up with Janice L. Jake in the early 1990s helped tip my focus to the morphosyntax of codeswitching because of her training in generative syntax. We did research together under a three-year NSF grant in the mid 1990s, the source of some of the codeswitching data reported in this volume. Next, we developed the 4-M model and the Abstract Level model together. We've also collaborated on field research at home and abroad, and have produced a number of articles and many conference presentations. Seeing how the premises of the MLF model apply beyond codeswitching—especially in concert with these two new models—pushed me to look at other types of contact phenomena. Jan Jake and I edited a special issue (2000) of the *International Journal of Bilingualism* consisting of articles by my former students that all use the three models (MLF, 4-M, and Abstract Level) to explain data beyond codeswitching.

At the University of South Carolina, I was fortunate during the 1990s and early 2000s to have a number of excellent graduate students; they did field work (largely in South Carolina) and wrote dissertations in contact linguistics that employed these models. They include Janet Fuller (convergence in Pennsylvania German varieties), Longxing Wei (morphological aspects of Interlanguage among Chinese and Japanese learners of English in second language acquisition), Maha Okasha (codeswitching and generational differences in Palestinian Arabic/English codeswitching), Agnes Bolonyai (codeswitching and attrition among Hungarian/English bilingual children in the United States), Steve Gross (codeswitching and attrition after forty years in the United States among German/English immigrants), Elena Schmitt (codeswitching and attrition among Russian/English bilingual child immigrants in the United States), Paola Sarullo (convergence between Italian and French in Valle d'Aosta), and Sue Jenkins (convergence on New Ireland, Papua New Guinea). Also, Silvia Milian wrote an MA thesis (on Spanish/English codeswitching) and a current PhD student, Raquel Blazquez, is studying English/Spanish in Interlanguage among United States learners of Spanish.

In addition, the findings from a number of researchers elsewhere who were writing doctoral dissertations that included testing of the MLF model were very useful. I just mention three especially: Ad Backus, who studied generational differences in the Turkish/Dutch codeswitching of Turkish immigrants in Tilburg, the Netherlands; Jim Hlavac, who explored codeswitching and convergence among Croatian/English speaking young adults in Melbourne, Australia; and Emel Türker, who studied codeswitching and convergence among Turkish/Norwegian speaking young adults in Oslo, Norway.

Research data by all of these doctoral candidates enriched my understanding of contact phenomena in general. In particular, I couldn't have written the sections on attrition in this volume without the help of data and insights from my students, Agnes Bolonyai, Steve Gross, and Elena Schmitt. The luck of having all of these outstanding students was an impetus for my own work; they have become good colleagues today.

I've also been fortunate to be able to exchange data and ideas with a number of colleagues elsewhere; they are too numerous to list every one. I just mention those that I've corresponded with regarding my writing of this volume: Philip Baker, Kees de Bot, Louis Boumans, Gerrit Dimendaal, Helena Halmari, Michael Klein, Yaron Matras, Maarten Mous, Christina Bratt Paulston, Carol Pfaff, and Li Wei. None necessarily supports any or all of my ideas, but I appreciate their help. I also single out Rosalie Finlayson and Sarah Slabbert who made it possible for me to spend a month in South Africa in 1995 collaborating with them in the analysis of South African data on codeswitching; two articles resulted from that collaboration.

I also appreciate the invitations to a number of conferences from Australia to Norway to South Africa to talk about my ideas about constraints on codeswitching. These began in 1990 when Penelope Gardner-Chloros brought my work to the attention of the organizers of a European Science Foundation project on codeswitching; I participated in three ESF-sponsored conferences in the early 1990s. I especially appreciate the early encouragement from one of the organizers, Georges Lüdi of the University of Basel, who hosted a research visit from Jan Jake and me in 1994.

Finally, of course, I'm ever so grateful to Jan Jake for more than ten years of collaboration. Without the help of her amazing intellectual acumen and encyclopedic knowledge of languages, I would have had less to say about contact linguistics. Perhaps more important, I would have learned less, had fewer ideas, and enjoyed the ride much less.

1

Introduction

1.1. Introduction

This is an investigation of what happens to the grammatical structure of languages when their speakers are bilingual and their speech brings their two (or more) languages into contact.[1] The volume provides (i) an overview of language contact research, but one more thorough in some areas than others; (ii) details on current research about language contact, taking some account of the work of others, but largely illustrated in terms of my own models; and (iii) a research agenda in the sense that the discussion indicates directions for further research.

Overall, contact linguistics is a little-studied area of linguistics, partly because most linguistic research is done on one language at a time, and regrettably often only on English. Further, the fiction is typically maintained that whether the speakers of a language are monolingual or bilingual has no significant bearing on the form of the variety under analysis. Nor do most linguists consider that how two languages come together (i.e. what options are possible) can lead to important insights into the very object of their investigations, abstract linguistic structure, or I-language (Chomsky 1995).

The effects of bilingualism on one or more of the languages of bilinguals can be either overt (i.e. obvious at the surface level) or covert (i.e. indirectly recognizable at the abstract level). But even bilingual speakers themselves are often unconscious of any effects, whether overt or covert. When speakers borrow a word from another language into their first language for an object or concept new to their culture, they must be overtly aware that their lexicon has been enlarged—at least at the time of the borrowing. Shona, the major Bantu language in Zimbabwe, has borrowed many words from English. Shona speakers came in contact with the English language during the colonial period when Zimbabwe (as Southern Rhodesia) was a British colony. Example (1) illustrates *ovhataimi* 'overtime', obviously a borrowing from English into Shona for a new way to look at one's working schedule in modern African society.[2]

[1] Throughout this volume, *bilinguals* refers to persons who speak two *or more* languages.

[2] The example also contains a reference to time, also a borrowed form (*wan oklok* 'one o'clock'), but not for a new object or concept. Probably because they are much more brief, English words for numbers are frequently preferred over their Shona counterparts.

(1) to-zo-pedza na **wan oklok**. . . . kana pasina kuti ndinenge ndashanda **ovhataimi** [ovataim] . . .
'we finish at one o'clock. . . . if I don't work overtime . . .

(Shona; Bernsten 1990: 128)

But many cases of how language contact affects speakers seem to pass unnoticed. For example, many speakers who codeswitch between two languages in the same sentence are not even aware of this very overt evidence of contact. Examples (2)–(4) illustrate such codeswitching. Example (2) comes from a conversation including Swahili/English codeswitching between two friends in Nairobi, Kenya, who do not share the same first language. Note the time adverbial *anytime* from English as well as the infinitival form *borrow* that is inflected with an object prefix. Inflecting verbs from one language with affixes from the other participating language is common in some data sets, but not in others; some possible reasons are discussed in Chapter 4.

(2)

Wewe	u-nge-rudish-a	hiyo,	halfu **anytime**
you	2S-CONDIT-return-FV[3]	DEM-CL9	then anytime

u-ki-hitaji	u-na-wez-a	ku-j-a	ku-i-**borrow**
2S-PROG-need	2S-NONPST-be able-FV	INF-come-FV	INF-OBJ-borrow

'If you would return that thing, then anytime you are needing [it] you can come and borrow it.'

(No. 34, Myers-Scotton Nairobi corpus 1988)

Example (3) comes from a Moroccan Arabic speaker who is an immigrant in the Netherlands. He switches to a Dutch noun *omgeving* 'environment' in a sentence that is otherwise all in Moroccan Arabic. Singly-occurring nouns are the most commonly switched elements in codeswitching corpora. Note that the inflected possessive form modifying this Dutch noun (*dyal-i* 'my') is in Arabic.

(3)

ah,	maši	bhal	l-mġarba	lli	ka-ne-ʕref-hŭm	ana
oh	NEG	like	DEF-Moroccan/PL	REL	ASP-1S-know-3PL	1S

f	l- . . . eh	**omgeving**	dyal-i
in	DEF-er	environment	of-1S

'Oh it's not at all like the Moroccans I know in my . . . er . . . environment.'

(Moroccan Arabic/Dutch; Boumans 1998: 190)

Example (4) illustrates not simply a single-word switch but a switch of a full prepositional phrase. The PP from French (*à front de rue*) occurs in a sen-

[3] FV = 'final vowel'. Words in Bantu languages normally show a CVCV pattern and verb forms end in a final vowel; however, it is difficult to attach a specific or independent meaning to this vowel. Usually, final *-a* occurs as part a set of affixes on a verb in the indicative mood.

tence framed by Brussels Dutch. This example comes from a conversation in Brussels.

(4) Je vijf of zes waren er, want die **à front de rue** waren
yes five or six were there for who at end of street were
'Yes, there were five or six, (for) who were at the street front.'

(Brussels Dutch/French; Treffers-Daller 1994: 223)

When the effect is even more covert (e.g. all the morphemes still come from one language), speakers are even less aware of it. For example, many languages have two different words for different types of 'knowing' (knowing a fact and knowing a person). But if such a language is influenced by a language that is more dominant in the speech community and this second language has only one word for 'knowing' (such as English), speakers may begin to use their 'knowing' words in free variation—at times mimicking the more dominant language. Example (5) illustrates just such an intrusion from English into the German utterances of a speaker of Pennsylvania German, a variety of German spoken in some Mennonite communities in the eastern United States. People in the community studied who speak a variety of Pennsylvania German are all fluent in English. Standard German distinguishes between *wisse(n)* 'to know a fact' and *kenne(n)* 'to be familiar with'. In this example, the speaker uses *wisse* for both 'to know a fact' and 'to know a person'.

(5) Ich hab-e sei Nome **ge-wiss-t.** Ich hab-e ihn net **ge-wiss-t,**
I have-1s his name PART-know I have-1s him/ACCUS not PART-know
net really.
not really
'I knew his name. I didn't know him, not really.'

(Pennsylvania German; Fuller 1997: 140)

Note that when referring to the use of two languages in the same clause, I use the term 'codeswitching', not 'mixing'. Like Haugen (1950*b*: 210) I think labeling such a phenomenon as 'mixing' has distinct disadvantages. In reference to 'mixing' as a term, Haugen writes, 'As a description of the process it might seem to have a certain vividness that justifies its use, but on closer inspection it shows disadvantages which led later linguistics, such as Sapir and Bloomfield, to abandon it. . . . Mixing implies the creation of an entirely new entity and the disappearance of both constituents; it also suggests a jumbling of a more or less haphazard nature' (210–11). (In Chapter 6 I discuss what are called mixed languages in the literature. Systematic study of these languages is relatively new, and perhaps a different name will catch on. I suggest 'split languages'. Certainly, those who study these varieties recognize that they are systematically organized, not accidental melanges.)

1.1.1. *The broad focus of bilingualism as a topic*

However, it is not the bilingual speakers themselves who are my main concern, interesting as their perceptions about their patterns of use may be. Rather, this volume, with its title of *Contact Linguistics*, centers on their bilingual speech as a reflection of the abstract structures of their languages, as well as linguistic competence in a general sense. I use the rubric 'contact phenomena' as an umbrella for the different structural outcomes in the languages involved and I use the rubric 'contact linguistics' for the analysis of these outcomes. That is, I give contact linguistics a more limited and specialized scope than do some researchers (cf. von Goebl, Nelde, Stary, and Wölck 1996, Nelde 1997). Nelde (1997) points out that the term contact linguistics was introduced at the First World Congress on Language Contact and Conflict held in Brussels in June 1979. While contact linguistics may have been intended by some as an umbrella for all processes associated with language contact, in fact the emphasis under this rubric has been on contact resulting in sociopolitical conflicts of various types. In contrast, the present study has an entirely different focus; the main interest is the lexicon and morphosyntactic aspects of the grammar in outcomes such as those in the examples. Of course, the phonology of languages also can be affected in contact situations; but that is not a topic here.

Contact phenomena include everything from the borrowing of words for concepts and objects new to the borrowing community (e.g. *beret* as a new word in English for a type of hat, new to English speakers, and worn especially in France) to changes in the morphosyntactic system of one of the languages (e.g. prepositions replace derivational verbal suffixes to signal various relations between elements). Such phenomena also include more radical changes, such as the attrition or total loss of one language as speakers shift to another language as their main medium. Even more radical is the development of pidgin and creole languages in a multilingual situation where speakers do not share any one common language. Another outcome not always considered as a contact phenomenon but mentioned here is Interlanguage, the grammar(s) of learners of a second language as they move toward learning the target second language. Its analysis is beyond the scope of this volume, but see Jake and Myers-Scotton (1997*b*), Jake (1998), or Wei (2000*a*) for analysis in line with the theoretical approach followed here.

As a topic, I see contact linguistics as different from bilingualism, a much broader topic that typically includes language contact and may include contact linguistics. The major difference is that bilingualism emphasizes the study of bilinguals themselves. That is, bilingualism has two main concerns: (i) the social factors involved in how people become bilingual and the ways in which they allocate their different languages to different uses, and (ii) childhood acquisition of two languages and organization of two languages in the brain. Further, the study of bilingualism also may include the study of provisions for bilinguals in a nation, i.e. language policy, especially regarding the rights of citizens and bilingual education.

Thus, in its study of bilinguals as members of communities, bilingualism is akin to sociolinguistics and the sociology of language, and in its study of bilinguals as individuals and their cognition, bilingualism is akin to psycholinguistics. While of course contact linguistics has affinities with both psycholinguistics and sociolinguistics, it is something else. It deals specifically with the grammatical structure of the languages of bilinguals.

1.1.2. *The more specific focus of contact linguistics*

Why study such phenomena, and codeswitching in particular? As I will argue, what outcomes are possible in contact phenomena are *empirical windows on the structures of the language in general.* Some linguists like to say that to speak of 'language contact' is erroneous, because it is the speakers who are in contact, not the languages. I beg to differ on where to place the importance. Of course what language contact typically involves is that speakers of one language meet speakers of another language and, then—for various reasons—one group may learn the other's language, although not necessarily in a target-like manner. While the circumstances of contact between speakers and the issue of who learns whose language are worth studying, what is significant to the structural linguist is that the two languages abut each other. That is, the languages are in contact in the sense they are adjacent in their speakers' mental lexicon and can impinge on each other in production.

Because of this juxtaposition of two languages and because of the availability of large corpora, contact data offer otherwise unavailable tests of hypotheses about the linguistic knowledge that underlies language (with a big L). Also, findings about the grammatical structure of languages in contact may reinforce existing analyses of individual languages, or may even offer new insights not available when a language is studied only on its own.

I discuss language contact in terms of models of language competence and production developed in cooperation with my associates, especially Jan Jake (e.g. Myers-Scotton and Jake 1995, 2000*a*, 2000*b*, 2001). In a general sense, evidence from contact phenomena suggests to us how parts of the mental lexicon may be organized and how different types of elements may be salient and accessed at different stages in production. More specifically, what is possible when languages come together tells us something about how certain aspects of grammatical structure may be bundled differently at the abstract level in one language in contrast with another. Thus, because of its concerns with the structural nature of language, contact linguistics belongs with theoretical studies of grammar; it can contribute to, and challenge, theories of syntax and morphology as well as phonology.[4]

[4] Roeper (1999) devotes a lengthy article to arguing that all linguistic phenomena are, at base, bilingual because children go through successive grammars in arriving at their adult grammar and mature speakers have different grammars for different uses within the same language.

However, as already indicated, only the morphosyntactic aspects of contact are discussed here.

1.1.3. *A theoretical, but limited, approach*

Thus, this study has a clearly theoretical orientation. Yet, I present many descriptive details in some cases of language contact, and treat a number of different contact phenomena. Still, I do not aim for an exhaustive survey of such outcomes. Earlier treatments in various handbooks (e.g. the handbook, *Kontaktlinguistic/Contact Linguistics* edited by von Goebl, Nelde, Stary, and Wölck 1996) and the recent volume by Sarah Thomason (2000) offer many more details. For some contact phenomena, I offer more of a 'survey of the literature' than for others. For example, I do this more for attrition than I do for codeswitching. The reason is that I cover the background on codeswitching up to 1990 rather thoroughly in Myers-Scotton (1993*a* [1997]). (However, I do review some other current approaches to codeswitching in Chapter 4.) Overall, more than offering extensive descriptions of data, I aim at making interpretative statements and explanations. But I have no illusions that what I offer is the 'last word'.

My main intention is to argue that the seemingly diverse types of language contact can be discussed synthetically and are amenable to unified explanations. That is, I will propose that the same abstract principles and processes structure all contact phenomena, even though the details of how they are played out in the various phenomena differ (e.g. first-language (L1) attrition compared with codeswitching or second-language (L2) acquisition compared with creole formation). What this volume offers, then, is a general treatment of the lexicon and morphosyntax of contact phenomena within a single perspective. At the same time, I aim to be fair and fairly comprehensive in reporting the main views of others that are relevant to understanding these phenomena.

The principles and processes that I refer to offer explanations for the underlying unity of contact phenomena. They are encapsulated in the models to be introduced shortly in this chapter. These models focus on the role of the mental lexicon as connecting a theory of grammar with language production and processing. This distinguishes the approach of this volume from approaches of most other language contact researchers; many focus on describing a contact phenomenon or labeling it, with the implicit view that such descriptions or labels (or typologies of labels) serve as explanations.

I propose to show how differences in structural patterns in contact phenomena depend on differences in the abstract nature of language in general and, sometimes, the participating languages specifically. Just like monolingual speech, bilingual speech is *not* best explainable in terms of surface configurations. At the same time, I recognize that the social and psycholinguistic factors that distinguish the milieu of one type of contact from another also make a difference in outcomes. However, the milieu influences selections from a set of structural options; it does not determine the set.

Throughout the discussions, the terms 'language' or 'linguistic variety' will be used interchangeably to identify the linguistic systems analyzed. These terms do not imply (i) that the examples portray the standard dialect of a language or (ii) that this dialect is necessarily the object of analysis or (iii) that linguistic systems are static and necessarily uniform. It hardly needs saying, but some critics miss the point that linguists usually refer to the objects of their investigation as 'languages' even when they are well aware that linguistic systems often cannot be pigeon-holed as this or that language. This is especially the case with contact phenomena.

Three models that are the basis for analyses of contact phenomena are introduced in this chapter. Some examples are included to make the models more comprehensible; however, the real utility of the models only becomes clear in succeeding chapters in which specific types of phenomena are analyzed in terms of the appropriate model or models.

Not all types of contact phenomena are analyzed; that is, I do not claim that this volume is entirely comprehensive. Nor do the analyses exhaust all there is to say about any particular phenomenon; this is especially true regarding my discussion of creoles. Rather, the goal of the analyses is to show how these models can provide a principled explanation for why certain structures occur in a specific phenomenon and for why others do not. Not all phenomena studied receive equal treatment. Not surprisingly, given the record of my interest in codeswitching, more space will be devoted to codeswitching than many other phenomena.[5] Codeswitching is a major subject in both Chapters 3 and 4.

Let me clarify terminology to be used in discussing structures within a language. I use the term 'bilingual speech' frequently. It refers to any utterance containing either actual surface-level morphemes or abstract lexical structure from more than one language. However, this term certainly does not refer *only* to utterances showing codeswitching—just because I have written extensively about codeswitching. Bilingual speech can refer to any type of contact phenomena; the context where it is used should make its referent clear.

Throughout this volume the terms 'constituent' and 'maximal projection' are both used for syntactic structures showing some hierarchical organization. All maximal projections are constituents, but not all constituents are maximal projections. A maximal projection includes the expansion of its head constituent to the phrasal level, resulting, for example, in NP. Therefore, for example, a single noun is a constituent, but not a maximal projection. The term 'maximal projection' highlights organizational aspects more than the term 'constituent' does. The point is that even though constituents also can show hierarchical structure, they do not necessarily have to be complete phrases (i.e. maximal projections).

[5] Contrary to what some imply, I do not think every contact phenomenon is a subspecies of codeswitching; however, I do argue that codeswitching is an important mechanism in many other contact phenomena, as is convergence.

'Constituent' was the main term used in Myers-Scotton (1993*a*); more use of 'maximal projection' now does not indicate any new orientation.

The term 'bilingual CP' is used as the unit of analysis in the volume. The term CP refers to the specific type of maximal projection or constituent, projection of Complementizer. The CP is at the highest level in a tree of syntactic structures. It follows that CPs contain other constituents or maximal projections, such as NPs, VPs, and the like. Both independent and dependent clauses are CPs. The motivation for using CP as the main unit of analysis is discussed further in Chapter 3.

The term 'classic codeswitching' refers to speech for which the speakers are proficient enough in the participating languages that they can produce well-formed monolingual utterances in the variety which becomes the source of what is called the Matrix Language (ML), the abstract morphosyntactic frame of bilingual utterances. They are also generally proficient enough in the other participating languages to do this.[6] Any general references to codeswitching are to classic codeswitching. However, another type of codeswitching may be more common in many communities.

This type of codeswitching is treated under a new term, 'composite codeswitching'. Utterances showing composite codeswitching include surface-level morphemes from two or more languages just as classic codeswitching does. However, composite codeswitching also shows convergence in regard to the source of some frame-building procedures, as well as in the features of the abstract grammatical structure in some lexemes. Composite codeswitching is defined in more detail and discussed in Chapter 3 and is a subject in Chapters 5 and 6.

1.2. General premises in the theoretical orientation

Four general principles guide the overall approach to all contact phenomena, not just codeswitching. (Of course, the parts of these principles that are not specific to bilingual speech also apply to monolingual data.) They are:

1. The Matrix Language Principle. There is always an analyzable or resolvable frame structuring the morphosyntax of any CP. This frame is called the Matrix Language. In bilingual speech, the participating languages never participate equally as the source of this Matrix Language.

2. The Uniform Structure Principle. A given constituent type in any language has a uniform abstract structure and the requirements of well-formedness for this constituent type must be observed whenever the constituent appears. In bilingual speech, the structures of the Matrix Language are always preferred, but some

[6] Classic codeswitching contrasts with other forms of contact phenomena in several ways: (i) in the relation between the Matrix Language as an abstract construct and the language that is the source of the Matrix Language and (ii) generally in the degree of bilingualism speakers have. Myers-Scotton (1993*a* [1997]) did not distinguish types of codeswitching, but it largely illustrates classic codeswitching.

Embedded Language structures are allowed if certain conditions are met. This principle is explained further in Chapter 4.

3. The Asymmetry Principle for Bilingual Frames. Bilingual speech is characterized by asymmetry in terms of the participation of the languages concerned. In what I now call classic codeswitching, only one of the participating languages is the source of the Matrix Language. In other contact phenomena (such as composite codeswitching), the Matrix Language may be a composite of abstract features from more than one language, but asymmetry still marks the contributory roles of the participating languages. This asymmetry is evidence of the universal drive in language to achieve uniformity in the structural frame of any variety, to avoid meaningless variation—although this outcome never entirely exists in any language. Still, the drive is always there, and in bilingual speech it is especially expressed as part of the movement toward the morphosyntactic dominance of one variety in the frame.

4. The Morpheme-Sorting Principle. All morphemes are not equal. This is an example of asymmetry of a different type. That is, at the abstract level of linguistic competence and production, there are different types of morphemes. In bilingual speech, the outcome of these abstract differences is that all the morphemes from the participating varieties do not have equal possibilities of occurrence.

Examples (6) and (7) illustrate the theoretical notion of Matrix Language in data sets showing classic codeswitching. In (6), an example from Chinese/English codeswitching, Chinese is the source of the Matrix Language or morphosyntactic frame. First, the word order clearly comes from Chinese (note sentence-final position of the verb *finish* in sentence 1 and of *jiaoshangqu* 'turn in' in sentence 2). Second, the other elements of the frame (function words and inflections) come from Chinese as well. Only what I call content morphemes (*paper, finish, term paper, slow*) come from English.

(6) ni **paper** hai mei **finish** a? wode san-fen
you paper yet not finish PART/AFFIRM my three-CLASSIF
term paper qiantian yijin
term paper the day before yesterday already
jiaoshangqu le. ni tai **slow** le.
turn in PART/PERF you too slow PART/AFFIRM
'You haven't finished your paper yet? My three term papers were already turned in the day before yesterday. You are too slow.'

(Chinese/English; Wei 1998 Chinese/English corpus)

Example (7) also illustrates the Matrix Language concept clearly, showing the asymmetry of the participating languages as sources of frame-building elements. That is, all inflections come from only one of the participating languages, Turkish. The example also illustrates the Morpheme-Sorting Principle because it shows that not all Dutch morphemes may occur freely; only Dutch-content morphemes occur (the nouns *student* and *baan* 'job' and the verb *afstuderen* 'graduate').

(7) coğu **student**-ler böyle ya, ooh, mesela bu sene **afstuder-en**
many student-PL such or INT e.g. this year graduate-INF
yap-ar-sa iyi **baan-ı** var
do-AOR-CONDIT(3S) good job-POSS is/EXIST
'Many students, it's like this, you know, if they graduate this year for example, they'll have a good job.'

(Turkish/Dutch; Backus 1999*a*: 261)

1.3. The Matrix Language Frame model and its setting

The Matrix Language Frame model (MLF) specifically was designed to explain structural configurations found in codeswitching, specifically classic codeswitching. However, with some modifications, my associates and I, as well as others, now use features of the model in offering explanations for structures in a wide variety of contact phenomena, from Interlanguage among second language learners of English to child bilingual acquisition, to child bilingual attrition and shift, to creole formation. My purpose here is just to introduce the MLF model in its near-original form. In Chapters 3 and 4, the model, as it applies to codeswitching, is updated from its 1993 and 1997 versions, and in Chapter 4 the model also is compared with other approaches to explaining the grammatical structure of codeswitching. In later chapters, the model is applied to other contact phenomena.

1.3.1. *Codeswitching as a subject*

Until recently, and arguably even today, most linguists who pay attention to codeswitching have been concerned about the social motivations for choosing to use one linguistic variety rather than another 'to say the same thing'. Few linguists who do not study codeswitching think of it otherwise; they assume that research on codeswitching automatically means sociolinguistic research. The evidence is that all conference papers analyzing codeswitching data are likely to be placed together, as if all studies of bilingual data belong with studies correlating social factors and dialectal variation—just because they all deal with more than one linguistic variety. However, as I try to make clear in writing this book, there are two sides to codeswitching research. There is the more widely recognized study of codeswitching as a social resource, something that I think of as a study of how individual speakers exploit their several languages (or dialects) to signal their perceptions of themselves and their interpersonal relations with others. I see this as the sociopragmatic side of codeswitching (cf. Myers-Scotton 1993*b*, Myers-Scotton 1998*b*, Myers-Scotton and Bolonyai 2001).

But there is also the study of the grammatical structure of codeswitching, an enterprise in which the social uses are not central and, in some cases, are not even mentioned. In Chapter 2, interrelations between the codeswitching structures a speaker chooses and their social messages are discussed. However, the rest of the volume devotes much more attention to showing how codeswitching patterns can be studied in regard to permissible grammatical structure and how such constraints relate to general linguistic structure. Both subjects are very inviting, not to mention worthy of study; however, in this book I find more challenges in what can be said about the grammatical structure of codeswitching and other contact phenomena. That said, I still side with the more socially oriented researchers who believe that study of language in use has essential theoretical value. For example, while grammaticality judgements (i.e. speaker intuitions) may have their uses, there is no substitute for studying naturally occurring data in regard to bilingual clauses.

1.3.2. *Codeswitching as the medium of inferential messages*

The expression *le mot juste* reflects what many ordinary speakers know: the medium—whether a single word, a grammatical construction, a style, or a language—makes a difference in the inferential message of any utterance. The relevant inferential messages here are social; they refer to the speaker's self-presentation, especially self in relation to others. Speakers who are able to switch languages have an additional resource to express such messages because of the sociopsychological associations that a community typically gives to the different languages in its collective linguistic repertoire.

Blom and Gumperz (1972), a study of a form of codeswitching in Norway published in a widely read sociolinguistics reader (Gumperz and Hymes 1972), was the main introduction to codeswitching that most linguistics students had, even though this was a study of dialect switching rather than language switching. Later works by Gumperz and others (e.g. Gumperz 1982, (Myers) Scotton and Ury 1977) promote the idea that codeswitching was worth studying because it so clearly shows how one variety conveys a different social message from another—after all, switches had to 'mean something'. Today, with the advent of the European Union and the renewed floods of immigrants to many European countries, but also to the United States, Canada, and Australia, hearing people speak two languages in the same conversation is no longer exotic. Recent sociolinguistic studies of bilingual communities, such as Zentella's (1997) study of Spanish-speakers of Puerto Rican origin in New York (who also speak English), devote much attention to how alternating languages in different settings or switching within the same interaction is a conversational resource.

At the same time, the study of grammatical structure in codeswitching has flowered. Even in the early days of codeswitching study, some linguists considered how codeswitching was grammatically possible (Hasselmo 1970, 1972, was one of the first; some of his insights still hold today). However, it was not until the 1980s and, even more so, the 1990s, that the structural nature of codeswitching was seriously investigated by more than a handful of linguists. But the early view of codeswitching has stuck in many minds: codeswitching is seen as an interesting social use of language, to be sure, but not necessarily as a phenomenon whose study can contribute to the serious enterprise of investigating the nature of linguistic structure. One goal of this volume is to change such views.

1.3.3. *Studying grammatical structure in codeswitching*

The Matrix Language Frame model appeared in the wave of interest in the grammatical structure of codeswitching in the last ten years. It was first fully explicated in a book-length study in 1993 as 'a model to account for the structures in intrasentential codeswitching' (Myers-Scotton 1993*a*: 5). In less complete forms, the model had been taking shape in the late 1980s in conference presentations and more conference papers and publications on the model followed in the early 1990s. In its 1993 version, the MLF model did accomplish much of what it set out to do; that is, the Matrix Language hypothesis and the two principles derived from it, as well as the Embedded Language Island hypothesis and the Blocking hypothesis, offer an explanatory account for nearly all of the data in intrasentential codeswitching in the literature. Of course, there are some counterexamples; Myers-Scotton (2001*a*) responds to representative examples.[7] (The discussions in Chapters 3 and 4 are also relevant.)

However, it is no surprise that the volume *Duelling Languages* (Myers-Scotton 1993*a*) was not the last word on the model. First, a lengthy co-authored article (Myers-Scotton and Jake 1995, reprinted in Li 2000) and then the Afterword to the 1997 second edition of *Duelling Languages* offered new developments. The Afterword included a revised and clearer notion of what is meant by 'Matrix Language' as a construct. I argued that the sentence is an unwieldly unit of analysis for codeswitching (because it can include more than one CP or reduced CPs); I clarified that the domain of the Matrix Language construct is the CP, not the sentence. Also, the role of cross-linguistic congruence received more attention, especially in regard to what types of codeswitching structures are possible within CPs in a given data set (cf. Jake and Myers-Scotton 1997*a*). Finally, two new supporting models were developed to refine the original MLF model's explanation of certain codeswitching constituents and to show how the model's basic provisions can explain aspects of other types of contact data. These models are introduced here; they are discussed in reference to codeswitching in Chapters 3 and 4 and in reference to other contact phenomena in later chapters. The models are the 4-M model and the Abstract Level model.

1.3.4. *Different approaches to codeswitching and its grammatical structure*

When it was introduced in the early 1990s, the MLF model was different—and remains largely different—from previous treatments and most of its contem-

[7] Counterexamples are few, but most seem to result from misinterpretations of the System Morpheme Principle, which is discussed in Chapter 3. This principle disallows a certain type of system morpheme from the Embedded Language, but does not disallow *all* system morphemes and certainly not all functional elements or closed class words. For example, sometimes plural morphemes from the Embedded Language occur, but this is not the type of morpheme disallowed.

poraries in several important ways. The same comment applies to the models that support the MLF model, the 4-M model, and the Abstract Level model. They all explain empirical distributions of bilingual data by making claims about universal aspects of competence that are not restricted to bilingual data, but which are especially visible in such data.

First, most of the researchers suggesting constraints on the structure of codeswitching in the 1970s and 1980s (and even into the 1990s) took a descriptive approach. Many researchers offered a list of (not necessarily related) lexical categories that they claimed could not be switched. These constraints were empirically based, but not motivated by any particular theoretical approach. Some of their restrictions are in line with claims of the MLF model (e.g. writing about codeswitching involving French, Timm (1975) states that pronouns could not be switched. The MLF model would agree that French clitic pronouns cannot be switched, but not because they are pronouns; instead, the reason is they are the type of system morpheme that violates the System Morpheme Principle.). Other early researchers took a linear approach to constraints. Among others, Poplack (1980, reprinted in Li 2000) proposed constraints based on such surface relations as linear equivalences between the participating languages. Because few of these approaches offered unified and motivated models for what elements they placed on the restricted list, sometimes the set of forbidden elements resembled laundry lists. Later researchers produced various counterexamples to these attempts of the 1980s.

Second, other researchers from the 1990s onwards are producing more theoretically based accounts of constraints on codeswitching. However, these accounts differ from the MLF model because the researchers attempt to explain the structure of codeswitching within existing syntactic models—especially generative models in the Chomskyan tradition—designed to explain monolingual phrase structures. Again, others cite many counterexamples. Major approaches are detailed in Chapter 4.

Third, some other researchers have analyzed codeswitching data sets to develop their own diverse ideas. Some make testing the claims of others a major goal in presenting data; others look at specific aspects of codeswitching, such as how codeswitching data varies across generations in the same community. Some of these researchers are listed in Chapter 4. In addition, there have been a number of Ph.D. dissertations on codeswitching, especially since 1995; some are discussed in Chapter 5. A number provide data supporting the MLF model (e.g. three of the most recent ones are Türker 2000 on Turkish/Norwegian codeswitching, Schmitt (2001) on Russian/English codeswitching, and Callahan (2001) on Spanish/English codeswitching in written literature).

1.3.5. *How does the MLF model differ?*

How does the MLF model differ from other approaches? First, in contrast with some approaches, the MLF model is not a slate of descriptively based constraints, but a model with interrelated parts that offer explanations for why its constraints take the form they do. Further, the constraints are motivated, not just by the empirical findings at hand (i.e. codeswitching data), but by findings about the nature of other linguistic phenomena (e.g. speech errors and aphasia, as well as from experimental psycholinguistic evidence on language in bilinguals).

Second, Levelt's (1989) psycholinguistic model for language production also motivates the emphasis the MLF model places on the lexicon as source of grammatical projections connecting intentions with surface forms. This means that in its discussion of what codeswitching involves, the MLF model suggests that the nature of language production is relevant. That is, the MLF model indicates that modeling language production is relevant to codeswitching, but *not* that the MLF model itself is a model of language production (*pace* Bhatia and Ritchie 1996). Certainly, it is not a model concerned with parsing theory or processing limitations, as some have suggested (e.g. MacSwan 1999: 52). Rather, as far as it discusses production, the model's main objection (and mine) is to show how surface realizations (i.e. production) are linked to how language is structured (i.e. competence). As stated in the 1993 exposition, the model 'sees codeswitching constraints as set by processes which operate well before the positional level at which surface orders and structures are realized' (Myers-Scotton 1993*a* [1997]: 6).

Third, the MLF model contrasts with models based on syntactic theories intended to elucidate and explain monolingual phrase structure. The premise underlying the MLF model is that while codeswitching and other bilingual data follow most of the same syntactic principles applying to monolingual data, syntactic models devised for monolingual data do not suffice for explaining codeswitching structures. Of course such models ought to be able to account for the phrase structures of the participating languages; but they account for these structures *as they are used in monolingual CPs.* It is quite another task to account for how elements from two languages can be combined in the same (bilingual) CP. Further, the premise of the MLF model is that bilingual data, such as codeswitching, cannot be sufficiently explained at the level of phrase structure alone.

Fourth, this means the model is lexically based. This means that it emphasizes the abstract procedures directed by lemmas in the mental lexicon. Some of these procedures necessarily refer to phrase structure, but also to the role of oppositions elsewhere at more abstract levels. Admittedly, to say a model is lexically driven seems to mean different things to different researchers. To me, what is most relevant to the discussion in this volume are the following points: as already noted, lemmas in the mental lexicon underlie surface-level lexical elements. The lemmas contain lexical rules and these rules contain all the necessary information to realize surface constructions. This means that a specific lemma entry contains (i) the morphophonological information that is associated with a surface-level content morpheme, (ii) syntactic properties (a subcategorization frame) of that morpheme, and (iii) a semantic and a pragmatic representation. Each type of information within a lemma forms the input for a particular type of formal operation; thus, in some sense lemmas are compounds of operations (cf. e.g. Hoekstra, van der Hulst, and Moortgat 1980, Aronoff 2000).

Thus, the MLF model is not primarily a phrase structure model (i.e. not a syntactic model). This does not mean that the MLF model is not potentially compatible with most contemporary syntactic models. Certainly, it seems to be very compatible with many of the views of Jackendoff (1997) on the relationship of the lexicon to syntactic and phonological components.

Fifth, two interrelated oppositions or hierarchies are the key to the nuts and bolts of the MLF model. Interestingly, both oppositions refer to asymmetries. That is, the members of the oppositions play unequal roles in codeswitching structures—and elsewhere in language in general, as it turns out.

1.3.6. *The key oppositions in the MLF model*

The MLF model is based on two oppositions: the Matrix Language – Embedded Language opposition and the content–system morpheme opposition. Here is how they are played out:

1. The participating languages in codeswitching do not contribute equally.[8] The language making the larger contribution is called the Matrix Language and the other language is called the Embedded Language. Within the terms of the MLF Model, 'contributing more' does not mean *more* morphemes, although this is often the case. Rather, contributing more means *more abstract structure and structure of a certain type.* Specifically, the Matrix Language – Embedded Language opposition is most salient in regard to mixed constituents. (Mixed constituents are those with morphemes from two or more languages or, as we will see when phenomena other than classic codeswitching are discussed, abstract structure from two or more languages.) The nature of the Matrix Language is discussed at length in Chapter 3.

2. The importance of recognizing the abstract structure behind surface phrase structures is largely encapsulated in the second opposition, that between content morphemes and system morphemes. Content morphemes are the main elements conveying semantic and pragmatic aspects of messages, and system morphemes largely indicate relations between the content morphemes. These divisions are discussed more thoroughly in the next section. Clearly, then, these two types of morpheme perform different functions in language in general, monolingual or bilingual. But because system morphemes are related to constituent structure, where they will come from—which of the participating languages—becomes more critical in bilingual speech than the source of content morphemes. All the participating languages may contribute content morphemes to bilingual CPs, but not all can contribute critical system morphemes.[9] This is the domain of the

[8] Others before me recognized the unequal participation of the languages involved in codeswitching (e.g. Joshi 1985, Sridhar and Sridhar 1980).

[9] The observations of numerous earlier researchers indicate they recognized differences between some functional elements and content elements, but they did not propose the general pattern that the content–system morpheme distinction captures (cf. Myers-Scotton 1993*a* [1997]: 82).

Matrix Language. Accordingly, this is why the Matrix Language – Embedded Language opposition is so important. I discuss this point further in Chapter 4 in relation to other approaches.

Note that neither of these oppositions refers to phrase structure; rather, they operate at a more abstract level. The Matrix Language – Embedded Language opposition refers to linguistic competence—in the sense that, psycholinguistically, the bilingual's two or more languages do not achieve equal activation in bilingual speech. Decisions (largely unconscious) made at the prelinguistic conceptual level result in one language dominating (the Matrix Language sets the grammatical frame of such speech). The less dominant language (the Embedded Language) participates largely by supplying lexical elements that are integrated into that frame. The content–system morpheme opposition refers to how lexical elements are organized in the mental lexicon and differentially accessed in the language production process. This affects how they participate in bilingual CPs as well. A theme in this volume will be that what these oppositions reflect is the universal division in language between the roles of content elements in the lexicon and grammatical elements.

1.4. The 4-M model

The MLF model not only accounts for a very wide range of codeswitching examples, but can explain most of them under the Matrix Language – Embedded Language and the content–system morpheme oppositions. But these oppositions do not explain them all on their own. A new supporting model, the 4-M model, refines the earlier content–system morpheme opposition to explain a wider range of codeswitching data. This model results from a collaboration with Jan Jake (cf. Myers-Scotton and Jake 2000*a*, 2000*b*, 2001). Like the three princes of Serendip, we made a fortunate discovery: the model not only helps explain codeswitching, but also offers plausible explanations for distributions in a wide range of other data, as will become clear in later chapters.

What the 4-M model does is take the content–system morpheme opposition in the MLF model and break down the class of system morpheme into three types. The MLF model had offered a formal way of distinguishing content and system morphemes (content morphemes participate in the thematic grid of an utterance by either assigning or receiving thematic roles, but system morphemes do not). Prototypical content morphemes that receive thematic roles are nouns (e.g. in the thematic role of Agent, nouns are often mapped onto the grammatical relation of Subject; in the role of Patient or Theme, they are often mapped onto the grammatical relation of Internal Argument or Direct Object). Prototypical content morphemes that assign thematic roles are most verbs and some prepositions. In contrast, system morphemes neither assign nor receive thematic roles. Most function words and inflections are system morphemes.

The content–system morpheme opposition is discussed further in Chapter 3, and the 4-M model is thoroughly described. Here, the purpose is only to introduce it. The classification is independently motivated because the four morpheme types can be distinguished by their formal syntactic properties. However, the model is more than a classification. It adds new specificity to the predictions of the MLF model and also predicts distributions across other types of linguistic phenomena rather than just systematizing what has been found already. These data distributions imply a hypothesis concerning abstract detail of language production, the Differential Access Hypothesis. This hypothesis is the following:

The different types of morpheme under the 4-M model are differently accessed in the abstract levels of the production process. Specifically, content morphemes and early system morphemes are accessed at the level of the mental lexicon, but late system morphemes do not become salient until the level of the Formulator.

Differences in surface distributions of these same morphemes support the hypothesis (cf. data in late chapters here and in Myers-Scotton and Jake 2000*a*), although, of course, evidence from psycholinguistic experimentation would provide valuable corroboration. (Such support seems to be found in the psycholinguistic and neurolinguistic evidence presented by Ullman 2001 to give credence to a declarative/procedural model that posits that 'lexicon and grammar are subserved by separable cognitive systems, with at least partially distinct neural correlates', p. 107.)

This much is evident: the 4-M model's most important virtue is that it makes a claim about how abstract entries in the mental lexicon are related to surface elements. Another way of saying this is that the 4-M model implicates a model of surface distributions of morpheme type that is based on abstract competence.

1.4.1. *Morphemes at the abstract level*

Throughout this volume, references to 'morphemes' may refer to actual surface-level morphemes, or references may be metaphorical. The name '4-M model' itself refers to morphemes in both senses of the term. Certainly, when referring to elements in regard to abstract procedures that precede surface realizations, the reference is metaphorical. That is, what are called 'morphemes' (in reference to how lexical elements are accessed) are really lemmas, not morphemes at all. 'Real' morphemes themselves are surface phenomena; lemmas are abstract entries in the mental lexicon that underlie morphemes. On this view, lemmas are the main link in the chain that begins with speakers' intentions and ends in surface-level linguistic forms.

1.4.2. *The 4-M model and its four types of morphemes*

The Differential Access Hypothesis of the 4-M model is that the four types of morpheme are related in different ways to the production process. First, content morphemes are the only morphemes whose lemmas link them directly to speakers' intentions. Speakers' intentions activate language-specific semantic/pragmatic feature bundles that underlie the conceptual information that content morphemes will convey. In turn, these bundles point to lemmas in the mental lexicon. The lemmas underlying content morphemes are directly elected and their content is salient at the level of the mental lexicon.

Second, the lemmas underlying one type of system morpheme also become salient at this level; these are called early system morphemes because of their early saliency. Their lemmas are activated when the lemmas supporting content morphemes point to them. These indirectly elected lemmas further realize the conceptual content of the semantic/pragmatic feature bundles. For example, in English the determiner *the* adds definiteness to its head noun in the sentence *Where is the book you borrowed yesterday?* The noun *book* is a content morpheme and the determiner *the* is an early system morpheme; the same semantic/pragmatic feature bundle activates both *the* and *book*. This conceptual link between content and early system morphemes means that Embedded Language early system morphemes have more potential for appearing in bilingual clauses framed by the Matrix Language than do the other system morphemes. We will see examples of this in later chapters.

Third, two other types of system morpheme become salient when their lemmas are activated at the level of the Formulator. They are called late system morphemes because the hypothesis is that their saliency is delayed until the Formulator level. They are activated by the directions sent to the Formulator by the lemmas underlying content and early system morphemes; these are directions to build larger linguistic units such as CPs and IPs.

The presence of one type of late system morpheme, 'bridges', depends on the maximal projection in which they occur. They integrate elements in a constituent when the well-formedness conditions for those constituents call for them. An example of a bridge system morpheme is *of* in the English construction *ball of Lena*.

In contrast, the second type of late system morphemes, 'outsiders', look outside their immediate maximal projection for information about their form. For example, subject–verb agreement in many languages is an outsider system morpheme as in the English sentence *The dog like-s bones* vs. *The dogs like bones.* Both types of late system morpheme are structurally assigned in contrast with both content morphemes and early system morphemes, which are conceptually activated.

Independent evidence for this classification is the way these different morphemes pattern in surface-level syntactic structures; this is discussed in Chapter 3.

1.5. The Abstract Level model

Another new model that grew out of earlier research on codeswitching is the Abstract Level model. The model was developed by Myers-Scotton and Jake, but a number of linguists have posited similar abstract levels. The model's outlines were introduced in Myers-Scotton and Jake (1995) and made more explicit in contributions to Myers-Scotton and Jake (2000*b*). This model enables us to discuss two aspects of language contact more precisely. First, in Chapter 3 and also in later chapters I show how the model is useful in delineating what will count as 'sufficient congruence' in codeswitching so that certain constructions are possible for certain language pairs. Second, we see in later chapters how the model provides a principled explanation for the nature of the abstract morphosyntactic frame that structures bilingual clauses in types of contact phenomena other than classic codeswitching. In these phenomena, we cannot argue that all the abstract structure is derived from the grammar of one of the participating languages; rather it is clear that more than one language is the source of structure. In Chapter 6, the Abstract Level model also offers an explanation for how 'structural' borrowing can come about in relation to convergence, which is seen under the model as the product of the splitting and combining of abstract lexical structure. In these cases, I refer to a *composite* Matrix Language (cf. Afterword in Myers-Scotton 1997, Myers-Scotton 1998*a*).

Once again, this model is based on premises about the nature of the mental lexicon. The major premise underlying the Abstract Level model is that all lemmas in the mental lexicon include three levels of abstract lexical structure. The three levels contain all the grammatical information necessary for the surface realization of a lexical entry. The levels refer to (i) lexical-conceptual structure, (ii) predicate-argument structure, and (iii) morphological realization patterns. These are exemplified below and discussed more thoroughly in later chapters when they are relevant.

Myers-Scotton and Jake suggest that lexical-conceptual structure is closest to the speaker's intentions. They write, 'In our view, pre-verbal intentions in the conceptualizer activate language-specific semantic/pragmatic feature bundles at the interface between the conceptualizer and the mental lexicon. These bundles are mapped onto entries in the mental lexicon (lemmas) as lexical-conceptual structure' (2001: 125).

The other two levels refer to how relations among content morphemes are encoded or structurally assigned in a specific language. The level of predicate-argument structure deals with how thematic structure is mapped on to grammatical relations. For example, in a specific language, this level may provide for the mapping of Agent to Subject, Beneficiary to Internal Object, etc. The level of morphological realization patterns refers to how grammatical relations are realized in surface configurations. This level includes morpheme order and agreement morphology.

1.5.1. *Applying the Abstract Level model to codeswitching*

Recall the Matrix Language – Embedded Language opposition in the MLF model. Under this opposition, the Matrix Language is the source of structure for the grammatical frame of the bilingual clause. The other language, the Embedded Language, may supply content morphemes that are inserted in this frame. For example, Embedded Language nouns are the most frequent form of Embedded Language material in bilingual clauses, although in many language pairs, Embedded Language verb stems also can appear. However, in order for these Embedded Language morphemes to appear, they must be checked for 'sufficient congruence' with their Matrix Language counterparts. This notion was introduced in Myers-Scotton and Jake (1995). This checking involves the three levels of abstract grammatical structure of the Abstract Level mdodel and it would occur in the mental lexicon at the lemma level.

However, the fly in the ointment is the issue of what sufficient congruence means. This notion has not yet been adequately refined. Very definitely, *sufficient* does not mean *complete* congruence—because, of course, content morphemes across languages are rarely completely congruent (*pace* Sankoff 1998). There are more questions to be answered than answers to date. For example, does an Embedded Language lexeme have to match a Matrix Language counterpart regarding lexical category? The evidence from many language pairs indicates the answer is no (Myers-Scotton and Jake 2000*b*). Myers-Scotton and Jake also note that while Embedded Language thematic role assigners can match Matrix Language thematic role assigners, in other instances the roles that they assign can be different. However, what constitutes congruence in contact phenomena is still largely unstudied. But this is no reason to set aside the possibility of making progress now.

Further, the reason congruence is worth exploring is that it seems that lack of sufficient congruence may explain why certain structures are avoided or impossible in switching between specific language pairs (and probably in other contact phenomena for which congruence is yet to be studied). One of the major claims of Myers-Scotton and Jake (1995) is that lack of sufficient congruence is what promotes speakers to use certain compromise strategies in codeswitching (reiterated in Jake and Myers-Scotton 1997*a*, Myers-Scotton and Jake 2001).

We explain three ways in which Embedded Language material appears in bilingual clauses as compromise structures. While these structures are not disallowed under the MLF model, they vary from what seems to be the optimal codeswitching construction from the psycholinguistic point of view.[10] The optimal constitutent is the mixed constituent, consisting of a Matrix Language grammatical frame with both Matrix Language and Embedded Language content morphemes inserted in the frame with full Matrix Language morphosyntactic integration. One reason to posit that this is the optimal codeswitching construction is that its production should cause the least 'psycholinguistic strain' of all bilingual projections: only one language must be sufficiently activated to direct morphosyntactic

[10] Obviously, this is only conjecture. The matter would benefit from experimental study by psycholinguists.

procedures and the other language's activation only involves inserting sufficiently congruent content morphemes in the Matrix Language frame. The mixed constituent, of course, is the domain in which the Morpheme Order and the System Morpheme Principles apply (discussed fully in Chapter 3).

We argue that there are three main compromise strategies that are promoted by insufficient congruence across the participating languages as an alternative to a mixed constituent. First, we suggest that Embedded Language islands arise because of congruence problems at one or more of the three levels of abstract grammatical structure. Embedded Language islands are constituents entirely in the Embedded Language and well-formed in the Embedded Language; they are embedded in the larger clause (CP) and are under overall Matrix Language control in various ways. Second, we say that rather than being fully morphosyntactically integrated into a Matrix Language frame, some Embedded Language content morphemes may occur as bare forms because of lack of sufficient congruence. Bare forms are Embedded Language content morphemes that lack the requisite Matrix Language system morphemes that would make them well-formed in a Matrix Language frame. They are often nouns. Third, in some language pairs, 'do' constructions (with the Matrix Language encoding 'do') occur instead of Embedded Language verbs with Matrix Language inflections. These strategies are discussed more fully in Chapter 4.

Just because these compromise strategies depart from optimal mixed constituents, ostensibly creating more strain in regard to both language competence and production, their explanation is important. After all, Embedded Language islands require a lowering of activation of the Matrix Language and an increase in that of the Embedded Language. And both bare forms and 'do' constructions require modifications in the morphosyntactic specifications sent to the Formulator. That is, these compromise strategies are potential production problems. But because speakers are able to create such constructions at all—presumably when they satisfy intentions better than monolingual constructions totally in either participating language—they tell us something about the nature of linguistic competence, too.

1.5.2. *Applying the Abstract Level model to other contact phenomena*

If the only major premises of the Abstract Level model were that abstract lexical entries consist of three levels of abstract grammatical structure, the model would add nothing to the conclusions of the linguists who have been considering monolingual data and lexical structure (e.g. Jackendoff 1990, *inter alia*). However, what makes the Abstract Level model different from such formulations is an innovation derived from investigating bilingual data (Myers-Scotton and Jake 2000*b*).

We suggest that the types of abstract structures found in bilingual data showing convergence indicate that any of the three levels posited in the Abstract Level model for one participating language can be copied to the other language in a bilingual clause. As I define it, convergence results when all the surface morphemes come from one language, but part of the abstract structure comes from another language. The net result is that a bilingual clause can be structured by levels from more than one contributing language. Put another way, abstract material can be split off from one language and combined with abstract structure from another language, resulting in a composite. Such results have gone under a variety of labels, such as 'transference' and 'interference' and even 'creolization'. However, labeling phenomena does not explain them. Positing a composite Matrix Language offers a more precise and principled way to characterize—and explain—what is happening.

That is, instead of having a Matrix Language for a bilingual clause that is largely isomorphic with a single language, in some contact phenomena, the Matrix Language itself is a composite. One can define a composite Matrix Language as an abstract frame composed of grammatical projections from more than one variety. It can result when speakers do not have full access to the desired Matrix Language, or when there is competition between languages for the role of Matrix Language (reflecting sociopolitical competitions that affect Matrix Language selection at the conceptual level). For example, when speakers are shifting from one language to another as their sociolinguistically dominant language, the structure of their bilingual clauses often can be characterized in terms of a composite Matrix Language. In Chapter 6, the Abstract Frame model offers an explanation of how such 'structural' borrowing can come about at all.

Predictions about the nature of a composite Matrix Language in such contact situations are presented in later chapters, especially in Chapter 6. Here, I simply point out some examples of how the abstract structure of a bilingual clause can represent a recombination of structural material from several sources. For example, quite a common occurrence in some bilingual clauses is a lexical item showing some lexical-conceptual structure from one language and some from another. Example (8) illustrates convergence at this level. It comes from the conversation of a Russian boy, who now lives in the United States, and for whom English is rapidly becoming his dominant language. (The example and the analysis come from Schmitt 2000: 20.) Also, recall example (5) in which English structure is implicated in the merger of verbs of 'to know' in Pennsylvania German.

(8) *a*	i	on	smotre-l	**cherez**	knig-u
	and	3S/NOM/S/M	look/IMPERF-PST/M/S	through	book-ACC/F/S
b	i	on	pro-smotre-l		knig-u (Standard Russian)
	and	3S/NOM/S/M	PERF-look-PST/M/S		book-ACC/F/S

'And he looked through the book.'

(Schmitt 2000: 20)

In example (8*a*) the preposition *cherez* 'through' is inserted into the grammatical frame. In Standard Russian, it is not present. Instead in (8*b*) only the Russian verb *prosmotret'* 'to look through' apears; it is perfective in form. Russian perfective verbs with prefixes do not encode only aspect, but also express the completion of the action or result. That is, in Standard Russian, the idea of 'through' is part of the lexical-conceptual structure of the verb itself. However, the speaker in (8*a*) simply uses the imperfective form of the verb and then adds the preposition *cherez* to convey the idea of completion. Clearly, the speaker is following the English pattern of encoding 'completion' through the use of the verb satellite with the meaning 'through'. Thus, the very frame of the utterance has been affected by English structure; a slot for a verb satellite (preposition) has been added.

1.6. Implications for a model of language production

Although I have been at pains to argue that these three models, the MLF model, the 4-M model, and the Abstract Level model, are not themselves models of language production, they do presuppose the model of language production portrayed in Figure 1.1. This figure reflects the premises that structure much of the discussion in this volume. The basic outlines of the model follow Levelt (1989), but there are modifications.

The model is based on the notion that production procedures begin at the conceptual level, well before procedures set in motion the projection of surface structures. At the conceptual level, speakers—whether the result is monolingual or bilingual speech—map their intentions onto language. They make a number of decisions, largely unconsciously. They consider the sociopolitical and psycholinguistic possibilities of this mapping and its consequences.

For monolingual speakers, this means they consider their dialectal and stylistic choices. For example, they consider the potential effect of speaking casually (e.g. *hey, dude*) versus much more formally (e.g. *excuse me, sir*). If the other speakers present speak a non-standard dialect of their shared language, our fictional speakers consider the effect of their own dialectal choice (cf. Bell 1984 on audience design). But primarily, speakers take into account their own goals about self-presentation and the costs and rewards associated with using one variety rather than another (cf. Myers-Scotton 1998*b*, Myers-Scotton and Bolonyai 2001). In sum, they consider the indexical value of linguistic varieties that they have the potential to use (i.e. sociolinguistic considerations) and they also consider their own proficiency and that of their audience in these same linguistic varieties (psycholinguistic considerations).

Bilingual speakers have even more to consider at this level. One consideration is simply the effect of producing bilingual speech rather than speaking one language at a time. That is, speakers must decide whether in a given community engaging in codeswitching is even acceptable or whether they will be denigrated for speaking 'broken language'. If they do engage in codeswitching or other forms of contact language, they will have to select—again generally unconsciously—a Matrix Language to provide morphosyntactic structure for bilingual speech.

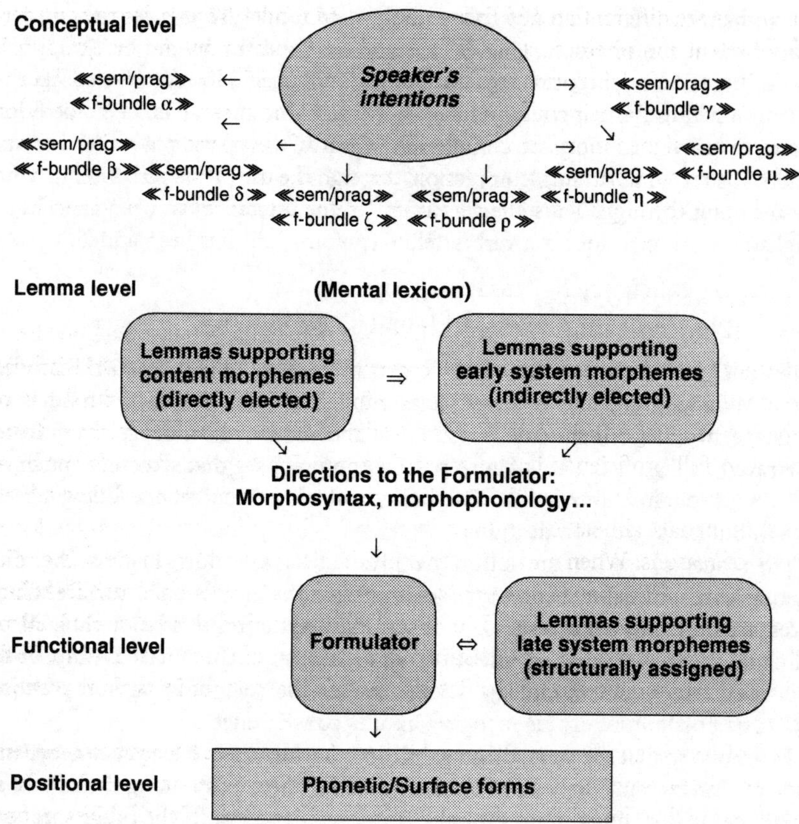

Figure 1.1. Production process diagram: lemma activation (adapted from Myers-Scotton and Jake 2000*a*)

Content morphemes will be their main means for expressing intentions, but again there are choices to be made because there is generally the option to select content morphemes from either Matrix Language or Embedded Language (and, of course, from both) to realize in the Matrix Language frame.

Speaker intentions now point to language-specific semantic/pragmatic feature bundles that, in turn, interface with language-specific lemmas in the mental lexicon. That is, these bundles, not syntactic units, are what mediate between the conceptual level and the mental lexicon (cf. Jackendoff 1997). Lemmas are tagged for specific languages in the speaker's repertoire. They contain all the necessary information that will result in surface-level morphosyntactic structures. This information is what is referred to in the Abstract Level model as the three abstract grammatical levels of lexical-conceptual structure, predicate-argument structure, and morphological realization patterns.

Lemmas are differentiated in line with the 4-M model. That is, lemmas underlying content morphemes are directly elected by speaker intentions (cf. Levelt 1989); those underlying early system morphemes are indirectly elected by the lemmas underlying their content morpheme heads. However, lemmas underlying structurally assigned morphemes (late system morphemes) are not activated until those lemmas supporting content morphemes send directions to the Formulator, switching on the morphosyntactic procedures resulting in surface utterances.

1.7. How proficiency figures in

Of course, it turns out that even in what I now call classic codeswitching, both languages usually cannot participate equally. (Recall that classic codeswitching is defined as codeswitching by speakers who have full proficiency in the participating language that becomes the Matrix Language, and anywhere from limited to full proficiency in the other language. That is, speakers *do not* have equal proficiency in the participating languages.) As students of bilingualism know, bilinguals almost never have equal proficiency in their languages for a variety of reasons. When and how they acquired the languages matters (e.g. did they acquire both languages more or less simultaneously as children? Did they learn their second language (L2) in a classroom situation as adults? etc.). Also, how often and where they use their languages today also matters. Finally, both their negative and positive attitudes towards the languages in their repertoire matter.

And of course another problem is that even L2 specialists have yet to come up with an all-encompassing definition of what it means to be proficient in a language. Further, it is even difficult to establish a speaker's level of ability in one area of a language (e.g. morphosyntax) because abilities in other areas (e.g. vocabulary knowledge, phonetic mastery) create 'background noise'.

However, fortuitously, it turns out that speakers need *not* have equal proficiency to use codeswitching as a test for at least some aspects of grammatical structure. At least under some models, notably the MLF model, the premise is that languages do not participate equally in codeswitching. In brief, this means that while speakers must be able to produce and recognize well-formed utterances in their dialect of one of the languages, they need not have full command of the morphosyntax of the other language.

The MLF model recognizes that one language, called the Matrix Language, is more responsible for morphosyntactic structure than the other language, called the Embedded Language. Specifically, the Matrix Language supplies essential morphosyntactic structure for mixed constituents, while the Embedded Language may supply content morphemes to be inserted into this frame. The Matrix Language also controls, in various ways, any monolingual Embedded Language constituents (Embedded Language islands) within the larger bilingual constituent. This is discussed fully in Chapter 4.

1.8. Competence and performance

Two interesting, but unresolved, issues are the following. First, how is unequal ability in participating languages related to the unequal participation of languages in contributing to various contact phenomena? Second, is unequal ability in participating languages only a result of a speaker's history and therefore solely part of linguistic performance rather than of linguistic competence? Yet, even if this is so, surely unequal ability has some relation to competence. How is this? First, some discussion of the problems with some definitions. It was always clear that Chomsky (1965: 3) wishes to separate '*competence* (the speaker-hearer's knowledge of the language) and *performance*, the actual use of language in concrete situations'. In later works, others (if not Chomsky himself) have used the term Universal Grammar (UG) as part of the universally present human language faculty. Further, UG has been used as if it were synonymous with competence. Researchers went on to include *principles and parameters* as the stuff that UG is made of and, further, to refer to acquiring a specific language as 'parameter resetting' (of the basic UG parameters). More recently, under the Minimalist Program (Chomsky 1995) feature value replaces parameters as most important. Now it seems that what is acquired is not a resetting of feature values, but rather the universal values themselves. But what is the relationship of a general innate competence to what is acquired? And if the acquired feature values become part of the well-formedness conditions of the grammar of a specific language, then are they not also part of the ability to speak that language? And how is ability related to performance? That is, for example, as I am 'performing' this English sentence, the surface structures are projected by abstract configurations of settings originating in UG or competence. Can we then say that the ability to speak a specific language is competence instantiated in a specific way? If so, then where is the line between competence and performance?

Recall the model of production in section 1.6 envisioned for this volume. At the prelinguistic conceptual level, the main decisions that are made have to do with how a speaker's intentions will be projected as linguistic material. This means especially mapping intentions onto language-specific semantic/pragmatic feature bundles. But another decision comes first: speakers decide on the linguistic medium to express intentions; that is, will speech be monolingual or bilingual? Many factors influence this decision; obviously, most important is the speakers' linguistic proficiencies and abilities to produce bilingual utterances. Other factors have to do with community norms. Is bilingual speech censured or is it the norm? If bilingual speech is chosen, will speakers engage in codeswitching within the same constituent? And if this option is chosen, which language will serve as the basis for the Matrix Language in such codeswitching? Speakers may follow the norms of their community, if there are such norms, or they may choose to make marked choices (cf. Myers-Scotton 1993*c*). Here, in the very inner circle of linguistic competence, how is it that the main considerations are performance issues?

At the same time, the very possibility that speakers are able to make such decisions must be part of linguistic competence. Most important for grammatical structure is that the very idea that in any utterance there is an abstract morphosyntactic frame at work. This means, of course, that the notion of a Matrix Language grammar applies to monolingual as well as to bilingual utterances. That there is a discernible frame with its own well-formedness conditions—and not some compromise solution—must be part of universal competence. In regard to bilingual speech in specific, the particular division of labor that the Matrix Language – Embedded Language opposition presupposes must be part of competence, even while it has an empirical underpinning (i.e. the speaker has to have sufficient proficiency in a language when it is used as the Matrix Language to project codeswitching frames).

This is the view that underlies the MLF model. It is not the premise of most other leading competitors, as we see in later chapters. For many, the focus is either on performance (i.e. theory-free describing and cataloguing of data) or competence (analysis aimed at validating a specific syntactic theory), but not both. In general, most researchers studying other contact phenomena outside of codeswitching concentrate on performance; that is, their goal is to describe and catalogue surface level phenomena. This is especially evident in most work on creoles (Bickerton 1981 is an exception, as are some of the contributions to DeGraff 1999*a*). It is also clear in the recent interest in mixed languages and in many overviews of language contact.

In section 1.3.4, I mentioned some approaches to codeswitching, and in Chapter 4 I elaborate on this discussion. The MLF model's perspective is different; it looks for explanations *in the interaction of competence and performance.* This approach defines not only the MLF model, but also its supporting models, the 4-M model and the Abstract Level model. For example, the premise of the 4-M model is that its proposed division of system morphemes is part of underlying competence because it is based on how linguistic units are accessed in production. In turn, accesibility is part of competence. Thus, the notion that different units are accessed differently offers an explanation for performance (observed differences in surface distributions of the system morphemes). This is how the 4-M model makes a clear connection between competence and performance data. Empirical evidence for differential distributions of system morphemes is found not only in codeswitching, but also in other performance data from diverse linguistic phenomena. For example, there is more variation across non-standard English dialects in how late outsider system morphemes are realized (e.g. what happens to forms of the copula) than in other types of system morphemes. Also, Myers-Scotton and Jake (2000*a*) reanalyze data on Broca's aphasics to show that not all grammatical elements are equal in the speech of these aphasics; instead, it is late system morphemes that are less accurate than other morphemes. They also show how accuracy in Interlanguage in L2 acquisition can be explained in terms of morpheme types.

In sum, the point that is developed throughout this volume is that the different statuses of morphemes in competence (that is, the lemmas underlying morphemes) affect their status in production. Cross-linguistic differences in how grammatical information is encoded at an abstract level and then accessed in language production also matter. As becomes clear in later chapters, this view leads to specific predictions about the form that various types of contact phenomena take.

1.9. Summary

The goal of this chapter has been to introduce the general orientation of this volume. The plan is to present an overview of language contact research, including the claims of current research, most especially those illustrated by my own models. Also, this discussion implies a research agenda for future research.

The overarching premise of this discussion is that the same principles and processes structure all language contact phenomena; the surface results differ because the sociopolitical and psycholinguistic circumstances of the contact phenomena differ. Although this premise receives little direct attention in this chapter, it becomes clearer in later chapters how basic it is to proposed explanations. Here, the more specific premises of the three models structuring discussions are introduced. These models are the Matrix Language Frame model (MLF), as well as its newer supporting models, the 4-M model, and the Abstract Level model. The models make concrete the general principles that were introduced in section 1.2 as applying to bilingual data: the Matrix Language Principle, the Uniform Structure Principle, the Asymmetry Principle, and the Morpheme Sorting Principle. In addition, the Differential Access Hypothesis, stemming from the 4-M model is introduced in section 1.4. These models are used to explain diverse contact phenomena in later chapters.

1.10. The coming chapters

Chapter 2 is the only one that does not focus on grammatical structures in specific contact phenomena; instead, it offers an overview of the sociolinguistic factors that promote bilingualism across societies and in individuals. Chapters 3 and 4 both deal with codeswitching. Chapter 3 discusses the MLF model as I see it today and also presents the 4-M model and the Abstract Level model in more detail, with examples. Chapter 5 is devoted to convergence (including convergence areas) and attrition. It offers an overview of how attrition has been treated and goes on to present a set of hypotheses that I offer to explain the structure of attrition. Chapter 6 has three topics, lexical borrowing, split (mixed languages), and creole formation. They are included in the same chapter, based on the argument that how they all are structured reflects the basic division in language between the lexicon and grammatical structures.

The final chapter (Chapter 7) offers a summary in the form of a set of hypotheses based on discussions in the earlier chapters.

2

The Roots of Language Contact

2.1. Introduction

This chapter provides an overview of the conditions that promote the cycle of language contact. Although the major subject of this volume is what happens to the structure of the participating languages in this cycle, appreciating how events bring speakers of different languages into contact is helpful in visualizing and understanding those structural outcomes.

The cycle begins when their environment puts monolingual speakers in interactions that prompt them to learn another language (second language or L2). (Alternatively, children are born into such a situation and they acquire two languages simultaneously (first language or L1).) The cycle may proceed with the learning of other L2s, replacing or duplicating the first L2. It may end with some maintenance of the L1, but along with one or more L2s in a speaker's repertoire. But if this happens, they will not be spoken with equal proficiency or equal use. One scenario is that the L1 will be maintained, along with less use of an L2 that was learned for special purposes at some point in the speaker's life. Perhaps more likely, the cycle will end with one L2 that is the dominant language in the community where the speaker lives being maintained, but the terminal, or near-terminal, attrition of the L1 or of any of the other L2s the speaker may have learned. That is, languages generally are only maintained if a use for them is also maintained. Thus, the cycle that begins with bilingualism often ends with language shift, entailing near or complete monolingualism in the language surviving the shift. Of course, there need be no shift to monolingualism at all; after all, there are many more bilinguals than monolinguals in the world.

Specialists on bilingualism point out that there are many different ways in which the term 'bilingualism' is used (cf. Mackey 2003). Of most relevance to this volume is the difference between *individual bilingualism* (an individual uses two or more languages) and *societal bilingualism* (a community houses speakers of more than one language, even though individual community members do not necessarily speak more than one language.) Clearly, we are interested only in those speakers who either are now using, or have used, two or more languages with some regularity. Further, although bilinguals may differ in what they use their languages for, we are mainly concerned with speakers who use both languages at least part of the time for in-group conversations.

2.2. Factors favoring adding a language

A number of circumstances promote the conditions in which bilingualism develops and also in which shift to another language for most purposes takes place (Fishman 1972, Lieberson 1982, Grosjean 1982, Clyne 1997, and Mackey 2003, *inter alia*). However, there are more frequently multiple causes for learning another language than for such a change being caused by any one factor. The main circumstances are the following:

1. *Military invasion and subsequent colonization.* These have been perhaps the important factors, especially if the conquest was followed by a long period of stability. That is, a population finds itself with speakers of an alien language in charge and finds it expedient to learn their language. In the ancient world, Alexander the Great and his armies spread Greek throughout the Middle East, and the Roman Empire spread Latin throughout Europe and North Africa. Arabic was spread in the Middle East by Muslim invasions. In many cases, indigenous languages were replaced; for example, Arabic replaced Egyptian in Egypt. Two centuries of close contact with France following the Norman Conquest in 1066 motivated bilingualism in French, at least for some members of the upper classes, in England, and mass French lexical borrowings and some structural changes to English. Spanish conquerors spread Spanish to all of Central and South America. More recently, European powers, especially England, France, and Portugal, spread their languages in Africa. Russian was spread in the former Soviet Union in the twentieth century.

2. *Living in a border area or an ethnolinguistic enclave.* Inevitably, because there are borders between nations and between ethnic groups within many nations, some people find themselves living next to speakers of another L1. For a variety of reasons, these border residents become bilingual; sometimes they learn each other's languages, but just as often, the learning is one-directional with the less numerous or less economically powerful group learning the other group's language. In many parts of Asia, Africa, and Central and South America in areas with numerous small language groups, many persons learn as many as three or four of their neighbors' languages. Sorensen (1972) details a remarkably multilingual area in the northwest Amazon. The area is culturally homogeneous, but each ethnic group has its own language and it is usual for individuals to speak a number of their neighbors' languages. In interethnic encounters, switching between languages is common, as Sorensen indicates in this description:

> Conversations in two or more languages indeed occur on occasion, as in visiting, but no one takes special note of it. Each individual initially speaks in his own father-language during such a conversation in order to assert his tribal affiliation and identification, but after a while the junior persons change, without comment, to the longhouse language, to Tukano as the lingua franca, or to another language, whatever one is most convenient for the others. A person usually cannot enumerate how many languages he knows, and is perplexed at being asked to do so. (p. 87)

While Europeans may not speak so many languages or switch so casually among them, persons at national boundaries, especially where more than two nations come together, such as in the Baltic area, or in the Balkans, often speak more than two languages.

Within nations—often because history redrew borders—there may be enclaves of L1 speakers who only speak the dominant or official language of the nation as an L2. For example, there are enclaves of L1 speakers of Hungarian in Slovakia and Romania. And in East Africa, many L1 speakers of Somali live outside Somalia in Kenya's northeast provinces.

3. *Migration for social and economic reasons.* The reason most people migrate is to find better living conditions. However, the conditions that immigrants find upon arrival in a new national home give them not only new social and economic opportunities, but also reasons to learn a new language. The nineteenth and early twentieth centuries especially saw mass migrations from Europe to North America, Australia, and New Zealand. Except for eastern Canada where French prevailed, learning English became a necessity for these immigrants. Today, there is continued mass voluntary migration all around the world, but particularly in Europe and North America.

Migration has not always been voluntary. Before slavery was outlawed by most countries by at least the early nineteenth century, Africans were imported to the New World as involuntary migrants, to work as slaves on plantations. In the process, they developed creoles and learned other languages. Further, throughout history, wars have created refugees who had to flee their home areas (e.g. refugees of the civil wars in West Africa, Angola, Congo, and Sudan today). Almost necessarily, these persons learn the dominant language of the nation that takes them in. Because they generally have access to language classes today, or at least have regular contacts with speakers of the new language, they learn a near-target-like version of this language; that is, they do not develop a creole.

4. *Education as a factor in bilingualism.* Because at all times in history, specific languages have been seen as the hallmark of the educated person, those languages have been studied in schools during their time of importance. For example, with the spread of Christianity in Europe, Latin became the language the educated person would learn. Today, of course, many students study English as a second language.

5. *Spread of international languages.* As the number of persons learning a given language increases, this increases pressure for others to learn the same second language even if their interaction patterns are unchanged. Greenberg (1965 [1971]) was one of the first to comment on the inherent momentum of a language when circumstances establish it as a lingua franca. This observation obviously applies to the spread of English in the world today, as mentioned again when the economic value of languages is considered below. In the Middle Ages, momentum applied to Latin in Europe among the educated and to French in the eighteenth and nineteenth centuries among the upper classes in Europe.

6. *Ethnic awareness.* There are other conditions that promote bilingualism, too, such as a new valuation placed on ethnic identity or the rise of nationalism. A major student of language and social identity, John Edwards, defines ethnicity as 'a sense of group identity deriving from real or perceived common bonds such as language, race or religion' (1985: 6). He defines nationalism as 'an extension of ethnicity in that it adds to the belief in shared characteristics a desire for political autonomy' (1985: 11). While nationalism may result in the formation of new nations—and possibly an atmosphere favoring monolingualism—expressions of ethnicity tend to promote bilingualism, with the ethnic language viewed as an additional language.

Either existing ethnic groups in a nation or new immigrants to a nation can clamor for conditions to preserve their languages or provide learning opportunities in these languages. Indigenous ethnic groups also can assert their cultural heritage by calling for opportunties to learn their almost forgotten ethnic language. A good example is the rise in interest in learning three Celtic languages, especially Welsh in Wales, but also Irish Gaelic in Ireland, and Breton in France. In addition, new language minorities may claim the right to have their children schooled in their mother tongue.

2.3. Bilingual competence

The degree and nature of bilingual ability depends on which languages are known, on when, why, where, and how they were acquired, and also how much of each, and how well, the languages were mastered and are presently known. Mackey (2003) comes up with a series of questions and indicates that their answers demarcate or describe bilingual competence. These include: (i) Which languages? (ii) What is the interlingual distance between the speaker's L1 and an L2? The less distance, the easier the L2 is to learn. (iii) Where was the L2 learned? Was it learned at home, on the street, in school, at work? (iv) When was the L2 learned? Was the language learned as a child or not? (v) Why did the speaker become bilingual? (vi) Was it by choice or necessity? (vii) How much and to which skills did learning apply? To speaking, reading, writing? (viii) To what extent was their learning in each of these skills? Measuring bilingual proficiency, however, is still a problem.

2.4. The costs and rewards of bilingualism in the international arena

2.4.1. *Bilingualism as an investment and a cost*

The relationship of bilingualism and money in the world—because they are both means of exchange—deserves mention. More than anyone else, Bourdieu (1991) has made us view language as a commodity through his use of economic metaphors. For example, he speaks of society as a '*linguistic marketplace*' in which languages are valued positively or negatively, and he observes that languages possess '*symbolic capital*'. He refers to linguistic exchanges as 'relations of symbolic power in which the power relations between speakers of their respective groups are actualized' (1991: 37).

Taking a more nuts-and-bolts perspective, Coulmas (1992) devotes an entire volume to the relationship of world bilingualism and the relative statuses of different languages to the workings of governments and businesses. Ways of looking at the relationship include such topics as language as the economic asset, especially the monetary values of specific languages. In characterizing individual languages as commodities, Coulmas writes that '[a language's] value increases by every speaker who acquires it, or, whom it acquires. . . . The more people learn a language, the more useful it becomes, and the more useful it is, the more people want to learn it' (1992: 80). The most outstanding example of this 'snowball effect' is English. English holds the preeminence it does today not because of some inherent value, but because of historical and economic developments. For example, because English-speaking countries are the largest import market in the world, 'it is . . . only economic common sense that export-oriented countries in the non-English-speaking world prefer English to all other foreign languages' (1992: 80). Another result is that English is a main language for communication between two non-native speakers of English, neither of whom has the same L1. French used to hold this position in the international community and still does, especially in some geographical areas, as does Spanish.

Another topic Coulmas raises is the costliness of the polyglot world, especially the everyday fact of language-related expenses for governments and businesses. For example, some nations spend a good deal of money promoting their languages in other nations by setting up 'cultural centers' abroad. The idea is that political and business alliances are easier if a nation's language is known by at least some citizens in the targeted nations. International governmental organizations spend a good deal on translation facilities. Businesses may also have to employ translators; certainly, they often shoulder the cost of teaching employees languages they will need in international trade.

In addition, getting across simple business messages to consumers may require ingenuity in multilingual areas. For example, a southern California utility (in an area with many non-speakers of English or L2 speakers of English) was able to save $252,000 per year by using a linguistically more transparent billing form, because, as a result, customer inquiries dropped drastically (Coulmas 1992: 147). An article in *The New York Times* reported that in some areas of the United States where there is a Hispanic concentration, telephone operators who are bilingual in Spanish and English are demanding—and receiving—extra compensation for having to field calls in Spanish.

Of course money also figures in why individuals become bilingual, or shift from an L1 to an L2. This topic is discussed in the next section as well as when language shift is considered in some detail.

2.4.2. *Language as political capital*

In any bilingual community, not all languages have the same political capital; this depends on how languages are allocated to official and other public functions in a society. Those languages with the greatest capital are the language of government business and the medium of higher education. These choices make a difference in the fate of individual speakers of a particular variety, whole classes of individuals, or whole ethnic groups. They also make a difference in the fate of the variety itself—whether it will be maintained and flourish.

All linguistic varieties in a community are rarely treated equally; I refer to how they are often treated as 'elite closure'. Elite closure is 'a type of social mobilization strategy by which those persons in power establish or maintain their powers and privileges via linguistic choices' (Myers-Scotton 1993*b*: 149). Who are these elite and what do they do? I refer not to the wealthiest individuals in a society; rather, the elite that I have in mind are the policy-makers. They are largely politicians or governmental administrators, but also can include educators and other non-governmental professionals. Obviously, such an elite can close off access to power by other groups through official language policies that they often control or at least influence. For example, in Sri Lanka one of the major causes of the ongoing civil war is that the ruling party made Sinhala the official language, thereby effectively excluding the large Tamil-speaking minority from political access. Also, in Belgium, until after World War II, French was considered the only appropriate language for serious, public discourse, with Flemish relegated to informal, in-group activities.

In addition, more informal decisions of the elite about patterns of language use also have political consequences for all groups in a nation. The elite can accomplish elite closure through their own non-formalized language-use patterns and because they control different linguistic varieties from the masses. In many developing countries, membership in the elite is synonymous with persons with advanced education and bilingualism in the language of higher education (although there are exceptions). Thus, often simply being able to speak a particular variety identifies the elite. Just as important, and often harder to master, a particular style of speaking may be the badge of the elite. For example, extensive codeswitching between the local language and an international language, such as English in many parts of the world or French in francophone Africa, may identify the elite. Essien (1995) writes about such codeswitching between English and Ibibio as identifying those with university educations in the Ibibio-speaking area in eastern Nigeria. Or, the elite may favor different language-use patterns with their children from others from their L1 group, such as using an international language in their homes.

Thus, either through formal means (official language policies) or through informal means (codeswitching patterns, lexical choices, etc.), but typically both, elite closure is a tactic of boundary maintenance. Such closure designates those who will have easier access to socioeconomic mobility and political power because it specifies the varieties to be used in these arenas. That is, such choices can serve 'to alter boundaries between people or to maintain or alter patterns of access to power, wealth, and prestige within a society' (Weinstein 1983: 11–12).

Some degree of elite closure exists in all societies. Where the differences in repertoire between groups are only dialectal differences, elite closure is obviously weaker (but still present!) than it is where there are differences in the languages that different classes or ethnic groups can speak. This stronger version of elite closure is found especially where only part of the nation's population in a bilingual nation speaks the main official language. For those who do not speak this language, the access that it affords to status is an obvious incentive to learn the language and the overall patterns of allocation that characterize interactions of the elite.

2.5. Motivations to become bilingual

Section 2.2 spelled out the main conditions that favor bilingualism. However, the presence of any of these circumstances is not a guarantee that widespread bilingualism will develop. In this section, I briefly consider two main reasons why individual speakers decide to learn a second language and then mention a reason why speakers decide to drop their first language. In most nations, as well as between nations, dominant groups exert powerful pressures on other groups to learn their language (i.e. the language of those with economic and social power). In turn, such pressures set up counterpressures in other groups to preserve their L1, and even to lobby for provisions for it to have various types of official recognition. Consider the pressures within the United States regarding pushes and pulls between English and Spanish; or consider competition within Europe over which languages are to have various official roles in the European Community. Haugen (1950*a*: 279–80) observes, 'One of the most useful quantitative measures of linguistic pressure and counterpressure is to be found in the number and prestige of people who learn the "other language".'

Prestige may be what counts; however, prestige has a compound nature. Roberts (1939: 29) not only captures its kernel meaning in this statement, but also implies that there is more than one kind of prestige. He writes, 'Prestige contains two elements: power and charm. People must not only fear; they must admire what they fear.' He goes on to say that the semantic development of the word 'prestige' is highly instructive. The etymon is Vulgar Latin *praestigium*, earlier *praestrigium*, from *praestringere*, 'to bind up the eyes'. Prestige means at first the performance of a magician; in its wider meaning the term connotes the mirage of power.

2.5.1. *A second language as an instrumental asset*

Many observers explain becoming bilingual in the dominant language of a community in terms of economic opportunity (Edwards 1985, 1992). The main reasons are that chances for socioeconomic mobility almost always require proficiency in the dominant group's language, and attempts at communication outside one's own language group normally take place in the dominant group's language. As Fase, Jaspaert, and Kroon note, 'The most likely norm for communication with members of the dominant group is, of course, the dominant group language' (1992: 5). Also, in introducing a set of case studies of shift, Paulston answers the question of why groups shift to a new language for most purposes with this observation: 'The main point is simply that ethnic groups within a modern nation-state, given opportunity and incentive, typically shift to the language of the dominant group' (1994: 9).

A related point is that the learning of a second language (L2) by adults frequently begins in work contexts; that is, people generally acquire an L2 because it is useful to them in their livelihood. When this happens, speakers do not necessarily intend to abandon their L1, but they see ways in which the L2 is more tied to either simply a way to earn a living or to socioeconomic mobility. This is how traders in Africa at ethnic-group borders come to learn the L1s of the peoples across the border; for example, Luyia traders on the border between the Luyia homeland in Kenya's Western Province and Nyanza Province, which is dominated by Luos, often learn some Dholuo.

Similarly, the first villagers in Gapun, a small Papua New Guinea community, who came to learn Tok Pisin did it on the job (Kulick 1992). Young males spent time as contracted workers on plantations elsewhere or as ship hands or road builders where they learned Tok Pisin, the main lingua franca in the nation and one of the official languages. They brought their knowledge of Tok Pisin and—significantly—its associations back to the village. For this village, the bilingual cycle continues with the use of the newly learned second language expanding into more and more contexts.

The link between becoming bilingual and employment figures especially in the lives of most migrants the world over. The reason for most migration is to improve one's lot through new job opportunities, and usually a necessary part of this process is learning the dominant language of the host country. Immigrants may be Chinese peasants who join the work force in Shanghai and learn the Shanghai dialect, if not the national standard dialect, Pu Tong Hua. Or, in Nigeria, in-migrants to the city of Lagos from other parts of the country find that there is value on the job in being able to speak not only Standard Nigerian English, but also Nigerian Pidgin English. If they do not already know it, they may learn Nigerian Pidgin on the job where they also may learn some Yoruba. Because Yoruba is by far the main L1 in the city and neighboring areas, non-native speakers of Yoruba find being able to speak Yoruba beneficial when interacting with fellow workers, many of whom—predictably—are from the Yoruba group.

In Europe, North America, and Australia, immigrants often travel further; they come from diverse homelands to diverse destinations and occupations. They are Moroccan construction workers in France learning French, Turkish factory workers in Germany learning German, Ethiopian street cleaners in Italy learning Italian, or Philippine hotel workers in Norway learning Norwegian. And in North America, even though there are immigrant ghettos, such as 'Little Russia' in Brooklyn and bilingual street signs in some areas of Toronto (e.g. Greek and English), immigrants to Canada and the United States quickly add English to their repertoires (or French in Quebec Province).

In Asia, the practice of indentured labor figured in mass migrations of workers from China and from India to other parts of Asia and overseas. As early as 1985, Swamy (1985: 4) estimates eight million workers had moved from China and three million from British India. The result is that today in such places as Singapore, speakers of a variety of Chinese dialects are one of the main segments of the population. These immigrants retain their own languages to a much greater degree than those in North America, for example, partly because of the large size of their communities. Still, there has been an increasing shift from the so-called Chinese dialects to both English and Mandarin (Gupta and Yeok 1995).

In a very different setting, an army camp in the Eastern Cape province of South Africa, it is clear that a measure of Ethnolinguistic Vitality (discussed in section 2.5), sheer numbers of speakers of one language, makes a difference in seeing the need—and willingness—to learn another language. The camp is located in the Xhosa-speaking area and most of the soldiers are L1 speakers of Xhosa. Other languages are spoken and heard less frequently and (if at all) in town. The perception of two speakers indicates a typical attitude toward Xhosa (Barkhuisen and de Klerk 2000: 108):

(1) *a The comment of a Sotho L1 speaker:*
'Yes, I'm a Sotho, because of the majority of the peoples here they are Xhosa speakers, you see. So that is why most of the time I try to learn Xhosa. The Sothos and Venda they try to learn Xhosa.'
b The comment of a Xhosa L1 speaker:
'It will be difficult for that guy to try to talk his Venda or ask me to try to speak Venda.'

While these attitudes definitely do not mean that Sotho speakers will shift to Xhosa in any permanent sense, they do show how the symbolic capital of a language in a specific setting is affected by such vitality measures as numbers of speakers.

2.5.2. *Self-perceptions and becoming bilingual and perceptions of bilinguals*

However, another major reason for becoming bilingual that is often overlooked is that exposure to outside lifestyles causes individuals and entire groups to change their interpretations of their own world. That is, becoming bilingual can be part of a change in how individuals perceive and express themselves. Under this view, becoming bilingual is not just a reaction to, or a recognition of, the economic value of a second language. On the one hand, for example, a university graduate in computer science in India could hardly expect to work for a firm with international business except as a lower level programmer without a good command of English. However, on the other hand, studying a language of wider communication or an international business language may also have more indirect motivations that have to do with one's persona as a 'modern person'.

This approach to bilingualism and language shift focuses on speakers as social agents (Gal 1996) and how they use languages to encode social identities (Hyltenstam and Stroud 1996). Gal calls for more attention, not just to the large social changes such as urbanization and industrialization that have been cited as promoting bilingualism and language shift, but to the relation between these changes and speakers' evaluations of languages and the social meanings associated with them. And Hyltenstam and Stroud argue that 'since the language encodes social identity, speakers chose the language that best accords with their needs for self presentation and identity negotiations in given situations' (1996: 572).

For example, true, knowing English may benefit a factory manager or an electrical engineer in China if he or she has to interact occasionally with traveling American businessmen. But such persons do not really *need* to be able to speak English (as long as they can read English technical documents). They certainly are not going to replace Chinese with English except for their handful of encounters with foreigners. Instead, they are motivated to learn English because they see some knowledge of English as a badge for people who are regarded as capable of participating in modernization strategies.

The psychological associations that a group has with specific languages also can promote bilingualism and language shift. While acknowledging that overarching social and economic factors promote bilingualism in a language of wider communication, Kulick (1992) argues that how these factors are interpreted in people's everyday lives may be as important in bringing about bilingualism and shift. Kulick details how Tok Pisin is being learned as an L2 in the Papua New Guinea village of Gapun and how this language is coming to be identified with a desirable aspect of *save* 'self' (in Taiap, the village's L1). Speaking Tok Pisin is associated with the sociable, cooperative side of a person. In contrast, the other side of personhood—what villagers call *hed*—is associated with the individualistic, selfish, and unbending side of personhood. Kulick writes, 'In using Tok Pisin, villagers are thus expressing an important and highly valued aspect of self. . . . But in doing this, they are constituting a situation in which their vernacular is becoming less and less desirable and important' (1992: 21). Language-use patterns in the village also do not favor Taiap. Caregivers of young children willingly translate their Taiap utterances into Tok Pisin. This means that 'the children come to understand that whatever is said to them in Taiap will be repeated in Tok Pisin, sooner or later' (p. 207). And, as of 1987, no village child under ten actively commanded the vernacular and the use of Tok Pisin was spreading, Kulick reports.

Although language is often considered an integral part of ethnic identity, there are examples of groups for whom this is not so and who readily accept bilingualism, even bilingualism that leads to the loss of their own L1. Barth (1972) details such a case. Two groups along the Indo-Iranian border, the Baluchi and the Pashto, differ in their attitudes toward language and therefore inevitably in their language practices. He cites the Pashto proverb that 'he is a Pathan who *does* Pashto, not who *speaks* Pashto' (1972: 457). While their Baluchi neighbors have a socially stratified and centralized form of group structure, the Pathans do not. Instead, Barth refers to the Pathans as 'independent men with separate interests who . . . can unite as a corporate body through joint decision making' (p. 460). Even though the Pathans greatly outnumbered the Baluchis at the time of his writing, Barth indicates that these differences in group organization and self-perception have made it easy for the Baluchi language area to expand, with Pathans assimilated into Baluchi tribal organization.

Edwards, who has been most associated with the instrumental view of bilingualism and language shift, makes an especially perceptive comment that recognizes speakers as rational agents whose decisions reflect not only their drive for socioeconomic mobility, but also their perceptions of self. He writes, 'I think it is both unlikely and unparsimonious to assert that some groups value their language less. What is *more* likely is that groups find themselves in different circumstances, requiring different adaptations' (1994*a*: 23).

This leads to a consideration of how others perceive bilinguals. Bilingualism may be envied, but it may be frowned upon, too. In communities with a hierarchical structure, it has typically been the educated classes who become bilingual in varieties associated with whatever the society values (e.g. certain types of literature, a glorious past, and always various sources of contemporary power). Armed with this commodity, they can practice 'elite closure' (as indicated in section 2.4.2.). Whatever they do, they form an envied and privileged class based partly on their bilingualism. This is even the case in supposedly egalitarian societies to an extent (e.g. the United States). However, even more frequently, an egalitarian society can perceive bilingualism as divergence from the norm of 'open communication'. That is, speaking a 'foreign language' may be considered an unwelcome sign of out-group allegiance. This perception gives especially immigrants a reason to avoid speaking their L1 in public and even to lose it as fast as possible.

2.6. Bilingualism and language-use patterns

Fishman (e.g. 1972) gave currency to considering language-use patterns in terms of domains. He (and others) have looked at language use in terms of these domains: family, friendship, religion, education, and employment, among others. Domain is an abstract construct, but Fishman argues that 'domains are as real as the very social institutions of a speech community, and indeed they show a marked paralleling with such major social institutions' (1972: 45). Just as important, speakers 'can come to have certain views concerning their varieties or languages because their varieties are associated (in behavior and attitude) with particular domains' (p. 46).

2.6.1. *Lexical borrowing*

The most obvious effect of bilingualism on the languages of individuals is it promotes the borrowing of lexical elements across languages. An obvious sociolinguistic characteristic of borrowing is that, for the most part, this borrowing is one-way: L1 speakers of the less prestigious group (however prestige is conceived of) take into their language words from the L1 of the more prestigious language. A psycholinguistic characteristic that differentiates borrowing from codeswitching is that not all the speakers who use borrowed forms (loanwords) need to be bilingual in the donor language. True, at least some speakers in the borrowing community need a measure of bilingualism to effect borrowing in the first place. More structural aspects of borrowing are discussed in Chapter 6.

While the status of borrowed forms vis-à-vis codeswitching forms in any model designed to constrain the structure of codeswitching is controversial, most researchers agree that borrowed forms and codeswitching forms differ in regard to predictability. While one cannot predict when a borrowed form will reoccur, one can predict it definitely will reoccur because it has a status in the recipient language. If it has a dictionary entry, its status is undisputed (although some clearly established borrowings take a long time to achieve dictionary status). The codeswitching form may or may not reoccur; it has no predictive value. Following Myers-Scotton (1993*a* [1997], chapter 6), I argue that any established borrowed form achieves the cognitive status of being projected by lemmas tagged for the recipient language (although lemmas supporting them certainly can remain in the mental lexicon tagged for the source language as well). In contrast, the premise is that those content morphemes that are labeled as codeswitching forms have entries tagged only for the Embedded Language in the mental lexicon. If they are used frequently enough, they can achieve status in the recipient language, too, as borrowed forms. This happens when lemmas for them as borrowed forms are added to the recipient language's store in mental lexicon to support them.

There are two types of content morphemes that can become borrowed forms: (i) Cultural borrowings are words for objects and concepts new to the culture (e.g. *hard drive*, *SUV*, or *global warming*). These borrowed forms are rapidly integrated into the recipient language, although they may retain phonetic features from their source language. Cultural borrowings appear abruptly in a language when influential speakers begin using them. These cultural borrowed forms may appear frequently in two outcomes, in the monolingual speech of either bilinguals or monolinguals (speaking the recipient language), or in the codeswitching of bilinguals. (ii) Core borrowings are words that more or less duplicate already existing words in the L1 (e.g. in French a word for a small truck, *pickup*, or *le weekend*).[1] I argue that such borrowed forms typically come into the recipient language through codeswitching. That is, in contrast to cultural borrowed forms, core borrowed forms only enter the recipient language gradually.

[1] Of course, core borrowings may not exactly duplicate an existing word; the semantic fields or the pragmatic force of the two elements may be different.

Haugen (1950*b*: 282) offers a graphic description of how core borrowed forms easily become part of an immigrant's life. Writing specifically about Norwegian immigrants to the United States, he suggests this scenario:

> Without affectation or snobbishness they were speaking an americanized tongue to each other before they were fully aware of what was happening to them. The needs of understanding and of social solidarity were most effortlessly met by a gradual infiltration of loans. These were not limited to actual cultural novelties or so-called 'necessary' words; the terms most characteristic of the new environment were often impressed on their minds by mere repetition in vivid situations. Their experience in the new language began to outstrip their experience in the old, and the discrepancy set up a pressure which led to linguistic change.

Established borrowed forms, whether they are cultural or core borrowed forms, often show some phonological integration into the recipient language; the degree of this integration depends on a number of factors, including differences in the phonology of the two languages, but also the degree of bilingualism of the speakers using the borrowed forms.

In contrast to their phonological characteristics, most borrowed forms are entirely—or almost entirely—morphosyntactically integrated into the recipient language. There are exceptions. For example, some borrowed forms retain some system morphemes from the donor language. However, these are almost always early system morphemes and, as such, are not part of the morphosyntactic frame (for example, *alchemy* is a borrowing originally from Arabic *al kimiya* with *al* as a definite article). A very few borrowings into English retain another early system morpheme, plural marking (e.g. at least in English-speaking academic circles, the pairs *datum, data; syllabus, syllabi* may be doggedly retained). In line with morphosyntactic integration that has structural consequences, what counts is that such borrowed forms conform to the recipient language's requirements for late system morphemes. For example, if *data* is recognized as a plural form, then subject–verb agreement indicates plurality (*data are*...); if it is considered a singular form or a mass noun, then it receives singular subject–verb agreement. One should note, however, that largely only academics (and not all of them) treat *data* as a plural; that is, retaining plurality for *data* becomes something of a 'boundary marker' for academics—in the same sense that *cacti* is for readers of the popular western American magazine *Arizona Highways*. When the readership was asked for vote for either *cacti* or *cactuses* as a plural for *cactus*, they much preferred *cacti*.[2]

In addition, some borrowed forms may not retain their original set of inflections, but they fail to conform to all the morphological requirements of the recipient language. For example, Arabic adjectives as borrowed forms in Swahili do not receive the agreement prefixes that indigenous Bantu adjectives receive (compare *m-tu Ø-hodari* 'person clever, intelligent' with *hodari* from Arabic, with

[2] Source: National Public Radio program, 'Morning Edition', October 2000.

m-tu m-kubwa 'person big'). Still, such adjectives of Arabic origin follow Swahili word order. Even though Arabic verb stems are not totally integrated into the Bantu frame (i.e. they do not show the final vowel *-a* in positive indicative mood), they are treated otherwise entirely like Bantu verb stems.

Still, most borrowed forms, as entries in the morphosyntactic frame of the recipient language, conform to its well-formedness conditions. Lexical elements can be borrowed, but they must leave behind their levels of predicate-argument structure and morphological realization patterns unless they match those of the recipient language. This is as the MLF model would predict. The structure of lexical borrowings is discussed further in Chapter 6 in contrast to one language's incorporation of grammatical elements from another language.

2.6.2. *Compartmentalizing varieties in a linguistic repertoire*

The most obvious effect of bilingualism on individuals themselves is that they generally do compartmentalize their use of the different varieties in their repertoires. That is, one variety is mainly used in certain domains, and another is used in other domains. At the same time, two other patterns are more frequent than is often reported in the literature: (i) Speakers may frequently engage in codeswitching in a given domain; codeswitching is discussed more fully in section 2.6.3. (ii) Or, the same language is not the 'unmarked choice' for all participants in the same interaction. Thus, when such individuals converse with each other, each person may speak her own language, as in the following example from Zentella's ethnographic study of language use among Puerto Ricans living in New York City:

> Lolita and her mother communicated in Spanish on occasion, but they were more likely to engage in non-reciprocal language dyads. Lolita understood everything her mother said in Spanish and Lourdes [the mother] understood what her daughter said in English, *but each preferred to respond in her stronger language.* (Italics added) (1997: 68)

Elsewhere family conversations show similar linguistic disjunctions. For example, in Singapore, even though '*everyone* except some members of the oldest generation is bilingual' (Gupta and Yeok 1995: 303), proficiencies and—accordingly—preferences vary. In their study of language use within a Chinese family in Singapore, Gupta and Yeok report that codeswitching is a way to bridge the communication gap between an older generation (generation 1 or G1) and a younger generation (generation 3 or G3). The intermediate generation may form the bridge. 'This often involves a G2 [generation 2] member speaking first in Cantonese to a G1 member, and then giving an English version for the benefit of a G3 member. This can create conversations in which all generations can participate through the mediation of G2' (1995: 309).

2.6.3. *The major social motivations for codeswitching*

When bilinguals add a language to their repertoire, they also add the possibility to codeswitch between languages in order to achieve various stylistic effects.

Codeswitching can take many forms, but it can be defined most generally as the use of two or more varieties in the same conversation. A popular view is that speakers switch codes because they cannot think of the right word in one language and so they go to their second language. Zentella referred to this as crutching because 'a bilingual who is stumped in one language can keep on speaking by depending on a translated synonym as a stand in' (1997: 98). However, Zentella also checked instances of codeswitching in the group of children she studied most intensively against their lexical inventories. She concluded that even non-fluent children use codeswitching as a 'lexical cover-up' much less than is assumed. Other observations also show that switching mainly to fill gaps is neither typically true nor the major reason that speakers switch codes. First, most bilinguals who engage in codeswitching are very proficient in both of their languages; that is, they do not *need* to search for a word in the other language. Second, most switch codes because of the stylistic resource that another language offers. By using more than one language in the same conversation, speakers can accomplish two social maneuvers: codeswitching can be either (i) a comment on the speaker's perception of self or (ii) it can be a comment on his/her perception of the tenor of the ongoing interaction, its participants, its topics, etc.

One reason many think that codeswitching is a stop-gap measure is that speakers are more conscious of their language use when they use codeswitching in this way. However, typically, speakers are not even aware that they are engaging in codeswitching. For example, a graduate student of mine from Malaŵi thought that he compartmentalized his languages while he was a student in England. Here's what he thought he did: speak exclusively his main Malaŵian language, Chicheŵa, with other Malaŵian students, and only speak English in outside interactions. However, when he made an audio recording of some fellow Malaŵian students and himself for a classroom assignment, he found their conversation was one stream of codeswitching between Chicheŵa and English. Or, to take another example, in her study of language use among the Tigak ethnic group on New Ireland island (in Papua New Guinea), Jenkins reports having been walking down a path with some Tigaks, discussing what languages they used in different contexts. One middle-aged man spoke up and claimed that he and his fellow Tigaks always use only Tigak. But he said this while speaking part in Tok Pisin *O-o mipela olgeta taim* 'oh, all the time'—and only part in the Tigak language, their vernacular:

(2)	**O-o mipela**	**olgeta**	**taim**	men	etok	lo	etok	siva!
	1PL	all	time	1PL/EXCLUS/SUBJ	talk	LOC	talk	place

'Oh, we always speak in [the] vernacular.'

(Jenkins 2000: 132)

Many researchers who are interested in discourse strategies have found grist for their mills in codeswitching. The idea behind the notion that codeswitching is a strategy is that speakers exploit the associations of the varieties in their repertoires to convey social meanings of various types. For example, one of the most prominent students of codeswitching, John Gumperz (1982) refers to codeswitching as a 'contextualization cue'. That is, switches within a conversation provide clues to other participants about the speaker's attitude or stance vis-à-vis other participants and/or their conversational contributions. This is a notion that has been taken up by Auer (e.g. 1998*a*) and others who study codeswitching within a methodological approach called conversation analysis.

I have written about codeswitching as a strategy of negotiation. I argue that speakers see code choices in general (not just codeswitching) as a way to index the set of rights and obligations that they wish to have in force between speaker and addressee in the current exchange (cf. 1993*c*: 113ff.). (That is, the rights and obligations set in effect in any exchange is open to negotiation.) As part of their communicative competence, speakers develop a sense of choices as more or less unmarked (according to community norms) for a particular rights and obligations set, and the motivation to switch codes is best understood in this light. To expand briefly on the motivations for codeswitching already mentioned, I argue that codeswitching can accomplish one of two main goals. (i) It can call for a change in the dynamics of a conversation (making a marked choice indexes a negotiation for a different relationship—a different rights and obligations set—from that which is unmarked for the current exchange or is ongoing in the exchange). (ii) Or, an overall pattern of switching codes can index the speakers' desire to project themselves as persons with the identities associated with more than one language; that is, they project dual identities. (This type of switching, what I call 'codeswitching itself as the unmarked choice', is the type that provides most of the examples of switches within a CP; such switches are the ones providing data that test the MLF model.)

For example, here is a portion of a conversation among a group of young men in Nairobi, Kenya. They come from different ethnic groups, but all speak both Swahili and English in addition to their separate first languages. By speaking both Swahili and English in the same conversation they can identify themselves with the associations of both languages. Swahili has positive connotations as the language of 'those who know the town', while English is associated with education and the higher-paying jobs, as well as with the wider world. Swahili is the Matrix Language in this conversation, as it is for most such conversations in Nairobi, even though the speakers have similar proficiency in both English and Swahili. Note that this conversation includes switching within the same bilingual CP as well as a full monolingual CP (*ambao wamebaki nyuma* 'they who remain behind'). Within a bilingual CP, there are three types of switches: (i) intra-word switching (*a-li-fall* 'third person singular-past-fall'; *ku-appreciate* 'infinitive marker-appreciate'), (ii) singly occurring forms (e.g. *deadly*, *fashion*, etc.) and Embedded Language islands, full constituents from English (*for me*, *so badly*, *people on the move*, etc.).

(3) *Two young men in casual conversation:*

G: Huyo Dorothy **a-li-fall kwangu ile deadly.**
'That Dorothy **fell for me so badly.**'
A: Ah . . . **fall kwako?**
'Fell for you?'
G: Kitu mmoja mbaya kwake ni kuvaa zile **miniskirts.**
'The bad thing with her is to wear [that she wears] **miniskirts.**'
A: **Miniskirts** huzipendelei?
'You don't like **miniskirts?**'
G: Ah hizo ni **fashion nyingine ovyo sana.**
'Ah, that's **another very lousy fashion.**'
A: Wewe unajua, bwana, hii **fashion** ni ya wale watu, **people on the move.** Sasa kama watu kama wewe ambao wamebaki nyuma hamuwezi. **ku-appreciate** hiyo.
'You know, mister, that is the **fashion** of those people, **people on the move.** Now, people like you who remain behind can't **appreciate** it.'

(Swahili/English Myers-Scotton; Nairobi corpus 1988)

2.6.3.1. Codeswitching in a rational-choice model

Most recently I have extended the notion that speakers exploit the markedness of the various codes in their repertoires by discussing code choices (and codeswitching specifically) as rational choices. That is, I interpret my Markedness Model as a Rational Choice Model (Myers-Scotton 1993c, Myers-Scotton and Bolonyai 2001). I expand the argument that speakers take account of readings of markedness when they make choices in using one language rather than another. What is emphasized is that choices are best explained as cognitively based calculations that depend on their estimations of what choices offer them the greatest rewards, given the available evidence. What this means is that a bilingual may see switching languages at some point in a conversation as a way to optimize rewards. A rational choice model does not view choices as objective, but rather very subjective; however, given their ongoing assessment of the situation, the premise is that speakers are making the choice they consider 'best'. Of course, as with the choice to speak one language rather than another in any interaction, there is no guarantee that switching codes accomplishes a speaker's goals.

Example (4) illustrates how codeswitching is a calculated strategy for an eight-year-old Hungarian boy who lives in the United States with his family. His mother prefers Hungarian as the unmarked choice for family dinner-table conversations and the boy, Kristóf, does begin in Hungarian. However, he switches to English when the issue of how he is going to be served salad comes up (*I'll make my own salad*). If one considers the associations of English in his life, his switch to English can be viewed as indexing his assertion of independence. After all, English is the language of the dominant culture; it is the language associated with his roles when he is independent of family constraints, such as his interactions with peers and at school. Note that such a switch cannot be explained under an analysis that looks only at the ongoing turn-taking features of the conversation (e.g. analyses under a Conversation Analysis framework, cf. Auer 1998*b*). Nor can the claim that bilinguals switch languages according to topic explain Kristóf's choices; note that he uses Hungarian for talking about school matters, a domain closely aligned with English, not Hungarian. (Note that Kistóf not only gets to make his own salad, but his mother gives him some extra ingredients!)

(4) *Making a salad at the dinner table* (Hungarian/English). K = Kristóf; M = Mother
M: Kristóf, mi volt az iskolában? Irtatok tesztet?
'Kristóf, how was school? Did you write any tests?'
K: Tessék?
'Pardon?'
M: Volt teszt? Milyen volt az AGP?
'Were there any tests? How was AGP?'
K: Most nem voltam. Nem volt még.
'I wasn't [in AGP] today. It hasn't started yet.'
M: Kedden van?
'Is it on Tuesday?'
K: Thursday-n van.
'It's on Thursday.'
M: Kértek salátát, úgy-e?
'Would you like some salad, wouldn't you?'
K: **I'll make my own salad.**
M: Mi?
'What?'
K: **I'll make my own salad.** Ilyen kicsi tányérokban csinálják a restaurant-okban.
'They make it in such small plates at the restaurants.'
(K making the salad)
K: **I need some salad, please.**
M: Odaadtam az egészet. Tegyél hozzá mást is.
'I've given you all. Add something else to it, too.

(Myers-Scotton and Bolonyai 2001: 7)

2.6.3.2. Codeswitching and group solidarity

When group social identities, rather than an individual's social identity, are the issue, and accommodation is a goal, codeswitching may be employed as a neutral strategy. This is so in situations where either ethnicity or socioeconomic status, or both, differ across participants (Myers-Scotton 1976). For example, in a car-assembly plant in Malaysia, codeswitching between English and Malay is very frequent in middle-level meetings, such as production meetings. The codeswitching 'may be explained by the fact that the membership cuts across communication networks, one based on socioeconomic differences and the other on ethnic divisions. These are the managers and their executive assistants who represent the top-level network, and the foreman and the charge hands who come from the shop-floor network' (Morais 1998: 99). The managers may use mesolectal varieties of English and Malay while the subordinates use more basilectal varieties, but through codeswitching they can maintain the fiction that they are speaking 'the same language'. This enables them to project themselves as on a similar level, at least regarding conversational strategies.

2.7. Language shift

Language shift is simply 'a change from the habitual use of one language to that of another' (Weinreich 1967: 68). Becoming bilingual can lead to such a shift; that is, for a host of reasons, speakers come to replace their L1 with a second language they added.

Lambert (1975) provides two ways that are useful in viewing bilingualism in relation to language shift, additive and subtractive bilingualism. Additive bilingualism occurs when speakers maintain their L1 but also learn an L2 for some of their activities. An example of this type of bilingualism is the learning and use of English in Switzerland by some L1 speakers of any of the four official languages of Switzerland (German, French, Italian, and Romansh). Subtractive bilingualism occurs when speakers learn an L2 that develops into a replacement for their L1, either in many of their daily activities or entirely. An example of this type of bilingualism is the learning of English by many immigrant groups in Australia or North America. A typical pattern is shift to the community's dominant language by the third generation.

No one would expect that a language that is transmitted to children and is used by both adults and children in many and varied contexts is in jeopardy. However, what about languages with less robust attributes? And, given the power differential between the majority language and the minority languages in any community, are not all minority languages vulnerable to losing speakers through shift to the majority language? That is, if access to important resources (e.g. jobs, schools, government) is all through the majority language, there is necessarily a power differential.

Most students of shift agree that the future of a language depends on the number of people using it, the existence of a community of speakers, and the domains in which a language is used. In most countries in the world and for most of its languages and dialects, all functions are not covered by a single language. Almost everyone would agree with Ryan and Giles that 'the more numerous and more important the functions served by the variety for the greater number of individuals the greater is the vitality' (1982: 4). Also, almost no one would disagree with Edwards that 'the relationship between language and economics is . . . a very strong one, and practical considerations underlie most linguistic patterns and alterations' (1985: 164). That is, there is no question that the language used in status-raising domains will certainly be maintained. Further, because economic, or at least instrumental, motives determine much language use, the language of such domains may well expand to other domains.

2.7.1. *Two major ways in which allocation matters*

The details of complementarity of languages and their domains in a community and allocation to solitary-stressing domains may be keys in predicting maintenance of the L1 of a minority group. For example, consider two aspects of allocation that are often mentioned: does diglossia exist and what do group speakers use with each other?

Diglossia refers to the rather strict and complementary allocation of the varieties in a community's repertoire to different domains. That classical Arabic and a regional colloquial Arabic are not used in the same situations in most Arabic-speaking countries is an example of diglossia in place (Ferguson 1959). This segregation of varieties applies elsewhere to unrelated varieties (Fishman 1972); for example, Portuguese immigrants in France may speak French at work, but continue to speak Portuguese at home. That is, as long as both varieties have their separate community roles, this diglossic pattern seems to help maintain the language that has the lesser prestige in the power arena. However, where codeswitching exists—especially in the younger generations—this neat division collapses, and possibly L1 maintenance with it. For example, the Russian immigrant boys that Schmitt studied (2000, 2001) and the Hungarian girls that Bolonyai studied (2000) engage with each other in codeswitching that includes English, even though their parents prefer Russian and Hungarian respectively.

Related to this, the language that an individual uses with fellow speakers of an L1 is considered a good predictor of a language's future in the community. Fase, Jaspaert, and Kroon assert, 'As long as there is a minority group, as long as the minority group is not demograhically broken up, the use of the minority language will not disappear unless the norms for language use within the group are changed' (1992: 7). Further, Harwood, Giles, and Bourhis also point to in-group language use as a predictor of the vitality of a group's language. They write, 'The density and multiplex nature of these everyday contacts provide the dynamic link between the objective vitality of the groups and the perceptual and behavioral developments that shape relations between ethnolinguistic group members' (1994: 179).

A language's profile in regard to a second set of factors that are less demographic and more psychological in nature may be even more important in predicting maintenance. In general, to what extent do the speakers of a language value it, and what do they value it for? Quite clearly, if speakers do not value their own language, it is on its way out. As Dorian points out, 'It's fairly common for a language to become so exclusively associated with low-prestige people and their socially disfavored identities that its own potential speakers prefer to distance themselves from it and adopt some other language' (1988: 3). However, it is just as clear that if a language is important as a salient mark of identity and as a symbol of political resistance for a low-prestige people, it may well be maintained; consider the Kurdish speakers in Turkey. Also, Hyltenstam and Stroud (1996) cite Smolicz (1981) on the notion of 'core values', the values that an ethnic group itself believes must be maintained to represent the group. If language is one of these values, the chances of an L1 being maintained has increased. For example, within Australia, not all immigrant languages have been equally maintained. 'Language as a core value would, in the Australian immigrant context, distinguish Latvian and Greek speakers, on the one hand, who have maintained their languages to a high degree from such groups as the Dutch on the other' (Hyltenstam and Stroud 1996: 573).

Clearly, the same psychological forces that convince individuals to add a language (such as adding Tok Pisin in the Papua New Guinea village discussed above (Kulick 1992)) also convince them in many cases to abandon their L1s. Obondo (1996) provides a case study from Africa in which even the ways that speakers discuss their L1s mirrors the words used in the Papua New Guinea village. Obondo studied attrition of Dholuo as an L1 among staff workers at a university in Western Kenya. Luos there are shifting to Swahili and, among the more educated, to English as their main languages. They are putting little effort into making sure their children acquire Dholuo. Swahili functions as the language of parental authority in many family interactions. In children's conversations, there are arguments over who speaks English better; also, English is used to exert control in games. When asked why a child spoke Swahili, not Dholuo, to a younger child, he responded, 'but *watoto* [Swahili for 'children'] they . . . cannot comprehend *Kijaluo* [Swahili for 'the Luo language']. . . . In fact they undersand Kiswahili more' (Obondo 1996: 87). Further, Obondo notes the signs in elicited narratives that indicate a shift is under way; that is, Dholuo narratives from urban Luos show both a good deal of codeswitching and many lexical borrowings from English and Swahili.

2.7.2. *Ethnolinguistic vitality*

Social psychologists have integrated sociopsychological variables into their accounts of language-use practices (cf. Giles, Bourhis, and Taylor 1977 and with more recent work by Landry and Allard, e.g. 1992, 1994). Specifically, the concepts of ethnolinguistic vitality and subjective ethnolinguistic vitality are useful in predicting when groups may become bilingual and, conversely, when they may replace their L1 in most, if not all, activities with an L2. A language's vitality is defined as 'the range and importance of the symbolic functions a variety serves, that is, the degree to which a variety is used' (Ryan and Giles 1982: 4). The measure of such vitality is based on demographics, status, and institutional-support factors (e.g. How many speakers? Is a variety standardized? Does it have a literary tradition? Does it have status in government and education?). Ethnolinguistic vitality is 'that which makes a group likely to behave as a distinctive and active collective entity in intergroup situations' (Giles, Bourhis, and Taylor 1977: 308). Later,

Bourhis, Giles, and Rosenthal (1981) added the notion of 'subjectivity' to ethnolinguistic vitality. They suggest that simply 'a group's subjective assessment of its relative position on the variables affecting EV [Ethnolinguistic Vitality] may be as important in determining its inter-ethnic behaviours as its more objective position on these variables' (Allard and Landry 1992: 172). The idea, of course, is that an individual's attitudes toward the group's ethnolinguistic vitality contribute directly to his/her desire to maintain the language tied to the group's social identity.

Allard and Landry conducted a study in eastern Canada that supported at least two conclusions about perceptions and language use and maintenance. First, even the use of one's L1 versus an L2 shows a high degree of relationship with beliefs regarding Ethnolinguistic Vitality (Allard and Landry 1992: 192). That is, if minority group members perceive their language's vitality as high, it influences their language-use patterns. Second, the results also convinced the authors that minority-group and majority-group individuals treat bilingualism differently in the following ways: (i) If majority group members have the necessary contacts, they will learn an L2 and maintain bilingualism. (ii) However, for minority-group members, especially in situations of low Ethnolinguistic Vitality, becoming bilingual means eventually dropping their first language. Allard and Landry see that attitudes are very influential as to whether bilingualism is additive or subtractive. Maintaining a minority language depends on 'the maintenance of a strong L1 ambience in the school and family milieu . . . with very few losses in L2 competence. . . . Just as important, L1 self beliefs and ethnolinguistic identity would also be maintained' (Landry and Allard 1992: 247).

Finally, consider a positive way of looking at language shift from Edwards. He writes that to see shift as negative 'implies a static conception of history which is, simply, unrealistic. It is much more useful to consider language shift as *alteration*; this accords with social dynamics and, in any event, there is never a question of a loss, sure and simple, with nothing to replace the abandoned form. Another languages comes to serve and, in the transitional period, bilingualism is the usual bridge' (1985: 159).

2.8. Structural results of bilingualism and language shift

The main goal of this chapter has been to detail the types of situations that promote bilingualism and a possible counterpart, language shift, as well as the reasons why individuals become bilingual and why some shift from their L1s to another language as their main medium of communication. A person's linguistic repertoire is necessarily dynamic, changing with other types of changes in the community.

Whatever its outcome vis-à-vis the speaker's repertoire, bilingualism—as a social and psychological phenomenon—almost inevitably produces the type of structural phenomena that are the main subjects in this volume. Of course, second-language acquisition itself is obviously also part of bilingualism; however, just because I have to limit the scope of this volume at some point, I only mention second-language acquisition. One reason is the large literature elsewhere on the subject.

The topics considered in this volume in relation to bilingualism include the following: (i) Lexical borrowing, a subject in Chapter 6, is frequent and pervades both monolingual and bilingual communities everywhere. Lexical borrowings are almost always content morphemes and they pattern along with content morphemes that are singly occurring forms in the relevant morphosyntactic frame (either the frame of the recipient language or of the Matrix Language) in codeswitching. (ii) Both among speakers who maintain their bilingualism and among speakers who are shifting from their L1s, codeswitching is widespread; it is discussed, or at least mentioned, in every chapter. (iii) Wherever there is bilingualism there is always a power differential between the languages involved—simply because access to sources of power (e.g. high-level jobs, educational facilities, governmental services) are not equally distributed. One result that may affect both languages, but almost certainly the language of the less powerful, is structural convergence. As we see in later chapters, convergence may be combined with codeswitching. Both codeswitching and convergence tend to figure in all other contact phenomena; this gives them special importance in this volume. (iv) When language shift is under way, attrition of an L1 is always a certain outcome, a topic in Chapter 5. (v) and (vi) Two other possible outcomes of bilingualism, mixed (split) languages and creole formation, are discussed in Chapter 6.

The social and psychological conditions discussed in this chapter promote such structural developments, and many of the ways in which these contact phenomena differ have to do with difference in the sociopsychological milieux in which they develop. However, this volume argues that a single set of structural principles is behind all the options that differentiate the outcomes, whatever their sociopsychological setting.

3

Explaining the Models and Their Uses

3.1. Introduction

After the general introduction in Chapter 1, this chapter offers more substantive premises about grammatical structure in relation to bilingual speech as they are articulated in the Matrix Language Frame model and its new supporting models, the 4-M model and the Abstract Level model. These premises are relevant to other chapters, especially Chapter 5 on convergence and attrition and Chapter 6 on mixed languages and creole development.

Because the MLF model is now augmented by the 4-M model and the Abstract Level model, one main purpose here is to show how the MLF model has changed since the 1993 version of *Duelling Languages*. Some of the discussion repeats statements from the Afterword in the 1997 second edition of this volume, a discussion overlooked by many commentators on the MLF model. Contrary to the views of some researchers (e.g. Park 2000: 39) the model has not 'changed radically'. Rather, the Afterword only elaborates on the model's basic principles and tries to clarify hypotheses; also, it acknowledges some rather superficial mistakes and misguided views in the 1993 version. However, the basic substance is the same. All the main premises of the MLF model still hold, highlighting the asymmetry that characterizes codeswitching data and seemingly all contact phenomena in general.

I try to accomplish two main goals in this chapter. First, I reiterate provisions of the MLF model that either were not well articulated by me, or not well understood by others—or a combination of the two. Second, I enlarge on the introduction in Chapter 1 of both the 4-M model and the Abstract Level model. I suggest how applying these models in concert with the MLF model results in better analyses and explanations not only of classic codeswitching, the original subject of the MLF model, but also other contact phenomena. No prior knowledge of the MLF model is necessary; that is, I try to explain here the basics of how the model works.

I begin by turning to the Matrix Language – Embedded Language opposition. As a preliminary, I argue for the CP (projection of Complementizer) as the best unit of analysis for examination of any contact phenomena. Second, I argue once again for the other basic opposition in the MLF model, the content–system morpheme opposition. I go on to describe in detail the new 4-M model and to show how this model refines the content–system morpheme opposition. Third, I show how codeswitching, analyzed within the bilingual CP and observing the refined content–system morpheme opposition, supports and clarifies the System Morpheme Principle of the MLF model and explains some other structures. Fourth, I give a more detailed introduction to the Abstract Level model, the other new supporting model introduced in Chapter 1. In Chapter 4 I discuss some problematic data in terms of these models.

3.2. Clarifying the MLF model

3.2.1. *CP as the unit of analysis*

Soon after *Duelling Languages* was published in 1993, I replaced 'sentence' with 'CP' (projection of complementizer) as the unit of analysis. Even in *Duelling Languages*, the CP is usually the implicit unit of analysis, with a few lapses. In a very few cases, I erroneously refer to what is clearly a separate CP as an Embedded Language island.[1] Embedded Language islands are Embedded Language constituents that show structural dependency relationships (and therefore must consist of more than one morpheme). While both Embedded Language islands and CPs are constituents, islands are contained within CPs. A CP (or S-bar) is a special type of constituent; it is the syntactic structure expressing the predicate-argument structure of a clause, plus any additional structures needed to encode discourse-relevant structure and the logical form of that clause.

From 1995 onwards, my associates and I explicitly refer to our analyses of codeswitching as *within the CP* (cf. Myers-Scotton and Jake 1995, Myers-Scotton, Afterword in 1997 edition, Bolonyai 1999, Gross 2000*a*, *inter alia*). The main tradition in codeswitching studies had been—and continues to be—to distinguish only between intersentential and intra-sentential codeswitching, with the sentence as the reference point for structural analyses. However, we find that CP is the unit of analysis that is easiest to apply and the one that offers comparability across examples not only for codeswitching, but also for other contact phenomena. I will use it throughout this volume.

[1] For example, in my discussion of Embedded Language islands (in chapter 5 of *Duelling Languages*) I sometimes claim that what is a full CP is an Embedded Language island. For example, in the sentence *it's only essential services ambazo zinafunction right now*, there are two CPs, the second one introduced with the complementizer *ambazo* 'which' (1993*a* [1997]: 130). The sentence translates as 'it's only essential services which are functioning right now'. My erroneous reference to the relative in an island must have confused Muysken (2000: 241). Muysken also finds my discussion of the example on p. 72 confusing; again, my error is to refer to the English part of an embedded CP as an Embedded Language island. That is, the CP (with a null in Comp position) is this: *the customer fills forms and surrenders kiasi fulani cha pesa say like 200 shillings every month for two years.* English is the Matrix Language in this CP, with a Swahili Embedded Language island (*kiasi cha pesa* '[an] amount of money'). There is no English Embedded Language island in this CP at all.

3.2.1.1. Why not use the sentence?

Obviously, grammatical constraints on codeswitching only become potentially interesting within a sentence. That is, if one sentence is in language X and the next one in language Y, the grammars of the two languages are hardly in contact. However, a moment's thought tells you that *even within a sentence*, the grammars may not be in contact. The problem with using the sentence as a reference point is that what is called intra-sentential codeswitching (i.e. a sentence showing morphemes from more than one language) can contain many different structural configurations. The source of bilingualism within the sentence may be two conjoined monolingual CPs, each in a different language (e.g. *I like my aunt Marie, mais je detest mon oncle Albert*). Or, a bilingual sentence may consist of a monolingual main clause and an embedded clause in a second language (e.g. *I think qu'il pleuvra apres midi* 'I think it will rain after noon'). And of course a bilingual sentence can consist of a single CP, as in *I like ma tante Marie.* Only in the third type of sentence, with bilingualism within a single CP, are the languages really in contact. Because a bilingual sentence has been used to refer to any—or all—of these configurations, using 'sentence' as a unit for analysis invites lack of comparability. Finally, how do we define even a monolingual sentence? And how is a sentence related to 'an utterance'?

Some researchers who can see the problem with sentence in analyses use 'clause', instead, as their unit of analysis. But clause also has its problems. Clause brings with it a history as more a semantic unit than a structural one. That is, for many, a clause is that unit that expresses a proposition. But are the limits of a single proposition always clear? In the sentence, *The man walking down the street broke his leg*, how many propositions—or clauses—are there? If this is one proposition or clause, then is it comparable with what is clearly a single proposition or clause in a sentence, such as *I walk to work*?

3.2.1.2. Why is CP better?

Why champion CP as a unit of analysis? First, in contrast with sentence or clause, its status is clear. A CP is the highest unit projected by lexical elements. It can be defined unambiguously in terms of phrase structure as a complementizer or an element in Specifier (Spec) position followed by an IP (cf. Myers-Scotton and Jake 1995: 982). Second, CP is a unit used by many syntacticians, no matter what model they espouse; because of this status, there is no reason to assume its use here implies preference for any specific syntactic theory. Third, because CPs can contain null elements in Comp (complementizer) position or elsewhere, using the CP as the unit of analysis avoids problems regarding the status of constituents with nulls. For example, what have been called examples of extra-sentential codeswitching (e.g. *What?* or *Never!*) have generated unwarranted discussion about their status by a number of codeswitching researchers. With the CP as the unit of analysis, their status is clear: such exclamations are simply monolingual CPs that include a number of null elements.

While of course the CP itself is a constituent, it only becomes a *bilingual* constituent when it either (i) contains one or more constituents (including other CPs) that are mixed constituents or (ii) contains one or more Embedded Language Islands that it dominates. That is, because a CP contains bilingual constituents, this makes the CP itself a bilingual CP.

3.2.1.3. Illustrating the CP

Examples (1) through (4) illustrate the divisions within sentences by CP and demonstrate the characteristics of the bilingual CP. To keep other considerations simple, these examples all come from the same language pair, Swahili/English codeswitching. All examples include morphemes from both Swahili and English, but their configurations vary in regard to how many CPs are in each example and what types of constituent make up the CPs. The examples come from conversations recorded in Nairobi, Kenya. The speakers in these examples speak Swahili and English as second languages, but speak them both with a high level of proficiency. In Nairobi switching between these languages is common between speakers who do not share the same first language and who have been educated through secondary school.

Example (1) illustrates a bilingual sentence, to be sure, but it is only bilingual because it contains two monolingual CPs, one in Swahili and one in English. For this reason, this is *not* the type of codeswitching that is studied with the bilingual CP as the unit of analysis. Specifically, the Matrix Language – Embedded Language opposition is not relevant.

Instead, examples (2), (3), and (4) illustrate the type of constituent in which two languages truly are in contact, the bilingual CP. Each illustrates a different configuration. Example (2) contains only one CP, but it qualifies as a bilingual CP. This is because it contains several mixed constituents, a bilingual NP (*nguo nyingine* ***bright*** 'clothes other bright') and a bilingual AdvP (*kama* ***color*** *ya* ***red*** 'as color of red'). Alternatively, (2) could be analyzed as containing a monolingual CP (*u-na-weza ku-m-pata* 'you can find her') followed by a subordinate CP with a null complementizer (*a-me-vaa nguo nyingine bright kama color ya red* 'she is wearing other bright clothes such as red ones'). Under either analysis, the basic question is easily answered within a CP analysis: What is the Matrix Language in the mixed constituents? (The morpheme order and the relevant system morphemes in the bilingual constituents show that Swahili is the Matrix Language.)

(1) [Ndio wa-zungu wa-na-sem-a]$_{CP}$ [**old habits die hard**]$_{CP}$
Yes CL2-European CL2-NONPST-say-FV
'Yes [as] Europeans say, old habits die hard.'

(Swahili/English; Myers-Scotton Nairobi corpus 1988)

(2) [U-na-wez-a ku-m-pat-a a-me-va-a
2S-NONPST-able-FV INF-OBJ-find-FV 3S-PERF-wear-FV
nguo ny-ingine **bright** kama **color** y-a **red**]$_{cp}$
clothes CL9-other bright as color CL9-ASSOC red
'You can find her (she is) wearing other bright clothes [such] as red [ones].'
'You can find her [that] she is wearing other bright clothes [such] as red [ones].'

(Swahili/English; Myers-Scotton Nairobi corpus 1988)

Examples (3) and (4) both contain two CPs, but they are different. Example (3) contains two full CPs. The first (*lakini sasa wewe angalia* ***profit*** 'but now you look at [the] profit') is bilingual because it contains the mixed constituent including ***profit***. The second one is also bilingual (*ambayo a-li-enda ku-**make*** 'that we went ahead to make'), but it is embedded in the first. In (4) there are also two CPs, but the second CP (*a-me-repeat mara nyingi* 'he has repeated many times') contains null elements, including a null Complementizer. The higher CP constituent is a bilingual CP for two reasons. First, it qualifies as a bilingual CP because it contains an Embedded Language island (*so many problems*). Embedded Language islands are discussed later. Second, (4) has a second CP embedded within the first CP, and this embedded CP has the mixed constituent (*a-me-repeat mara nyingi*). The second CP has a null in COMP position (referring to *problems*). Alternatively, *mtu* 'person' could be interpreted as a CP in its own right with nulls (the full form would be something like *yeye ni mtu* 'he is a person'). Then there would be three CPs in this sentence, the monlingual CP (*mtu*) with its null forms and two bilingual CPs.

(3) [Lakini sasa wewe angalia **profit** [amba-yo a-li-end-a ku-**make**]$_{cp}$]$_{cp}$
But now you look at profit REL-CL9 3S-PST-go-FV INF-make
'But now you look at [the] profit that he went [ahead] to make.'

(Swahili/English; Myers-Scotton 1988 corpus)

(4) [Lakini a-na **so many problems**, mtu [a-me-**repeat** mara ny-ingi]$_{cp}$]$_{cp}$
but 3S-with so many problems person 3S-PERF-repeat time CL9-many
'But he has so many problems, [that] [he is] a person [who] has repeated many times.'

(Swahili/English; Myers-Scotton Nairobi corpus 1988)

3.2.2. *The basic constituents under the MLF model*

The MLF model and the distinction between the Matrix Language and Embedded Language allows for three types of constituents in classic codeswitching that are structurally different. Two types of possible constituents in the bilingual CP are made up entirely of one language or the other(s). These are either Matrix Language or Embedded Language islands. Islands must show structural dependency relations (meaning almost necessarily that they must consist of two or more morphemes). Also, they must be well-formed in their language; however, the placement of Embedded Language islands within the CP depends on Matrix Language procedures. I will have little to say about Matrix Language islands; given that the Matrix Language is the source of the frame for the CP, constituents entirely in the Matrix Language are almost 'expected' and do not present any problems (e.g. *mara nyingi* 'many times' in (4) is a Matrix Language island). Embedded Language islands deserve more comment and will be discussed further in Chapter 4 (e.g. *so many problems* in (4) is an Embedded Language island). A third type of constituent consists of morphemes from both languages; this is the Matrix Language + Embedded Language constituent (hereafter mixed constituent). For example, see *a-me-repeat* 'he has repeated' in (4). Note that mixed constituents themselves may contain either Embedded Language islands or Matrix Language islands. In fact, the bilingual CP itself is a large mixed constituent.

3.2.3. *When does the Matrix Language – Embedded Language opposition apply?*

As indicated in Chapter 1, the MLF model is based on the premise of asym-metry between the participating languages in codeswitching, but always within a bilingual CP. That is, one language, called the Matrix Language, has a more central role in the relevant CP. The MLF model states unequivocally that this role matters for grammatical structure in bilingual speech. At the same time, one should recognize that there is always a Matrix Language in monolingual *or* bilingual speech—because the Matrix Language is simply a label for the abstract morphosyntactic frame for an utterance. However, the Matrix Language is obviously transparent in monolingual speech. It is only in bilingual speech where the Matrix Language, the frame, becomes much of an issue, because—theoretically—either language participating in the utterance could be the source of the Matrix Language. Again, in codeswitching, there is only a reason even to discuss the Matrix Language *if* the issue is constraints on codeswitching within a bilingual CP (where there is a Matrix Language – Embedded Language opposition). In monolingual CPs—even if they are part of a bilingual conversation—there is no Matrix Language – Embedded Language opposition within a CP. I stress this because some readers still try to apply the opposition to intersentential codeswitching or inter-CP codeswitching.

Return again to examples (1) through (4). Even though example (1) contains morphemes from both Swahili and English, there is no Matrix Language – Embedded Language opposition for this sentence, simply because there is no bilingual CP. Instead, there are two monolingual CPs, one in Swahili and one in English. In examples (2) through (4), which do include bilingual CPs, Swahili is the Matrix Language, with English as the Embedded Language. The opposition Matrix Language – Embedded Language only takes on meaning within a bilingual CP. To those who point out that the MLF model doesn't apply to alternations of codeswitching from one sentence to another (or, even alternations across CPs), all I can say is their observation is true, but shows a lack of understanding of what the intended object of investigation is under the MLF model.

3.2.4. *But how can the Matrix Language be identified?*

How to identify the Matrix Language is the most frequently asked question about the MLF model. However, there is less of a question here than there seems to be. Still, here are two answers. First, if the Matrix Language must be defined, it is defined by the role it plays in the Matrix Language – Embedded Language hierarchy, realized in the Morpheme Order Principle and the System Morpheme Principle. Second, the definition of the Matrix Language is not circular, as some have suggested. To begin at the beginning—a basic premise of the MLF model is that the languages referred to as Matrix Language and Embedded Language do not participate equally in structuring intra-CP codeswitching. This unequal participation is referred to as the Matrix Language – Embedded Language hierarchy, and the Matrix Language is the label identifying the language with the larger structural role. But which language is the Matrix Language? The MLF model provides the two principles as tests of the premise of unequal participation and as a way to identify the Matrix Language. If the terms of the principles, morpheme order and one type of system morpheme, *both* are satisfied by one and the same language, then the Matrix Language can be identified as that language. Further, the basic theoretical notion that there is a Matrix Language – Embedded Language hierarchy is supported, because the two languages do not both satisfy the roles of the Matrix Language contained in the principles.

The principles are repeated here from Myers-Scotton (1993*a* [1997]: 83).

> The Morpheme Order Principle: in Matrix Language + Embedded Language constituents consisting of singly occurring Embedded Language lexemes and any number of Matrix Language morphemes, surface morpheme order (reflecting surface syntactic relations) will be that of the Matrix Language.
>
> The System Morpheme Principle: in Matrix Language + Embedded Language constituents, all system morphemes which have grammatical relations external to their head constituent (i.e. which participate in the sentence's thematic role grid) will come from the Matrix Language.

These principles are the formal statement of the Matrix Language – Embedded Language opposition. The terms that they contain (i.e. 'morpheme order' and 'system morphemes which have grammatical relations external to their head constituent') are independent of the theoretical construct, the Matrix Language. That is, they do not depend on the predicted Matrix Language – Embedded Language hierarchy for their existence; morpheme order and the type of system morpheme specified have an objective reality. Once more, the terms can be defined objectively. This is what makes the principles testable hypotheses. If only one language, the one labeled the Matrix Language, supplies morpheme order and the one relevant type of system morpheme, then the hypothesized relation of the Matrix Language to the Embedded Language is supported. Once more, in discussing codeswitching structure, the terms 'Matrix Language' and 'Embedded Language' become more than just useful heuristics.

The language whose structural role is critical—*within the terms of the principles*—is the one that receives the label 'the Matrix Language'. By extension, 'the Matrix Language' becomes the label for the frame providing morphosyntactic structure for the bilingual CP—because the source of this frame is the language so-named (because it satisfies the terms of the principles). Of course this frame includes various abstract specifications, more than just the specifications stated in the two principles. A circular definition would state that the Matrix Language is the frame (or is a label for the frame) providing structure for the bilingual CP because the Matrix Language is the frame. Instead, the label for the frame is derived from the relationship of the frame of one of the participating languages and the frame of the bilingual CP. The other participating language is called 'the Embedded Language'.

3.2.4.1. What others have had to say

Many other researchers who have examined codeswitching have seen that the roles of the participating languages are not the same. The only difference in their assessments from mine is that they have not often gone beyond passing observations, or they have not produced formal statements about these roles similar to the Morpheme Order Principle and the System Morpheme Principle. For example, two of the early 'greats' of bilingual research recognized the notion of a grammatical frame from one language only in bilingual speech. Weinreich wrote in reference to clauses with both Yiddish and Russian, 'An equivalent sentence could be constructed using Yiddish vocabulary in a Russian grammatical frame; it would then be assigned to Russian. "No amount of lexical penetration can dislodge the grammatical barriers."' (1967: 68, quotation from Roberts 1939.) One of the earliest researchers on codeswitching, Hasselmo (1970, 1972), who studied English and Swedish codeswitching in America, clearly saw that both languages did not participate equally in the same clause in his data. He remarks, 'The inflections and the function words that express definiteness all belong on the same level, i.e. that they all have to be English or Swedish' (1972: 269).

Many researchers in the 1980s noticed that both languages in codeswitching did not contribute the same affixes and function words to a mixed constituent. The MLF model explicitly builds on Joshi (1985), which referred to the differential roles of the participating languages and labeled them as a matrix language and an embedded language.

More recently, several researchers have espoused the notion that verbal inflection is the key to defining a base language (e.g. Klavans 1983, followed by Treffers-Daller 1994, *inter alia*). In his Monolingual Structure Approach (MSA), Boumans (1998) adopts Klavans's notion as part of his definition of the Matrix Language, but with some reservations. He writes, 'At this point I can only infer that the verbal inflection and the constituent order tend to be attributable to the same language' (p. 76). And a few pages later, he recognizes, 'Obviously, the admission of the possibility that the finite verb itself is an insertion drastically damages the MSA . . . since it is precisely the finite verb which designates the ML [Matrix Language]' (p. 100).

Data from Palestinian Arabic/English codeswitching offer just such examples of the main tensed verb of the bilingual CP (and all its inflections) as part of an inlay into the Matrix Language frame. That is, the finite verb appears in a large Embedded Language island called either an IP (Inflectional Phrase) or TP (Tense Phrase). In either case, they represent a phrase headed by the syntactic category Tense. These data show many IP/TP Embedded Language islands occur, generally with only the complementizer (or Specifier in Comp position) in the Matrix Language (these islands are major topics in Jake and Myers-Scotton (1997*a*) and Myers-Scotton and Jake (2001)). Such islands are briefly discussed and illustrated in Chapter 4. Clyne (1992: 31) also concludes that Klavans's claim that 'all sentences can be assigned to a matrix language according to the linguistic affiliation of the verb' is not practical in Dutch/English codeswitching spoken by Dutch immigrants in Australia.

It is true that in many data sets, the inflections on the tensed main verb in a mixed constituent *do* come from the Matrix Language; that is, this statement is observationally adequate, if only for those data sets. However, it does not achieve explanatory adequacy because it ignores *the general pattern in the entire mixed constituent.* Instead, the Morpheme Order and System Morpheme Principles capture this generalization because not just inflections on tensed main verbs must come from the Matrix Language, but also other system morphemes of the type specified by the System Morpheme Principle (the type called 'late outsiders' under the 4-M model). The Uniform Structure Principle introduced in Chapter 4 augments the System Morpheme Principle by applying to *all* types of system morpheme, as well as to other aspects of clause structure.

3.2.4.2. Other ways to identify the Matrix Language

In the 1993 version of the model (Myers-Scotton 1993*a*), I tried to support the Matrix Language – Embedded Language opposition with other types of empirical data. Notably, I claimed that the Matrix Language can be identified as the source of more morphemes in a discourse sample. That claim was abandoned. Unfortunately, some researchers trying to apply the MLF model still read only the 1993 version of the model. As early as 1995, the claim was modified (Myers-Scotton and Jake 1995: 984) and it was explicitly rejected in the Afterword in Myers-Scotton (1997: 246) and does not appear in publications after 1993. The reasons for abandoning that claim are twofold. First, even though the language that is the source of the grammatical frame (as specified in the Morpheme Order and System Morpheme Principles) often supplies more morphemes in a bilingual CP, this is not always the case. Second, as stated, the criterion was to apply to a 'discourse sample'; but exactly what would constitute such a sample is ambiguous. (Yet, it is worth noting that in a recent application of the MLF model, Paradis, Nicoladis, and Genesee (2000) use morpheme counts to identify the Matrix Language to their satisfaction in their bilingual-child language data.)

Part of the reason some have trouble with the notion of the Matrix Language may be that the language that meets the specifications for the Matrix Language under the two principles of the MLF model often occupies the same position in discourse as languages that go by other names. I have in mind *dominant language* in the psycholinguistic and bilingual-child language literature (cf. Lanza 1997), and also *unmarked choice* in the sociolinguistic literature (cf. Myers-Scotton 1993*c*). Both also apply in bilingual speech; however, dominant language refers to the language in which the speaker is most proficient and unmarked choice is a label for the variety considered most appropriate (and therefore typically most frequent) in a specific interaction type in a specific community. The Matrix Language differs from both of these designations because it is a grammatically based construct.

3.2.5. *Even a Matrix Language in 'street' varieties*

The reality of the Matrix Language – Embedded Language opposition is even very obvious when one examines urban 'street talk' varieties that appear to be a disorganized jumble of slang and/or lexical input from many sources. Even in such codeswitching corpora, only one variety is clearly the source of the morphosyntactic frame. Applying the Morpheme Order Principle and the System Morpheme Principle to the data makes the division of roles between the Matrix Language and the Embedded Language very clear. I briefly consider African urban varieties.

In multilingual and multicultural Nairobi, two codeswitching varieties are the basis of informal speech among the youth. One is Sheng, a variety that developed in the Eastlands area of Nairobi, home to a number of low-rent housing estates. Especially among adults, the use of Swahili and English as lingua francas promotes interethnic communication there; ethnic group languages are also used. Based on these languages, Sheng developed as a peer-group language among teenagers and younger children as well in the early 1970s. While Sheng includes content morphemes from many languages, Swahili is clearly its Matrix Language. This is evident from the description of Sheng in Abdulaziz and Osinde (1997). They report, 'The most common morphological structure of Sheng is the affixation of Swahili affixes to roots that are drawn from Kikuyu, Dholuo, English, and other donor languages' (p. 56). Significantly they go on to say, 'Coined words are similarly given Swahili affixes. However, there are no coined affixes in the language' (p. 56). Thus, it is clear that while content morphemes can come from other languages, critical system morphemes (affixes) come from Swahili.

In contrast to Sheng, Engsh (*sic*) is a more recent creation and is spoken by the more upscale youth in the Westlands area of Nairobi. Most of the African residents in Westlands have higher education and they can speak English fluently as well as Swahili. According to Abdulaziz and Osinde, the African children there 'have English as their first and primary language of daily communication, at home, at school, and in social domains' (p. 50). The in-group language of children there is Engsh, a variety that 'has English as the dominant donor language, which also provides most of the grammatical framework within which words from other languages are blended' (p. 49).

In urban South Africa, two varieties that also are in-group markers exist. Slabbert and Myers-Scotton (1997) cite examples from these varieties, with data largely coming from conversations recorded in Soweto, a major township outside Johannesburg. As in-group languages, they are characterized by a good deal of 'private' slang. The older of the two, Tsotsitaal, has a non-standard version of Afrikaans as its Matrix Language, even though it includes many English-content morphemes. It also has some words from local African languages and others of unknown origin. The second in-group language is Iscamtho; versions of this variety have a South African Bantu language—usually Zulu—as their Matrix Language.

Two abbreviated examples make the source of the Matrix Language clear in both varieties. Example (5) comes from Tsotsitaal. Note that the morpheme order (finite verb in final position) clearly comes from an Afrikaans variety (see *group join*). English and the local African languages are not verb-final languages.

(5) . . . want ou Tex laat ons daa i(daardie) **group join**
because old Tex make 1PL DET group join
'. . . because old Tex made us join the group.'

(Tsotsitaal; Slabbert and Myers-Scotton 1997: 332)

Example (6) is an extract from a conversation in Iscamtho with Zulu as the Matrix Language. The evidence is that morpheme order and the relevant system morphemes clearly come from Zulu. Note that the English verb *recruit* is inflected with Zulu affixes, as is the Afrikaans verb *vay*. Also, note the English Embedded Language islands, *first half* and *second half*. Neither is used with its standard English meaning.

(6) . . . u-ya-ku-**recruit**-a na-we u-thi ma- -si -**vay**-e-ni,
. . . 3S-PRES-2S-recruit-FV and-2S/TOP 2S-say HORT 1PL-go-FV-PL
na-we u- bon-a . . . u-ya -**vay**-a **first half**
and-2S 2S-see-FV . . . 2S-PRES-go-FV for the first time,
uma u-phumelel-a u- ya- **vay**-a **second half**
COMP 2S-succeed-FV 2S-PRES-go-FV for the second time
'You will [be] recruit [ed] and you, you say, let us go, and you, you see . . . you go for [the] first time, and when you succeed, you go for [the] second time.'

(Iscamtho; Slabbert and Myers-Scotton 1997: 335)

3.2.6. *Can the Matrix Language change?*

Can the Matrix Language change within an utterance? Yes, but it is not so frequent—and certainly not so haphazard—as some assume is possible under the MLF model (cf. Muysken (2000: 69) writes, 'Myers-Scotton even suggests that the Matrix Language could change during a sentence (1993: 70)'; MacSwan (2000: 42) states, 'The definition of the matrix language may change at any time in production, even mid-sentence.'). What, in fact, is stated in *Duelling Languages* is the following (Myers-Scotton 1993*a* [1997]: 70):

> Synchronically, a change within the same conversation is possible; an extreme case would be a change within the same sentence. Diachronically, a change may occur when the socio-political factors in the community promote some type of shift to an L2.

Nowhere is it written that the Matrix Language 'may change at any time', etc. I stand by my original statement. I should have been more precise and stated that no change is possible within a CP, I admit, but in 1993 I was still operating as if the sentence was a reasonable unit of analysis. However, note my statement says that a change within the same sentence would be 'an extreme case', not the usual state of affairs. In fact, there are very few corpora in the codeswitching literature in which the Matrix Language changes *at all.* Note this is not to deny there are some corpora in which the Matrix Language does change from one sentence to the next or even one CP to the next, but again I emphasize not within the same CP. For example, in conversations between young adult Turks in the Netherlands, Backus (1996) reports cases of Turkish as the Matrix Language at times and Dutch at other times. However, I repeat that the Matrix Language does not change at all in most corpora. Certainly, many other researchers have found that the Matrix Language is a robust and stable construct in classic codeswitching. To take some recent examples, see Türker (2000) on Turkish/Norwegian codeswitching; Hlavac (2000) on Croatian/English codeswitching; Amuzu (1998) on Ewe/English codeswitching.

Here is what Amuzu (1998: 134) reports about his corpus:

> The consistency with which Ewe supplies all directly elected system morphemes and also determines the order of morphemes in all mixed constituents is a firm support for the MLF model's recognition of the asymmetry between languages involved in intrasentential codeswitching. Specifically, the Matrix Language Hypothesis of the MLF model, which is operationalized in the System Morpheme and Morpheme Order Principles, is fully supported by the codeswitching data. The MLF model, however, anticipates that the Matrix Language may change from one discourse to another as topic, for instance, changes such that English becomes the Matrix Language and Ewe the Embedded Language. This did not happen in the data but it does not in any way imply that it is impossible; neither does it imply that the MLF model over-predicts; codeswitching data sets involving some other language pairs have shown that the Matrix Language is dynamic and changes over discourse situations.

As already noted, changes in Matrix Language in a single speaker's conversation are not very frequent and may even be rare in most codeswitching corpora. Example (7) from Swigart (1992), a study of Wolof/French codeswitching in Dakar, is an example of many switches of languages within a conversational turn. And even here, there is no change of the Matrix Language within a CP.

Up to the point in the discourse at which example (7) occurs, the speaker has been engaging in Wolof/French codeswitching, with Wolof at the Matrix Language. In the example of seven CPs, French is the Matrix Language for the first CP. (Note this is a bilingual CP only because it includes the Wolof self-standing pronoun as a Topicalizer; otherwise, it is entirely in French.) He continues with three monolingual French CPs (2 to 4). This is followed by a bilingual CP (5) that includes the French verb *comprendre*, but with Wolof as the Matrix Language. CP 6 also has Wolof as the Matrix Language; it is bilingual only because it includes *mais* 'but'. The final CP (7) is a monolingual Wolof CP. Although there is switching between Matrix Languages from one CP to the next, note at no point is there a change in the Matrix Language *within a CP.*

The switch from Wolof as the Matrix Language in previous turns to predominantly French may be motivated by the fact that the interlocutor has switched from codeswitching to speaking only French (both participants are highly educated and the speaker himself is a television journalist). Another obvious motivation is the new topic at this point in the conversation—whether the speaker's children are studying French in school.

This is also an interesting example because it shows that pronouns (when they are self-standing content morphemes, as they are in these examples from Wolof, and not clitics) do occur in mixed constituents (cf. Jake 1994). *Ñoom* 'them' is an initial Topicalizer (and an Embedded Language pronoun in the French frame of the first CP). The other pronouns (self-standing *ñu* 'they' and *ko* 'it') occur in the Wolof frame in the fifth CP as subject and object of the verb *comprendre*, which is treated as a verb stem by the Wolof frame. In the last two CPs (monolingual Wolof CPs) *ko* occurs again as a self-standing object of the Wolof verbs and *ñu* occurs as a suffix.

(7) [**Ñoom**, ils parlent français]$_{1}$, [ils parlent parfaitement le français]$_{2}$. [Y a pas
3PL they speak French, they speak perfectly DET French there no
de problèmes]$_{3}$. [Tu leur dis un bonjour]$_{4}$, [ñu **comprendre** ko]$_{5}$.
of problems. You them say a hello, 3PL understand 3S
[**Mais** nag, bindu-ñu ko]$_{6}$, [jàngu-ñu ko]$_{7}$
but then write not-3PL 3S read-not-3PL 3S
'[As for] them, they speak French, they speak French perfectly. No problem. You say hello to them, they understand it. But then, they don't write it, they don't read it.'

(Wolof/French; Swigart 1992: 149)

3.2.7. *Quantitative evidence of a single Matrix Language within any CP*

Further, a study of codeswitching in a South African township tested a hypothesis not part of the original MLF model, a precise and stringent hypothesis about a stability of the Matrix Language in classic codeswitching (cf. Finlayson, Calteaux, and Myers-Scotton 1998). This hypothesis is that the Matrix Language does not change at all within a single bilingual CP. The speakers, all indigenous Africans, live in a large African township near Pretoria and they are all bilingual in at least several languages. In this data set, the languages used in conversation were Zulu, Sotho, and English. Some conversational turns included monolingual CPs representing switches from one language to another. *But when bilingual CPs were produced (predominantly either in Zulu/English or Sotho/English), there were no instances of a switch in the Matrix Language.*

Altogether, the corpus consisted of 124 bilingual CPs, all with a single Matrix Language maintained throughout each CP. (Some CPs included Embedded Language islands (from English).) One of the virtues of using the CP as the unit of analysis is that it is true that many sentences are complex, consisting of more than one CP. Part of the definition of CP is that the unit of structure includes Comp position; this definition disposes of the problem of where to put elements in Comp position (with one part of the sentence or which clause) if either sentence or clause are used as the unit of analysis.

Yes, the Matrix Language can—and does—change from one CP to the next for some speakers in some corpora, even though there are not many examples of this in the codeswitching literature. This fact does not change the finding that *within a single CP itself*, evidence to date indicates the Matrix Language does not change within that unit.

3.2.8. *What, then, is the Matrix Language in classic codeswitching?*

From the discussion so far in this section, it appears that the Matrix Language can be identified as identical to one of the participating languages. For example, in any of the codeswitching examples in later sections, the morphosyntax of the bilingual CP is clearly identical to the morphosyntax of one of the participating languages. Yet, the Matrix Language is not that language, or even any 'language' as such. This is a misguided notion, and one that I have been at pains to correct from the 1997 Afterword onwards. Admittedly, this is a notion that—unfortunately—I encouraged with my discussion of the Matrix Language in the 1993 edition of *Duelling Languages*. The Matrix Language is *not* to be equated with an existing language; rather one should view the Matrix Language as an abstract frame for the morphosyntax of the bilingual CP. But, then, there are two issues to be considered.

First, what is the Matrix Language's relation to the source variety that the Matrix Language frame so closely resembles? It turns out that the Matrix Language and its source do not have exactly the same requirements for constituent structure. There are two points to be made here.

1. If the bilingual CP contains a mixed constituent, with one or more singly occurring Embedded Language content morphemes that are fully morphosyntactically integrated into the Matrix Language, then yes, the Matrix Language is entirely identical with the morphosyntax of one of the source languages.

2. However, there are elements and phrases in the mixed constituent that are not completely integrated into the morphosyntax of the source of the Matrix Language. These are what I have called 'bare forms' and Embedded Language islands. Bare forms are Embedded Language content morphemes that do not show all the function words and inflections that would make them fully integrated into the Matrix Language (Myers-Scotton 1993*a* [1997]: 112–15). For example, Boumans (1998) finds bare nouns in his Moroccan Arabic/Dutch corpus. In example (8), the Dutch noun *cultuur* 'culture' is such a bare form. That is, it does not receive an article (or its counterpart) from Arabic, the Matrix Language.

(8) ta-te-qra-y **Ø-cultuur** dyal-ek . . .
ASP-2-learn-F culture of-2S . . .
'You learn about your culture . . .'

(Moroccan Arabic/Dutch; Boumans 1998: 189)

Further, there also are what I have called Embedded Language islands (Myers-Scotton 1993*a* [1997]: 136 ff.). Again, these are constituents that show structural dependency relations and are well-formed in the Embedded Language, not in the Matrix Language. In the case of both bare forms and Embedded Language islands, their placement in the bilingual CP is under Matrix Language control, but they are not optimally morphologically integrated into the Matrix Language. The existence of bare forms and Embedded Language islands in classic codeswitching, along with the possibility of a composite Matrix Language (discussed later in this chapter under the Abstract Level model) obviously invites speculation about how conditions of well-formedness in language production involving bilingual CPs are seemingly more flexible than those resulting in monolingual data.

These two types of 'aberrant' Embedded Language material in classic codeswitching clearly show that the Matrix Language, as the frame of the bilingual CP, does not place *exactly* the same requirements on the elements it contains as the source language does. The relationship of the Matrix Language and the Embedded Language in the mental lexicon, including their respective levels of activation (they are both 'on', but to different degrees at different times), is discussed further in Chapter 4. From this discussion here, two things are clear: the Matrix Language as frame of the bilingual CP is not its source language, but represents an abstraction from it, and, at times, the Embedded Language beats out the Matrix Language in sending morphosyntactic directions to the Formulator. Even so, if all the above is recognized, 'Matrix Language' may be used as a label for the source language as a short cut.

3.2.9. *The Matrix Language as a theoretical construct*

The Matrix Language is an abstract construct because, although it is empirically verifiable, it is only indirectly verifiable. (For example, the Morpheme Order and System Morpheme Principles directly support the claim that both morpheme order and one type of system morpheme come from the same language in intra-CP codeswitching; it is this finding that indirectly supports the claim of a single, unified frame in such codeswitching.) Like many other theoretical constructs, the Matrix Language refers to an abstract architecture. The Matrix Language is an *abstract frame*. This means it does not include actual morphemes nor is it isomorphic with any fully fleshed-out linguistic variety. Instead, it includes *specifications about slots* and how they are to be filled, based on directions from lemmas in the mental lexicon. These lemmas include the three levels of abstract lexical structure outlined in the Abstract Level model (cf. section 3.6). Typically, they are specific to the source language of the Matrix Language. However, the Matrix Language lemmas themselves need not always underlie an existing surface-level morpheme that appears from the Embedded Language in codeswitching. Instead, the Embedded Language morpheme is allowed if it meets critically the relevant well-formedness requirements of the Matrix Language that are found in language-specific Generalized Lexical Knowledge in the mental lexicon.

Muysken (2000: 275) apparently does not accept the notion that such knowledge exists. He cites an example from my earlier work (the example, in turn, comes from Bentahila and Davies 1992) in which Moroccan medical professionals are conversing about medical matters in a combination of Arabic and French. There are two NPs from French (*la regulation* and *les naissances*), both embedded in larger Arabic-based NPs (they qualify as internal Embedded Language islands, as discussed extensively in Chapter 4). The example is cited here as (9):

(9) Tajẓiw tajdiru dak **la régulation** djal **les naissances** . . .
'They come and do that the limitation of the births . . .'
(Moroccan Arabic/French; Bentahila and Davies 1992: 106, cited by Myers-Scotton 1993*a* [1997]: 106)

Muysken argues, 'What Myers-Scotton would have to propose here is that the French elements are replacing abstract Arabic lemmas . . . but the assumption that the medical discourse is regulated by abstract Arabic lemmas is implausible . . . it is clear that the Moroccan doctors or interns are talking **in Arabic** [original] about the **French** [original] universe' (p. 276). He goes on to say that this 'suggests the selection of a morphosyntactic frame is not linked directly to lemma-selection, but is a separate process' (p. 277).

Yet, in Myers-Scotton and Jake (1995: 1017 ff.) we explicitly state that, indeed, there is a separate—but clearly related—process. We write, 'If there is no existing ML lemma as a counterpart, the EL lemma is matched with relevant prototypical material that exists in the mental lexicon in an unbundled state as ML lexical knowledge. In order to form new words (fill lexical gaps) and change the meaning or grammatical patterning of existing lexemes, the existence of prototypical ML material as undifferentiated lexical knowledge, alongside fully specified lemmas, seems necessary.'

That is, we agree with Muysken that Arabic may not have exact counterparts to terms used in the French medical discourse; however, this does not prevent Arabic speakers from matching the lemmas supporting French nouns with undifferentiated Matrix Language lexical knowledge at the same three levels as are involved when existing Matrix Language lemmas are the match (lexical-conceptual and predicate-argument structures, and morphological realization patterns). Thus, congruence checking is possible and French nouns that are not sufficiently congruent with frame requirements would be rejected. This type of matching has parallels in learner strategies in second-language acquisition, an observation made by Ad Backus in regard to Myers-Scotton and Jake (1995). Muysken (2000: 276) also questions the definition of a lemma in Myers-Scotton (1993*b*); I maintain a lemma is an abstract entry in the mental lexicon that can and does trigger language-specific morphosyntactic procedures. That view has not changed. But, as the Differential Access Hypothesis states, I argue more explicitly now that not all procedures are salient at the level of the mental lexicon; those involving late system morphemes only are accessed at the level of the Formulator.

3.3. Content vs. system morphemes

As indicated in Chapter 1, the division between content morphemes and system morphemes has been one of the two major underpinnings of the MLF model from *Duelling Languages* (1993*a* [1997]: 98–110) onwards. Now, with the addition of the 4-M model to the MLF model, the division takes on even more importance (Myers-Scotton and Jake 2000*a*, 2000*b*, 2001). The new model accomplishes two things: (i) it provides more precise explanations for what occurs in classic codeswitching, and (ii) with extensions, it offers a different approach from what is generally found in the contact literature to explain the form of other contact phenomena.

The content–system morpheme distinction is motivated by the way the two types of morpheme pattern according to frame-building properties. An established tenet of syntactic theory is that different morphemes relate differently to the thematic grid of an utterance; this is independent motivation for the content–system morpheme distinction. In *Duelling Languages*, content morphemes are defined by the feature [+thematic role assigner/receiver] while system morphemes have the feature [–thematic role assigner/receiver]. Admittedly, for some linguists, the status of some lexemes in relation to this dichotomy is an open issue; that is, there is not a consensus on the thematic status of some elements, such as adjectives. However, there is general agreement that all nouns receive thematic roles and most verbs (but not the copula) and most prepositions assign thematic roles. Thus, the status of the most central elements bearing content in the CP is clear. They definitely assign or receive thematic roles and therefore are not system morphemes, and the main basis of the content–system morpheme opposition is intact.

Another issue is the status of discourse markers. Along with my colleague, Janice Jake, I argue that they can be considered content morphemes *at the discourse level.* We argue that whatever can appear in the position of Comp in a CP and whatever can occur in the position of Spec of Comp can also be a discourse-thematic element. (However, in some languages, e.g. Arabic, complementizers may be multimorphemic, including a system morpheme in addition to the discourse marker itself.) Discourse markers are discussed again in Chapter 6.

A second feature, [+/–quantification] also distinguishes the two types of morpheme (cf. Myers-Scotton 1993*a* [1997]), although the [+/–thematic role assigner/receiver] feature is sufficient alone. Under the notion of quantification, one can argue that 'any lexical item belonging to a syntactic category which involves quantification across variables is a system morpheme' (1993*a* [1997]: 100). I have seen no evidence to change this view; however, whether [+quantification] is a feature of *all* system morphemes may merit more study. Certainly, [+quantification] includes quantifiers (e.g. *all, any, no*). It also includes determiners and possessive adjectives, as well as degree adverbs (e.g. *very, too*). But it is also a property of categories, such as tense and aspect, which involve quantification across events (cf. Dowty 1979). Data examined support the claim that quantifiers pattern as system morphemes in classic codeswitching data. In fact, Jake and I (Jake and Myers-Scotton 2001) find quantitative evidence supporting this claim further: if a quantifier is to be produced in the Embedded Language, then the phrase must be 'finished' in the Embedded Language, too. A Chinese/English codeswitching corpus (Wei 1998) supports this claim: one finds Embedded Languages islands beginning with a degree adverb, e.g. English *very* and then the island, *very big.* However, crucially—as the model (this classification) predicts—there are no instances such as ****very*** *nan* 'very difficult' in the corpus. There are also constituents with the quantifier from Chinese (e.g. *hěn dá* 'very big') as well as mixed constituents (*tai busy* 'too busy'), but of course *busy* is an adjective, a content morpheme.

3.3.1 *Why refer to content and system morphemes?*

The MLF model introduced the content–system distinction. Some other researchers have adopted it; yet, many other researchers persist instead with earlier classifications. Further, they do not typically endow them with the meaning of the content–system distinction.

Why should anyone adopt the terms content and system morphemes? Why not just continue with open and closed classes of words (the division most psycholinguists use and some linguists)? Or why not accept thematic as opposed to functional elements (a division widely used by generative syntactitians following Abney 1987)? In this section, I try to explain once again the value of discussing morpheme types in terms of the content vs. system morpheme opposition (cf. Myers-Scotton and Jake 2000*a*).

Because 'content' is an easily understood term, it causes few problems; it is superior to 'thematic' just because it is more semantically transparent, even though it is true that all content morphemes are thematic. The term 'system morpheme' requires more discussion. First, the term comes from Bolinger (1968), who used this as a cover term for both inflectional morphemes and function words. (However, note that in my use of the term, not all functional words are system morphemes; for example, not all prepositions are system morphemes.) Second, my reason for using 'system morpheme' is *not* to be a contrarian in a world that habitually uses the terms 'open' and 'closed elements' or 'thematic' and 'functional elements'. Rather, 'system morpheme' is used because it identifies a class of morpheme more precisely than either of the other widely used terms, 'closed class word' or 'functional element'.

3.3.2. *Why not use 'closed class' or 'functional element' as labels?*

What is the problem with 'closed class'? First, the unit of analysis is unclear: is it only a word, and what counts as a word? Second, the relation of closed (and open) classes to an entry in the mental lexicon is not clear. In contrast, the status of a morpheme as a unit of analysis is better; it is a surface realization supported by a lemma entry in the mental lexicon, although there are, of course, multimorphemic units at the surface level. Third, the distinction closed vs. open class is only a truly valid distinction for the purpose for which it was originally intended: open classes are those that are open to taking in new members—whether borrowings or neologisms—while closed classes are not. Under this definition, the lexical category of noun is an open class while the category of preposition is not. The distinction takes on a new and questionable life when some researchers, especially psycholinguists, use the terms as the canonical descriptive labels for lexical categories—as if whether an element is a member of a class open to new members is its critical defining feature from a linguistic point of view. A third problem with referring to closed-class elements is that the terms of the open–closed opposition, strictly speaking, refer only to words; however, it is often used for affixes as well. Fourth, and most important, not all closed-class elements pattern alike when their distribution in actual utterances is considered. For example, non-clitic pronouns (e.g. English *I*, *me*) are closed-class items; yet in most languages they pattern in syntactic structures with nouns, which are open-class elements. Ironically, these pronouns also pattern with nouns in the data on accuracy of production by Broca's aphasics in the psycholinguistic research where the terms open and closed are typically used.

What is the problem with 'functional element' as a term? First, this is a classification based on lexical-category membership. But not all members of the same lexical category have similar distributions in codeswitching and other data. Non-clitic pronouns are a case in point, as are prepositions. Once more, not all affixes or clitics have similar distributions in many linguistic phenomena. Also, the distribution of prepositions in English supports the notion that, under the 4-M model, some prepositions are content morphemes, some are early system morphemes, and some are late system morphemes. My claim is that these differences in distribution suggest a problem with treating what is classified under 'functional element' as a coherent category.

Alternatively, is there a meaningful division involving bound vs. free morphemes? My answer is 'no'. It is true that all open-class elements are free-standing words; most of these are content morphemes in my classification. It appears that all bound forms are system morphemes, but this feature does not define the class of system morpheme. Some system morphemes are free-standing, such as certain prepositions (e.g. English *in* in many contexts) and determiners such as English *the*.

3.3.3. *The empirical evidence*

The empirical evidence in almost all examples in codeswitching corpora is that Embedded Language elements form two classes, based on their opportunities to occur in mixed constituents. These classes coincide with the content–system morpheme opposition. While Embedded Language content morphemes (especially nouns) occur with relative freedom in these constituents, Embedded Language system morphemes have little or no freedom of occurrence. Specifically, under the System Morpheme Principle of the MLF model, certain types of system morpheme cannot come from the Embedded Language, but must come from the Matrix Language. The principle appears in section 3.2. It is further discussed when late outsider-system morphemes under the 4-M model are introduced in this section. It will turn out that the same type of system morpheme patterns differently from other morphemes in other contact phenomena.

Further, one can demonstrate this same division between content and system morphemes in other linguistic data. For example, Myers-Scotton and Jake (2000*a*) demonstrate that the incidence of errors in the speech of Broca's aphasics reflects the divisions of content–system morpheme. Under analyses employing the open vs. closed class distinction, the speech of such patients has long been referred to as agrammatic because these patients often have trouble producing closed-class items accurately or at all. However, it turns out that this generalization about closed-class items is inaccurate. Researchers overlook the fact that closed-class elements that are content morphemes (e.g. self-standing pronouns, certain prepositions) are produced more accurately than those that are system morphemes. In section 3.4.9, I show how the content–system morpheme distinction, as well as divisions within types of system morpheme, matter in speech errors.

3.4. What the 4-M model adds

As indicated in Chapter 1, the 4-M model takes the content–system morpheme opposition of the MLF model and refines it by dividing the class of system morpheme into three types: early system morphemes, and two types of late system morphemes, bridges and late system morphemes. I emphasize that cross-linguistically the classification of morphemes in terms of the 4-M model can differ; that is, the same lexical categories or types of affixes are not necessarily the same types of 4-M model morphemes. However, I also emphasize that the oppositions on which the 4-M classification is based, as well as how they are to be applied, are universal.

3.4.1. *Oppositions in the 4-M model*

The relevant oppositions are explained in this section. Figure 3.1 represents how they join and divide the four types of morpheme. The oppositions are:

[+/–conceptually activated]
[+/–thematic role receiver/assigner]
[+/–looks outside its immediate maximal projection for information about its form]

Note that the content–system morpheme distinction in the MLF model is largely motivated by theoretical notions about syntactic or semantic structure. Whether or not a linguistic element participates in the thematic grid refers to an element's syntactic nature; whether or not an element is

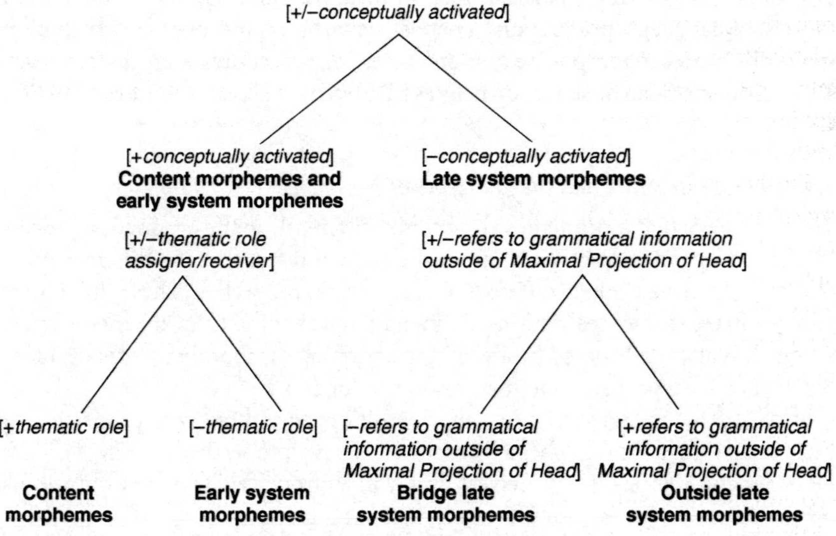

Figure 3.1. Feature-based classification of morphemes in the 4-M model

[+quantification] refers mainly to its semantics. The assumption is that these distinctions are universally observed and originate in Universal Grammar or linguistic competence.

The 4-M model adds another abstract opposition. This opposition is motivated by the hypothesis that some of the lemmas underlying types of morpheme are more directly linked to speaker's intentions than others and are salient at the level of the mental lexicon; others are not. These notions are captured in the opposition [+/–conceptually activated]. It emphasizes not the status of elements in phrase structure, but their status in the abstract procedures that produce surface statuses. Again, the assumption is that this status is part of UG or linguistic competence. We see how once more performance interacts with competence.

Note how this new opposition enlarges the basis of explanation. The [+/–conceptually activated] opposition refers to hypotheses about the differential nature of lemmas in the mental lexicon and, as will become clearer, how morphemes are differentially elected in the production process.

3.4.2. *Empirical and theoretical value*

The motivation to devise the 4-M model, to divide morphemes into four types, is empirical; that is, it can be demonstrated that they differ in their distribution in many types of data sets, from codeswitching to Interlanguage in second language acquisition to speech errors to speech production by Broca's aphasics. Thus, on one level the 4-M model is a means to classify morphemes to reflect distribution patterns. However, the real value of the 4-M model is that these differences in distribution imply an explanation that, in turn, has implications for theoretical aspects of language production. That is, patterns of morpheme distribution imply differences in morpheme type and accessing procedures at an abstract level. These differences can be stated formally as a Differential Access Hypothesis (section 3.4.5).

3.4.3. *Phrase structure and the four types of morpheme*

The hypothesis that morphemes are accessed differently in the production process receives independent motivation from the empirical fact that the different morpheme types have evident different lexicosyntactic properties. These differences are clear in the surface realizations of different morphemes. Thus, the model offers a formal, syntactically based means of distinguishing the morphemes that is independent of its hypotheses about access in production.

Such differences give rise to an opposition regarding two properties of morphemes in building phrase structures. These properties are the familiar [+/–thematic role assigner/receiver] and a new property, [+/–looks outside its own maximal projection for information about form].

1. First, consider the formal status of content morphemes in phrase structure. The lemmas underlying content morphemes are directly elected as the heads of their

maximal projections; e.g. a noun heads an NP,[2] a verb heads a VP, an adjective heads an AdjP, etc. Lemmas supporting content morphemes include information about well-formedness conditions for the entire phrase that the heads project, including the hierarchical structure of mapping arguments and predicates. All nouns and most verbs are the prototypical content morphemes.

2. Next, consider the first new type of system morpheme, early system morphemes. Their syntactic profile is this: they appear in the same surface-level maximal projections as their heads, and they depend on their heads for information about their forms. Examples of these morphemes are forms under Det (determiner, including articles and possessive adjectives) and 'plural'. This means early system morphemes include the relevant *phi*-features of person, number, and gender in relevant languages. (Thus, for example, in Spanish a determiner depends on its head noun for information about its gender and number.)
   These morphemes are called 'early' because the hypothesis is that the lemmas underlying them are salient in the level of the mental lexicon. As I will argue below, they share the plus feature with content morphemes in the opposition [+/–conceptually activated]. In relation to their reading for this feature, I also argue that lemmas underlying early system morphemes are indirectly elected by their head content morphemes.

3. Finally, consider the two types of late system morphemes; they have different syntactic specifications from each other. They differ in regard to the feature [+/–looks outside its own immediate maximal projection for information about its form] (or [looks outside] as an abbreviation).
   'Bridge' system morphemes are the first type. Like early system morphemes, bridge system morphemes receive information about their form within their own maximal projection. However, early system morphemes are closely tied to their heads; they depend on the specific semantic/pragmatic properties of a content head and add semantic/pragmatic information to that head. In contrast, bridge system morphemes are projected when the grammatical configuration of a maximal projection in a language-specific grammar requires such morphemes to complete the projection. Thus, bridge system morphemes connect content morphemes with each other *without reference to the properties of a head.* The information they add is in the form of integrating elements or structures. Possessive *of* and *'s* (and their counterparts in other languages, such as *de* in French, as in *beaucoup de gens* ('much of people' > 'many people'), are examples of bridges.
   In contrast with bridge system morphemes, 'outsider' late system morphemes depend for their form on information *outside* their immediate maximal projection. That is, they are coindexed with forms outside the head of their

[2] Jake and I do not accept the Det as head of NP analysis (Abney 1987). While it provides symmetry with the Infl or T as head analysis of VP in tree diagrams of phrase structures, it obscures the role of the noun in underlying structure.

maximal projections. Under the Differential Accessing Hypothesis (introduced in Chapter 1), this information becomes available when larger constituents (e.g. CPs and IPs or Infl phrases) are constructed. Examples of these morphemes include subject–verb agreement, clitics/affixes, and case affixes in many languages.

The two types of late system morphemes are called 'late' because the hypothesis is that the lemmas underlying them are not fully salient in language production until the level of the Formulator where larger constituents are assembled. This hypothesis figures prominently in explanations of contact data in the coming chapters.

3.4.4. *Activation in the mental lexicon*

I turn now from the evidential basis of the 4-M classification (i.e. surface phrase structure) to more abstract and implicational grounds for the classification. Recall the new opposition the 4-M model adds that refers to the mechanisms by which morphemes are accessed, [+/–conceptually activated]. It cuts across the content–system morpheme distinction. It refers to activation to satisfy what the speaker intends to communicate in producing linguistic elements. Under this opposition, content morphemes and one type of system morpheme, the early system morpheme, have the feature [+conceptually activated] and the other two types of system morpheme, called late system morphemes, have the feature [–conceptually activated].

Simply put, when an element is [+conceptually activated] it is salient as soon as a speaker's intentions are encoded as language, at the lemma level in the mental lexicon. Conceptual activation also means that such elements have semantic content—what speakers hone in on to convey their intentions.

It becomes clear in later chapters that the opposition [+/–conceptually activated] is an extremely useful heuristic to explain distributions of data in diverse phenomena. To offer a quick example, while every linguist knows that nouns are the most frequently borrowed lexical category and every codeswitching researcher knows that nouns are the category most often inserted from the Embedded Language in Matrix Language frames, no one offers an explanation. The explanation hinges on a plus reading for conceptual activation. While verbs also are [+conceptually activated], they are more difficult to borrow (or to insert from the Embedded Language in codeswitching) from one language to another because—unlike nouns—they are [+thematic role assigner] and therefore carry more 'syntactic baggage' than nouns, meaning their fit with the recipient language may be harder to make. For a related reason, in reference to the Abstract Level model (see section 3.6), one could make the point that *sufficient congruence* across grammatical systems in different languages is more an issue with verbs than nouns.

What is the motivation of this opposition based on conceptual information? Recall the production model from Chapter 1. In this model, speakers' intentions select the language-specific semantic/pragmatic feature bundles at the conceptual level; these bundles point to lemmas in the mental lexicon that underlie content morphemes. This means that the lemmas underlying content morphemes are *directly elected*, as Levelt has hypothesized (1989). In turn, these lemmas may point to other lemmas that further realize the bundles of semantic/pragmatic features. These lemmas underlie early system morphemes. They are referred to as early because they are conceptually activated and salient at the level of the mental lexicon. Bock and Levelt (1994) refer to some lemmas as *indirectly elected*; my associates and I also use this term following Bock and Levelt. However, it is not clear that Bock and Levelt are designating exactly the same lemmas as those underlying early system morphemes in the 4-M model.[3] The early system morphemes contrast with the other two types of system morpheme, which are not salient at this level, meaning those two have a minus reading for [conceptually activated].

3.4.5. *Structurally assigned morphemes: later activation*

Together, the lemmas underlying content morphemes and early system morphemes send directions to the Formulator to build larger linguistic units. That is, these directions contain instructions about assigning late system morphemes to these larger structures. When the Formulator receives these directions, late system morphemes may be activated.

Instead of conveying essential conceptual structure, these late system morphemes are essential in another way: they are crucial in building the larger syntactic units because they indicate relationships in the mapping of conceptual structure onto phrase structures. There are lemmas underlying late system morphemes in the mental lexicon as well as specifications for their slots when they are called by an utterance under construction. However, these slots and the form of morphemes filling the slots are not salient until they are projected at the level of the Formulator. Projection depends on directions sent to the Formulator from lemmas underlying content morphemes in the mental lexicon. (Refer again to Figure 1.1.)

Late system morphemes are of two types that are identified by the second new opposition. This opposition is represented by [+/–outside information] for short. There are two types of late system morpheme. In neither case is information about form available until directions are sent to the Formulator to assemble larger constituents.

[3] Bock and Levelt (1994: 953) discuss indirectly elected elements as 'words that do not correspond to lexical concepts'. The example they give is *to* in *listen to the radio*. Such a morpheme as *to* in this utterance, of course, is exactly what qualifies as an early system morpheme in the 4-M model. Bock and Levelt go on to describe how *to* is activated: 'The lemma for the transitive verb *listen* requires the preposition *to*, so the lemma *to* must be activated via an indirect route at the lemma level. We refer to this as INDIRECT ELECTION' (1994: 953). However, they do not identify indirectly elected morphemes in other ways and so it is difficult to be sure their notion of indirectly elected words corresponds exactly to early system morphemes. Still, the idea of Bock and Levelt 1994—that some forms are 'indirectly elected'—is behind the formulation of the class of early system morpheme in the 4-M model.

One type of late system morpheme is called a 'bridge'. Bridge system morphemes do what the name implies; they serve as bridges in that they integrate morphemes into larger constituents. Their positioning indicates the hierarchical relationships between the morphemes they unite. Bridge system morphemes depend on the grammatical configuration of their immediate maximal projections to active them.

The second type of late system morpheme is called an 'outsider'. Outsider system morphemes also integrate morphemes or XPs into larger constituents, but contrast with bridges in regard to the source of information about their form. For outsider system morphemes, this information (usually) is not available until the highest-level projection, the CP, is assembled. This is why they are called late. Further, outsider system morphemes perform the arguably more important function of showing coindexical relationships across maximal projections. These hypothesized differences in how morphemes are accessed in language production are formalized in the Differential Access Hypothesis:

> Relevant information in lemmas supporting surface-level morphemes does not all become salient at the same level of language production. Information supporting content morphemes and early system morphemes is salient in the mental lexicon, but information about late system morphemes does not become salient until the level of the Formulator when larger constituents are assembled.

3.4.6. *Exemplifying morpheme types*

Now that the different types of morpheme have been defined and described, the following examples can illustrate them. In example (10*a*), *dog* is a content morpheme and its determiner (*the*) is an early system morpheme. *Dog* receives the thematic role of Patient or Goal; *the* depends on its head (*dog*) for its form.

While the phrase structure of English requires that definite nouns have determiners, and that determiners in general precede the nouns they modify, the choice of *the* as the selected determiner is not structurally assigned. Instead, like *dog*, *the* is conceptually activated. It occurs in order to add specificity to *dog*. Note also that the *-s* plural suffix on *dogs* is an early system morpheme (example (10*b*)). Again, its presence depends on the fact it adds conceptual information to *dog*, making it plural. That is, while English well-formedness conditions require that plural is conveyed by an affix and that this affix is a suffix on the relevant noun, there is nothing about the structure of English that requires nouns to be plural. Rather, it is the speaker's intention to convey a certain message that results in the plural affix's appearance.

(10) *a* I want *the dog* with the waggly tail.
b *Dog-s* can be very friendly.

The satellite prepositions (also called verb particles) in phrasal verbs are also early system morphemes in English. They depend on their heads (verbs) for their form. Note that the addition of a satellite conveys a different meaning from that of the verb on its own. Compare *look* with *look at* in (11*a*) and (11*b*).

(11) *a* Lena *looked* terrific in the photos.
b Miles *looked at* the photos.

Example (12) offers more examples of both content morphemes and early system morphemes. In this example, *relative, past,* and *think* are content morphemes while *my,* plural *-s,* and *the* are early system morphemes, depending on their head noun for their form. They add conceptual information to their heads, with *my* making explicit the reference of *relatives, -s* conveying plurality, and *the* adding definiteness to *past.* The finite verb *think* is a content morpheme and its satellite, *about,* adds meaning so that *think about* conveys a different meaning from what simply the verb *think* does. As content morphemes, *relatives, past,* and *think* participate in the thematic grid of the CP. The verb *think* assigns the thematic role of Goal to *past,* and *relatives* receives the role of Experiencer.

(12) My relatives think about the past.

In (13), two NPs are integrated into a larger constituent by the bridge late system morpheme *of.* Like early system morphemes, bridges depend on information inside the maximal projection in which they occur. But unlike early system morphemes, bridges do not convey conceptual structure; their role is to unite structural units. Also, while an early system morpheme is coindexed with its head, a bridge system morpheme is not coindexed at all. Rather, consider example (13*a*) and *of* in the construction *book of Jan.* Directions originating in lemmas supporting nouns in the mental lexicon, but activated at the level of the Formulator, require that case be realized in this type of [NP [NP]] construction. The English possessive suffix *-'s* in (13*b*) is also a bridge system morpheme. Like *of,* it expresses genitive/possessive case. However, *Jan,* the possessor NP in the construction [[NP] NP] receives genitive/possessive case from the construction itself, not from the possessed NP.[4]

[4] Jake (personal communication) has the following interpretation of such constructions. The possessive *of* in English constructs a grammatical structure out of a possessor NP and a possessed NP. Essentially, the *of* assigns possessive case to an NP that otherwise has no case. The possessive does not assign a thematic role as do some other prepositions in English. For example, *from* in *book from my sister* assigns Source; *to* in *trip to France* assigns Direction, etc. However *of* is notoriously vague and undefined. Consider *of* in *the destruction of the army.* Is *the army* a Patient or Agent? At best, we can say that it is a Theme, and when a larger constituent is structured, *of* is selected because the Theme requires overt case. While context clarifies how the Theme is to be interpreted in terms of its thematic role, case assignment is not a property of nouns. So *of* is selected as a late system morpheme, building a PP out of an NP within a larger NP. But the form of the preposition *of* need look no further than the NP within its own maximal projection for its form. Chomsky has a somewhat different argument for these types of constructions. He writes that in *the destruction of the city,* 'Destruction theta-marks its complement *the city* and, therefore, assigns it genitive case' (1986: 198). In Chomsky (1995: 114) he writes that 'A and N [in these types of constructions] are, in fact genitive Case assigners'.

(13) *a* The *book of Jan* is on the table.
b *Jan's book* is on the table.

Another example of a bridge system morpheme is expletive/existential *it*, as in *It is a nice day*. Again, as a bridge system morpheme, *it* facilitates, if not 'creates', a construction. Similarly, in French, *il* performs the same function and is also a bridge system morpheme, as in *il pleut* 'it is raining'. In codeswitching corpora, bridge morphemes typically come from the Matrix Language, although the MLF model does not require this. There are many examples from languages with a bridge between NPs in NP+NP constructions, with the NPs from the Embedded Language, but the bridge from the Matrix Language (e.g. *puis il y avait des games* ***de*** *ball* 'and there were ball games', Poplack 1987: 58).

Example (14) illustrates a late outsider system morpheme. English subject–verb agreement is only overtly expressed in present tense. All persons except third person singular receive zero affixes, with *-s* as a marker of third person singular present tense. This marker is under Agr (agreement) in Infl (inflectional phrase), but cannot be realized until it is coindexed with a third person singular NP.

(14) *Bora eat-s* her food rapidly.

Morphologically richer languages have more outsider system morphemes than English has. For example, in Hungarian, certain case affixes are late system morphemes, as is the accusative suffix *-t* in (15).

(15) Kris meg akar-t-a enni az almá-*t*
Kris PREVwant-PAST-3SG.OBJ eat/INF the apple-ACC
'Kris wanted to eat the apple.'

(Bolonyai 2000: 89)

Languages in which modifiers of nouns are linked in some formal way with their head noun supply other examples of outsider system morphemes; they perform the coindexing. For example, in Swahili and other Bantu languages, most adjectives receive an agreement prefix. Consider the adjective *-dogo* 'small' in (16*a*, *b*). The form of the prefix in the resulting AdjP depends on information outside its immediate maximal projection. It depends on the noun class of its head noun in the maximal projection of NP. Thus, in *m-toto m-dogo* 'child small', we have an outsider system morpheme on *dogo*; it receives information about its form from the noun *m-toto*. The same adjective is marked with a different prefix when it modifies a noun of a different class, for example *ki-kombe ki-dogo* 'cup small'. In this case, the form of the prefix is coindexed with its head noun, *ki-kombe*. Note that the prefixes on these nouns (*m-toto* and *ki-kombe*) are not late system morphemes, but early system morphemes. The reason? They add conceptual information to their head nouns (information about the noun class, which—in some cases—has semantic import, but which always has information about the agreement patterns it controls).

(16) *a* **m**-toto **m**-dogo a-na-li-a.
CL1-child CL1-small 3S-NONPST-cry-FV
'The small child is crying.'
b **ki**-kombe **ki**-dogo ki-me-anguk-a
CL7-cup CL7-small CL7-PERF-fall down-FV
'The small cup fell down.'

3.4.7. *All phonetic shapes are not equal*

Other examples from English make the point that the same phonetic shape may stand for different types of morpheme. While *the* as a definite determiner is an early system morpheme (as in (10*a*)), it is a bridge system morpheme in certain set collocations. Example (17) exemplifies *the* as a bridge system morpheme. In this phrase, *the* does not necessarily add definiteness to *hospital*; all it does is satisfy the requirements of the constituent structure.

(17) A: Where's John today?
B: Haven't you heard? He's *in the hospital.*
A: Oh, which one?

To take another example from English, consider *of.* Above in example (13) I argue that *of* is a bridge system morpheme in [NP [NP]] constructions. However, it is an early system morpheme when it occurs as a verb satellite in the phrasal verb *think of* as in (18*a*). Note that *think of* ('call to mind') contrasts in meaning with *think* ('consider') alone, as in (18*b*).

(18) *a* *Think of* a number, any number!
b *Think* positively!

3.4.8. *Multimorphemic lexemes*

Some lexemes are multimorphemic. For example, determiners in the Romance languages encode person, number, and gender. It happens that these features are all encoded by early system morphemes, as in *la maison* 'the house' in which *la* encodes third person singular and feminine gender. However, in some cases there is more than one type of morpheme within a single lexeme. For example, German determiners encode gender, number, and case. They are notoriously hard to learn for second-language speakers, perhaps because they encode so many morphemes simultaneously, but it is more likely they are hard to learn because case is not assigned in the same way as gender and number. Gender and number in German, as in most languages signaling these relationships, are early system morphemes. Thus, these features of the determiner are activated at the lemma level (they are indirectly elected by their nouns). However, case in German is assigned by verbs or prepositions; it is a late system morpheme, with the form not available until the larger constituent (not just an NP) is assembled.

Under the 4-M model, if the morphemes differ, outsider system morphemes take precedence. The fact they are hypothesized as accessed 'late' can make a difference in regard to favored constituents in codeswitching (cf. Myers-Scotton and Jake 2001: 113–14 on a Swiss German/Italian corpus). Chapter 7 includes a hypothesis predicting that in multimorpheme forms, the late system morpheme takes precedence and 'pulls down' the multimorphemic form so that it patterns with late system morphemes in its distribution in bilingual CPs, but also in other types of data.

3.4.9. *Speech errors as independent motivation for the 4-M model*

Data from diverse data sets, both monolingual and bilingual, motivate the 4-M model's classification. For example, as I have already indicated, Myers-Scotton and Jake (2000*a*) detail differential distributions that reflect the 4-M model's divisions in data from Broca's aphasics and Interlanguage in second language acquisition. Here, I will discuss briefly how speech error data support the model.

Psycholinguists have long recognized that speech errors show that inflectional elements and some function words behave differently from content morphemes in speech errors (cf. Garrett 1988, *inter alia*). These errors show the exchange of content morphemes within the same clause and the stranding of their affixes (cf. discussion in Myers-Scotton 1993*a* [1997]: 52 ff.). See example (19).

(19) How many pie*s* does it take to make an apple?
Target: . . . apples . . . to make a pie

(Garrett 1988: 76)

Stemberger (1985*a*: 165) points out that, in a corpus of 135 errors where stranding is possible, affix stranding does occur in 120 cases (88.9 percent), more often than expected by chance. Obviously, these exchange and stranding errors imply there is a difference in how content morphemes are accessed in comparison with system morphemes. (See Stemberger (1985*b*: 175 ff.) for a detailed argument citing four types of speech-error data that 'argue that regular inflected forms are analyzed into a base and an affix by speakers'.)

The potential implications of two facts about speech errors are especially relevant to the divisions of system morphemes within the 4-M model. First, consider what happens to the plural affix. In his corpus, Stemberger (1985*a*) found that more plurals (i.e. English *-s*) were involved in speech errors than any other affix (48/135 or 36 per cent). Like other early system morphemes, plurals are subject to stranding. However, in Stemberger's data, more plurals resisted stranding than would be predicted by chance. That is, they moved with their heads when their heads exchanged places with another content morpheme in the clause (eight out of the fifteen affixes that moved were plurals). Examples (20) and (21) show plurals that move with their heads. Of course a systematic examination of speech-error data to see the extent to which other early system morphemes also tend to move with their heads would be useful. However, the finding regarding plurals supports the assumption underlying the 4-M model that early system morphemes are more closely tied to their heads than other system morphemes, presumably because of the abstract features they share with their heads (i.e. they are salient in some sense at the lemma level).

(20) Well you can cut rain in the tree-s
Target: . . . cut trees in the rain

(Garrett 1982, cited in Levelt 1989: 222)

(21) I presume you could get light in poorer picture-s
Target: . . . get pictures in poorer light

(Stemberger 1985*b*: 162)

Second, while another type of error, syntactic accommodation errors, were already discussed in *Duelling Languages* (pp. 63–4), this type of error takes on new meaning in light of the 4-M model. In such errors, a content morpheme accommodates to a frame slot—in the sense that it takes on the system morpheme that is associated with that slot (e.g. it takes on the case of the slot). See (22) for an example of the English pronoun for first person singular that accommodates to nominative case when it appears in the subject slot.

(22) If *I* was done to that.
Target: if that was done to *me*

(Fay 1980, cited by Levelt 1989: 248)

Under my analysis, here is what happens: the speaker intended to use the objective form of first person (*me*). Frame-building operations in the Formulator (in language production) receive directions from a lemma in the mental lexicon that supports the first person pronoun. However, in the interaction between the lemma and the Formulator there is an error: the pronoun goes to the wrong syntactic slot, a slot that calls for a nominative case. That is, the net result is that those syntactic procedures in the Formulator (that come from the lemma for first person singular) call for a nominative form in subject position; they are blind to the speaker's intention to access *me* as a recipient. One may argue that the error occurred at the lemma level (*I* was accessed there); it is more economical to assume that the pronoun is neither *I* nor *me* at the lemma level and that procedures at the Formulator produce the form that fits the syntactic slot. By error, *that* went to the slot in the prepositional phrase (*to that*). Then, what mattered is that the Formulator had a slot for subject to fill. It filled it with what would be a pragmatically unmarked subject (the pronoun as Agent). This meant the pronoun received a nominative form (*I*). Such a form fits the English frame-building procedures for subject that the Formulator had at its disposal.

For an example of accommodation of subject–verb agreement, see (23). Here, with *cities* moved to the subject slot, the verb changes with singular to plural in agreement with *cities.*

(23) Most *cities are* true of that.
Target: that is true of most cities.
(Stemberger 1985*b*: 154)

What do accommodation errors tell us that is different from the implications of stranding errors? In regard to stranding, Levelt commented that the stranding of any inflection is 'supportive of the notion that the corresponding diacritical features are assigned *after* the lemma is inserted into its grammatical frame' (1989: 249). I agree, but only in part. I agree that *all* system morphemes are accessed *differently* from their content-morpheme heads, but the evidence regarding plurals and stranding indicates that early system morphemes are not necessarily activated *significantly later*. (This is an issue for psycholinguistic testing.) That is, Levelt's statement may only apply to late system morphemes.

Certainly, accommodation errors indicate that late system morphemes are entered in the grammatical frame at a later point than content morphemes that are not combined with late system morphemes (compare what happens to *cities* in (23) vs. English first person singular pronoun in (22) and the copula verb in (23)). That is, accommodation errors in these examples tell us that the nature of a content morpheme at the conceptual level (e.g. speaker's intentions to access a first person singular pronoun) need not be the same as it is when it becomes a multimorphemic linguistic unit (combined with a late system morpheme) at the level of the Formulator. That is, at the Formulator, the form of English first person singular in (22) as a linguistic unit depends on the slot it fills *when the larger constituent is assembled* (when it receives case). This is evidence that late system morphemes depend on information at this 'late' level to realize their form. In turn, this is evidence for differentiating early and late system morphemes along the lines of the 4-M model.

Based on German data, Berg (1987) argues explicitly against syntactic accommodation as a common occurrence in speech errors. However, if his examples are examined in light of the 4-M model, it is clear that most of his misaccommodation examples are *not* late system morphemes (as are featured in (22) and (23)). Berg's data consist of articles on nouns that require adjustment because they precede nouns that have been exchanged with the original nouns that stood in the slot. In thirty-one out of thirty-six cases, Berg states there is no accommodation; that is, the original article is retained.

However, upon examining at least the four examples Berg presents, one can see that the misaccommodation involves the early system morphemes of gender, not the late system morpheme of case. For example, the original noun may have called for a masculine article (e.g. the proper name *Helmut* and therefore *der Helmut* would be correct), but with the exchange a feminine noun appears in the slot with the masculine article (*der Christa*). However, *der* is the nominative singular form (what *Christa* as well as *Helmut* would require) and so the only 'error' involves the *phi* feature of gender that would be encoded by an early system morpheme. Under the 4-M model, one can argue that early system morphemes, such as gender, are salient at the level of the mental lexicon and therefore are already in place before the noun exchange takes place. For this reason, it is no surprise that the article *der* does not accommodate to *Christa*. That is, the 4-M model would predict that the division between early and late system morphemes would be evident in speech errors. To be fair to Berg, he himself recognizes that a reasonable prediction is that errors would not show up in case. He notes that 'since case information is not inherent to the moving noun but assigned to it via the syntactic structure, it is not often involved in errors' (1987: 285).

In sum, while the differential behavior or content words and function elements has long been recognized in speech errors, the discussion here supports the notion that the recognition of different types of system morphemes offers an even better explanation of how speech errors arise. That all functional elements do not pattern alike in speech errors adds independent motivation for the 4-M model.

3.4.10. *The value of the 4-M model*

The 4-M model adds precision to the MLF model, but also its implications seem to explain configurations in data well beyond the scope of the MLF model (i.e. beyond classic codeswitching). First, because of these wider applications, the 4-M model connects a theory of grammar with language production and processing in some more general ways than the MLF model. Remember that the MLF model implies that the Matrix Language – Embedded Language opposition and the content–system morpheme distinction are universal features underlying language production when classic codeswitching data is involved. However, the 4-M model offers indirect evidence about how language production *actually works*. This shows one way in which competence and performance are linked. It does this—its major virtue—by showing how surface morpheme distributions can be explained if they are related to abstract entries in the mental lexicon. The argument is that particular instances of morphemes are classified as a consequence of the abstract mechanisms that activate them.

Second, on the practical level, the model provides a more precise account of codeswitching by elaborating the classes of system morpheme, leading to a more satisfying explanation of certain distributions. This becomes apparent in the discussion of examples (24) through (35) in sections 3.5.1 and 3.5.2. Third, because the distinctions among morpheme types apply universally, in later chapters, the model shows how diverse linguistic phenomena are connected. This final point is especially relevant to the stated goal of showing how puzzles in the grammatical structure in all contact phenomena yield to explanations based on the same principles.

3.4.11. *A related way to classify morphemes*

The closest analogue to the 4-M model is the view of the Dutch linguist Geert Booij that inflectional morphemes divide into two types, inherent and contextual inflection. His definitions are rather unspecified. For example, in Booij (1996), he writes that 'inherent inflection is the kind of inflection that is not required by the syntactic context, although it may have syntactic relevance' (p. 2). The category number for nouns is an example of inherent inflection. Contextual inflection 'is that kind of inflection that is dictated by syntax, such as person and number markers on verbs that agree with subjects and/or objects' (p. 2). Clearly, Booij's inherent inflection corresponds to those inflections that are early system morphemes and his contextual inflection corresponds to those inflections that are late outsider system morphemes.

However, the 4-M model has greater scope and there are distinct differences in the details of the two classifications. First, Booij's main interest in setting up his division seems to be to account for word-formation properties. That is, his main criterion for dividing inflectional morphemes is their participation (or not) in word-building. Second, he does not offer formal lexicosyntactic criteria to motivate their differences in feeding word formation. Third, he is especially interested in the similarities between inherent inflection and derivation in word-building and gives examples of how inherent inflection can feed derivation and compounding. Fourth, he does not consider the difference distributions of his morpheme types across various forms of language, except for noting their relevance to orders of acquisition in child language. Finally, and most important to the 4-M model, while he seems to recognize that his two types of morpheme participate differently in language production, he does not suggest explicitly that there is a basis in language competence and production for such differences or their relation to word formation. Still, the division he makes has proven useful in describing differences in the inflectional systems of various languages.

3.5. The MLF model plus the 4-M model: revisiting classic codeswitching

Examples (24) through (29) (as well as examples (1) through (4) above) illustrate typical examples of mixed constituents in codeswitching that support the MLF model (i.e. they support the Morpheme Order and the System Morpheme Principles). Viewing such examples in terms of the 4-M model as well as the MLF model, I can add new precision to the definition of the type of morpheme that must come from the Matrix Language in mixed constituents. Then, with examples (30) through (37), I offer better explanations for two other distributions of data in mixed constituents. These are (i) 'double morphology', a configuration of a single content element (noun or verb) that is doubly marked by certain function words or inflections from both the Matrix Language and the Embedded Language, and (ii) Embedded Language non-finite verb forms that appear in codeswitching with their early system morphemes.

3.5.1. *Misunderstandings: the System Morpheme Principle*

One of the problems with applying the two principles for mixed constituents of the MLF model, and thereby identifying the Matrix Language to their satisfaction, has been that the meaning of the System Morpheme Principle has not been clear to all researchers. That is, some researchers have produced examples that they claim are counterexamples to the principle; they then go on to claim that, therefore, the Matrix Language – Embedded Language opposition is problematic. Unfortunately, they misinterpret the principle. The principle does not state that *all* system morphemes must come from only one participating language (the Matrix Language); it states that only those that 'have grammatical relations external to their head constituent' are the system morphemes that must come from the Matrix Language. Yet, its actual wording notwithstanding, some fault must lie with the way the principle is stated.

Further, an additional problem may be that, in fact, *most* system morphemes in mixed constituents *do* come from the Matrix Language, not just the type required by the System Morpheme Principle. For example, affixes for plural, an early system morpheme, generally come from the Matrix Language in codeswitching data sets (e.g. in Shona/English codeswitching, an English noun typically receives a Shona plural prefix, e.g. *ma-bus* 'busses'). Because most system morphemes come from the Matrix Language, this may be one reason why some researchers misunderstand the limits of the principle when not all system morphemes come from the Matrix Language.

The misunderstanding is compounded because some of the examples that appear in *Duelling Languages* (pp. 102 ff.) just after the statement of the System Morpheme Principle include Matrix Language system morphemes, but they are a mixed bag: some are the type of system morpheme to which the principle refers, but some are not. I admit this gives the impression that all system morphemes should come from the Matrix Language. In one example cited on p. 107 (from Poplack 1988: 99) there is a mixed constituent including a mixed NP with a French determiner and an English noun (*le brain* 'the brain'). I claim that French is the Matrix Language and because the example includes a system morpheme (*le*), one might suppose this is relevant to the System Morpheme Principle. But it is not; instead, it is an early system morpheme. Such morphemes do not have relations external to their heads—what the System Morpheme Principle specifies.

One of the benefits of the 4-M model is that it offers another, possibly more precise, way to state the syntactic qualities of the type of morpheme that must come from the Matrix Language under the System Morpheme Principle. The 4-M model calls this type of morpheme *a late outsider system morpheme.* Recall that the label 'outsider' refers to the fact that such a morpheme must look outside its immediate maximal constituents for information about its form. For example, in subject–verb agreement, the verbal affix looks to the subject for this information. Another way to think of late outsiders is that they build larger constituents—larger than just an NP, for example. This description may make the relevant type of morpheme easier to recognize. Also, because the 4-M model explicitly contrasts the three types of system morpheme with each other, this may also make the definitions of each type easier to apply. The distinction is important because it becomes clear in later chapters that recognizing late system morphemes is important in analyzing more than just codeswitching data.

Four examples, (24) through (27), are cited specifically as evidence that the System Morpheme Principle makes the right predictions for mixed constituents in codeswitching. Examples (24) through (26) show Embedded Language verbs inflected with Matrix Language affixes. In (24) note that the speaker inflects the English verb *comment* with Swahili prefixes for subject–verb agreement and tense/aspect. Morphemes signaling these relations depend on information outside their immediate maximal projection for their form; this means they are co-indexed with outside information. For example, in this case, the previous discourse must indicate that the subject of the verb is a first person singular entity. The System Morpheme Principle states that such morphemes must come from only one of the languages participating in codeswitching. Thus, *si-ku-comment* 'I didn't comment' supports the principle, and Swahili is identified as the Matrix Language because it is that language supplying the relevant system morphemes. If the speaker had produced either a Swahili verb with English subject–verb agreement or an English verb with English subject–verb agreement, these would be counterexamples to the System Morpheme Principle. The speaker also produces an English AdjP, *very new.* This is an Embedded Language Island; nothing in the MLF model prohibits such constituents. They are discussed again in Chapter 4. Note that *very* is a system morpheme, but an early, not a late outsider, at least in the case of English (equivalents in other languages may be multimorphemic and include late system morphemes). Still, if the speaker's intentions are to access an English intensifier adverb and it is accessed *initially* in the phrase, then the phrase must be finished as an island in the Embedded Language. Otherwise, the phrase would violate the Morpheme Order Principle. This principle requires the order to be from the same language as the language of the type of morpheme satisfying the System Morpheme Principle; in Swahili, modifiers follow their heads. There are examples in the same Nairobi corpus including English modifiers in mixed constituents, but they follow Swahili word order (e.g. *mambo mengi new* 'things many new').

(24) Ile m-geni, hata si-ku-**comment.**
DEM/CL9 Cl1/S-visitor even 1S.NEG-PST.NEG-comment
Si-ku-mu-uliza manaake ni-li-ku-w-a **very new.**
1S-PAST/NEG-3S.OBJ-ask because 1S-PST-INF-COP-FV very new
'That visitor, I did not even comment. I did not even ask him because I was very new.'

(Swahili/English; Myers-Scotton Nairobi corpus 1988)

Amuzu notes an interesting construction in his corpus that still maintains the Matrix Language frame with its Matrix Language system morphemes. English verbs that take prepositional satellites (that are early system morphemes) appear with their satellites in a discontinuous pattern that accommodates an Ewe suffix on the verb. It is the Ewe suffix (*-e*) that is the late system morpheme. See *keep away from* in (25).

(25) ɗe me dzí be má **keep**-e **away from** Eun . . .
FOC 1S want COMP 1S-FUT keep-3S away from Eun . . .
'I had wanted to keep him away from Eun . . .'

(Ewe/English; Amuzu 1998: 53)

English verbs can also occur in serial verb constructions in Ewe; as the System Morpheme Principle predicts, they take Ewe verbal inflections, as in (26).

(26) wo tsɔ-na wo fe asi-wo tsɔ-na
3PL take-HAB 3PL POSS hand-PL take-HAB
weed-na **garden**-a me-ɛ
weed-HAB garden-DEF in-FOC
'They take [use] their hands to weed in the garden'

(Ewe/English; Amuzu 1998: 56)

That the System Morpheme Principle holds just as well in an analytic language, such as Ewe, as it does in an agglutinative language, such as Swahili, should lay to rest comments that the MLF model only can be supported with Swahili-like languages. Further, example (27) in Croatian, a highly inflected language, comes from another language type, further illustrating the domain of the MLF model. Example (28) comes from Turkish/Norwegian codeswitching. Turkish is an agglutinative language, but also has rich morphology; Norwegian has less morphology, but more than English.

Examples (27) and (28) are included specifically to illustrate how Embedded Language nouns can receive Matrix Language case marking. Example (27) comes from a corpus recorded in Australia, with young adult second-generation Croatians as the speakers. All are bilingual in Croatian and English. The researcher (Hlavac) has reproduced a phonetic version of the English nouns (*pack*, *container*) that occur in this CP. Note that these nouns receive inflections that integrate them morphosyntactically into the Croatian frame. These inflections are multimorphemic. The first inflection (*-ujem*) encodes person, number, and tense, and the second (*-e*) encodes plural, gender, and case. Plural and gender are early system morphemes; the other morphemes (late) are all co-indexed with elements in the discourse outside the immediate maximal projection. Recall that in multimorphemic elements that include a late system morpheme, it is the late system morpheme that is most salient in testing the System Morpheme Principle. Again, its form becomes salient only at the level of the Formulator when larger constituents are assembled.

(27) i tako [**pak**]-ujem one . . . [**kontejner**]-e i tako dalje . . .
and so pack-1S/PRES those . . . container-M/PL/ACC and so on . . .
'And so [I] pack those . . . containers and so on . . .'

(Croatian/English; Hlavac 2000: 392)

Example (28) comes from a conversation among young adult Turkish immigrants to Norway. All had lived in Norway for at least four years. The example shows instances of Norwegian nouns with affixes that correspond to Turkish well-formedness conditions. That is, Turkish as the Matrix Language sets the frame. What is especially interesting here, from the standpoint of the Matrix Language – Embedded Language opposition is that nominal constructions (*herkes-in oppgave-si* 'everybody his own duty / everybody's duty') follow Turkish specifications entirely. In Turkish such a genitive construction consists of N-GEN + N-POSS. In this example, the complement noun is in Turkish and receives the genitive suffix. The head noun comes from Norwegian, but it shows the Turkish possessive marker. This marker is an outsider late system morpheme, as is the case marker (LOC) on the Norwegian noun **kjøkken.**

(28) **kjøkken**-de herkes-in **oppgave**-si vard-dı
kitchen-LOC everybody-GEN duty-POSS exist-PST-1PL
'Everybody had his own duty in the kitchen.'

(Turkish/Norwegian; Türker 2000: 151)

What about counterexamples to the System Morpheme Principle in the literature? Often, what are cited as counterexamples are early system morphemes (e.g. plural or determiners) or even content morphemes (e.g. *there* as a locative). In some cases, they are bridges. I know of very few actual counterexamples; to find a few would not be a surprise. In Myers-Scotton (2001*a*: 46 ff.), I argue against several supposed counterexamples. For example, both Bentahila and Davies (1998: 40) and Boumans (1998: 48) cite the use of Arabic *djal* in a frame that is clearly from French as possible violations of the System Morpheme Principle. Example (29) comes from a conversation in Moroccan Arabic and French, but the particular phrase in question is all in French, except for *djal*.

(29) . . . de quel degré de connaissance *djal* la personne . . .
'. . . on which degree of knowledge of the person . . .'

(Moroccan Arabic/French; Bentahila and Davies 1998: 38)

It is true, as Bentahila and Davies point out, that I identify *djal* as a system morpheme in *Duelling Languages* (p. 106) and do so in such a way that I imply that *djal* is the type of system morpheme relevant to the System Morpheme Principle. I admit I am guilty of this implication; either I was confused myself or my wording was an oversight. The 4-M model makes the status of morphemes such as *djal* very clear: it is a bridge late system morpheme, *not* an outsider. Therefore, its presence (ostensibly from the Embedded Language in (29)) does not violate the principle. Although bridge late system morphemes pattern with outsider late system morphemes as [–conceptually activated], bridges are then differentiated from late outsiders by another opposition, [+/–look outside maximal projection]. Bridges build structure within a maximal projection; they are structurally assigned to do so by the well-formedness requirements of the relevant constituent. But they do not look outside their immediate maximal projection for their form; they are not co-indexed with an element outside that maximal projection, as are late outsider system morphemes. This is a crucial difference. In this case, *djal* functions very much like English *of* or French *de* in joining together two NPs.

So, why should Arabic supply *djal* in this case? I have no ready answer to this question. In fact, as example (9) above shows—along with many other data sets (e.g. Acholi/English as discussed in Chapter 4 in relation to the Uniform Structure Principle)—the more usual circumstance by far is to have a NP + bridge + NP associative construction, with at least one of the NPs from the Embedded Language, but the bridge morpheme always from the Matrix Language. Here in (29), of course, *djal* is from the apparent Embedded Language.

3.5.2. *Double morphology in classic codeswitching*

Ever since the MLF model was introduced in *Duelling Languages*, other researchers and I have noted the occasional doubling of some system morphemes on content morphemes. The most frequent system morpheme to be doubled is the plural affix (e.g. *ma-storie-s* from Swahili/English codeswitching, with *ma-* as the noun class 6 prefix signaling the class and also plural). Contrary to the understanding of some researchers (e.g. Muysken 2000: 173), when Embedded Language plural affixes appear in mixed constituents, they do not violate the System Morpheme Principle. Plural affixes are not the type of morpheme at issue under the specifications of this principle; they are discussed in *Duelling Languages*, but not as counterexamples. Their status becomes even clearer under the 4-M model in which they are explicitly differentiated from late outsiders and classified as early system morphemes. (It should be clear why they are earlies; they add conceptual structure to their heads and their form depends on their head.)

In *Duelling Languages*, double morphology already was described as a type of 'mistiming'. The hypothesized scenario is the following: the speaker wishes to express her or his intentions by using an Embedded Language noun along with the concept of plurality. However, when the lemma for that noun is accessed, at the same time, its plural affix 'slips in', too.

Specifications for system morphemes under the 4-M model provide for a more explanatory way to view double morphology. Yes, double morphology occurs as a type of mistiming, but why does it occur only with certain system morphemes? The 4-M model answers this question and motivates a hypothesis referring to double morphology:

The Early System Morpheme Hypothesis is: Only early system morphemes may be doubled in classic codeswitching.

The motivation for the hypothesis is that—of all system morphemes—only early system morphemes have the special relation to their heads that would promote their accessing when their Embedded Language heads are called in codeswitching. Like their heads, earlies are conceptually activated, and a hypothesis under the 4-M model is that early system morphemes are salient at the same level as their content morpheme heads (at the lemma level—i.e. in the mental lexicon). Thus, they are 'available' if any mistiming is going to occur. In contrast, late system morphemes are not available yet, but only become salient at the level of the Formulator. There are no examples in the literature to show they are doubled in codeswitching, although I can imagine they could be doubled when a composite Matrix Language is being structured (cf. Thomason (2000: 77) on doubled person/number suffixes in Megleno-Rumanian).

All examples in the codeswitching literature showing double morphology are early system morphemes; that is, they all support the Early System Morpheme Hypothesis. Even though many of the examples I have cited here and elsewhere come from language pairs involving a Bantu language as the Matrix Language, double morphology is by no means a feature most found in Bantu languages. It is true that almost all involve nouns and their plurals, although there are a few doubled infinitive markers. There are also a few doubled determiners; for example Boyd (1997: 270) reports that 3.4 per cent (3/88) of Swedish nouns in a data set (English is the Matrix Language) drawn from American bilinguals in Sweden showed double marking of determiners (e.g. ***the** folkhögskola-**n*** 'the folk high school'). Examples (30) and (31) illustrate double morphology with nouns; in (30) the Matrix Language is a Bantu language and in (31) it is a totally unrelated language, a Nilotic language. In both cases, the doubling morpheme is a suffix and the Matrix Language morpheme doubled is a prefix.

(30) **ma-day-s** a-no a-ya ha-ndi-si ku-mu-on-a
but CL6-day-PL CL6-DEM CL6-DEM NEG-1S-COP INF-3S/OBJ-see-FV
'But these days I don't see him much anymore.'

(Shona/English; Crawhall 1990 corpus, cited in Myers-Scotton 1993*a* [1997]: 111)

(31) bene o-nwongo gi-**using** **Swahili** ka-**terrorizing** lu-**civilian-s**
also 3S-find/PERF 3PL-using Swahili INF-terrorizing DET/PL-civilian-PL
'One finds they are using Swahili to terrorize the civilians.'

(Acholi/English codeswitching; Myers-Scotton and Bernsten corpus 1995)

In (32), with Turkish as the Matrix Language, both doubling and doubled morphemes are suffixes. Example (33) shows doubling of infinitive markers in Congo Swahili/French codeswitching, the same type of doubling that I have cited elsewhere (e.g. Myers-Scotton 1993*a* [1997]: 111) as occurring in Lingala/French codeswitching (from Bokamba 1988: 37).

(32) **Pol-en-***lar*-a Holandaca ders verdi.
Pole-PL-PL-DAT Dutch lesson give/PRET-S
'He taught Dutch to Poles.'

(Turkish/Dutch; Backus 1992: 90)

(33) Siku hile **j'étais sur le point** ya ku-**renvoy-er**
CL9/day CL9/DEM 1S/PAST/be at DET/M point CL9. ASSOC INF-return-INF
mon épouse kwa wa-zazi wa-ke . . .
POSS/M wife LOC CL2-parent CL2-POSS
'That day I was at the point of returning my wife to her parents . . .'

(Congo Swahili/French; Kamwangamalu 1987: 172)

One might ask why the Matrix Language goes ahead and contributes its versions of the system morphemes—if they are already accessed with their heads from the Embedded Language. Psycholinguistic experimentation may provide better solutions, but the answer seems to be that the Matrix Language is the more activated of the two languages, no matter what. Therefore, for it to supply as many system morphemes as it can seems simply more efficient. And, of course, all system morphemes can be considered part of the morphosyntactic frame; some are simply more essential parts from the standpoint of constituent building (late ones).

3.5.3. *Embedded Language non-finite verb forms*

Some researchers have raised bare non-finite verb forms from the Embedded Language as a counterexample to the System Morpheme Principle. Again, they are not relevant counterexamples because they do not contain any outsider late system morphemes. I cite several examples from language pairs with diverse

African languages as the Matrix Language. These can easily be augmented by many examples from the codeswitching literature; for example, Backus (1996: 226) cites examples from three other data sets. Examples (34) and (35) come from Acholi/English codeswitching in Uganda. No finite English (Embedded Language) verb forms appear in this corpus (except one in the apparent imperative: *imagine*). However, the English present participle appears frequently, apparently as a congruent enough match for an Acholi non-finite form. In fact, in a rather small corpus, there are forty-eight English present participles, with only one functioning as a finite verb. This present participle functions in three ways. Half (24/48) function as part of a reduced relative clause or otherwise subordinate clause (e.g. *gi-doing* 'they doing/they who do' as in (34)). Another 29 per cent (14/48) are infinitives, either with or without the Acholi infinitival prefix (as in (31) above *ka terrorizing* 'to terrorize'). Finally, 21 per cent (10/48) are gerunds or other types of nominals (as in *labongo considering life* 'without considering life' (as in (35)) or in *chances me surviving* 'chances of surviving'). These gerunds (and other nominals in [NP + bridge + NP] constructions are discussed in Chapter 4 under the Uniform Structure Principle.

(34) jo ma-pol i kom kare ni camo **meal** acel keken
people COMP-many in body/LOC period this eat meal one only
gi-**doing** labongo **lunch** a gi-camo **supper** keken
3PL-do without lunch then 3PL-eat supper only
'People [who are] many in this period eat only one meal, [people who] do without lunch, then they eat supper only.'

(Acholi/English; Myers-Scotton and Bernsten corpus 1995)

(35) Gin gi-mito cente ma-dwong labongo **considering life** pa dano
3PL/TOP 3PL-want money COMP-much without considering life POSS people
'As for them, they want a lot of money without respecting people's lives.'

(Acholi/English; Myers-Scotton and Bernsten corpus 1995)

Examples (36) and (37) also show non-finite Embedded Language verb forms appearing in a codeswitching corpus as holistic forms; these examples come from the Nairobi Swahili/English corpus. Swahili contrasts with Acholi as a Matrix Language in that Swahili not only employs the English present participle form as a gerund, but also employs many English verb stems in finite verb forms. In Swahili/English codeswitching (as is the case with other Bantu languages), actual English verb stems (with no English inflections) easily receive Swahili inflections to result in finite verbs. That is, speakers can strip off any English inflections from an English verb stem. However, they treat English participles as indivisible units. In (35) *teaching* appears as a gerund and in (37) *confused* appears as the past participle form functioning as a predicate adjective.

(36) Ni-na m-pango w-a **teaching**
1S-NONPST CL3-plan CL3-ASSOC teaching
'I have a plan of teaching.'

(Swahili/English; Myers-Scotton Nairobi corpus 1988)

(37) Sasa unaweza nieleza juu ya dini, tu-ko **confused**
now you can tell me about religion 1PL-LOC confused

(Swahili/English; Myers-Scotton Nairobi corpus 1988)

Taken together, such examples as (34) through (37) indicate that codeswitching treats English participles as holistic forms and (33) shows this is also the case for French infinitives. They appear categorically as full forms, never as only verb stems. This implies that they are holistic forms in the mental lexicon (i.e. the verb stem and any affix in a single lemma). Evidence that non-finite forms are holistic forms in the mental lexicon is that they (perhaps especially present participles) are acquired early in both child-language acquisition and second-language acquisition (cf. Klein 1993 as part of an extensive study of informal second-language acquisition in a number of European countries).[5]

There are reasons why such forms are acquired earlier and are easier to integrate into a Matrix Language frame than finite verb forms. Under the 4-M model, the Embedded Language affixes on present participles and on at least English past participles and on infinitives in some languages (e.g. French) are early system morphemes; their form depends on their relation to their heads and they add conceptual information to their heads. Because they contain early system morphemes (and not late system morphemes), their congruence with Matrix Language counterparts is less problematic (i.e. they do not encode tense or aspect, features that are more likely to vary crosslinguistically than the meaning of infinitives or participles). For this reason, one would expect that they match Matrix Language counterparts sufficiently to be integrated into the Matrix Language frame, and this match offers one explanation for their frequent appearance. Note that Acholi, for example, is a language encoding aspect on finite verbs (Noonan 1992 on Lango, a near-identical variety to Acholi), not tense; this may be a reason why English finite verbs do not seem to be easily integrated into an Acholi frame, but non-finite English verbs fit readily.

[5] Klein (1993) states that in the basic variety of the adult immigrants who are informal second-language learners, lexical verbs occur in a base form. He writes, 'Thus, most learners of English use the bare stem (V), but also *Ving* is not uncommon. Learners of other languages may use the infinitive' (p. 105). Note that the English infinitive (*to* + verb stem) is not a holistic unit under my view; *to* is a late system morpheme whose appearance depends on features outside the infinitive itself (e.g. it does not occur as part of the infinitive form in such sentences as *Let him go*; I thank Jan Jake for this observation).

3.5.4. *What the 4-M model adds*

Although both the notions of double morphology and holistic non-finite verb forms have been discussed before, they can be better explained under the 4-M model. The explanation rests on the relationship between content morphemes and early system morphemes. Note that under the MLF model, these two types of morpheme show no special connection; content morphemes are defined only as assigning or receiving thematic roles and system morphemes are defined as lacking this ability. However, under the 4-M model, new connections between early system morphemes and their content morpheme heads become more plausible. First, both are conceptually activated; this means they convey speaker intentions, with the earlies adding to the meanings of the content morphemes (e.g. adding definiteness or plurality, etc.) or in the case of non-finite verb forms adding derived meanings (nominalizations or modification). Because of this link between these morphemes, it is easy to see two outcomes: (i) through mistiming, double morphology, with earlies accessed along with their heads, could result, and also (ii) both parts of non-finite verbs (content morpheme and an early system morpheme) form a conceptual unit and do not build structure in the same sense as late system morphemes do, making it easier to establish sufficient congruence crosslinguistically.

3.6. The Abstract Level model further explicated

The second model that can support the MLF model, as well as explain structure in other contact phenomena on its own, is the Abstract Level model. Recall from Chapter 1 that the heart of the Abstract Level model is the claim that there are three levels of abstract grammatical structure in any lexical item. These are: (i) the level of lexical-conceptual structure (semantic/pragmatic features), critical in the semantic/pragmatic feature bundle that is matched at the conceptual level with an intention that the speaker wishes to convey; (ii) the level of predicate-argument structure (relations between thematic role assigners—verbs and some prepositions—and the arguments they map onto phrase-structure units); and (iii) the level of morphological realization patterns (elements and constituent orders required by well-formedness constraints for surface-level realizations).

A number of linguists have posited abstract structures similar to those in the Abstract Level model. They have investigated the ways in which these levels provide a formal means to describe and account for certain properties of lexical items (cf. Jackendoff 1990, Pinker 1989). The discussion in Rappaport and Levin (1988) refers to the levels of lexical-conceptual structure and of predicate-argument structure, and Talmy (1985, 2000) discusses how languages differ at the abstract level in ways that motivate the third level of the model, morphological realization patterns.

3.6.1. *The Abstract Level model and classic codeswitching*

The Abstract Level model matters for analyses of classic codeswitching because one or more of these levels is implicated when there is matching (i.e. some form of feature matching) across the participating languages to check for congruence.[6] Specifically, when speaker intentions implicate lemma selections that promise a resulting Embedded Language element, this checking begins. However, the Embedded Language content morpheme can only appear at the surface level, fully integrated into the Matrix Language frame, if this checking turns up sufficient congruence between the Embedded Language morpheme and its Matrix Language counterpart (cf. Myers-Scotton and Jake 1995). That is, the premise of the Abstract Level model is that when Embedded Language singly occurring forms occur with morphosyntactic integration into a mixed constituent in a Matrix Language frame, they have passed checking for congruence at all three levels of abstract grammatical structure. Recall my earlier discussion in this chapter; the counterpart need not be a specific Matrix Language element, but Lexical Knowledge (generalized but specific to the Matrix Language). This knowledge is also present in the mental lexicon, but in addition to entries for specific lemmas.

However, this does not mean that the Embedded Language content morpheme is totally congruent with its Matrix Language counterpart—just sufficiently congruent so that the features they encode satisfy the requirements of the Matrix Language frame.

Always keep in mind that the impetus for codeswitching is at the level of lexical-conceptual structure. Sometimes the desired Embedded Language element can be accommodated morphosyntactically in a Matrix Language-framed mixed constituent. At other times the levels of predicate-argument structure or the morphological realization patterns that the prized Embedded Language element implicates means that the only path open is by accessing it as a bare form or in an Embedded Language island. I develop these arguments in Chapter 4; here, I only offer some examples.

3.6.2. *Ways to integrate Embedded Language material*

In (38) the English verb *buy* is an example of an Embedded Language form selected to satisfy special intentions of the speaker; *buy* better conveys what the speaker wishes to say than its Swahili counterpart. The English verb receives nearly full

[6] Muysken (2000) refers to 'congruent lexicalization' as one of the three processes that he sees as central to what he calls code-mixing. However, his use of 'congruence' is different from mine. For him, congruent lexicalization seems to obtain when the structures of two varieties are very compatible to the extent that he claims there are no constraints on which elements in a bilingual clause must come from one variety or the other. However, for me, congruence and constraints go hand in hand. Congruence has to do with what features must be checked and the results of checking that must obtain in order for certain elements to occur in certain codeswitching patterns (cf. the Blocking Hypothesis of Myers-Scotton 1993*a* [1997] and 'matching' in Myers-Scotton and Jake 1995).

morphosyntactic integration.[7] This is evidence that there is sufficient congruence at all levels for *buy* to occur, including the crucial level of lexical-conceptual structure—but not total congruence; otherwise, there is no need for it at all. Its use could just mean that it 'came to the speaker's mind'; without psycholinguistic evidence that this is so, I think it is safer to assume that *buy* carries different connotations from its putative Swahili counterpart *-nunua* 'buy'. 'To buy someone a beer' implies that someone is the speaker's guest; in contrast *a-li-m-nunulia* (applied form from *-nunua*) 'he bought for him' has more of an implication of simply 'making a purchase for someone', not necessarily for someone as one's guest.

(38) Hau-ku-on-a a-ki-ni-**buy**-i-a **beer** siku hi-yo?
2S/NEG-NEG/PAST-see-FV 3S-PROG-1S/OBJ-buy-APPL-FV beer day CL9-DEM
'Didn't you see him buying beer for me that day?'

(Swahili/English; Myers-Scotton 1993*a* [1997]: 115)

What happens if there are congruence problems? If the semantic/pragmatic feature bundle that satisfies the speaker's intentions creates a congruence problem, the bundle can be retained by accessing compromise strategies (cf. Jake and Myers-Scotton (1997*a*)). Forms accessed as compromise strategies are not counterexamples to the MLF model, but neither are they optimal choices. These are bare forms and Embedded Language islands. Chapter 4 considers such forms in some detail; here, they are only illustrated.

Example (39) includes a bare form (*prijs* 'price') from Dutch, the Embedded Language, in Turkish/Dutch codeswitching in Tilburg, the Netherlands. That is, *prijs* occurs without the case suffix that would make it well-formed in the language of the Matrix Language, Turkish. (To be well formed in Turkish, the Dutch noun should have a possessive third person singular suffix because of the reflexive that precedes it. Also, because of the possessive, which makes it specific/definite, it needs an accusative suffix, too. Thus, *prijs-i-ni* is expected.) Why, then, is *prijs* accessed at all? The claim is that it is selected because it better conveys the speaker's intentions than the Turkish counterpart (*fiyat*) when the subject is how business is conducted in the Netherlands.[8]

(39) bunlar herkes kendi **prijs** söyl-üyor
these everyone self price say-PROG/3S
'Everyone says his own price for these.'

(Turkish/Dutch; Backus 1996: 109)

[7] To be completely morphosyntactically integrated into a Swahili-based frame, a verb has to include a final vowel (generally *-a*). This vowel carries little information on its own; it is part of a discontinuous morpheme that generally marks mood and sometimes negation.

[8] Ad Backus (personal communication) suggests a possible pragmatic difference between the Dutch *prijs* and its Turkish counterpart, based on the association of the Dutch element with life in the Netherlands. He does not see a great semantic difference between the two words.

Do such compromise strategies require possible feedback (e.g. consider 'do' verbs discussed in Chapter 4), resulting in a change in the method of conveying intentions? Levelt (1989) argues against feedback in his model of monolingual production. There is not necessarily feedback in our bilingual model, either, but the issue is not closed. The question remains: in order to access the 'do' verb, is feedback to the lemma level from the Formulator involved? That is, is does the process of activating a 'do' verb *follow* the attempt to integrate an Embedded Language verb into the Matrix Language frame? If it does, then there must be feedback in the production process.

Example (40) illustrates an Embedded Language island, with English as the Embedded Language. This example contains a very common island type, a set collocation in the Embedded Language (*for personal purposes*). A set collocation in one language often does not have an exact counterpart in another language at all levels of abstract structure. Thus, the Abstract Level model provides one motivation for accessing material in an Embedded Language island in classic codeswitching.

(40) a-na-i-tumi-a **for personal purposes**
3S-NONPST-OBJ-use-FV for personal purposes
'He uses it for personal purposes' (refers to his car mentioned in previous discourse).

(Swahili/English; Myers-Scotton 1988 corpus)

3.6.3. *The Abstract Level model and other contact phenomena*

In the previous section just the notion that there are three levels of abstract lexical structure offers us a way to suggest with some precision how congruence figures in explaining why there is more than one way for Embedded Language elements to occur in classic codeswitching. In this section, quite a different notion is development.

Now, not only are there three levels of abstract structure in every lemma, but the contents of these levels are open to revision. This supposition is motivated by evidence in the lexicon of any language that the meaning of content morphemes can and does change; even their predicate-argument structure can change. Consider all the nouns that add a new dimension to their existence as inflected verbs (e.g. *The student* ***researched*** *that topic*). But the Abstract Level model adds a new twist to making changes: In bilingual CPs, the abstract lexical structure underlying a given element, with its surface form entirely in one language, can represent the splitting off of one or more levels from an element in one language and its combining with levels in another language. This premise offers us a way to explain resulting structures in many contact phenomena outside of classic codeswitching. When this happens—when speakers produce structures for which the source of structure is split between two or more varieties—the result is what is called a composite Matrix Language.

In many contact phenomena, there is typically a difficulty in using any one of the participating languages as the source of the Matrix Language. This is the case when—for whatever reason—speakers do not have sufficient access to the morphosyntax of a desired target for the Matrix Language. This happens in second-language learning, but also in creole formation. It is also the case when sociopolitical conditions militate against using one of the speaker's languages as the Matrix Language. For example, in various situations, speakers may need to avoid using their L1 (although one's L1 is not necessarily the Matrix Language). Or, they may be shifting from their L1 to a more dominant language in the community. In these instances, the Matrix Language that provides morphosyntactic structure for bilingual CPs is typically a composite Matrix Language.

In sum, a composite Matrix Language is an abstract frame for the morphosyntax of a bilingual CP with abstract lexical input from more than one language. This means that not all levels or parts of levels of abstract lexical structure come from only one participating language.

3.6.4. *Congruent lexicalization*

Note that Muysken (2000) makes a good deal of use of the term 'congruent lexicalization'. When he initially defines it, he refers to 'congruent lexicalization of material from different lexical inventories into a shared grammatical structure' (2000: 3). He lists it as one of the three patterns of intra-sentential code-mixing (his term). While it is not always clear exactly what he means by this term, it does seem clear that he is arguing that when the features of two languages are congruent in various ways, a certain type of codeswitching that is different from other types (what he calls insertion—presumably mixed constituents in the MLF model, and alternation—islands or even full clauses in alternation from the participating languages). Later he states that 'congruent lexicalization often involves bidirectional code-mixing, since there is no dominant matrix language' (2000: 132). Some of the examples he cites come from codeswitching involving creoles (Sranan with Dutch), not from classic codeswitching per se, or else from codeswitching between closely related languages, such as Frisian and Dutch.

Such contact data sound a good deal like what I have been claiming results when there is a composite Matrix Language setting the frame for a bilingual CP (cf. 1997 Afterword: 258, Myers-Scotton 1998*a*, *inter alia*). A composite Matrix Language may be the product of either convergence alone or convergence in concert with codeswitching. However, I do not see such data (or the process of convergence as a whole) as bidirectional; rather, I see a movement from dominance by one language to dominance by another (i.e. a Matrix Language turnover in progress). And I also see the composite as complicated, yes, but still orderly in the sense that one can make predictions as to which grammatical structures come from one participating language rather than the other.

3.6.5. *Convergence*

Convergence is a familiar term in language-contact studies for the influence of one language on the structure of another. Often convergence is the term invoked to describe the source of changes in surface-level phenomena (e.g. changes in word order or expected inflections are not present). The motivation for convergence is clear: the influence of one language on another reflects generally asymmetrical sociopolitical relations between the native speakers of the languages involved, with the language that is influenced often in the less dominant role.

However, offering a motivation does not give us an exact characterization of the structural nature of convergence, let alone an explanation. The Abstract Level model does this. First, it provides for a more precise characterization of convergence. Under this model, convergence is both a process and an outcome. As an outcome, it is a linguistic configuration with all surface morphemes from one language, but part of its abstract lexical structure from another language. As a process, convergence is a mechanism in the progressive outcomes of attrition, language shift, language death, and creole formation. The explanation of convergence that the model offers is that utterances showing convergence are created when a composite Matrix Language is the frame of the CP involved.

The premise of the Abstract Level model is the following: convergence (as both a mechanism and an outcome) is initiated in the mental lexicon when lemmas underlying content morphemes from what was the lesser dominant language (the Embedded Language if codeswitching had been involved previously) achieve a level of activation more similar to that of the more dominant language. That is, one language is waxing and the other is waning to some extent. To put it simply, the waning language loses its undisputed role as the source of the Matrix Language frame in bilingual CPs. When this happens, there can be splitting and recombining at one or more of the three levels of abstract lexical structure from these lemmas so that a surface morpheme is supported by abstract material from both languages.

This waxing–waning process happens initially with content morphemes (and their supporting early system morphemes). That is, the first result of splitting and combining is that content morphemes in the waning language show the effects of waxing language lexical-conceptual structure. But that is not all. Bear in mind that the lemmas underlying content morphemes are not simply comprised of 'meanings'; they include grammatical specifications. Thus, not only does the waxing language insinuate itself into the lexical-conceptual structure of lemmas supporting content morphemes in the waning language, but also into the morphosyntax. This means that lemmas from the newly vigorous waxing language also can bring their own well-formedness conditions about predicate-argument structure and morphological realization patterns. When this happens, what some call structural borrowing (actual surface-level morphemes from both languages make up the morphosyntactic frame) can occur. I avoid the term 'structural borrowing' because I see the processes involved as quite different from those for lexical borrowing. This will become clearer in Chapter 6. How the Abstract Level model illuminates the issue of what is involved in attrition is a major topic in Chapter 5, and modifying and building the morphosyntactic frame is a major subject in Chapter 6.

3.6.5.1. Examples of convergence

3.6.5.1.1. CONVERGENCE AT THE LEVEL OF LEXICAL-CONCEPTUAL STRUCTURE

Examples (41) and (42) illustrate splitting and recombining at the level of lexical-conceptual structure. Hill and Hill (1986) devote a good deal of attention to detailing how Malinche Mexicano (Nahuatl) has been influenced by Spanish. However, when Spanish-content morphemes are used in utterances largely in Mexicano, their gender marking does not follow Spanish requirements. Rather, masculine gender becomes the default gender in the composite frame that is influenced by Mexicano. Hill and Hill report that 'when speakers use Spanish adjectives with Mexicano nouns, they generally will use the masculine form, regardless of any natural gender of the noun' (1986: 266). They cite examples such as (41) and (42).

(41) In nonāntzīn, **poderoso**
'As for my mother, she is powerful.'

(42) Noxōchih, **mal.**
'My flowers, ruined.'

(Malinche Mexicano; Hill and Hill 1986: 266)

Hill and Hill point out that Malinche speakers do make mistakes (from the standpoint of standard Spanish) when speaking monolingual Spanish, but not at the frequency that occurs when they are engaging in codeswitching with Mexicano as the Matrix Language (when they perceive themselves as 'speaking Mexicano'). Hill and Hill conclude, 'We believe that speakers are quite aware of Spanish gender, but feel that gender concord is not part of "speaking Mexicano"' (1986: 267). Within the terms of the Abstract Level Model, it is as if the abstract lexical structure of these Spanish adjectives includes specifications only for masculine gender, and the composite Matrix Language that frames this variety (mainly Mexicano input) includes a slot for gender, but the specifications for filling that slot—at least in this context—are not for the gender that would make the adjectives well-formed in standard Spanish.[9] That is, the speaker is accessing only part of the lexical-conceptual structure for these Spanish adjectives from Spanish, but part of it comes from Mexicano or the notion of a composite frame.

[9] In Standard Spanish, the feminine form for 'powerful' is *poderosa*; the feminine form for 'ruined' is *mala* and 'flower' in Spanish is feminine. Jane Hill points out (personal communication), 'The speaker here is perfectly aware that *mal* and *poderoso* are Spanish words and she probably uses them to add some weight to her accusations.'

3.6.5.1.2. CONVERGENCE AT THE LEVEL OF MORPHOLOGICAL REALIZATION PATTERNS

Example (43) is monolingual at the surface level, but bilingual at the abstract level where it shows convergence regarding morphological realization patterns. Under the influence of Spanish, Pipil, a Uto-Aztecan language spoken in El Salvador, has developed the means to produce conjoined clauses (Campbell 1987). (According to Campbell, the few hundred speakers of Pipil remaining in the 1980s were all bilingual in Spanish, many with Spanish as their dominant language.) Pipil has borrowed many conjunctions from Spanish, but at least one of its indigenous elements has been modified at both the level of lexical-conceptual structure and of morphological realizations patterns. This is *wan*, which formerly was only a bound form, meaning 'with' as in *nu-wan* 'with me' or *tu-wan* 'with us'. It could also occur with possessive pronominal prefixes to conjoin nominals (e.g. *Juan i-wan Maria* 'John her-with Mary'). In its new usage it can stand as a free form serving to conjoin clauses, as in (43).

(43)	ne ta:kaa-t	k-itshik	ne mich-in	**wan**	ki-kwah
	the man-ABSOL	it-caught	the fish-ABSOL	and	it-ate

'The man caught the fish and ate it.'

(Pipil; Campbell 1987: 257)

Example (44) shows another change in morphological realization patterns, this time a change in Spanish under the influence of English. In a study of Puerto Rican Spanish, Morales (2000) reports a number of examples in which an infinitive appears in a construction that calls for a tensed verb in the subjunctive mood in Standard Spanish. While many cases, cross-linguistically, of loss of the subjunctive may also be explained as instances of simplification, this particular example more clearly shows English influence. Note that not only does an infinitive (*meter* 'deal') replace a tensed form (*metiera*), but the position of the object clitic (as a clitic on the infinitive) follows English order, not Spanish order (*yo me metiera*). In Standard Spanish, the clitic precedes the tensed verb. Thus, employing an infinitive rather than a tensed verb in the subjunctive allows the speaker to follow English order.

(44)	Era	duro	para	yo	meter-me
	3S/IMP	hard-M/S	for	1S	deal-1S/INDOBJ
	con	esos	niños		ingleses
	with	DEM/M/PL	boy-M/PL		English-M/PL

'It was tough for me to deal with those English boys.'

(Morales 2000: 48)

Standard Spanish: era duro que yo me metiera esos niños ingleses.

3.6.5.1.3. CONVERGENCE AT THE LEVEL OF PREDICATE-ARGUMENT STRUCTURE

Another example shows how the level of predicate-argument structure can be split when a composite Matrix Language is structuring an utterance. In their usage of Swedish in the 1980s, at least some long-term immigrants to the United States (who left Sweden in the 1920s) used the Swedish verb *ha* 'have' in ways parallel to the English verb *have.* They used Swedish *ha* as a causative, after a permissible patterns for English *have.* In Swedish, the verb *få* ('cause' is one of its possible meanings) would be required instead to convey causation, in the construction, *få en amerikanare att komma hit.* See example (45). Even though all the morphemes are from Swedish, I argue that part of the predicate-argument structure of *ha* comes from English.

(45) de ksa va väldit intressant å **ha** en amerikanare komma hit å arbeta.
'It will be very interesting to have an American come here to work.'

(American Swedish; Klintborg 1999: 77)

Example (46) illustrates another common way in which abstract lexical structure in a bilingual CP is a composite from two languages. Savič (1995: 488) reports that college-age Serbians living in the United States have merged the accusative paradigms for animate and inanimate NPs, with the inanimate paradigm prevailing. In Standard Serbian, animate NPs receive an overt accusative marker, but inanimate ones do not. Thus, in (46) we see that the NPs for two of the family members mentioned have no overt accusative marker. In Serbian as spoken in Belgrade, *ota* 'father' would occur instead of *otac,* and *brata* 'brother' would occur instead of *brat.* She reports this leveling of the animate/inanimate masculine paradigms in the accusative was the most frequent form of leveling (twenty-two instances) in her data set. One can argue that such a merger is occurring because the level of morphological realization patterns for these speakers is a composite from English and Serbian. That is, English does not mark accusative case overtly and its specifications influence those of Serbian. However, others might argue that this merger (resulting in no overt case marking) is a case of simplification and no more. This issue of simplification vs. case realignment is discussed more fully in Chapter 5.

(46)	Ja	imam	**otac**	i	majku	i	starijeg	**brat**
	I/NOM	have/1S/PRES	father-Ø	and	mother/ACCUS	and	older/ACCUS	brother-Ø

'I have a father, a mother, and an older brother.'

(Serbian; Savič 1995: 485)

3.7. Codeswitching and convergence

Codeswitching and convergence have a special status among contact phenomena in that they are both mechanisms and outcomes, while other contact phenomena are best characterized as outcomes. Codeswitching and convergence are mechanisms because they—individually or together—figure in the outcome of other contact phenomena, either as triggers or as components in the outcome itself. In most cases, other contact phenomena are progressive outcomes, e.g. second-language learning, attrition, and language shift.

When contact phenomena show surface-level morphemes from two or more languages, some type of codeswitching is involved. From now on in this volume codeswitching is discussed as one of two types:

1. *Classic codeswitching.* Classic codeswitching has already been introduced and named as such. Recall that it is characterized as bilingual speech within a CP, with the morphosyntactic frame derived from only one of the participating languages. Classic codeswitching occurs when speakers have full access to the morphosyntactic frame of one of the participating languages (the source of the Matrix Language). Speakers also have enough proficiency in the other language (the Matrix Language) either to (i) insert Embedded Language content morphemes into mixed constituents framed by the Matrix Language or (ii) produce well-formed Embedded Language islands, or both (i) and (ii) (i.e. produce both mixed constituents and Matrix Language islands).

2. *Composite codeswitching.* The term composite codeswitching is new; however, the notion it captures is present when the theoretical notion of a composite Matrix Language is raised in earlier discussions in this chapter, as well as in my earlier publications. Composite codeswitching can be characterized as a phenomenon with morphemes from two languages within a bilingual CP, and with the abstract morphosyntactic frame derived from more than one source language. Composite codeswitching occurs in such phenomena as language attrition and shift. It occurs when speakers—because of psycholinguistic or sociopolitical factors—do not have full access to the morphosyntactic frame of the participating language that is the desired source of the Matrix Language. Or, possibly the notion of a target Matrix Language is not clear to the speakers themselves. The result is that a composite Matrix Language frames the resulting bilingual CP. Thus, in effect, composite codeswitching necessarily entails convergence.

3.8. Conclusion

This chapter offers a detailed introduction to the three models that are invoked in much of the discussion in following chapters. These are the MLF Model, as it applies to classic codeswitching, and two newer supporting models that apply on their own, or with the MLF model, to both classic codeswitching and other forms of contact phenomena. All of the models emphasize the link between abstract level competence and surface performance. Their goal is the same: to provide theoretical mechanisms operating at abstract levels as explanations for surface distributions of data.

I devote a good deal of space to explicating problematic details of the MLF model and to citing examples that support the model. I bring in the 4-M model to explain some of the types of structures that the MLF model only describes. I also revisit speech-error data, offering explanations of certain distributions and seemingly odd examples, based on distinctions made by the 4-M model.

I go on to summarize the claims of the two new models. After introducing the 4-M model in Chapter 1, I deal at length with it here. The model refers to both the surface and the abstract characteristics morphemes. Its distinctions hold across all languages; however, not all languages encode the same conceptual or structural information by the same type of morpheme.

The 4-M model's classification of morphemes results from an intersection of two sets of distinctions. These distinctions result in four types of morphemes, based on three binary oppositions. I repeat that the term 'morpheme' is used to cover two related elements, the actual surface-level morphemes, but also the lemmas that support them, abstract entries in the mental lexicon. The context should make clear when the referent is a surface level form or an abstraction.

The first distinction refers to the mechanisms by which morphemes are accessed. Thus, it refers to the lemmas underlying morphemes. It is based on the opposition [+/–conceptually activated].

Along with content morphemes, early system morphemes have a plus rating for the opposition. This means that they carry the semantic content that the speaker wishes to convey. Related to this and their early activation, they are salient at the level of the mental lexicon.

Late system morphemes are not conceptually activated, but only become salient when they are structurally assigned following directions to the Formulator. Their role is not to add content so much as it is to convey relationships. Of course this does not deny that all morphemes have content of some sort.

The second distinction refers to two properties of phrase building operations. This distinction is captured in two oppositions. The first opposition, [+/–thematic role assigner/receiver], sets content morphemes apart from all system morphemes.

Content morphemes either assign or receive thematic roles, but system morphemes do not. (This distinction was part of the content–system morpheme opposition under the 1993 version of the MLF model.)

The second opposition under phrase building operations applies only to late system morphemes; it divides them into two classes, [+/–outside information].

Bridge late system morphemes do not need any information outside their immediate maximal projection in order for their form to be realized.

However, outsider late system morphemes do require co-indexing with an element outside their immediate maximal projection.

Although it was mentioned in Chapter 1, the Abstract Level model also receives a more complete introduction in this chapter. There are two main points to make about the Abstract Level model: (i) All lemmas contain three levels of abstract lexical structure, the levels of lexical-conceptual structure, predicate-argument structure, and morphological realization patterns. These are realized in surface structures. How abstract levels match up across languages figures in classic codeswitching and affects what structures can occur. (ii) Because the three levels can be split and recombined with levels in another lemma (or in the Generalized Lexical Knowledge that exists alongside specific lemmas in the mental lexicon), new combinations can arise in monolingual data. However, this splitting and recombining is especially relevant to bilingual speech and I argue it goes on in various contact phenomena; it is a form of convergence. Such convergence is especially evident when a language is undergoing attrition and in creole development, as we will see.

4

Considering Problematic Codeswitching Data and Other Approaches

4.1. Introduction

The basic constraints of the MLF model for classic codeswitching and the oppositions underlying them are among the subjects of the previous chapter. This chapter continues the discussion of classic codeswitching in several directions that, at first glance, seem to present problems for the MLF model. Admittedly, not every single example in the literature is amenable to a satisfactory analysis under the MLF model. However, most of what appear to be problems can be accommodated under the provisions of the model, or expansions of how the provisions can be interpreted. I also show that what is really interesting about many of these 'difficult' examples is that, even more than the 'easy' examples (discussed in Chapter 3), they provide implications about various aspects of language competence and production, especially about the interaction of the two participating languages and their levels of activation.

Thus, this chapter includes the following. First, I elaborate on the discussion from Chapter 1 of how relative proficiency in the languages involved impinges on how speakers exercise the codeswitching options available under the model. Second, I discuss a number of morpheme configurations that are found across data sets that are not disallowed under the MLF model, but which are not unmarked elements in the optimal codeswitching constituent, either. (Recall that I suggest that a mixed constituent, framed by the Matrix Language, including both Matrix Language elements and some Embedded Language content morphemes that are basically morphosyntactically integrated into the Matrix Language, is the optimal constituent.) I argue that many of these difficult constructions occur because of certain mismatches between the participating languages with what is allowable in codeswitching, offering us an empirical window on psycholinguistic flexibility—or the lack of it—in various levels of language. I also elaborate on the Uniform Structure Principle (stated in Chapter 1) and how it applies. This principle formalizes the general notion that the basic syntactic frame of the Matrix Language, with its requisite requirements at the level of morphological realization patterns, must be observed in bilingual CPs in classic codeswitching.

Most prominently, constructions considered here include bare forms and Embedded Language material in the Matrix Language frame larger than singly occurring Embedded Language forms (i.e. Embedded Language islands). Most bare forms are singly occurring Embedded Language nouns, but those Embedded Language non-finite verb forms that are bare from the point of view of the Matrix Language merit special attention, too. Also discussed are such phenomena as 'chunking' (Embedded Language collocations) and 'triggering' (the claim that one Embedded Language form triggers others or that stretches of Embedded Language elements often/always should be seen as morphosyntactic units). In addition, the discussions occasion limited comparisons of how the MLF model treats some basic issues in comparison with other approaches to codeswitching data. These discussions include the issue of whether a satisfactory approach includes the Matrix Language – Embedded Language distinction and also whether singly occurring Embedded Language forms are borrowings or codeswitching elements.

That the constructions considered exist is not new; they were largely detailed in the 1993 edition of *Duelling Languages*. However, what has changed is that I now benefit from the research and commentary by others in the codeswitching literature, as well as my own data collection and deliberations since the early 1990s. That is, this work has given me corpora and analyses to consider, making it possible for me to reckon with the nature of these 'outlaw' constructions in a more informed way now.

4.1.1. *The MLF model reviewed*

I recapitulate the main theoretical premises of the MLF model. The first premise is that the participating languages do not participate equally; the Matrix Language – Embedded Language hierarchy captures this assumption.[1] Yet, there has to be some provision for how they do participate. Monolingual CPs (projection of Complementizer), the reference point of some models of codeswitching, obviously also have an abstractly based morphosyntactic frame, but in such CPs, only one language is the candidate as the Matrix Language and therefore no special provision is needed to identify it. Bilingual CPs present another set of possibilities: theoretically, both participating languages could be the source of the grammatical frame (the Matrix Language), either together or in tandem. Thus, the corollary of the first premise is that only one of the participating languages is the source of critical morphosyntactic structure in the bilingual CP in classic

[1] A premise of the MLF model is that there will be asymmetry between the Matrix Language and the Embedded Language in their roles in setting the morphosyntactic frame of the codeswitching clause; however this is not the same thing as having 'a priori assumptions about which language will serve as the matrix language' as Boumans suggests as a feature of the MLF model, differentiating it from his model (1998: 361).

codeswitching. When the Morpheme Order and System Morpheme Principles are tested, they support the notion that one language is more structurally dominant. This language receives the label of Matrix Language in the Matrix Language – Embedded Language hierarchy, and the term 'Matrix Language' is also used to refer to the morphosyntactic frame of the bilingual CP as well.

The second premise of the model is that the extent to which Embedded Language morphemes can appear in mixed constituents (framed by the Matrix Language) is limited. Their participation is in line with the distinction between content and system morphemes and then the further division within system morphemes. Only Embedded Language content morphemes can appear with any real freedom and Embedded Language late outsider system morphemes are explicitly excluded (by the System Morpheme Principle).

4.1.2. *What is classic codeswitching?*

The MLF model was formulated to explicate the constraints on classic codeswitching. This is defined as switching between speakers who have sufficient proficiency in one of the participating languages to use it as the sole source of the morphosyntactic frame of bilingual CPs (this language is called the Matrix Language or ML). The discussion in this chapter assumes that examples come from classic codeswitching. In Chapters 5 and 6 other types of codeswitching whose morphosyntactic structure cannot be explained as derived from a single language are considered; their structure has multiple sources and I refer to a composite Matrix Language to explain it.

Obviously, speakers engaging in classic codeswitching also must have some proficiency in the non-frame language(s) present in such CPs, the Embedded Language(s). Still, the extent of their proficiency can be considerably less than what is needed for them to produce well-formed Matrix Language morphosyntactic frames, along with syntactically relevant Matrix Language grammatical elements. For example, because speakers are proficient in the framing language, they know which slots in the frame must be filled with nouns and their required positions in the NP and of NPs in the overall CP. In fact, nouns are the most frequent singly occurring Embedded Language forms in codeswitching (cf. Poplack 1980, Myers-Scotton 1993*a* [1997], Treffers-Daller 1994, 1999, *inter alia*). Of course, the same proficiency also guides speakers in assessing whether other Embedded Language contact morphemes can appear in the Matrix Language frame.

Provided they meet these frame requirements, Embedded Language content morphemes can be selected to satisfy speakers' intentions as long as these morphemes have sufficient congruence with Matrix Language counterparts at the three levels of abstract structure (cf. the Abstract Level model discussed in earlier chapters). As is shown in sections 4.2 to 4.8, congruence requirements are flexible in some language pairs or for some lexical categories or phrase types, but rather rigid for other matches. (Again, I admit that what constitutes sufficient congruence is not well defined independently of what does occur.)

Grammatical proficiency in the Embedded Language must be considerably more if speakers are to produce Embedded Language islands in a bilingual CP (e.g. *in the morning, against all odds*). This should be obvious because such islands include not just content morphemes, but all relevant system morphemes. More important, the islands must show the internal structure dependency relations that make them well-formed in the Embedded Language grammar. They are discussed in section 4.9.

4.1.3. *Stable bilingualism is implied*

The MLF model was drawn up to explain codeswitching patterns of speakers whose linguistic proficiencies in the languages involved were fairly stable. Of course, the condition of a bilingual's abilities to speak the different languages in his or her repertoire is never really stable! For a variety of internal motivations and conditions external to the speaker, a bilingual's control over linguistic varieties waxes and wanes. However, the main data set exemplifying the MLF model in Myers-Scotton (1993*a* [1997]) of Swahili/English bilingualism comes from a relatively stable bilingual condition (recorded in Nairobi, Kenya, mainly in 1988). There are many other similarly stable cases of bilingualism, such as Spanish/English bilingualism among some long-established Latinos in the U.S. West and Southwest, or among certain francophone French/English bilinguals in parts of Canada, or at some national borders (e.g. among some Danes on the Danish/German border).

I am not claiming that any of these cases is not constantly changing; but the point is they all contrast with many more fluid cases of bilingualism, such as those involving recent immigrants. For example, Türker (2000) found that the Turkish of the young adult Turks in Norway shows a number of loan translations from Norwegian. Norwegian has become—or is becoming—their most proficient language for such Turks who have been in Norway for at least four years and have gone to Norwegian schools. In other places, changes in life styles are accompanied by major changes in both their repertoires and characteristics of their linguistic varieties. For example, in parts of Papua New Guinea, some members of certain ethnic groups that previously had little contact with outsiders now have jobs in local administrative centers. For example, Jenkins (2000) reports that the Tigak spoken by Tigak ethnic group members with such jobs is converging to local varieties of Tok Pisin. Tigak is spoken on the island of New Ireland, Papua New Guinea, and Tok Pisin is the pidgin/creole that is one of the official languages of Papua New Guinea.

In its original formulation, the MLF model cannot account for all the structures in the codeswitching of speakers in those communities where the relative status of the languages—in terms of both speaker proficiency and sociopolitical prestige—is more fluid than not. A composite source for the frame structuring bilingual CPs must be posited and the Morpheme Order and System Morpheme

Principles do not apply categorically. I refer to such codeswitching as composite codeswitching. Such corpora receive some attention in Chapter 6.

4.1.4. *Stability of the Matrix Language*

When data studied come from relatively stable bilingual communities, one can expect certain related structural consequences regarding stability of the Matrix Language. Although the MLF model presents the Matrix Language as a dynamic construct, what this means has been misinterpreted by some to mean I suggest that the Matrix Language changes often. The following statements about the Matrix Language are implicit in the original explication of the MLF model and still hold for classic codeswitching when the bilingual situation is relatively stable. Some statements (1 through 3) can be considered as testable hypotheses; the others (4 through 7) are simply assumptions. All are implied in all the discussions in this chapter.

1. One variety is consistently the single source of the frame of bilingual CPs; thus, the source of the Matrix Language does not change within any single bilingual CP.
2. Theoretically, the source of the Matrix Language may change in a conversation (but not within a CP) as topics or some participants change; however, even such changes are rare or non-existent in most corpora.
3. When what I label compromise strategies (bare forms, Embedded Language islands, etc.) occur within a bilingual CP, the Matrix Language for the entire CP does not change.
4. As a pragmatic strategy, structures that are marked for the Matrix Language frame (e.g. marked word order) are allowed. Yet, this is not intended as an escape hatch, allowing many apparent counterexamples to be explained as 'marked'.[2]
5. At most, the Matrix Language shows only minor, infrequent instances of convergence toward structures in the Embedded Language as long as the bilingual situation remains relatively stable.
6. Some communities with many near-balanced bilinguals provide a different pattern from the prevalence of bilingual CPs. The MLF model still applies, but it is relevant to less data because the number of monolingual CPs increases and of bilingual CPs decreases.
7. For such bilinguals, the dominant pattern may be alternation between monolingual CPs in each of their languages. That is, the Matrix Language still does not change within a bilingual CP; however, the Matrix Language may well change *within a conversation* (e.g. second-generation Turks in Tilburg, the Netherlands, Backus (1996)).

[2] In *Duelling Languages* (1993*a* [1997]: 236), I cite a single example of a marked word order for a Swahili frame (*no ordinary mbuzi* 'no ordinary goat'); it illustrates an exception to the Morpheme Order Principle. The point of this example, missed by some observers, is that marked choices do not have any real frequency in classic codeswitching; if they did, the two principles of the MLF model would not hold, of course. When such rare examples do occur, I suggested that they are typically pragmatically driven.

4.2. Bare forms

Bare forms are Embedded Language content morphemes appearing in mixed constituents framed by the Matrix Language, but they are missing the Matrix Language system morphemes that would make them well-formed elements in such frames. The MLF model does not disallow them as long as the System Morpheme Principle is satisfied. Under that principle, if there are late outsider system morphemes, then they must come from the Matrix Language. However, there is nothing in the MLF model requiring early system morphemes or bridge late system morphemes to come from the Matrix Language—although most of them do. However, in the next section, I discuss a case for which Embedded Language early system morphemes can stand in place of Matrix Language counterparts.

4.3. Nouns and their determiners when Arabic is the Matrix Language

There are several types of bare forms, and I deal with only three cases to any extent in this volume. In this section, North African Arabic nouns without Matrix Language articles are considered. (However, it is important to remember that these articles are typically early system morphemes, not the late system morphemes that must come from the Matrix Language, according to the System Morpheme Principle.) The data come from corpora with Moroccan Arabic as the Matrix Language, and—unfortunately—the details when Arabic is involved are many. I try to limit discussion to the main points.

The most striking examples in these corpora are bare nouns in Moroccan Arabic/Dutch data sets where Arabic definite articles are omitted before Dutch nouns (Nortier 1990, Boumans 1998). What makes such examples provocative is that they contrast with North African Arabic/French corpora where French nouns almost always have articles, but often occur with their own articles in an Arabic frame (Boumans and Caubet 2000). Arabic is the Matrix Language in most CPs in all corpora, and of course the usual state of affairs in codeswitching is to have any slots in the Matrix Language frame for articles filled with system morphemes from the Matrix Language. Thus, both of these data sets with Arabic as the Matrix Language are very atypical regarding how determiners are treated, although in different ways. I go on to compare French in Algerian Arabic/French data with French in other data sets (Wolof/French and Lingala/French).

Both French and Dutch articles convey gender and number, but gender in Dutch is reduced; masculine and feminine articles have merged into one form (feminine), leaving a contrast between feminine (*de*) and neuter (*het*). The extent of gender marking is reduced, too; for example it is not marked on demonstratives. However, French marks both masculine and feminine, as does Arabic, and all modifying elements are specified for gender.

4.3.1. *Moroccan Arabic/Dutch codeswitching and bare forms*

First, consider how articles are realized—or not—in the Moroccan Arabic/Dutch data sets. Arabic requires what I will call a determiner complex before a noun when a demonstrative (e.g. *dak* 'that' or *waħed* 'one') is used. The complex consists of two elements, the demonstrative and a determiner (e.g. *dak l-* + N). (Such a complex is illustrated schematically in Figure 4.1; note that the details of this complex are intended to apply only to the North African varieties of Arabic in the data sets discussed here.) The crucial point about Arabic/Dutch codeswitching is that in neither of the data sets (of Nortier and Boumans) is the Arabic determiner complex often present in its full form (i.e. both elements). Sometimes neither element is present. Still, the Dutch article never appears, either. As Nortier notes, 'When the article is used at all it is always in Moroccan Arabic' (1990: 200–1). Arabic determiners seem to occur less frequently than demonstratives. In Nortier's data, the Arabic demonstrative occurred in six cases, but without the Arabic determiner that the determiner complex requires (e.g. *had Ø uikering* 'this unemployment benefit'). Nortier reports that an expected Arabic determiner was omitted thirty-two times before a Dutch noun and was present in only seventeen cases in her corpus (1990: 147, 200).

Boumans does not give absolute numbers, but states that the definite prefix *l-* is the only Moroccan Arabic affix that is at all productive with Dutch (content) morphemes. However, even though this Arabic article appears occasionally in his data set with Dutch nouns, 'Yet all respondents tend to omit it in contexts where it is obligatory in MA [Moroccan Arabic]' (1998: 187). Not all of Boumans's speakers use the relevant forms alike. For one subject, at least, the definite prefix (*l-*) is often realized after the preposition *f* 'in', although not always (e.g. Arabic followed by Dutch underlined in *f l-<u>vrij-e tijd</u>* 'in your spare time' (1998: 190)).

Example (1) shows a case in which *l-* fails to appear before a Dutch noun; the expected Arabic determiner complex is the indefinite demonstrative *waħed* + *l-* as a definite article. In his sample of fifteen subjects, Boumans notes that the full *waħed l-* form only appears before Dutch nouns in the speech of one speaker. In (2) the same article is omitted before the Dutch noun *opleiding* after the definite demonstrative *dak* where it is also required (i.e. in a determiner complex).[3]

(1) u ʕad te-bqa waħed **Ø-probleem** dyal **'je moet zoveel**
and still 3F-remain INDEF DEM problem of You must so many

[3] Note in (2) that *dyal*, a bridge system morpheme, comes from Arabic in the NP–NP constructions of two Dutch nouns. The System Morpheme Principle does not specify that bridges must come from the Matrix Language, but they almost always do across many data sets. Also, in example (5) Arabic *f* in the French phrase *pas de rèduction f le billet* 'no reduction in the ticket [its price]' is another bridge system morpheme. Admittedly, it is unusual to find an Arabic morpheme in this otherwise French NP–NP construction since the rest of the CP is all in French. However, such a bridge is not blocked by any provisions of the model.

diploma-s heben om dat te doen'
diploma-PL have for this to do
'And there'll always remain a problem of "you need so many diplomas to do this".'

(Moroccan Arabic/Dutch; Boumans 1998: 187)

(2) ka-n-tebbeʕ dak ehm **∅ opleiding** dyal **leraar-opleiding**
ASP-1S-follow DEM er training of teacher-training
'I follow that training, the teacher training.'

(Moroccan Arabic/Dutch; Boumans 1998: 187)

The Arabic indefinite article *ši* fares better than the definite article in these Arabic varieties; it is often used with Dutch nouns in Boumans's data. (In other varieties of Arabic *ši* is not necessarily used or is used in a different sense (Jonathan Owens, personal communication).) Also, there are contexts where a zero article is expected (e.g. the predicate in copula constructions). When Dutch nouns do receive Arabic articles, Boumans also notes a tendency for his subjects to produce the article and then hesitate before producing the accompanying noun, but this also happens in monolingual Arabic, he points out.

4.3.2. *Algerian Arabic/French codeswitching*

Why these Dutch nouns never appear with Dutch articles and only occasionally with Arabic articles is open to speculation. They contrast with French nouns in various corpora, also with a North African variety of Arabic as the Matrix Language; French is the Embedded Language (e.g. Boumans and Caubet 2000 on Algerian Arabic/French). For a number of Det + N combinations, French articles appear with French nouns; that is, they fill slots for required articles in an Arabic frame. Before French (Embedded Language) nouns, the French articles *l'*, *la*, and *les* 'are used as if they were the Algerian Arabic article *əl-*' (Boumans and Caubet 2000: 152).

However, the story for the French definite article *le* (masculine singular) is different, at least in the data of Boumans and Caubet. Before French masculine singular nouns, Arabic *əl-* (also masculine singular) may occur instead. However, there may be some variability across North African speakers in this usage; for Moroccan Arabic, Hind (personal communication) cites examples with French *le*, such as *da:k le verre* 'that the glass'. Furthermore, in Moroccan Arabic/French codeswitching, *le* can occur as the masculine determiner; see example (5) for *le jour* 'the day'.

Example (3) illustrates a full French NP (*la scoliose*), and example (4) shows a French NP preceded by Arabic *waħed*. (Note that in both cases, the French NP is considered an Embedded Language island under the MLF model. In (4) *les histoires* is an internal Embedded Language island (under a node with *waħed* as its highest left branch).) Lahlou (1991: 133) reports similar examples for Moroccan Arabic/French codeswitching, as well as examples showing assimilation of the determiner to the following French noun (e.g. *dak s-systeme* 'that the system').

(3) tə-hkəm-l-u **la scoliose**
3F-strike-to-3M DEF/F scoliosis
'He gets scoliosis.'

(Algerian Arabic/French; Boumans and Caubet 2000: 152)

(4) yə-t-haka-w waħed **les histoires,** waħed **les histoires**
3-MP-tell-PL INDEF DEF/PL stories INDEF DEF/PL stories
taʕ **le temps passé**
of DEF/M time past
'They tell each other some (fantastic) stories, stories of past times.'

(Algerian Arabic/French; Boumans and Caubet 2000: 154)

(5) **le jour** djæl **l'mariage** djælhæ, mæt bbæhæ
DEF/M day of DEF/M marriage of/3FEM die/PERF father/3FEM
'the day of her wedding, her father died'

(Moroccan Arabic/French; Lahlou 1991: 208)

Note that in both monolingual Arabic and in most codeswitching data sets, the article assimilates to the initial consonant of the noun (e.g. in Moroccan Arabic/French *had s-système djal les étudiants* 'this the system of the students', with French supplying *système* and *les étudiants* (Lahlou 1991)).

French indefinite articles (*une, un, des*) also generally accompany French nouns. Boumans and Caubet note that 'they cover the distribution of three markers in Algerian Arabic: the "zero" article ø, *waħed əl-* and *kaʃ*' (p. 154).

4.3.3. *Summary: North African Arabic as the Matrix Language, Dutch or French Embedded Language*

Thus, the bottom line is this: (i) Dutch articles do not occur at all in Moroccan Arabic/Dutch corpora; instead, Dutch nouns are sometimes accompanied by an Arabic article; however, more frequently they are bare (no Arabic determiner). (ii) In contrast, in most North African/French corpora, French articles (except variably for the masculine singular determiner) typically accompany a French noun. I return to these articles in the next section and section 4.4 to consider possible explanations.

4.3.4. *Explaining Embedded Language nouns in Arabic corpora: Bare or not*

At least several linguists, dealing mainly with the Moroccan Arabic/Dutch cases, have tried to explain the occurrence of bare Embedded Language forms. Nortier gives six possible explanations, but notes there are counterexamples to all of them. They include such notions as 'syntactic simplification occurs in code switching environments' and 'phonological differences between French and Dutch may play a role' (1990: 202ff.; 1995). Muysken (2000: 83) offers his own set of relevant considerations, some overlapping with those of Nortier. He notes several phonological points that have been made by others as well (e.g. Heath 1989): the resemblance between French *le/la* and Arabic *l*, and also the fact that French *le/la* can cliticize to a following noun, but the Dutch articles *de/het* do not. French articles are obligatory; Dutch ones are not always. (Still, it can be argued that English articles also can cliticize to their nouns and they are not brought in along with the noun in Arabic/English codeswitching, as are French determiners. As indicated below, English nouns appear with Arabic determiners.) Further, Muysken does not mention the fact that the French masculine singular determiner (*le*) is replaced by Arabic *el* before French nouns, at least in some North African corpora.

Muysken (2000: 86) then hypothesizes that both French and Dutch determiners correspond to the category D (= determiner), as do Arabic *waħed* 'one/indefinite' and *dak* 'that'. (Although he does not state it, presumably his idea is that since all these elements correspond to D, it would be redundant to have French or Dutch articles at D-level replace their Arabic counterparts.) He then goes on to state that 'the definite marker [presumably in Arabic] would possibly correspond to a subordinate functional category of definiteness/number/gender (DNG) and project a DNG-P[Definiteness–Number–Gender Phrase]' (p. 86). He does not spell this out, but if one refers back to a phrase structure tree on his p. 61 (redrawn as Figure 4.2 below), it seems that he intends that DNG (Definiteness–Number–Gender) is not a sister node to D (Determiner), but rather a node under DP (Determiner Phrase). (DP would also project N-bar in his tree.) The D node (in Arabic) would include the demonstratives that are the first elements in the Arabic complex DP (e.g. *dak*). He then suggests that French determiners (which are under D in French and therefore parallel to Arabic demonstratives, not to Arabic articles) *can be reinterpreted* as DNG in Arabic (referring specifically to Moroccan Arabic/French data).

Muysken's analysis has its good points, but is not convincing overall. I think he is correct to place French determiners under DNG, *but not because they need to be moved there.* Based on Muysken's analysis of French determiners as *originally* under D, not DNG, one would expect them to be inserted in the Arabic frame under D. Instead, what appears under D are the Arabic elements under D (e.g. *waħed, dak*). Because the French determiners do not appear under D, but appear instead under DNG, he has to propose that they move to DNG in order to be realized, a notion that lacks motivation. His analysis of the end result is descriptively accurate; French determiners do occur under DNG. However, I offer another analysis in section 4.4 that does not include movement.

4.3.5. *French nouns and determiners elsewhere*

First, consider the issue of the link between French nouns and their determiners. The tie is not as binding as it appears at first glance. Evidence from other codeswitching corpora argue otherwise, as becomes clear below.

This evidence goes against interpretations relying on the strength of this tie (Determiner + Noun) to explain why French determiners can appear where Arabic determiners are expected. Largely on the basis of phonological evidence, a number of researchers have implied that a major reason for French determiners to appear with their nouns in codeswitching with Arabic is the special relationship of French nouns and their determiners (cf. Boumans 1998, Muysken 2000). And, at first, the relationship seems to be a 'tight fit'. Even the 4-M model offers another reason for claiming such a fit; under the model, determiners generally include early system morphemes that are indirectly elected by their nouns. When their nouns are inserted in Matrix Language frames, other early system morphemes (e.g. plural) are sometimes accessed with them (as in 'double morphology' in Chapter 3). Why can French determiners not also be accessed with their nouns in codeswitching? Additional evidence is that in other contact phenomena French nouns and determiners show the same tight fit. For example, they surface as units in many creoles for which French is the lexifier (superstrate) language (e.g. *lepain* < *le pain* 'bread', *leau* > *l'eau* 'water'). And in the mixed language Michif (with primary input from Cree and French), for which Cree is the main source of morphosyntactic structure, French nouns are almost always (always?) preceded by French determiners. (But French determiners prevail in general; even Cree nouns can be preceded by French determiners, as noted in Chapter 6.)

However, data from *other codeswitching corpora* (after all, codeswitching is our subject here) in which French is the Embedded Language provide a good reason to argue against the 'tie that binds' explanation for why French determiners can appear in Arabic/French codeswitching. Data from codeswitching corpora in which two distantly related African languages are the Matrix Language and French is the Embedded Language show that French nouns never appear with their own determiners. Instead, NPs including French nouns conform to the specifications of the Matrix Language; in one language, the specifications call for Matrix Language determiners, and in the other, they call for no determiners.

One of these languages is Wolof, which has its own determiners; however, in Wolof they follow the noun. Example (6) comes from a corpus of Wolof/French codeswitching recorded in Dakar, Senegal (Swigart 1992). The French noun *carnet* is followed by the Wolof determiner *bi*. Example (7) includes a possessive construction, with Wolof clearly as the Matrix Language (Wolof supplies the bridge system morpheme, *bu* 'of'); the construction includes a Wolof determiner.[4]

(6) Am **carnet** bi, seet ko
take notebook DET look at it
'Take the notebook; look at it.'

(Wolof/French; Swigart 1992: 119)

(7) bësal **bouton** bu **rouge** bi
press button of red DET
'Press the red button.'

(Wolof/French; Swigart 1992: 172)

[4] There are only a few examples of French nouns in the discussion of Wolof/French codeswitching in Meechan and Poplack 1995; however, one example shows a French noun as an indefinite but with no French article (*croissant rek, xam nga* . . . '[a] croissant, you know . . .' (1995: 170)). In Wolof, *rek* stands for 'only'. The absence of a French indefinite article supports my analysis that Embedded Language early system morphemes can only convey speaker intentions when such morphemes match the Matrix Language frame requirements.

The other language with French as the Embedded Language is Lingala. In contrast to Wolof, Lingala has no determiners at all. In this case, French nouns appear as bare forms. Example (8) comes from Kamwangamalu (1989), showing how French nouns appear in Lingala/French codeswitching. Kamwangamalu himself also refers to the lack of a slot for an article in the Lingala frame as the reason for such bare forms (1989: 119).

(8) ezali **probleme** mo-nene te
COP problem big NEG
'It's not [a] big problem.'

(Lingala/French; Kamwangamalu 1989, cited in Myers-Scotton 1993*a* [1997]: 154)

From these examples, one can conclude that it is not the relationship of French and its determiners that can explain why they appear in Arabic/French codeswitching. Instead, these examples suggest that the requirements of the Matrix Language are what matter and whether French can satisfy them. This line of reasoning is pursued below under the Uniform Structure Principle.

4.3.6. *One view on Dutch nouns*

The second issue regarding bare forms when Arabic is the Matrix Language is the situation with Dutch nouns. Why do they often appear as bare forms in Arabic frames and never appear with Dutch determiners, only Arabic determiner complexes or its parts, but not even those very frequently? Muysken suggests that 'for Dutch an integration strategy is developed in which null counts as a DNG' (p. 86). That is, to explain the lack of anything in either the D (Determiner) or the DNG (Definiteness–Number–Gender) slots when Dutch nouns appear in an Arabic frame, he posits that a null satisfies the frame. Given the high salience of the Determiner complex in Arabic, why should Arabic accept a null in place of its own Determiner complex? It is very counterintuitive to posit nulls having any role at all here.

4.4. Another view: Uniform structure

I suggest the entire issue may be approached in another way. Embedded Language determiners (French here) can appear *if they show sufficient congruence with their Matrix Language counterparts* at all three levels of abstract grammatical structure. French determiners seem to pass this test when Arabic is the Matrix Language. They fail it in other corpora, as do most Embedded Language determiners in most corpora, including Dutch nouns in Arabic/Dutch corpora.

4.4.1. *The Uniform Structure Principle*

This observation gives rise to an explanation that accounts for the bare and not-so-bare nouns, both in the corpora with Arabic as the Matrix Language and in the Bantu corpora. I begin by suggesting that, as part of Generalized Lexical Knowledge in the mental lexicon, every language has a Uniform Structure Principle. This principle is intended as a substantive universal and is based on empirical evidence found across languages; that is, constituents in any language have a characteristic categorical structure. Generalized Lexical Knowledge in the mental lexicon is, as the name states, general; that is, it is not lemma-specific. However, of course, it must be language-specific. Such lexical knowledge covers many default features of a language. For example, it covers morpheme order in some constituents, such as NPs. It also includes general provisions about predicate-argument structure (e.g. whether the thematic role of Experiencer can occupy the syntactic slot of subject is language-specific).

The Uniform Structure Principle (USP). A given constituent type in any language has a uniform abstract structure and the requirements of well-formedness for this constituent type must be observed whenever the constituent appears.

As it stands, the principle is compatible with the MLF model, but it goes beyond it. The System Morpheme Principle of the MLF model rules out Embedded Language late outsider system morphemes, a provision that is completely compatible with the Uniform Structure Principle. (After all, it is the nature of late system morphemes that they observe uniform structure across the CP because their forms depend on coindexing across the CP.) Note that the System Morpheme Principle does not rule out Embedded Language early system morphemes, or even Embedded Language bridge late system morphemes—even though many interpreters of the System Morpheme Principle mistakenly think it does. However, the Uniform Structure Principle goes beyond the System Morpheme Principle; it predicts early and bridge late system morphemes from the Matrix Language as the unmarked choice—just because it gives preference to keeping structure uniform across the CP. (However, for bilingual speech, some additional provisions are needed. For example, below, I introduce two addenda to the Uniform Structure Principle to accommodate early system morphemes from the Embedded Language.)

4.4.2. *Feature agreement*

Note that the theoretical notions behind the Uniform Structure Principle are not new. They have been perhaps most clearly expressed (at least, for me) in Generalized Phrase Structure Grammar and its general principles that control feature distribution in phrases or across phrases (Gazdar, Klein, Pullum, and Sag 1985).[5] The basic goal of GPSG is to show 'how grammatical rules that are under-specified with respect to feature detail, together with lexical entries that are more fully specified can determine the full structural and featural [sic] detail of a structural description for a linguistic expression' (1985: 12).

[5] GPSG has been further developed as Head Phrase Structure Grammar (HPSG), but the original generalizations of Gazdar *et al.* are the ones most relevant to this discussion.

The GPSG model aims to achieve this goal largely through applying three global principles. (i) The Head Feature Convention requires 'the set of HEAD features that get instantiated on heads to be identical to (or a superset of) the HEAD features instantiated on the mother category' (p. 51). That is, feature specifications of the subconstituents of a phrase depend on head features. (ii) The Foot Feature Principle requires that 'any FOOT feature specification which is instantiated on a daughter category in a local tree must also be instantiated on the mother category in that tree' (p. 81). (Note that this principle takes care of the co-indexing across maximal projections that spreads features to late outsider system morphemes.) (iii) Finally, the Control Agreement Principle refers to 'the relation of control [that] holds between pairs of categories in a local tree that meet certain semantic criteria' (pp. 84–5). For example, this principle provides the mechanism for ensuring that the VP does in fact agree with the subject NP. Under the GPSG notion of control, which constituents actually agree is a language-specific matter (e.g. whether certain elements in a given phrase are specified for plural is language-specific).

In an overview of GPSG, Horrocks (1987) makes a point about the model's approach to features and consistency within a phrase structure (in reference to monolingual data, but one that can be employed in bilingual speech to maintain the Matrix Language frame when Embedded Language material is incorporated into the frame). He writes, 'The crucial thing is that these features recur in all the right places, that the necessary agreement patterns are enforced when the features are instantiated elsewhere' (p. 183). Of course GPSG was designed to cover monolingual data; however, its basic features reinforce the Uniform Structure Principle, which I formulated especially for bilingual data (although it applies to monolingual data, too, of course). The principle is a way to capture the ideas that Head features (of the Matrix Language) must be observed throughout a maximal projection and that Foot features and the control features (of the Matrix Language) under the Control Agreement Principle must apply across maximal projections (e.g. whatever specifications there are for subject–verb agreement or case assignment).

Of course, many other syntactic models deal with how features are spread and checked; some of the provisions of Chomsky's Minimalist Program (1995) are reminiscent of the feature instantiation principles of GPSG. I only cite GPSG to indicate the tradition behind the Uniform Structure Principle and feature checking in general.

4.4.3. *French determiners again*

We now apply the Uniform Structure Principle to the case of French determiners in Arabic/French codeswitching. In his seminal discussion of universals about word order, Greenberg (1966) makes the point that word order in NPs is very strict across his sample of thirty languages. With the strictness of order in the Arabic determiner complex in mind, let us consider why French determiners can appear in this constituent. I suggest the reason is that French has more than a determiner that resembles the Arabic one; more important, it has *a determiner complex that closely matches that of* Arabic—at least in the North African Arabic varieties. Because of this, even though Arabic is the Matrix Language, French determiners can satisfy the requirements of the Arabic complex and appear with French nouns. In fact, they are so compatible, they can appear in two ways, either following *dak* or *wahed*, as in *di:k la fille* 'that the girl'), or in the place of Arabic determiners with French nouns (*la fille*). Not only does French have a determiner complex with the same structure as that of Arabic, but within this complex, French determiners (under DNG) have features that provide a sufficient match to those of Arabic determiners. Note that those French elements under D (quantifiers, demonstratives, etc.) do not replace Arabic ones in a mixed constituent; this is evidence that these features are not equally congruent with those in French. But my point is that the overall determiner complexes are sufficiently congruent to support the configurations that do occur.

Under my analysis, the relevant phrase-structure tree that includes determiners must be different from that drawn by Muysken (2000: 61). Like Arabic, French has a determiner complex that also has both a D (determiner) node and a DNG node, with determiners themselves under DNG. Under D in Arabic, one finds the previously discussed demonstratives. Under D in French, one finds demonstratives and quantifiers, as well as partitives (e.g. *tout* in *tout le monde* 'all the world' or 'everybody'; *de* in *je voudrais de la salade* 'I would like some salad'). See Figure 4.1 for my tree and Figure 4.2 for Muysken's tree. Under DNG, French and Arabic share the obligatory marking of masculine or feminine gender on singular determiners.[6] Of course in both languages these determiners are early system morphemes, so the System Morpheme Principle is not violated by the presence of French ones. In addition, note that the USP is at least minimally satisfied because of the close match across the French and Arabic determiner complex.

Thus, the major reason that French nouns can be placed in the North African Arabic determiner complex with their French determiners intact is that the structure of the two complexes is nearly identical, and no reanalysis involving movement along the lines suggested by Muysken is required. Further, indirect evidence indicates that the relation of the two determiner complexes is crucial, not the relation of the French determiner and its noun. See Figure 4.1 for my version of the determiner complex and Figure 4.2 for a rendition of Muysken's view.

The indirect evidence indicates a different outcome when French nouns occur in mixed NPs with such languages as Wolof or Lingala as the Matrix Language. What is the reason for no French nouns with their determiners occurring in these

[6] Note that under the MLF model, the French part of the mixed determiner complex and the French noun is considered an internal Embedded Language island. See *wahed les histoires* in (4). But the entire node (of D + DNP + N) is under N-bar in a larger constituent with an abstract Matrix Language NP as its head. That is, the DP node does not govern the French NP in the analysis.

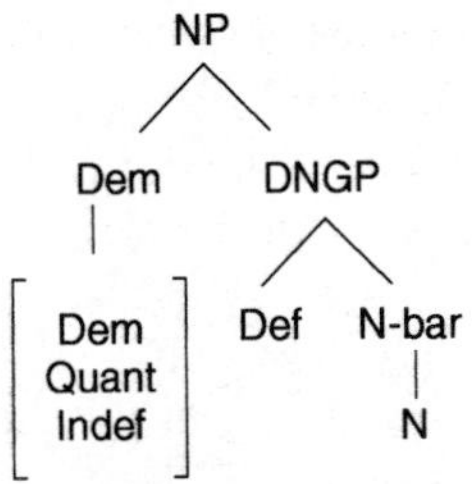

Monolingual phrase structures, with a demonstrative
Arabic: [*dak* [*l* + N]]
French: [*cette* [∅ + N]]

Bilingual NP, with Arabic ML, French EL:
[*dak* [*el~le, la* + French N]]
wah̄ed les histoires
Indef Def/Pl stories
'one of the stories' (ex. 4)

Monolingual phrase structures, with a definite article only
Arabic: [∅ [*l* – N]]
French: [∅ [*le/la* N]]

Bilingual NP, with Arabic ML/French EL:
[$_{\text{DNGP}}$*el~le* + French N]
f-el-carrefour
in-the-crossroads
'at the crossroads' (Caubet 1997)

French EL island, with Arabic as ML:
[$_{\text{DNGP}}$*la~le* + French N]
la scoliose
'[the] scolioisis' (ex. 3)

NP
Dem/Def N-bar
Dem
Quant
Indef
Def
N

Monolingual phrase structures, with a demonstrative
Dutch: [*die* [∅ + N]] → [*die* + N]

Bilingual NP, with Arabic ML, Dutch EL:
[*dak* [∅ + Dutch N]] (rare)
dak ehm ∅ *opleiding*
Dem er training
'that training' (ex. 2)

Monolingual phrase structures, with a definite article only
Dutch: [$_{\text{NP}}$*het* + N]

Bilingual NP, with Arabic ML/Dutch EL:
[$_{\text{DNGP}}$*l-* + Dutch N]
l-waarheid
'the truth' (Boumans 1998: 184)

Figure 4.1. Structure of NPs in Arabic, French, and Dutch. The definite, gender, and number features of the DNGP (Definite/Number/Gender Phrase) may be realized on the Def (the definite article itself), the N-bar/N, or both. The unspecified D can be coindexed—and also agree—with some or all of features of the DNGP (e.g. French *ces* 'these' is plural, but is not inflected for gender and occurs without the definite determiner).

corpora? The answer is that the fit regarding determiners is *not* perfect at all. Wolof has determiners following the noun and no gender and Lingala has no determiners. Thus, French determiners are nowhere to be found in these corpora (unless there is a full French NP as an Embedded Language island). Instead, the well-formedness conditions of the Matrix Language languages themselves satisfy the slots they project.

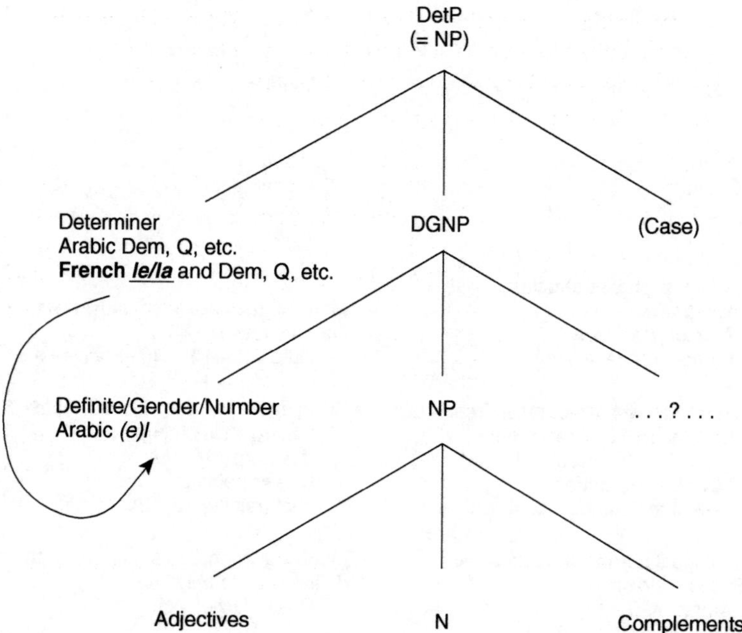

Figure 4.2. French definite article (under D) 'reinterpreted DNG in Moroccan Arabic' (Muysken 2000: 68; Determiner Phrase figure adapted from Muysken 2000: 61)

4.4.4. *Dutch nouns again*

Now, what about the case of Dutch nouns as bare forms in Arabic frames? Although the MLF model does not require this result, under the USP one would expect the Arabic determiner complex, or single Arabic determiners, to occur with Dutch nouns. To be consistent, one has to conclude some structural feature from Dutch is strong enough to block the Arabic elements. There are several potential sources of incongruence.

First, Dutch does not have a determiner complex to match that of Arabic. (Compare the trees for Arabic and Dutch in Figure 4.1.) Even so, as the Matrix Language, Arabic should still be able to project its own slots. In fact, Arabic does just this when English is the Matrix Language, and English has no determiner complex either (except in a few English constructions such as *all the X*) to match that of Arabic. In a large Palestinian/English corpus, Arabic determiners or the full Arabic determiner complex appear freely in mixed NPs with English (Embedded Language) nouns (Okasha 1999, *inter alia*). The same finding applies to a Jordanian Arabic/English corpus (Mustafa and Al-Khatib 1994). See (9), for example. What is so different about English and Dutch nouns?

(9) ʔil **communitie-s** s-ṣaɣiira tṣallamu ʔistṣmaal l- **manure**
DET community-PL DET-small learned/3PL using DET manure
'The small communities learned using the manure.'

(Jordanian Arabic/English; Mustafa and Al-Khatib 1994: 220)

This question leads to the second potential source of incongruence: gender marking may be a problem. One obvious point is that English nouns lack grammatical gender and therefore do not present a competing gender in an Arabic frame while Dutch nouns do. Recall that Dutch articles mark feminine and neuter while Arabic ones mark feminine and masculine. But can this conflict be basic enough to block Matrix Language determiners? In Spanish/English corpora, English nouns receive Spanish determiners in mixed NPs (cf. Myers-Scotton and Jake 2001). Spanish and English determiners certainly are not congruent, but of course the Embedded Language (English) lacks gender. The importance of gender as an inherent feature of nouns is not well understood; however, it is hard to accept the conclusion that Dutch gender is able to block the Arabic determiner complex.

4.4.5. *A synthesis regarding outcomes*

I apologize for the protracted discussion in the entire section 4.3, but the details do require a good deal of explication if they are to be understood at all. Let us review the situation, paying special attention to the determiners just discussed. We can assume that very little Embedded Language material, if any, *totally* satisfies feature requirements of the Matrix Language. Yet, for example, we also know that Embedded Language nouns occur frequently in mixed codeswitching constituents framed by the Matrix Language. Their occurrence requires that we make two assumptions. (i) First, we assume that the USP gives preference to the Matrix Language morphosyntactic provisions, not those of the Embedded Language. That is, as applied to bilingual speech, this principle affirms the morphosyntactic dominance of the Matrix Language. (ii) Second, even in the face of this principle, the Arabic/French corpora seem to show us that structural uniformity is not always maintained.

This leads to a compromise assumption that maintains the USP, but accounts for the Arabic/French data: those Embedded Language system morphemes that do not violate the System Morpheme Principle may come from the Embedded Language if the structure of the relevant constituent is (nearly) identical to a corresponding Matrix Language structure. In this case, the relevant constituent is the determiner complex, of course.

Under the USP, three outcomes for nouns and their determiners are possible in mixed constituents. The unmarked case is the first scenario.

Under this first scenario, Matrix Language determiners appear freely, either with Matrix Language or Embedded Language nouns, and no Embedded Language determiners are present (except in occasional Embedded Language islands). This scenario fits the Palestinian and Jordanian Arabic/English corpora, but also the Wolof/French and the Lingala/French corpora.

This explanation also fits the Spanish/English corpus discussed in Myers-Scotton and Jake (2001). In Spanish/English codeswitching (Spanish is the Matrix Language) mixed NPs (Spanish Determiner + English Noun) occur freely. English, of course, does not have gender features to compete with those of Spanish.

In Halmari (1997), the combination of a case-marked element in the Determiner slot and an English noun that lacks case marking (*si-* + *olive farm*) seems to satisfy possibly related Matrix Language requirements (Finnish) about how Embedded Language nouns are to be marked. Case-marking on nouns is the issue here. Operating within a Government-based model of codeswitching, Halmari argues that 'When a language carrier which shows case is present, the Government constraint is fulfilled' (1997: 148). The Finnish element in the determiner slot is considered the Lg-carrier under her model. This element can substitute for case marking on the noun itself, Halmari argues. Under her model, this means an English noun that lacks a required case affix is well-formed enough according to Finnish requirements (i.e. not bare). What makes this corpus similar to the other corpora discussed above is that once more, the Embedded Language (English) noun does not project a feature to compete with the Matrix Language feature. In this situation, English has no overt case marking to compete with Finnish case marking. In (10) Finnish *si-* receives the partitive case marker.

(10) . . . se mikä hoiti si + tä **olive farm**
it which took care it + PART olive farm
'. . . the one who took care of the olive farm'

(American Finnish/English; Halmari 1997: 148)

In the second scenario, Matrix Language determiners appear only variably and Embedded Language determiners never appear with Embedded Language nouns; they are bare nouns because of lack of congruence across the Matrix Language and the Embedded Language for the relevant structure. Embedded Language determiners never appear (again, except in occasional Embedded Language islands). This scenario fits the Moroccan Arabic/Dutch corpus. Somehow, an Embedded Language feature offers sufficient competition to impede the Matrix Language procedure.

Only in the third scenario can Embedded Language determiners appear with Embedded Language nouns. There may be two different outcomes from the same set of features. (i) The Matrix Language projects its own elements in the determiner complex, as would be predicted under the Uniform Structure Principle. (This scenario applies to French nouns with an Arabic determiner complex or determiner.) (ii) Embedded Language heads may project their own early system morphemes. This is possible even if all Embedded Language head features are not entirely identical to those of Matrix Language head features (e.g. how masculine and feminine gender is assigned may vary from lexical item to item or in some other manner). The crucial point is that the constituent structure in which they occur is (nearly) identical (as in Figure 4.1). This scenario applies to French determiners in Arabic frames, with or without Arabic demonstratives.

4.4.6. *A first addendum to the Uniform Structure Principle*

The different outcomes for the language pairs considered in this section motivate an addendum to the Uniform Structure Principle referring to determiners that are early system morphemes. A second addendum refers only to early system morphemes that are noun-class prefixes, specifying that alien nouns in Bantu corpora must receive noun-class prefixes.

Addendum I. In classic codeswitching, Matrix Language early system morphemes can be displaced in the Matrix Language frame for determiner complexes under two conditions: (i) If the abstract grammatical structure of Embedded Language early system morphemes is (nearly) identical to that of Matrix Language counterparts, then Embedded Language forms may satisfy Matrix Language structural requirements for the determiner complex (French in Arabic/French codeswitching). (ii) If crucial abstract features of Embedded Language early system morphemes in determiner complexes (gender?) conflict with those of Matrix Language counterparts, then even Matrix Language early system morphemes are variably blocked in the determiner complex (Dutch in Arabic/Dutch codeswitching). Otherwise, Matrix Language procedures for early system morphemes in the determiner complex prevail.

4.5. Bare nouns without Bantu noun-class prefixes

In many East and Southern African corpora showing codeswitching between a Bantu language and English, there also are what appear to be bare English nouns because they do not show any noun-class prefix. However, in most of these languages, there is a pair of Bantu classes (9/10) for which the noun-class prefix can be realized with a zero allomorph. When Swahili is the Matrix Language and English (Embedded Language) nouns are at issue, other agreement prefixes in the CP (subject–verb agreement, the prefix on the 'associative a' construction, etc.) are evidence that either class 9 or 10 is the intended class of the Embedded Language noun showing no overt prefix. Thus, in (11) the agreement of *y-* on the associative form *y-a* 'of' indicates that *date* is considered a class 9 (singular) noun. Note that a Swahili noun, *pesa* 'money' (probably originally a borrowing from Hindi) also shows no class prefix, but its agreement forms (*z-enyewe* and *zi-ta-toka*) with *zi-* as the agreement prefixes make clear that *pesa* is a class 10 noun (plural). (Note that *ya* is a multimorphemic unit consisting of a late outsider system morpheme (coindexed with the zero prefix on *date*) and the bridge system morpheme *-a* 'of' (required in an NP–NP construction).) Examples (12*a*) and (12*b*) show the variable co-indexing that bare nouns for humans receive in Swahili. In (12*a*), the class 9 agreement prefix on *y-ako* 'your' indicates *brother* is operating as a class 9 noun. But in (12*b*), another speaker treats another bare noun, *doctor*, also controlling an agreement marker on a possessive, as a class 1 noun (*w-ako* 'his' shows a class 1 agreement prefix). Sometimes, English nouns, especially plurals, do have overt Swahili prefixes and they are typically *ma-* (for class 6).

(11) hu-yo, ni-li-ku-w-a ni-me-m-p-a
CL1-DEM 1S-PST-INF-COP-FV 1S-PERF-IO-give-FV
(Ø)date y-a **this weekend** na (Ø)pesa z-enyewe
CL.9-date CL.9-of this weekend and CL.10-money CL.10-itself
si-ju-i zi-ta-tok-a wapi
1S/NEG-know-FV/NEG CL10-FUT-come from-FV where
'This one, I had given her a date of this weekend and [the] money itself I don't know where it will come from.'

(Swahili/English; Myers-Scotton Nairobi 1988 corpus)

(12) *a* Yu-le ni **brother** y-ako
CL1-DEM COP brother CL9-POSS/2S
'That one is your brother.'

(Swahili/English; Myers-Scotton Nairobi 1988 corpus)

(12) *b* A-li-ku-w-a a-na-tak-a
3S-PST-INF-be-FV 3S-NONPST-want-FV
a-w-e karibu na **doctor** w-ake
3S-be-SUBJUNC near with doctor CL1-POSS/3S
'He was wanting to be near to his doctor.'

(Swahili/English; Myers-Scotton Nairobi 1988 corpus)

In a Shona/English codeswitching corpus there are many singly occurring English nouns, but most show overt Shona noun-class prefixes. (Shona is the major Bantu language in Zimbabwe.) If there is a bare form (i.e. with no overt class prefix), it is more likely to be a singular form than a plural. If a singular does receive an overt class prefix, it is often a class 9 prefix (*i-*). For example, *i-holiday i-pi* 'which holiday'. Some nouns may show a class 13 prefix in the singular (e.g. *ka-small thing*) to convey the intent that the thing named is small (this is the class of diminutives). However, whatever the singular, the plural counterpart class is overwhelmingly class 6 (*ma-*).

In contrast with Swahili, Shona rather regularly treats many English nouns that represent plural concepts as members of class 6 (the plural member of the class 5/6 pair); that is, they receive the class prefix *ma-*. If they control any agreements on other elements in the clause, these elements also receive class 6 agreements (e.g. the demonstrative in *ma-wages a-ya* 'these wages', or see (13)).

(13) . . . ma-we ma-**property** ma-kuru a-no-di-w-a ne-munhu
CL6-any CL6-property CL6-big CL6-PRES-need-PASS-FV by person
'. . . any big property needed by [a] person . . .'

(Shona/English; Bernsten and Myers-Scotton 1988 corpus no. 22)

Further, where it is appropriate, English nouns often occur with a locative class prefix (*ku-*) as well as the class 6 prefix *ma-* (see (14)). (Note that *three* in (14) can be considered a plural as 'three hours'.) Singular English nouns may also receive an appropriate locative class prefix, but they may not have a non-locative class prefix as well. See *mu-Ø-paper bag* in (15). Note that *bhasikiti* 'basket' in this example is an established loan word with an initial aspirated voiced bilabial (it is in the Shona dictionary).

(14) ku-ma-**three**, ndo-svik-a kumba ku-ma-**three**
CL17-CL6-three 1S-arrive-FV home CL17-CL6-three
'At three, I get home at three.'

(Shona/English; Bernsten and Myers-Scotton 1988 corpus no. 11)

(15) Ti-no-takurir-a mu-ma-bhasikiti kana mu-**paper bag**
1PL-HAB-carry-FV CL18-CL6-basket or CL18-paper bag
'We carry [it] in baskets or in [a] paper bag.'

(Shona/English; Bernsten and Myers-Scotton 1988 corpus no. 11)

In summary, in neither the Swahili nor the Shona data sets are the alien nouns truly bare. Still, these nouns present an interesting question about alien nouns in general. One might suppose that agreement is a feature of the Matrix Language frame itself, but a moment's reflection indicates that while the frame may include the notion of agreement, which agreement feature to access has to depend on information originating outside the frame. In any sense do the Embedded Language nouns themselves 'become' Matrix Language nouns in order to spread agreement?

4.5.1. *A second addendum to the Uniform Structure Principle*

Addendum II. In classic codeswitching, the agreement features of late outsider system morphemes in any construction must be provided for. That is, if the construction calls for late outsider morphemes, they must be present and appropriate. To provide for agreement spreading from a nominal head, alien nouns in mixed codeswitching constituents receive the default spreading element (e.g. class prefix) of the specific language.

4.5.2. *Explaining agreements in Bantu*

Based on this addendum, I propose an explanation for how alien nouns in Eastern and Southern Bantu codeswitching corpora receive noun class membership in mixed constituents. Bantu nouns must be specified for noun class because other elements in the CP are co-indexed with the prefix on nouns. However, it seems self-evident that lemmas underlying non-native nouns do not include the type of information about noun-class membership that every native Bantu noun has.

What about nouns' ability to project class agreements (or variably to project class 1/2 agreements if the nouns stand for humans)?

Where do these provisions come from? In Chapter 3, I refer to Generalized Lexical Knowledge and now invoke it again here. In Myers-Scotton and Jake (1995), Jake and I argue that when the Embedded Language lemmas underlying all Embedded Language content morphemes are selected to convey the speaker's intentions, they must first be checked for sufficient congruence with the Matrix Language. This checking is either with an actual Matrix Language counterpart in the mental lexicon or with Generalized Lexical Knowledge for the relevant language in the mental lexicon.

Empirical evidence shows that if Embedded Language nouns in Bantu frames have a class-assigning property, it must come from the Matrix Language Generalized Lexical Knowledge in the mental lexicon. This knowledge must be part of the entry for the abstract NP that is the head of the construction in which the alien noun appears. One must assume that the Uniform Structure Principle contains a provision similar to the Head Feature Convention of GPSG. This convention specifies that the head features of the highest bar of the construction (the abstract NP in this case) should agree with those of the next highest bar categories (in this case, the alien nouns and their modifiers) and that the features of the these categories agree with those of any X category (the noun itself) (cf. Horrocks 1987: 184).

As it applies to Bantu languages, the Uniform Structure Principle must stipulate that every noun has to have a noun-class membership. Therefore, the principle would add specifications for a noun class to the lemma (in the mental lexicon) of any alien (Embedded Language) noun. The default noun class for alien nouns in Swahili would be class 9/10 while in Shona it would be class 9 for singulars, but class 6 for plurals. However, there would be a provision general to Bantu languages to allow any noun class with a zero as one of the allomorphs for its prefix to be available to Embedded Language nouns. A general provision (still in line with the Uniform Structure Principle) could override the first provision and variably allow any alien noun for humans to govern class 1/2 co-indexing properties, while still receiving the default noun-class prefix for the language.

Why is it important that Embedded Language lemmas underlying Bantu nouns receive these agreement properties? Note how the second addendum is different from the first one that applies to early system morphemes. That addendum provides only for early system morphemes; this second addendum deals with early system morphemes as a means to providing that late ones be present. When cases of a composite Matrix Language (grammatical input from more than one source) are discussed in Chapter 6, we will see that late system morphemes from the dominant contributor to the composite Matrix Language are not always present and their absence will be the best indicator that a turnover in dominance (and perhaps a total language shift) is under way.

Note that this addendum to add class membership to Embedded Language nouns when a Bantu language is the Matrix Language is necessary, not so much for the noun as for the elements that must show agreement with an overt noun. Recall that in many Bantu languages other elements in the CP must show overt agreement with a head (e.g. adjectives, possessives, the associative construction, and subject–verb agreement as well as object agreement). It is of no small importance that all these agreement affixes are late outsider system morphemes; they all must look outside their immediate maximal projections for information about their forms. (Recall the use of Swahili adjectival prefixes and agreements in the '*-a* of association' construction to illustrate outsiders in Chapter 3.)

4.5.3. *Implications of Addendum II*

Although a mechanism such as the Uniform Structure Principle is necessary to motivate what indeed happens, i.e. a reanalysis of alien nouns as Bantu nouns, this is not the most interesting outcome of the principle. Rather, more consequential is that this reanalysis provides for an abstract NP as the head of the alien noun, but also as the source of the proper late system morphemes of agreement in the larger clause. That is, integrating content morphemes (nouns in this case) into the Matrix Language is not an end in itself but a means to a more important end. I would want to argue that in those data sets including Embedded Language verbs that are able to be inflected with Matrix Language affixes, these verbs also must have received Matrix Language specifications from the Matrix Language's store of Generalized Lexical Knowledge. All this suggests a good deal of interaction between the Matrix Language and the Embedded Language at the level of the mental lexicon.

4.6. Explaining other codeswitching phenomena with the Uniform Structure Principle

The implications of the Uniform Structure Principle may turn out to be many. For example, the USP offers an explanation why there are so many NP + bridge + NP constructions in an Acholi/English corpus that consist of two English nouns or an English noun and an English present participial form, but an Acholi form *me* for 'of' (associative). There are forty-two constructions with English nouns or participial forms in at least one of the NP slots. Of these, eighteen have English in both NP slots (e.g. *taxis me long routes* 'long route taxis') and twenty-four have English in one of the NP slots (e.g. *lok me employment* 'conditions of employment'). These compare with only twelve monolingual Acholi ones and only one entirely in English (the formulaic *cost of living*).[7]

Why are there not more entirely in English (accessed as an English Embedded Language island), but so many with at least one English noun or participial form?

[7] This analysis follows the general argument on non-finite English verbs in Acholi in Jake and Myers-Scotton (2001). In Chapter 3, such non-finite forms are also discussed.

Table 4.1. Associative *me* constructions in Acholi/English codeswitching

	Tokens	%
Acholi monolingual associative construction	12	21.8
One associative element from English	24	43.6
Both associative elements from English	18	32.7
Formulaic English Embedded Language island: associative of (cost of living)	1	1.8
Total	55	99.9

Example (1): Both associative elements from Acholi:

I mwaka ma-okato, gi-twey-a kunu pi **lok me mucoro**, . . .
in year REL-pass, 3PL-tie-1SG/OBJ there for **issue of tax**
'In the past year, I was imprisoned [they imprisoned me] there due to the matter of taxes.'
(Note: *mwaka* is from Swahili)

Example (2): Both associative elements from English:

Costs me education i-**private institutions** tye **high** *tena*
costs of education in-private institutions COP high again
'The costs of education in private institutions are high once more'
(Note: *tena* is from Swahili)

Adapted from Jake and Myers-Scotton 2001

The USP provides one answer: the Matrix Language frame (e.g. from Acholi) is uniformly maintained if the bridge system morpheme comes from the Matrix Language (e.g. Acholi). That is, maintaining the frame uniformly overrides activation of Embedded Language framing procedures that would be required in order to form an Embedded Language island (i.e. the entire construction in English).

4.7. Other lexical categories and system morphemes

In contrast to my extended treatment of nouns, I simply mention other types of Embedded Language content morpheme that do not seem to be integrated into a Matrix Language frame at all easily. My intention is no more than to raise issues here, not try to offer explanations. Very few Embedded Language adjectives modifying Matrix Language nouns occur in codeswitching corpora, possibly because of congruence problems at all levels. In Schmitt (2001), there are only 5 English adjectives out of 146 English elements in one of her Russian/English corpora. True, there are 27 adjectives (types) in the Nairobi Swahili/English corpus; yet, they are all bare, indicating congruence problems (and compare this number with 141 nouns (types)). See example (16) from this corpus, in which *new* follows a noun and a quantifier inflected for class 6; yet *new* does not receive a class 6 prefix.

(16)

. . . na	u-ta-ku-w-a	na	ma-mbo	mengi	**new**
. . . and	2S-FUT-INF-COP-FV	with	CL6/PL-matter	CL6/PL/many	new

'. . . and you will be with many new things'

(Swahili/English; Myers-Scotton Nairobi 1988 corpus)

A general reason may be that adjectives are notorious for not translating directly. What is encoded by an adjective in one language may be conveyed by a tensed verb in another language. Or, to take another example, in some languages physical experiencer adjectives are predicate adjectives, but in other languages they can be both attributive and predicative (*the hungry dog* and *the dog is hungry*). In other languages, physical experiences are encoded as nouns, requiring a dative case in some languages and a nominative in others.

4.7.1. *A compromise strategy for adjectives*

Meechan and Poplack (1995) report on a compromise strategy that is similar to the 'do' construction discussed in the next section; however, it provides for a way of inserting French (Embedded Language) adjectives into Fongbe frames, not for inserting verbs. This is the *dò* 'to be' construction (note *dò* does not equal 'do'). In monolingual Fongbe, *dò* only occurs with adverbials and locatives. But Meechan and Poplack report, 'By far the greatest proportion of *dò* . . . occurs in the context of French adjectival phrases' (1995: 186). Also, this particular construction does not occur with Fongbe adjectival complements in their corpus at all. They conclude, 'It seems inescapable that the Fongbe semi-auxiliary *dò* is being used as a device for handling French-origin adjectives' (p. 186). See (17) for an example of *dò* + the French feminine adjective *importante*.

(17)

Donc	ɔ	nyɛ	mɔ ḍɔ	**que langue**	ɔ	e	ḍò	**importante**
so	TOP	I	see tell	that language	DEF	she	be	important

'So, me I see that language is important.'

(Fongbe/French; Meechan and Poplack 1995: 187)

4.7.2. *Finite verbs and the Embedded Language*

Inflecting Embedded Language verbs with Matrix Language inflections does not seem to be very easy. We have seen in Chapter 3 that at least in one corpus (Acholi/English) non-finite verbs from the Embedded Language occur freely, but not finite verbs. Even in those data sets where Embedded Language finite verbs do occur, they certainly are not as frequent as Embedded Language nouns (e.g. Halmari 1997; at least the discussion considers only seven inflected English (Embedded Language) verbs, but at least thirty-six inflected English nouns). The major compromise strategy to integrate at least the lexical-conceptual structure of Embedded Language verbs into the Matrix Language frame is discussed in section 4.8.

4.8. Another case of bare elements: the 'do' construction

When many languages around the world participate in codeswitching as the Matrix Language, they do not accept Embedded Language verbs as tensed forms (i.e. with Matrix Language inflections). To solve the problem of carrying speaker intentions that an Embedded Language verb is intended to convey, they construct what has come to be called a 'do' construction (cf. for a general discussion Romaine 1995, Muysken 2000). This construction includes an Embedded Language verb that is the reflex of those intentions at the level of lexical-conceptual structure. However, the construction also includes the Matrix Language verb for 'do' and it is this verb that carries the inflections that the Matrix Language requires for well-formedness from a tensed verb construction. Note that at least some of these inflections are the type of system morpheme that both the System Morpheme Principle and the Uniform Structure Principle require to come from the Matrix Language.

Thus, the Embedded Language verb occurs without any of the inflections that are required by the Matrix Language. This is what makes it a bare form from the standpoint of the Matrix Language frame. In Chapter 3, non-finite Embedded Language verbs occurring in Matrix Language frames are discussed. Here, the major subject is how these non-finite verbs also occur in 'do' constructions, with the entire complex a substitute for a finite verb. Often the Embedded Language verb is an infinitive and it typically occurs with the Embedded Language infinitival suffix if it is an early system morpheme. (In some language pairs (e.g. Hausa/English) a 'do' construction is formed with the Embedded Language verb as a present participle.) A typical construction is illustrated in (18) in which the Dutch infinitive (*kij-en*) 'watch/look at' occurs with the Turkish 'do' verb (*yap-*). Example (19) from Turkish/Norwegian codeswitching includes a case-marked Turkish object complement as well as the Norwegian infinitive *vask-e* 'wash'.

(18) **ja, maar toch**, millet **kijk-en** yap-ıyor
yeah, but still, everybody watch-INF do-PROG/3S
'Yeah, but still, everybody is watching you.'

(Turkish/Dutch; Backus 1996: 238)

(19) Adam-lar yer-i **vask-e** yap-ıyor
man-PL floor-ACC wash-INF do-PROG/3S
'The men are washing the floor.'

(Turkish/Norwegian; Türker 2000: 113)

4.8.1. *The 'do' construction discussed*

A number of researchers have discussed such 'do' verb constructions in various languages. This construction knows no typological or geographic limits. It occurs when the Matrix Language is an agglutinating language such as Turkish (Backus 1992, 1996, Türker 2000) or Chicheŵa (Myers-Scotton and Jake 1999*a*), as well as when it is Japanese (Azuma 2001). South Indian agglutinating Dravidian languages also use the construction (Annamalai 1989). It also occurs with more fusional languages as the Matrix Language, such as the North Indian languages (Sankoff, Poplack, and Vanniarajan 1990, Romaine 1995) as well as with such mixed isolating-inflectional languages as Acholi/Lango (Myers-Scotton and Bernsten 1995) or inflectional languages such as Hausa (Bickmore 1985).

In most of these cases, the 'do' construction is the only means for introducing an Embedded Language verb into a codeswitching construction. Many of the languages involved are verb-final languages, but not all. Nor do only verb-final languages employ the construction. Chicheŵa (a Bantu language in Malaŵi) is such a language. In a corpus with Chicheŵa as the Matrix Language, English verbs only appear in the 'do' construction, although examples have been found with only four English verbs (for example (20)).

(20) Ngoni, ku-khomo w-a-**chit**-a **check**, eti?
Ngoni, CL18-door 2S-PERF-**do**-FV check right
'Ngoni, you have checked the door, right?'

(Chicheŵa/English; Simango corpus 1995)

Shona (another Bantu language spoken in Zimbabwe) variably uses the 'do' construction with English verbs, but the preferred strategy is to fully integrate an Embedded Language verb with verbal affixes. In the corpus of 132 interviews in both urban and rural Zimbabwe, Bernsten (2000) found 87 English verbs that received Shona inflections (93 tokens), but only 8 English verbs in 'do' constructions (9 tokens).

Bernsten notes that the most common use of the 'do' verb construction in Shona/English codeswitching is with English phrasal verbs (a verb + an early system morpheme satellite), as in (21). Example (22) from another Shona/English corpus shows the Shona 'do' verb (*-ita*) also used with an English phrasal verb. Example (22) also contains an example of how an English noun is integrated into the Shona noun class system as well as an example of double morphology in the same element (*mu-ma-lesson-s*).

Not all Bantu languages make use of the 'do' construction; a Swahili/English corpus shows no examples at all and researchers informally observe that they do not occur frequently, if at all, in South African Bantu languages (Finlayson, personal communication). It has been suggested that the underlying structure of Bantu languages is SOV, but because not all Bantu languages have 'do' constructions, even if the SOV characterization is correct, it does not explain why 'do' constructions occur in some Bantu languages and not others.

(21) a-ka-**it**-w-a **run over** ne-bhazi
3S-PST-**do**-PASS-FV run over by-bus
'He was run over by [a] bus.'

(Shona/English; Bernsten 2000 MS; Bernsten and Myers-Scotton 1988 corpus no. 46)

(22) . . . va-no-nok-a ku-**it**-a **catch up** mu-ma-**lesson-s**
CL2/PL-HAB-be late-FV INF–**do**-FV catch-up CL18-CL6/PL-lesson-PL
'. . . they are late to catch up in (their) lessons'

(Shona/English; Crawhill unpublished corpus cited in Myers-Scotton 1993*a* [1997])

It may be that, at least for some languages, the 'do' construction is an especially easy way to integrate Embedded Language phrasal verbs into the Matrix Language frame. A Shona counterpart to either *run over* or *catch up* would probably be a verb with a derivational suffix (i.e. the applied suffix); but such a suffix would only convey general 'movement towards' without the different meanings in the English phrasal verbs. Bernsten found that five out of the eight English verbs with the 'do' construction were phrasal verbs.

4.8.2. *An attempted solution, but no final word*

No discussions in the literature offer a satisfactory explanation of why the 'do' construction seems to be required if an Embedded Language verb is to be accessed. Most of them refer to codeswitching corpora with Turkish as the Matrix Language. Boeschoten and Backus (personal communication) certainly are correct in viewing the entire complex (Embedded Language infinitive + inflections + *yap*) as a substitute for the Turkish inflected verb. In monolingual Turkish, verbs can be derived from native nouns and adjectives by an affix *-la-* (Backus 1996: 225). Backus (1996: 250 ff.) offers an extended discussion of the continuum of meanings of the *yap* 'do' construction and its structural variations in Turkish/Dutch codeswitching. Türker (2000: 89 ff.) offers a similar discussion, referring to Turkish/Norwegian codeswitching. Backus hypothesizes that it is the entire complex of Embedded Language infinitive + *yap* that takes the inflections, not just *yap*. In this sense, he views *yap* as an auxiliary, suggesting that it is in the early stages of grammaticalization as an affix. In general, Turkologists point out that this construction is traditionally used in Turkish to integrate alien verbs as borrowings. Tradition also prevails in Japanese; for centuries, Chinese verbs have been taken into Japanese via the 'do' construction. Whatever the case, these suggestions about the nature and origin of the 'do' verb construction do not explain why the construction is required in the first place.

Several researchers consider structural features of the 'do' construction. Jake and Myers-Scotton (1997*a*) claim that incongruence between the tense/aspect systems of the participating languages makes the 'do' verb construction a necessary compromise strategy, but they offer little evidence. Ritchie and Bhatia (1999) offer a treatment of the 'do' construction in Hindi/English codeswitching within the Minimalist Program that describes the phenomenon very neatly, but does not explain why it occurs in the first place. Its parsimony is helped along by the implicit assumption that Hindi functions as what I would call the Matrix Language. Muysken (2000) illustrates many 'do' constructions across language pairs, but provides no explanation for why they are needed.

A relevant piece of data may be that in Greenberg's study of the typology of word order, he labels a group of languages as a 'rigid' subcategory of SOV languages. His claim is that not only do these languages have a subject–object–verb order, but they also allow no elements at all to follow the verb (1966: 79). This 'rigid' group includes the categorical 'do' verb construction languages—not only Turkish, but also Japanese and Hindi, but it excludes such verb-final languages as Quechua. Note that Quechua is a language in which the 'do' construction does not figure. The explanation for 'do' verb constructions may have to do with the strictness with which the 'rigid' subgroup maintains left-branching and the verb as clause head. Perhaps no alien verb (from a non-left-branching language) can fulfill this role. The scenario is this: the tensed verb assigns predicate-argument structure and has to assign it to the left. If an Embedded Language verb fills the tensed verb slot, the assignment fails. That is, at the lemma level the Embedded Language verb is not congruent with a Matrix Language counterpart (Embedded Language Generalized Lexical Knowledge regarding branching is not congruent with Matrix Language branching) and therefore cannot appear in the tensed verb slot to control left branching. However, Backus (personal communication) points out that in Turkish, at least, branching is not always to the left of the verb (i.e. verbs are not always the final element in a clause). Further, not all languages with 'do' constructions are verb-final with left-branching. Certainly, strict left-branching does seem to prevail in those languages where the 'do' construction is the categorical means of integrating an Embedded Language verb into the Matrix Language frame. However, this is obviously not the last word on 'do' constructions.

4.8.3. *Similar constructions*

Many other language pairs have a structure similar to the 'do' verb construction, although it is not necessarily recognized as such by the researchers who describe it. For example, Eze (1998) reports on a serial verb construction in Igbo/English codeswitching with the Igbo verb for 'do' *me* as the initial verb. The second verb is from English. In monolingual Igbo, *me* does not occur in this position. For example, see (23). Eze states that ninety per cent of all English verbs appear in this type of construction; the others are treated as Igbo verbs (and therefore are not bare forms). In line with Poplack and her other associates, Eze treats English verbs in the *me* construction as nonce borrowings; he says they differ from established loan words 'in lacking widespread diffusion' (p. 191).

(23) à-chọghi m ime gị **offend**
CL-want/NEG I do you offend
'I do not want to offend you'

(Igbo/English codeswitching; Eze 1998: 190)

4.8.4. *Verbs in other data sets*

In some other language pairs, Embedded Language verbs receive Matrix Language inflections with no apparent problems. These include languages of different morphological types, from agglutinative to analytic. For example, in the Swahili/English Nairobi corpus, there were ninety-one inflected English verbs and thirty-one infinitive forms with Swahili prefixation (Myers-Scotton 1993*a* [1997]: 88). There are several studies in the codeswitching literature of analytic West African languages as the Matrix Language in which English verbs easily receive Matrix Language inflections. Nartey (1982) gives examples of English verbs with Adaŋme verbal inflections; Forson (1979) reports the same for an Akan cluster language, Akuapem, as does Amuzu (1998) for Ewe. Amuzu illustrates English verbs taking these Ewe suffixes: ingressive aspect, present progressive tense/aspect, habitual aspect, and subjunctive mood (p. 49).

However, admittedly, there are also language pairs where very few Embedded Language verbs appear inflected with Matrix Language affixes. For example, in a German/English corpus of 265 bilingual CPs, there is only one example of an English tensed verb with German inflections (example (24)) (Fuller 1997). There are a few examples of bare English verbs (e.g. . . . *wo wir so hang around* 'where we just hang around'), and five German-inflected English infinitives (e.g. *install-en*) and three German-inflected English past participles (e.g. *ge-hired*).

(24) Ich weiß nicht wie viele **transfer**-en
1S know not how many transfer-3PL
'I don't know how many (will) transfer.'

(German/English; Fuller 1996 corpus)

Similarly, in other data sets, there are few Embedded Language verbs and fewer ones receiving any inflection. So far I have no completely satisfactory explanation for this state of affairs; lack of congruence across tense/aspect systems seems very likely, but no researcher has provided convincing details for such an argument.

There is some evidence that simply familiarity with codeswitching as a medium of communication may result in new structures developing that were not present in earlier data sets. This comment applies especially to the treatment of verbs. For example, in Spanish/English data sets gathered before 2000, there are few, if any,

English verbs inflected with Spanish affixes. However, new corpora, especially those from speakers who are very aware of their language use (e.g. university graduate students in linguistics or Spanish departments) report that they increasingly are using English verbs inflected with Spanish in their informal speech.

4.9. About Embedded Language islands

Embedded Language islands are full constituents consisting only of Embedded Language morphemes occurring in a bilingual CP that is otherwise framed by the Matrix Language. An Embedded Language island shows structural dependency relations; minimally it can be two content morphemes (e.g. noun and modifier) or a content morpheme and a non-derivational system morpheme. However, sequences of Embedded Language morphemes that are only juxtaposed are excluded, such as *building high-rise* in (25). The problem here is that these morphemes follow the word order of the Matrix Language, French, not English; therefore, this is simply a sequence of two Embedded Language content morphemes in a mixed constituent under Matrix Language order. Example (26) illustrates a typical Embedded Language island, a set phrase (*nihongo de* 'in Japanese'), as does (27). Note that both of these are PPs, as are many Embedded Language islands. Example (28) includes another typical island (that is another PP), a locative construction (*chez les pauvres vieux* 'at the house of those poor old people').

(25) À côté il y en a un autre gros **building high-rise.**
at [the] side there is ART other big building high-rise
'Next door there is another big high-rise bilding.'

(French/English; Poplack 1987: 59)

(26) How do you say this **nihongo de**?
How do you say this Japanese in
'How do you say this in Japanese?'

(English/Japanese; Azuma 1991: 193)

(27) Ní féidir é a chur as an tír **on any account**
NEG can 3S PARTICLE put/VN from the country on any account
'He can't be put out of the country on any account'

(Irish/English; Stenson 1990: 173)

(28) wat gaat ge doen **chez ces pauvres vieux**?
What go you do at house these poor old
What are you going to do at the house of those poor old people?'

(Brussels Dutch/French; Treffers-Daller 1994: 208)

Embedded Language islands represent a break in the Matrix Language frame. Is this a problem for the MLF model? No, but it does indicate that characterizing the relationship of the participating languages and their level of activation during production is more complex than simply stating that the Matrix Language is in continuous control of the morphosyntax in the bilingual CP. However, accepting the idea that the Embedded Language is 'on' in some sense when Embedded Language islands are produced does not imply the same level of activation for the Embedded Language as when singly occurring Embedded Language forms are introduced into Matrix Language frames.

Islands are well-formed at all three levels of abstract grammatical structure in the Embedded Language[8] and differ from singly occurring Embedded Language forms integrated into a mixed constituent in this regard. That is, at least in classic codeswitching, of the three levels of abstract grammatical structure, only the lexical-conceptual level need be implicated in single-form insertions, especially in the case of Embedded Language nouns. An obvious example of Embedded Language nouns that do not bring along their morphological realization patterns is the case of nouns from a prepositional language, such as English; they occur easily in PPs with postpositions in a postpositional language, such as Hindi. The same can be said for Dutch or Norwegian nouns with Turkish as the Matrix Language (Turkish also has postpositions). Another piece of evidence is that although Embedded Language islands must be well-formed in the Embedded Language to qualify as islands, a constituent including a noun may be well-formed *only* at the N-bar level, but not at the NP level from the standpoint of the Embedded Language. That is, because the Matrix Language controls the larger constituent, it may inhibit formation of a full NP in the Embedded Language *if such an NP is not what would be well-formed in the Matrix Language.* For example, the Embedded Language may require a phrase including a determiner to be well-formed, but the Matrix Language may not have this requirement. Examples illustrating the outcome of such a difference in requirements, such as (29), occur in a Chichewâ/English corpus. In Chichewâ, there are no determiners as integral parts of NPs; thus, *very expensive costume* is a well-formed NP according to the Chichewâ frame. It is also well-formed *as an N-bar in English,* even though (because it lacks a determiner) it is less than an NP in English.

(29) Mu-ku-on-a zi-mene a-val-a. A-val-a **very expensive costume.**
2S-PROG-see-FV CL10-DEM 3S-wear-FV 3S-wear-FV
'You see what he's wearing. He's wearing [a] very expensive costume.'

(Chichewâ/English corpus 1995)

4.9.1. *Islands as conceptual units*

However, even though the evidence provided by Embedded Language islands is that Matrix Language procedures are at the very least inhibited when Embedded

[8] Note that Embedded Language islands meet the same requirements that Sridhar and Sridhar (1980: 412) set for what they call guest constituents under their Dual Structure Principle.

Language islands are produced, it is important to note two characteristics of the bulk of Embedded Language islands across diverse data sets that imply a relatively lower level of activation for Embedded Language islands than for the mixed constituents under Matrix Language control.

First, many Embedded Language islands are adverbial phrases of time or place; that is, they are adjuncts (cf. Treffers-Daller 1994 who notes this, too). This means that they are outside the predicate-argument structure projected by the main clause verb. True, within such Embedded Language islands, thematic roles are assigned (e.g. in the PP, *outside the gate, outside* assigns the role of Goal to *gate*) and morphological realization patterns are projected. But these features just serve to differentiate islands structurally from singly occurring insertions.

Second, because their structure is often very formulaic, many Embedded Language islands can be subsumed under what Backus (1999*b*) called 'chunks' and now also calls 'composite expressions' or 'complex units' (personal communication). Consider the typical adjunct Embedded Language islands, e.g. *next week, pour les vacances* 'for a holiday/the holidays' or even an NP that may be part of the argument structure of the CP, such as *cost of living.* Further, a number of islands are true idioms or set collocations, making them even more formulaic (e.g. *once in a blue moon*). This raises the issue of the comparable level of activation of Embedded Language islands and mixed constituents, which are arguably more innovative.

In his 1999*b* article, Backus defines a chunk as a conventional unit, stating that 'reference to conventionality is crucial: a chunk must be current. . . . Novel combinations are put together on the spot, chunks are not' (p. 94). Backus's overall notion of chunks is influenced by Langacker (1987) and is in line with other work done under the rubric of Cognitive Linguistics. Backus's idea of what constitutes a chunk is very broad and his hypothesis, at least in this 1999*b* article is that 'every multimorphemic Embedded Language insertion is a chunk' (p. 97). His examples include everything from some phrasal verbs (*disgusted with*) to some full CPs (*it was a piece of cake*). Clearly, full CP chunks or complex units cannot be part of a bilingual CP, because they are CPs themselves, but the possible claim that all Embedded Language islands are such units is not discussed.

Backus's overall idea certainly has some appeal just because it does capture a generalization. Of course, the main problem with the notion of chunks or complex units is that there are no clear bounds on those combinations that are conventional and those that are not. Also, his ideas about how certain combinations are assembled are open to dispute. He suggests that 'if two or more Embedded Language morphemes are used in codeswitching and they form a conventional combination in the Embedded Language, then it would be too coincidental if the speaker had produced them by two or more independent switches, compositionally building up a composite expression' (p. 97). I can agree that idioms, like irregular plurals and irregular past tenses in English (and other languages), may well be contained in single lemmas and therefore are not compositionally assembled. However, it is hard to argue that an Embedded Language island such as *at the gate* is accessed as a unit when similar phrases such as *inside/outside the gate* exist. Of course producing such phrases compositionally would seem to involve a higher level of activation than producing them as whole units.

4.9.2. *Triggering*

A number of researchers favor an idea related to Backus's claims, triggering. The name most associated with triggering is Michael Clyne. In characterizing triggering, Clyne suggests that 'certain words may constitute an overlapping area between two languages which causes the speaker to lose his linguistic bearings' (1967: 84). In studying language use by Dutch and German immigrants in Australia, Clyne noted that a word in one language seems to trigger a switch to another language, especially if that word is phonologically similar to a counterpart in the second language or otherwise ambiguous. For example, he states that *in* is a common trigger word for these speakers. See example (30) where he would argue that *in* triggers more English. Others use the notion of triggering more broadly; for them, triggering occurs if the presence of any Embedded Language morpheme is followed by another Embedded Language morpheme or phrase.

(30) Dieses Bild ist in Melbourne, Collins Street, is it?
DEM/3S/F picture is in Melbourne, Collins Street, is it
'This picture is in Melbourne, Collins Street, is it?'

(Clyne 1967: 95)

Triggering is not something that the MLF model provides for, although neither does it disallow it. However, quantitative studies of the effects of supposed triggering on the segment that follows are lacking, and what evidence there is, goes against triggering as a very salient factor in codeswitching. For example, two codeswitching forms/core borrowings-in-progress from English to Shona are discussed in Myers-Scotton 1993*a* [1997]: 203. They are *but* (as a doublet/replacement for Shona *asi*) and *because* (as a doublet/replacement for Shona *nokuti*). A quantitative study showed that neither did English preceding these discourse markers nor English following them occur as often as—instead—Shona material surrounded the English forms. For example, *because* occurred sixteen times both preceded and followed by Shona elements; in only four instances was *because* preceded by English and it was followed by English only once. The distribution of *but* is similar. One could argue that these forms are not true tests of triggering, at least as Clyne envisioned it, because *because* and *but* are not cognates of their Shona counterparts and do not resemble them phonologically.

4.9.3. *Is adjacency a form of triggering?*

Muysken (2000: 62) offers a variation on the triggering argument. At least for the example he cites, he argues that if an Embedded Language verb stem occurs with

Matrix Language inflections and then the Embedded Language verb is followed by a complement in the Embedded Language, the verb stem and the following Embedded Language material form a unit. Thus, he argues that *-wash all the clothes* is a unit. (Note that Muysken cites only part of example (31).[9] Also, he cites the original incorrectly; the NP following *nikawash* is *all the clothing*, not *all the clothes*.)

(31) Ni-me-maliz-a ku-tengenez-a vi-tanda
1S-PERF-finish-FV INFIN-fix-FV CL8/PL-bed
Ni-ka-**wash** **all the clothing** na wewe bado maliz-a na **kitchen**
1S-CONSEC-wash all the clothing and you still/not finish-FV with kitchen
Ni nini u-na-fany-i-a huko?
[it] is what 2S-PROG-do-APPL-FV there
'I have finished making [the] beds and I washed all the clothing and you haven't yet finished with [the] kitchen. What are you doing there?

(Swahili/English; Myers-Scotton 1993*a* [1997]: 80)

Muysken introduces an Adjacency Principle that he states 'would predict *wash all the clothes* to be a single switch (e.g. an entire switched VP)' (2000: 62). His Adjacency Principle is the following:

If in a code-mixed sentence, two adjacent elements are drawn from the same language, an analysis is preferred in which at some level of representation (syntax, processing) these elements also form a unit. (2000: 61)

I argue against Muysken's specific interpretation of (31) and the principle, as well as the idea of triggering as a categorical rule, for the following reasons. First, a general argument. The notion of triggering is attractive, for the same reasons that the notion of chunking is attractive. However, the problem is that not all instances of singly occurring Embedded Language content morphemes are followed by further Embedded Language material. Therefore, when it does happen, what is the evidence that any 'triggering' is responsible? Or, to put it another way, if triggering is at work sometimes, why is it not at work all the time?

Second, I have a more specific argument against Muysken's Adjacency Principle and his view of the unity of an Embedded Language verb stem and the following Embedded Language NP (*-wash all the clothes/clothing*). Yes, at the prelinguistic conceptual level, *wash all the clothing* may well be a unit in the speaker's intentions. However, *at linguistic levels*, it is not a unit. (The same comment applies to Backus's ideas about chunks and their unity.) (In his principle, Muysken himself hedges on the level at which adjacent Embedded Language morphemes are a unit.) I argue that singly occurring Embedded Language forms

[9] Here, I have altered the morph-by-morph glosses (but not the actual text) in the original citation to make them more precise and to conform to the notation used elsewhere in this volume.

(e.g. *-wash*) are projected differently from the mental lexicon than are full maximal projections (e.g. NPs, such as *all the clothing*). The reasons are the following:

1. Singly occurring Embedded Language forms require less checking and undergo less processing at all levels of abstract grammatical structure than do Embedded Language phrases (phrases that will include grammatical as well as lexical elements). Above, I have argued that singly occurring nouns simply must be sufficiently congruent with a Matrix Language morpheme counterpart at the level of lexical-conceptual structure to occur. (If there is not a counterpart, then—under the Uniform Structure Principle—even this congruence is not necessary as long as the Embedded Language nouns follow the relevant language's procedures regarding potential Matrix Language predicate-argument structure and morphological realization patterns.) In the case of verbs, congruence may be more difficult to establish with a Matrix Language counterpart, since predicate-argument structure is at issue, too. However, for *-wash*, congruence with a Swahili counterpart (*-fua*) that projects the same arguments (Agent, Patient) seems likely. And, if there were not a verbal counterpart, as long as the Embedded Language verb projected arguments in line with the Matrix Language's permissible matching of thematic roles with syntactic positions (General Lexical Knowledge), the Embedded Language verb could be employed. However, it is certain that the speaker is not simply translating Swahili into English; in Swahili, *kufua nguo* 'to wash clothes' is a common collocation, but not one that parallels *wash all the clothing* in its phrase structure.

2. That is, both the issue of activation for a full maximal projection, such as *all the clothing* and its phrase structure are at issue. For such a constituent, the Embedded Language is activated to such a level that the frame-building procedures of the Matrix Language are inhibited and those of the Embedded Language take over. Further, the noun *clothing* does more than match its Swahili counterpart (*nguo*) at the lexical-conceptual level. True, it receives the same thematic role of Patient as *nguo* would receive (here assigned by the Matrix Language verb underlying the projection of its Embedded Language counterpart *wash*). However, the English noun projects morphological realization patterns that are not the same as its Swahili counterpart (i.e. the possibility of *all the clothing* as well as *all clothes* or *the clothes*, or even *the laundry*, etc.).

It is true that many Embedded Language islands are adjuncts. That is, Embedded Language islands, such as *all the clothing*, that are part of the argument structure of the CP are more unusual (*clothing* receives the thematic role of Patient from the verb). Still, such islands do occur, especially if there seems to be a pragmatic or grammatical motivation. In the next section, I discuss the relation in this particular case between these two types of motivations for *all the clothing*. Further, even Embedded Language islands that encode all the thematic structure of a CP are possible. Embedded Language islands that are full IPs are discussed in section 4.9.5.

Admittedly, the principle of Occam's Razor does support the notion behind Muysken's Adjacency Principle. That is, the principle offers the simplest explanation for a stretch of Embedded Language material in a Matrix Language frame. However, data on other inflected English verbs in the Swahili/English corpus definitely do not support the notion implied by the principle that once an Embedded Language verb is accessed, it will take Embedded Language complements. Only 13 per cent (12/91) of the finite English verbs in the Nairobi corpus were followed by English material, and four of these were phrasal verbs (e.g. *a-na-make sure* 'he/she makes sure') (Myers-Scotton 1993*a* [1997]: 88–9). Further, I have outlined an argument against the Adjacency Principle in this specific case: a full NP is accessed differently from a lone verb stem.

4.9.4. *Pragmatic motivations for islands*

I argue that many Embedded Language islands, and specifically *all the clothing* in this case, occur for the same reason that singly occurring Embedded Language elements occur. That is, there is a semantic or pragmatic mismatch between the two languages at the lexical-conceptual level and the speaker's intentions are better satisfied by producing the Embedded Language element or the Embedded Language island (cf. Myers-Scotton and Jake 1995). True, it is difficult to make a watertight argument on this point since we are not dealing with discrete features when semantics and pragmatics are concerned. Still, let us return to *all the clothing* and consider the compelling argument that can be made. The speaker is a woman who is annoyed with her house servant for having done so little work. She could have produced the closest Swahili equivalent of this island and said, *ni-ka-wash nguo zote* (*nguo zote* = 'clothes all' = 'and I washed all clothes'). Instead, producing *all the clothing* places the focus on the quantifier, and the *all the X* phrase adds definiteness in ways that the Swahili counterpart cannot. Thus, my argument is that the speaker did not continue in English beyond *ni-ka-wash* simply because of a linguistic preference for staying in the same language. Instead, she wanted to emphasize the extent of what she had done.

For another example of an Embedded Language island that carries a different connotation from what its Matrix Language counterpart would, note *from a good family* in (32). The speakers are university personnel who know English well. In English, *good family* in this phrase has the connotation of high social status of long standing; the context in which (32) occurs (*from a good family* is contrasted with *from a poor family*) indicates a near Acholi equivalent has more the meaning of 'wealthy' and not necessarily a good standing. That is, an argument can be made that the pragmatic force of the two expressions is different.

(32) I-ngeyo en pe tye **from a good family** tutwal
2s-know 3s NEG COP from a good family really
'You know she is not really from a good family.'

(Acholi/English; Myers-Scotton and Bernsten 1995 corpus)

4.9.5. *Grammatical motivations for islands*

Embedded Language islands can also occur because of structural mismatches, and in some data sets they are as frequent as pragmatically motived islands, if not more so. There can be structural mismatches at the abstract level (the case with the large Embedded Language islands in the Palestinian Arabic/English corpus discussed shortly) or at the surface phrase level. Example (33) illustrates a mismatch that is largely at the phrase-structure level. The speaker apparently wanted to use the English verb *bring up*. Whether there is an exact Spanish semantic equivalent is not so much the issue as the fact that, with a pronoun as object, this English construction positions the object between the main verb and its satellite. There is no structural equivalent in Spanish; object clitics cannot break up a phrasal verb.

(33) no va-n a **bring it up**
no go-3PL to bring it up
'They are not going to bring it up'

(Spanish/English; Pfaff 1979: 296, cited in Myers-Scotton and Jake 1995)

Structural motivations at the abstract level can promote even larger Embedded Language islands. In Jake and Myers-Scotton (1997*a*) and Myers-Scotton and Jake (2001), Jake and I argue that many Embedded Language islands that are full IPs occur in Palestinian Arabic/English codeswitching. In the corpus studied, two types of Embedded Language islands—those with English finite verbs or with English Control verbs—account for 79 per cent (86/109) of English verbs in the corpus. Further, these large Embedded Language islands were not marked structures for the corpus. Instead, they constitute 21.3 per cent (86/403) of the English constituents; only singly occurring nouns were more frequent.

Table 4.2 illustrates one such Embedded Language island and there are two more in example (34). The first is *we get in the mood* in the IP in the CP headed by the inflected subordinating conjunction *liʔannu* 'because' in complementizer position. The second is *it is difficult* following *bas* 'but'.

(34) hunak binikhi aktar **liʔannu** **we get in the mood**
1P/IMP/speak more because/1P we get in the mood
bas hooni **it is difficult**
but here it is difficult
'There we speak more because we get in the mood but here it is difficult.'

(Arabic/English; Okasha 1996 corpus, cited Jake and Myers-Scotton 1997*a*: 30)

In brief, the argument is that Arabic verbs do not exist as verbs until they are specified as perfect/imperfect at the lemma level. In contrast, English verbs are only stems at this level. Therefore, the Arabic frame does not accept English verbs in slots to receive inflection because they do not meet the tense/aspect specifications

Table 4.2. Occurrence of English elements in Palestinian Arabic/English codeswitching corpus: lack of cross-linguistic congruence at the lemma level (mental lexicon) in Aspect/Tense in verbs results in English islands (at the IP level), not mixed constituents

Category	Number	%
N	139	34.5
IP islands(projection of Infl)	**86**	**21.3**
Adj	42	10.4
NP	39	9.7
*All other categories**	*97*	*24.1*
Total	403	100.0

*each category is <6% (range is 5.7%–.2%)

Example of IP Embedded Language Island (**you feel like a queen**)

ʔana ʕindi **job security** wa ma feeš **pressure** xaaliaħ.
I with/1S job security and NEG exist/NEG pressure at.all
Kwanik el-waħeeda [$_{CP}$ **hina** [$_{IP}$ **you feel like a queen**]]
GER/be/2F the-one here you feel like a queen
'I have job security and no pressure at all; being the only one here, you feel like a queen.'

Palestinian Arabic/English Okasha Generation I corpus: adapted from Jake and Myers-Scotton 1997*a*, Myers-Scotton and Jake 2001, Jake and Myers-Scotton 2001

that a well-formed Arabic verb exhibits at this level. (Of course English verbs can make this specification, but tense/aspect is realized on English verbs only at the level of the Formulator.) When the English verb matches the speaker's intentions better than an Arabic verb, the Arabic frame still blocks the English verb for the slot specified for an Arabic verb. Therefore, the only way to access an English verb is in an Embedded Language island, with all the elements under Infl also from the Embedded Language. Such islands also occur in other corpora with other varieties of Arabic as the Matrix Language and other languages as the Embedded Language (cf. Nortier 1990: 166); however, when French is the Embedded Language, at least some French verbs do receive Arabic inflections in some corpora from North Africa.

Another structural motivation for Embedded Language islands is related to the speaker's desire to use an Embedded Language quantifier. Note that a quantifier occurs initially in *all the clothing.* I suggested in the 1993 *Duelling Languages* that if an Embedded Language quantifier is selected, the speaker often continues in the Embedded Language (i.e. producing an island). Recent quantitative research supports the prediction that many Embedded Language islands are headed by quantifiers, and in some data sets they are numerically dominant among Embedded Language islands (Jake and Myers-Scotton 2001).

Why should one expect accessing Embedded Language quantifiers to trigger islands? Yes, quantifiers are system morphemes under the MLF, but only early system morphemes, not the late system morphemes specified under the System Morpheme Principle. However, under the Uniform Structure Principle, the preferred option is to maintain uniform structure. This means that Matrix Language forms for all structural features of the frame are preferred. However, the principle also can be interpreted as meaning that once an Embedded Language system morpheme is accessed (generally for pragmatic reasons), the constituent is better completed as an Embedded Language island because an island also involves uniformity.

4.9.6. *Embedded Language islands and proficiency*

The relative presence of Embedded Language islands seems to tell us two different contradictory conclusions about the proficiency of the speakers depending on the community:

1. When the overall prevailing pattern includes many bilingual CPs (with many mixed constituents), singly occurring forms (typically nouns) prevail. If speakers employ relatively many Embedded Language islands, they seem to be among the more proficient speakers. That is, it seems that higher language proficiency in the Embedded Language is necessary to feel at home producing islands. Quantitative evidence from a study in an urban township of multilingual Black South Africans supports this explanation (Finlayson, Calteaux, and Myers-Scotton 1998). English was typically an Embedded Language in this study, with either Zulu or Sotho as the Matrix Language. Although speaker samples were small (N = 8 in each of two samples), the differences in number of Embedded Language islands is significant. The groups differed in terms of education level and presumably therefore differed in English proficiency.

   The differences between the two groups regarding the composition of their bilingual CPs was significant (X^2 = 17.87 (sig. at 0.001)). The more educated group (at least ten years of schooling) produced a total of eighty bilingual CPs. Of these CPs, 40 per cent (32) included Embedded Language islands. The less educated group (secondary school or less) produced 117 bilingual CPs, but only 14 per cent (16) included Embedded Language islands. That is, although the less educated group produced more bilingual constituents, their CPs were much more often bilingual on the basis of including singly occurring English lexemes.

   Overall statistics on the two groups mask this difference and are not significant. For example, just looking at the number of bilingual CPs across groups is not significant. Of all the CPs of the more educated group 44 per cent (49/112) were bilingual, while 51 per cent (75/149) of all the CPs in the less educated group were bilingual. Other measures that also were not significant included frequency of codeswitching constituents per the total number of CPs in the conversation.

2. However, there is also evidence that when speakers are nearly equally at home in both languages, almost ironically, Embedded Language islands lose their importance. Instead, switching *between* CPs becomes very frequent as well as switching between sentences, which, of course, may include more than one CP. This is the case with a younger generation of Turkish immigrants in the Netherlands who speak Turkish, but who also have become very proficient in Dutch (Backus 1996: 190). Backus's conclusions about differences in codeswitching patterns among Turkish/Dutch speakers are especially valuable because they are based on an analysis of quantitative data. Interestingly, he argues that 'there is no predominately EL islands stage' (1996: 334). That is, as bilinguals reach more and more proficiency in the Embedded Language, they do produce more islands, but at some point islands lose their numerical importance. What happens is that bilingual CPs in general, whether they include islands or singly occurring Embedded Language content morphemes, lose out to monolingual CPs and switching between sentences. As Backus puts it, 'At some point, intersentential CS [codeswitching] takes over, and the frequency of EL [Embedded Language] islands goes down again, along with that of intrasentential CS in general' (1996: 334). I will return to such findings in the concluding chapter when I argue again for the push to uniformity within a syntactic unit, if not within a conversation.

Further, there is another reason not to expect increased bilingual proficiency to result in more Embedded Language islands. One must not forget that from a psycholinguistic standpoint, producing mixed constituents with only singly occurring Embedded Language forms should cause less stress. Bear in mind that the activation level of the Embedded Language must be raised considerably to project Embedded Language islands and inhibit the frame-building procedures of the Matrix Language. Not just content morphemes are at issue, but the Embedded Language frame and its system morphemes. That is, bilinguals can remain bilingual and switch between languages, even within conversations, but the architecture of language may well resist meaningful variation that depends on having more than one variety contributing structure within a single CP frame.

4.9.7. *Internal Embedded Language islands*

Of course some islands require much less grammatical proficiency than others. For example, Embedded Language nouns plus a plural affix are probably the Embedded Language islands requiring the least proficiency in the Embedded Language (cf. examples in almost every codeswitching corpus such as *ghost-s* in the Swahili/English corpus in Myers-Scotton (1993*a* [1997], or *employer-s* in Hlavac (2000: 404)). (I note that Boumans (1998) specifically refers to nouns and their plurals as Embedded Language islands, and I agree. In the earlier expositions of the MLF model, they were not discussed one way or the other.) In many data sets, these plural nouns are what I refer to as internal Embedded Language islands. That is, the N + plural is part of a larger constituent in which they constitute a sister to a Matrix Language element under N-bar (in X-bar theory), with the entire constituent projected under NP (or DP in the Minimalist Program). For example, see (35) from Finnish/English codeswitching (*täs-step-s* and *ne step-s*), (36) from Brussels Dutch/French *ne mauvais point*, and (37) from Arabic/Dutch codeswitching (*duk artikel-en*).

(35)

tässon	st-	täs- **step-s**	tosson	ne **step-s**
here are	(false start)	here (false start) step-PL	over there	DET step-PL

'Here are (the) st- here- steps over there are the steps.'
(American Finnish/English; Halmari 1997: 27)

(36)

Ik had	altijd	ne	**mauvais point**
1s had	always	INDEF ART	low/M point

'I always had low marks.'

(Brussels Dutch/French; Treffers-Daller 1994: 163)

(37)

duk	**artikel-en**	ila	bġi-ti	t-teržem-hŭm
DEM/PL	article-PL	of	want-2S	2-translate-3PL

is echt moeilijk
is really difficult
'Those articles, if you want to translate them, that's really difficult.'

(Moroccan Arabic/Dutch; Boumans 1998: 37)

I argue these internal Embedded Language islands (such as *artikel-en* in (37)) take the form because they match a feature (plurality here) that is part of the abstract NP heading the maximal projection that is activated to satisfy the speaker's intentions. In this case, the speaker wishes to use the Dutch noun and wishes to express plurality. Inflecting a Dutch noun with Arabic procedures to encode plurality can present a problem, given that plurality in Arabic is most commonly conveyed by ablaut procedures and insertion of vowels, at least in the relevant Arabic variety. Possibly because of this incongruity with Dutch, the compromise strategy is to project the Dutch plural suffix with the Dutch noun. The speaker also wishes to convey the deictic information encoded in an Arabic demonstrative. The result is an internal Embedded Language island (*artikulen* in the larger constituent *duk artikulen*). At the same time, plurality must appear on those elements for which plural agreement is stipulated by rule in Arabic. This means that the demonstrative must be plural. In addition, the object suffix on the verb must be plural to reflect the speaker's intentions.

In summary, the speaker's intentions call for a plural complement of the verb 'translate'. The plural suffix on the verb satisfies those intentions. *Duk artikel-en* 'those articles' appears as a topicalized NP with the Dutch noun + plural as an internal Embedded Language island in the NP. The NP itself is under Matrix Language control. At the conceptual level, the Dutch plural satisfies the speaker's intentions; at the phrase structure level, it also satisfies the frame's specifications for a noun to occur in the NP.

Boumans (1998: 36) goes a step further and views such 'EL plural nouns [as functioning] as ML plurals'. He argues that 'these EL plurals, whether they occur as EL islands or within mixed constituents, typically trigger agreement where appropriate according to the ML grammar'. I cannot agree. The notion of plural satisfies the speaker's intentions. The abstract NP under Matrix Language control maps these intentions onto phrase structure. That is, the abstract NP projects plural in the right places, not the actual Dutch noun in the slot for a plural noun. (This claim is similar to the Head Feature Convention of GPSG that was discussed in section 4.4.2 and then in section 4.5.1 especially in relation to alien nouns in Bantu frames.) My reasons for this claim are two related points. First, the structure of the CP outside of the Dutch plural follows Arabic (Matrix Language), not Dutch (Embedded Language) well-formedness requirements.[10]

Additional evidence on the limited status of plural Embedded Language forms in Matrix Language frames comes from Simango (2000). He shows that plural Embedded Language forms (*slippers* in (38) and *apples* in (39)) trigger singular agreements. In (38), *yako* 'yours' is a singular form from class 9 and in (39) *apples* is modified by the singular form *imodzi* 'one' from class 9 as well. That is, even though the English nouns are plural in form, Simango remarks, 'This evidence supports the claim that it is the Chicheŵa system morphemes that are active in mixed constituents consisting of Chicheŵa and English forms' (p. 495).[11]

(38) Timothy, ta-dz-a tend-a **slipper-s** y-ako
IMPER-come-FV get-FV slipper-PL CL9-your
'Timothy, come get your slipper.'

(Chicheŵa/English codeswitching; Simango 2000: 494)

(39) Ngoni, ta-mu-send-er-a mw-ana **apple-s** i-modzi
N. IMPER-OBJ/3S-peel-APPL-FV cl1-child apple-PL CL9-one
'Ngoni, peel one apple for the child.'

(Chicheŵa/English codeswitching; Simango 2000: 494)

A second argument against the notion that Embedded Language plurals can control agreement is this: if the Dutch noun controlled the co-indexing of the

[10] Boumans also interprets the Embedded Language plural morpheme as the type of system morpheme that would challenge the System Morpheme Principle; however, it is not a late outsider system morpheme, but an early system morpheme.

[11] The alert observer may remember that in Swahili/English codeswitching, an English noun marked with an English plural, but no Swahili noun prefix, often takes modifiers in Swahili class 10, a plural class. That is, a noun such as *slippers* is treated as a plural in Swahili. However, in Swahili, class 10 has a zero allomorph as one of the realizations of the class 10 prefix and therefore the English nouns qualify as class 10 nouns with no overt Swahili prefix. In contrast, the Chicheŵa class prefixes for classes 6 or 10 (possible plural matches for *slippers* and *apples* as singular nouns) are overt. In fact, Simango remarks in order for these nouns to be plurals, they would have to receive Chicheŵa *ma-* (class 6).

object suffix with the noun, this would mean that Embedded Language islands can project Matrix Language morphological realization patterns. Evidence in this and other bilingual constructions does not support this notion. For instance, in an Arabic frame, if the agreement suffix in question were for a singular noun, it would reflect a gender-feature value and this would be the value of the Matrix Language, not the Embedded Language (Arabic singular nouns are feminine and masculine, not neuter and feminine as in Dutch).

In other data sets, many of those Embedded Language islands that are not adverbial phrase adjuncts are internal Embedded Language islands—perhaps many more than has been recognized. That they are internal Embedded Language islands implies more Matrix Language control and less Embedded Language independence. For example, *lauw water* in (40) is such an island, occurring in a PP with the Turkish postposition as its case marker. In line with my argument above, I claim that the entire PP is under the control of the Matrix Language. (I made a similar argument for ML control of an NP in section 4.9 for (29) from Chicheŵa/English; there, the internal EL island is [*very expensive costume*] and the larger frame is [∅ + *very expensive costume*].) In (40), the Dutch NP has its own word order, but it is congruent enough with a Matrix Language counterpart NP at the level of lexical-conceptual structure to be able to appear in this PP. The postposition itself is assigned by the Turkish verb. Note that Turkish, not Dutch, projects placement of the overall structure (left-branching in relation to the verb), additional evidence that when Embedded Language islands are projected, the Matrix Language is not entirely inhibited.

(40) . . . ondan sonra [**lauw water**'nan] yıkayınca
. . . then early lukewarm water-with wash/when
'Before I wash it with lukewarm water'

(Turkish/Dutch; Backus 1992: 112)

4.9.8. *Summary on Embedded Language islands*

In summary, Embedded Language islands are clear evidence that the Embedded Language is 'on' to some extent in the bilingual CP. However, the type of constituents that occur in Embedded Language islands (largely formulaic expressions that are often adjuncts or internal Embedded Language islands under an abstract Matrix Language larger phrasal category) indicates the level of activation is not the same as that of the Matrix Language when the major constituents of the clause are constructed. In addition, when there is a conflict in word order between the two languages, placement of Embedded Language islands always follows Matrix Language requirements. However, the actual degree of difference in levels of activation across Embedded Language islands of different types compared with mixed constituents is a subject for testing by psycholinguists.

Motivations for Embedded Language islands vary. In earlier work, I indicated that sociopragmatic motivations provide explanations for why most Embedded Language islands occur. Now I am less sure that this is the only reason for islands; more and more islands seem to depend on structural (grammatical) constraints. These may well be in addition to the sociopragmatic motivations, but they are definitely identifiable. Still, saying something in the Embedded Language often conveys a desired connotation—or simply has more cachet. Another argument is that Embedded Language islands are easier in some psycholinguistic sense (rather than just accessing a singly occurring element, access a full collocation or a frequently occurring complex unit).

4.10. Borrowing vs. codeswitching

A discussion that will not go away concerns the issue of distinguishing borrowing from codeswitching. The list of researchers who treat singly occurring Embedded Language forms as codeswitching forms along with Embedded Language islands is long (e.g. Backus 1996, Halmari 1997, Boumans 1998, Hlavac 2000, Türker 2000, *inter alia*). Yet, others continue to devise models that treat only full constituents or full clauses as codeswitching material. They are discussed briefly below.

Elsewhere I have argued that, from a synchronic point of view, there is no need to make the borrowing vs. codeswitching distinction (Myers-Scotton 1993*a* [1997]: Chapter 6). My reasoning is twofold. First, a single model (the MLF model) can cover all singly occurring elements from the Embedded Language in the Matrix Language frame; that is, both established borrowings and singly occurring codeswitching forms largely are integrated into the morphosyntactic frame of the recipient or Matrix Language. With no evidence to the contrary, the same processes seem to be involved. (The only sense in which there is a serious difference between singly occurring codeswitching forms and established loans is in regard to their status in the mental lexicon. Presumably, lemmas underlying codeswitching forms are only tagged for the Embedded Language, while borrowed forms have lemmas tagged for *both* the donor and the recipient language, at least in the mental lexicon of bilinguals in those languages.) Second, the same model can cover phrase-level stretches of Embedded Language material, Embedded Language islands. The bottom line is that a model that can cover all Embedded Language forms within the bilingual CP arguably is superior to one that cannot.

There are many similarities between the two types of Embedded Language structures that are covered under the MLF model. True, I have argued in the previous section that singly occurring codeswitching forms and Embedded Language islands may well involve different activations (i.e. islands generally require activation involving all three levels of abstract grammatical structure and singly occurring codeswitching forms—especially nouns—generally require only activation at the level of lexical-conceptual structure). However, one should not overlook their major similarity. This is that motivation to access any type of Embedded

Language material at all has a socio-psychological basis. Embedded Language forms appear because, at a variety of possible levels, they convey a different semantic/pragmatic interpretation than their putative Matrix Language counterparts (cf. Myers-Scotton 1993*c*). For this reason alone, simply achieving descriptive adequacy in codeswitching research means proposing a model that can explain the social motivations for both singly occurring forms and Embedded Language islands. In addition, as I have argued in earlier sections, no Embedded Language material is accessed in a bilingual CP without some interaction between the Matrix Language and the Embedded Language; although Matrix Language features prevail, there is congruence checking between the two grammars at the abstract level of the mental lexicon. This checking occurs for both singly occurring forms and islands.

4.10.1. *Researchers who differentiate codeswitching and borrowing*

Those researchers who consider most (or all) singly occurring Embedded Language forms as borrowings and who therefore do not attempt to explain them in their codeswitching models vary considerably in their theoretical orientations. On one side stand Poplack and her associates with an extensive presence in the literature dating from Poplack (1980) or even earlier. Most recently, they have concentrated their efforts to argue that singly occurring Embedded Language forms are nonce borrowings, not codeswitching forms (e.g Poplack and Meechan 1998). Employing the methodology of the Labovian variationist tradition, they devote a good deal of energy to demonstrating that these Embedded Language forms show similar levels of morphosyntactic integration to that of native forms when they appear in the same native frame. On this basis, they state that these alien forms are nonce borrowings.

Here is a sampling of some of the ways that Poplack and Meechan (1998) characterize their approach to singly occurring Embedded Language forms. First, they argue that 'codeswitching and borrowing differ as *processes*' (p. 129). They see codeswitching as involving the alternation of the procedures of one language with those of another. Borrowing does not involve this alternation—although it is not clear how borrowing would be accomplished under this view. That this is their view of codeswitching becomes clear when they write, 'Since codeswitching implies *alternation* between two (or more) language systems, (single word) codeswitches should show little or no integration into another language' (p. 129). That is, not only is there alternation in codeswitching, but it results in compartmentalization of the languages involved in any resulting bilingual CPs. They go on to argue that since the singly occurring forms in question do show integration, they cannot be codeswitching forms. That is, they seem to accept as codeswitching only what I call Embedded Language islands—or, and this is a huge difference in our models—even full monolingual CPs in the same sentence. What I call mixed constituents do not qualify as codeswitching for them. (I argue, of course, that monolingual CPs are not of the same order of theoretical interest as bilingual CPs if the object of study is how two grammars divide the labor of constructing a bilingual clause.) Second, applying their premises to specific data sets with English elements, they state that 'if according to some diagnostic criteria, lone English-origin nouns are observed to pattern like their counterparts in the (unmixed) recipient language . . . we conclude that only the grammar of the recipient language is operating, that is, that they [English-origin nouns] were borrowed' (p. 131). On the same page, they say, 'If the contentious lone English-origin nouns pattern like attested loanwords, this can be taken as further confirmation that 1) the former are borrowings, if only for the *nonce* . . . and 2) nonce borrowings and dictionary-attested loanwords are not distinct linguistically' (p. 131).

For a specific example of this approach, consider the analysis by Budzhak-Jones (1998) of a Ukrainian/English corpus. Based on an item-and-arrangement type analysis, she concludes that English nouns are integrated into the Ukrainian frame in various ways. Among the points she makes are the following: (i) 'English-origin nouns are assigned gender in exactly the same way as it is assigned to their Ukrainian counterparts' (p. 177); (ii) 'lone English-origin nouns with overt Ukrainian morphology participate in all grammatical operations required by Ukrainian grammar in precisely the same way as Ukraininan nouns' (p. 179); and (iii) the evidence shows 'that they are borrowed . . . refuting hypothesis III, that they are codeswitched' (p. 179).

Of course, I argue that these *same* forms are codeswitching forms in mixed constituents. My prime evidence is the extent to which they conform to the Matrix Language frame, the same evidence that Poplack *et al.* interpret differently. That is, we are both in agreement that there are bilingual CPs framed by a Matrix Language and that lone English nouns can appear in these frames with Matrix Language morphosyntactic integration. We are also in agreement that the codeswitching/nonce borrowing and attested loan words are not distinct linguistically.

Where we are *not* in agreement is in recognition of the role of abstract grammatical structure in codeswitching. My claim, of course, is that when mixed constituents are accessed, there is necessarily interaction of the two grammars at an abstract level, even while the Matrix Language is more activated than the Embedded Language. It is this interaction that differentiates codeswitching from monolingual data. Although the same abstract procedures may result in (i) monolingual Ukrainian discourse and (ii) discourse with a Ukrainian frame but English insertions, the two outcomes do not have the same history. The form of the bilingual outcome depends on both universal principles for bilingual clauses (e.g. one language dominates in the grammatical frame) and restrictions that depend on congruence/incongruence regarding the typological characteristics of the participating languages.

As I do here, Jake and I have argued in many publications that this interaction takes the form of congruence checking. For example, as noted in section 4.9.5, in order to explain why English IP Embedded Language islands are very prevalent in Palestinian Arabic/English codeswitching, one must accept the premise that English verbs are somehow blocked by the Arabic frame. What is this blocking, if not some level of activation for both languages? Further evidence is what happens in other language contact phenomena that include convergence, a subject for the next chapter. Convergence is interaction between the two grammars par excellence. A systematic, precise way to consider convergence is as a splitting and recombining of abstract grammatical structures. Such a process necessarily means that the grammars of both languages must be 'on' even though, as in classic codeswitching, one language is the major source of the Matrix Language frame.

How Meechan and Poplack (1995) decide that French adjectives in a Fongbe frame must be codeswitching forms is another indication that Poplack and her associates do not see that both languages can be activated at the same time in a bilingual CP. French adjectives are codeswitching forms for them just because they have not shed their French indications of number and gender. For them, this means such adjectives are based only on French activation. They state that the lone French-origin adjectives in otherwise Fongbe contexts pattern 'with French structures and not Fongbe ones' (p. 187). Yet, Fongbe sets the grammatical frame, not French. What *is* French is the fact that these adjectives show French number and gender. (See *importante* in (17) repeated here as (41), agreeing with *langue* as feminine.) However, there is no base form of the French adjective; all adjectival forms show number and gender. So that there is French inflection is hardly an argument that the presence of these adjectives in a Fongbe frame has nothing to do with Fongbe. (Fongbe is an isolating language with little or no inflection with which to mark adjectives, so there are no Fongbe affixes to expect on these French adjectives.) I agree that the French adjectives are codeswitching forms, but not for the reasons Meechan and Poplack give. Their argument seems to be that they are codeswitching forms because they are not integrated into Fongbe. Yet, the French adjectives can take no other form than they do, and the *dò* construction clearly is a Fongbe compromise strategy—designed just to allow Embedded Language elements to appear in Matrix Language frames. I would argue that the stimulus to activate this compromise strategy (this *dò* construction) is the mismatch between how French and Fongbe encode attributive features. In order for this mismatch to be recognized, French has to be activated at some abstract level, *but activated along with Fongbe.* The same type of checking (but for verbs, not adjectival elements) results in 'do' verb constructions in other language pairs. Thus, both languages are 'on' to some degree at the abstract level where checking takes place.

(41) **Donc** ɔ nyɛ mɔ dɔ **que langue** ɔ e dò **importante**
so TOP I see tell that language DEF she be important
'So, me I see that language is important.'

(Fongbe/French; Meechan and Poplack 1995: 187)

Poplack and her associates have an ally in Muysken, who does not distinguish codeswitching and borrowing based on surface distributions, but rather on formal, surface characteristics. In Muysken (2000: 69 ff.), he states that 'code-mixing can be viewed as involving words with different languages indexes inserted into a phrase structure for a clause C . . . while lexical borrowing may be seen as involving formatives inserted into an alien word structure' (p. 75). Elsewhere he states that 'code-mixing has the ordinary, supra-lexical, productive properties of syntax' (p. 72). He also states that 'insertion is constituent-internal, alternation is phrase- or clause-peripheral' (p. 75).

Muysken is correct in making this superficial distinction between singly occurring Embedded Language forms and full Embedded Language constituents (Embedded Language islands). I can hardly disagree that codeswitching phrases (Embedded Language islands) only result when the language's own phrase structure procedures are activated; that is, they have productive properties. In contrast, singly occurring Embedded Language forms are inserted in phrase structures that are not their own. Yet, he ignores the fact that both types of Embedded Language material occur *in the same frame, the Matrix Language frame.*

Muysken emphasizes their surface level differences. Instead, the 'right' difference to consider is this: are the two types of insertions into the bilingual CP very different at a more abstract level? I argue they are not—because the move from speaker's intentions to language-specific lemmas (that in turn will activate phrase-structure procedures) is very similar for both singly occurring forms and full phrases. I have already argued that one common type of Embedded Language phrase, an internal Embedded Language island, is under the control of a larger Matrix Language phrasal category, making them even less different from singly occurring Embedded Language forms. In addition, the fact many adjunct Embedded Language islands are formulaic raises questions about just what type of Embedded Language activation is necessary to activate them (i.e. are they accessed as units?).

However, as I have already argued in this section, there is a more important similarity between the two types of Embedded Language material: whether either singly occurring forms or Embedded Language islands are accessed at all requires cross-linguistic congruence checking at an abstract level. And this, in turn, requires some activation of both languages. For me, this dual activation is a kernel feature of codeswitching.

4.10.2. *Approaches under government and binding*

More recent arrivals on the borrowing vs. codeswitching scene are researchers within the Chomskyan tradition. In general, they also imply that codeswitching represents bilingual speech, but with one language activated at a time. Their goal is to explain constraints on phrasal switching under syntactic models designed to explain monolingual data (Woolford 1983, DiSciullo, Muysken, and Singh 1986, Belazi, Rubin, and Toribio 1994, Toribio and Rubin 1996, Halmari 1997, MacSwan 1999, *inter alia*). What is relevant to this section is that, like Poplack, these researchers do not consider (most) singly occurring Embedded Language forms as codeswitching material. That is, their models are devised to treat only phrasal constituents.

Even so, there are many counterexamples to proposals based on a GB framework. For example, the claim of DiSciullo *et al.* that the lexical governor and a governed maximal projection must be in the same language does not hold. For example, on the basis of Panjabi/English data, Romaine (1989) argues that switching between V and its NP predicate is possible. I also cite counterexamples in Myers-Scotton 1993*a* [1997]: 43–4.

Belazi, Rubin, and Toribio propose a Functional Head Constraint: 'The language feature of the complement f-selected by a functional head, like all other relevant features, must match the corresponding feature of that functional head' (1994: 228). They rule out singly occurring forms as borrowed forms and therefore such mixed NPs as occur frequently in data sets (e.g. Spanish/English *la potato*). Even so, the constraint runs into trouble in a number of instances and most notably in the occurrence of dependent clauses with a complementizer head from one language and the IP from another language. Further, in an experiment involving Spanish/English bilinguals Dussias (1997) demonstrated that reading-time data do not support the constraint.[12] One of her conclusions is that 'items in which a switch occurred between a functional head and its complement took significantly less time to read than items in which the switch occurred at the functional head [i.e. before the head]' (pp. 144–5).

4.10.3. *A Minimalist Program approach*

More recently, the Minimalist Program model (Chomsky 1995) has been employed in codeswitching research. One of the model's basic tenets is 'Mismatch of features cancels the derivation' (Chomsky 1995: 309). He goes on to say, 'If the optimal derivation creates a mismatch, we are not permitted to pursue a nonoptimal alternative' (p. 309). Applying the model to monolingual data may be possible, but such provisions create a fatal problem for applying the model to codeswitching. The problem is that feature mismatches (across languages) in codeswitching do not invariably lead to unacceptable structures. Instead, in most cases, codeswitching is still possible and any mismatch is resolved in favor of the Matrix Language.

MacSwan (1999, 2000) is most prominently associated with employing the

[12] Note that Dussias's results (that response time is shorter for a Matrix Language complementizer followed by an Embedded Language IP than for a switch in mid-sentence of the entire CP to the Embedded Language) support both the MLF model and Poplack's views. Under the MLF model, one assumes less activation for singly occurring forms than for mid-sentence switches consisting of a full CP. Therefore, response time is predicted to be shorter for the combination of a Matrix Language complementizer and an Embedded Language IP than for a switch to a full Embedded Language CP. Poplack might view the complementizer as a nonce borrowing and the entire CP as a single unit. Thus, in her approach, response time would not be adversely affected by the fact the complementizer and the IP are in different languages.

Minimalist Program model to explain phrasal codeswitching. Like most minimalist approaches, his model rules out singly occurring lexemes as codeswitching (from the Embedded Language under the MLF model). He does this in two ways. First, any Embedded Language form that is inflected with Matrix Language morphemes is simply considered a borrowing. Second, any Embedded Language form without Matrix Language inflections is a borrowing if its grammatical features (such as *phi*-features within DP/NP and agreement on Infl/TP) differ from those of the monolingual frame of the other language. For example, English nouns in a Spanish frame would be borrowings because they do not match the gender feature of Spanish. These two provisions leave a minimalist approach with little to account for since the most frequent Embedded Language forms in codeswitching are nouns and many Embedded Language forms are inflected with Matrix Language morphemes.

MacSwan goes into some detail to reject Embedded Language forms with Matrix Language inflections. His argument is encapsulated in a PF Disjunction Theorem. The argument is that 'the PF component consists of rules or constraints that must be (partially) ordered/ranked with respect to each other, and these orders can vary cross-linguistically' (1999: 45). He next states his assumption that 'phonological systems cannot be mixed' and for this reason 'codeswitching at PF generates "unpronounceable" elements which violate FI [full interpretation]' (p. 45). He concludes that 'codeswitching below X^0 is not permitted' (p. 45). Of course this line of assumptions and arguments means that any switches involving bound morphemes from the Matrix Language (affixes) in the same word as an Embedded Language content morpheme are not permitted, making the PF Disjunction Theorem very reminiscent of Poplack's Free Morpheme Constraint (1980), which also disallows intra-word switches.

MacSwan then argues when there are alien singly occurring forms in a seemingly bilingual constituent, the constituent is simply monolingual, not bilingual. That is, these alien forms are borrowings. One can see why MacSwan would like to rule out these forms because he can then say that any features these forms have that are different from those of the base language are not relevant to the derivation. Thus, any cross-linguistic feature mismatches are irrelevant and this explains why a derivation does not crash.

The major problem with the PF Disjunction Theorem is that MacSwan's approach ignores empirical evidence about the realization of Embedded Language forms in Matrix Language frames. His claim that 'phonological systems cannot be mixed' (p. 45) does not stand up to scrutiny; the phonetics of Embedded Language singly occurring forms belies this claim. In fact, a feature distinguishing codeswitching forms from the base language is that they generally retain their Embedded Language phonology—even while they are morphosyntactically integrated into the base language. For example, the phonemic oppositions of Hungarian vowels are not observed by English vowels in singly occurring English forms in Hungarian/English codeswitching (Bolonyai 1999). And in Gross

(2000*a*), while bilingual speakers of German living for years in the United States may inflect an English past participle with a German past participle prefix (*ge-*), the German rule for word-final obstruent devoicing does not apply to the form (e.g. *ge-cured*). English verb stems in Swahili/English codeswitching retain English phonetics and do not follow Swahili CVCV phonotactics (e.g. for *ni-me-suggest* 'I have suggested', the first vowel in *suggest* is a schwa [ə], not a [u], and the final element is a consonant cluster, not a vowel). Further, what experimental evidence there is supports the view that Embedded Language singly occurring forms retain their phonology (cf. Grosjean and Miller 1994 on voice-onset time duration for word-initial consonants in English with French as the 'host' language). For my approach to how Minimalism can combine with the Matrix Language construct to explain distributions in codeswitching data, see Jake, Myers-Scotton, and Gross (2002).

4.10.4. *A Tree Adjacency Grammar model*

Although the Tree Adjacency Grammar (TAG) model (Mahootian 1993, Mahootian and Santorini 1996) is also within the generative syntax tradition, it takes a somewhat different approach to codeswitching. It relies on general principles of phrase structure rather than on constraints specific to codeswitching. The basic premise is that heads impose their syntactic requirements on their complements. Although Mahootian's model resembles the MLF model in some ways, it differs in important details. For example, it does not see a need for the Matrix Language – Embedded Language distinction (however, the initial corpus motivating the model is Persian/English data in which Persian is the putative Matrix Language in all clauses). The Mahootian model considers both lexical and functional elements as heads, whether lexical or functional (therefore including determiners, complementizers, adpositions, case-marking morphemes, and inflection elements as potential heads). (Under the MLF model, only lexical elements (= content morphemes) are heads.) Mahootian's model does assume that both languages involved in codeswitching are 'on'; however, the basis of this premise is the assumption that syntactic structure is projected from a single lexicon and that bilingual speakers have access to the lexicon and therefore the syntactic structures of both languages. Under the MLF model, there is a single mental lexicon, but lemmas are tagged as language-specific and, in line with the Matrix Language – Embedded Language distinction (and the newly introduced Uniform Structure Principle), these lemmas are not equally available in codeswitching. Thus, the TAG model makes different predictions in many of the same ways as the other generative models discussed above. An overview of these differences is given below.

4.10.5. *Other recent approaches*

There are a number of other relatively recent approaches to codeswitching that are somewhat outside the themes sketched above. Some researchers make testing earlier models one focus of their work (e.g. Bentahila and Davies 1997, Boumans 1998, Park 2000, Türker 2000). In a series of publications, Muysken emphasizes a typology of types of codeswitching (e.g. Muysken 1995, 1998, 2000). Under what he calls insertion, it seems as if the grammar of only the language of the grammatical frame is 'on' while under what he calls alternation, there is an alternation between activation of the two participating varieties. Finally, under congruent lexicalization, the lexicons and grammars of both languages are involved, although it seems that the participation of neither variety is constrained in its role. Backus (1992, 1996) employs the MLF model's notion of a Matrix Language, but is exploring the role of 'chunking' within a cognitive grammar approach. Boumans (1998) takes the MLF model as a starting point, but develops his own notion of a Matrix Language. Generational difference in codeswitching patterns figure especially in Bentahila and Davies (1992), Backus (1996), and Okasha (1999).

4.11. Conclusion

In this chapter, I have considered some problematic data, from bare forms to Embedded Language islands. I have introduced a Uniform Structural Principle to help explain some of these data. Of course such a principle is self-evident in monolingual data, just as is the theoretical notion of an abstract morphosyntactic frame structuring all constituents. However, stating the principle explicitly is more important for bilingual data; it affirms the structural integrity of any constituent and of the CP as a whole. Further, the requirement of uniformity biases the principle in favor of the structure of the Matrix Language.

Bare nouns are one major topic. I apply the Uniform Structure Principle to the case of nouns with and without determiners in several data sets. It can help explain how it is possible for Embedded Language early system morphemes to occur in place of Matrix Language ones in the case of French determiners with French nouns in North African/French codeswitching. The claim is that these French determiners meet the Matrix Language requirements for structural uniformity. This is not so when French is the Embedded Language with Wolof or Lingala as the Matrix Language. In the case of Embedded Language nouns in Bantu frames, I employ the principle to explain why it is important to posit an abstract NP that carries the default noun class of the relevant language. This abstract phrasal category can assign this feature to an Embedded Language noun and the other elements that must be co-indexed with a head outside their own maximal projections.

Another topic considered is the often-mentioned 'do' construction that is employed in codeswitching, especially when a number of languages that are verb-final (SOV) are the Matrix Language. In these cases, Embedded Language verbs occur in codeswitching only as non-finite forms in this 'do' construction. The construction consists of a 'do' verb preceded by an Embedded Language infinitive (or another Embedded Language non-finite form) and any complements of the verb.

Because the 'do' verb carries any necessary Matrix Language inflections, the Embedded Language non-finite form can be considered a bare form. On the basis that most of these languages are SOV and require left-branching, I suggest that a conflict of branching requirements between the Matrix Language and the Embedded Language may be behind the need for the 'do' construction. That is, Embedded Language verbs may be blocked from projecting predicate-argument structure because they are not congruent enough to pass the Uniform Structure Principle of the Matrix Language. However, a complete explanation is still needed for 'do' constructions.

The chapter also includes an overview of Embedded Language islands, with special attention to two areas: how islands are accessed and the motivations for islands. I argue that Embedded Language islands require Embedded Language activation at more levels of abstract grammatical structure than do singly occurring Embedded Language forms. Still, there are distinct similarities between the two types of Embedded Language forms. For example, many Embedded Language islands are either formulaic or routine collocations, perhaps making them similar to the activation required to access singly occurring forms. Also, many other Embedded Language islands are internal Embedded Language islands; as such, they are similar to singly occurring forms because one can argue such islands are under the control of an abstract Matrix Language head element. Other Embedded Language islands can be explained as the result of cross-linguistic incongruence at abstract levels (e.g. in Arabic/English codeswitching, abstract specifications for verbs prevents English verbs from appearing in mixed constituents framed by Arabic, leaving only Embedded Language islands as a way to access English verbs). I suggest that it may turn out (based on more quantitative work) that many more Embedded Language islands are the result of structural (grammatical) constraints than previously thought.

Finally, I offer a brief overview of the views of those researchers who make a point of differentiating singly occurring Embedded Language forms as borrowed forms and who therefore consider only phrasal (and larger) switches as data to be explained under a codeswitching model. This includes the work of Poplack and her associates (e.g. Poplack and Meechan 1998), but also those researchers who have analyzed codeswitching within developments of the generative Chomskyan tradition (e.g. most recently MacSwan 1999, 2000). In contrast to these approaches, I think, of course, that the same model (the MLF model) can account for both types of Embedded Language material. Further, while these other approaches offer explanations of phrase-level switches, they offer no model at all to explain any constraints on the nature of singly occurring forms or their derivational history. That is, if they are going to disallow singly occurring forms as codeswitching, then a separate model to explain these forms is needed.

A major difference in our approaches seems to be twofold. First, these researchers seem to place most weight on phrase structure as the source of constraints on codeswitching; in contrast, I place most weight on higher-level, more abstract procedures in the production process and the nature of entries in the mental lexicon. Second, their view seems to be that the only time that the Embedded Language is activated in codeswitching is when there is a switch of languages at the phrase level. (However, I note that at least under his process of 'congruent lexicalization', Muysken (2000) sees both participating languages simultaneously activated.) I argue, of course, that the Matrix Language is always more activated than the Embedded Language, but that the Embedded Language also is 'on' when congruence checking occurs (when the lemmas underlying Embedded Language content morphemes are accessed). This checking implicates the Uniform Structure Principle and its bias in bilingual CPs for the structural requirements of one source, the Matrix Language.

These other models also differ from the MLF model in ways related to frame-building properties, specifically the source of the Matrix Language or morphosyntactic frame of the bilingual CP and the designation of heads to project structure in that frame. First, there is the notion of the Matrix Language – Embedded Language opposition under the MLF model. This is rigorously enforced by the Morpheme Order Principle and the System Morpheme Principle and otherwise generally enforced by the Uniform Structure Principle. Under this opposition, the Matrix Language cannot switch within a CP. For all the models discussed here, one language is not necessarily structurally dominant within a CP; therefore, these models predict that Matrix Language switches will occur within a CP. These are over-predictions, as analysis of any naturally occurring codeswitching corpus shows.

Still another major difference is the type of lexical element that can project structure as a head (largely content morphemes) and therefore determine many aspects of constituents they select. Under the MLF model, conceptual saliency is paramount and is derived from the speaker's intentions. This means content morphemes are paramount. Such an approach provides for a unification of both discourse-level and argument-level thematic elements and better explains switching that—after all—is pragmatically, as well as structurally, motivated. Grammatical structure is important in the MLF model; after all, the model provides for congruence checking (grammatical feature checking) and its most specific constraints refer to permissible phrase-structure configurations (e.g the source language of late system morphemes). Still, the MLF model is basically a cognitively based and lexically driven model of codeswitching.

5

Convergence and Attrition

5.1. Introduction

From a structural standpoint, convergence and attrition are very similar as outcomes, perhaps even identical. As outcomes, they have two distinctive features: (i) all surface morphemes come from one language; (ii) the abstract lexical structure projecting these morphemes no longer comes from one language, but includes some abstract structure from another language. The result is a composite morphosyntactic frame or Matrix Language. (Of course, there is always the possibility of lexical borrowings from another language, but their presence does not affect the basic lexical and grammatical profiles.)

Arguably, one could see convergence more as both a mechanism involved in other contact phenomena and as an outcome, while attrition is only more of an outcome. As a mechanism, convergence is the process that promotes a splitting of abstract lexical structure in one variety and its combining with such abstract lexical structure from another variety, often resulting in a restructuring of grammatical relations and even surface-level grammatical morphemes from the stronger group in the equation, as we will see in Chapter 6.

Convergence and attrition may well be perceived as more different than they are. The very term 'attrition' implies the first steps toward loss of a language and its replacement by another—probably the language that is one of the contributors to the composite frame. Of course, convergence may also lead to language shift, but because there are many cases of convergence without shift, the assumption of a sure link between convergence and shift is much weaker than that between attrition and shift. Still, a person's language may undergo what researchers call attrition without arriving at final loss of that language and shift to another.

There are real resemblances in the sociolinguistic and psycholinguistic factors that promote convergence, attrition, and shift. As de Bot (1999: 348) points out, 'If we look at the processing side of language loss, we see more overlap between shift and attrition than differences'. Along with many other researchers (discussed in the ensuing sections on attrition), he argues that frequency of use (necessarily including frequency of activation) is the main factor in the change in language skills. Related to frequency of use is level of language input. For example, in his study of language loss among speakers of Moroccan Arabic living in the

Netherlands, El Aissati (1996: 158) concludes that '[t]he obvious answer to the question of why participants with low proficiency are the locus of more changes than those with a higher proficiency has to do with language input. Simply stated, those who were born in the Netherlands were exposed less to MA [Moroccan Arabic] than those who spent long periods of their lives in Morocco.' Typically, speakers receive limited input and use a language infrequently when it is spoken in a community where another language is dominant and that language is used in most settings.

More important in this volume and as I have already indicated, there are strong resemblances in the grammatical structures that characterize all of these phenomena. Both convergence and attrition necessarily involve a composite Matrix Language. That is, the source of the grammatical frame for the relevant CP is not a single language, but more than one. Thus, we speak of the frame as a composite. Along with other phenomena with a composite Matrix Language, convergence and attrition often involve codeswitching. In an earlier chapter, I introduced the term composite codeswitching to characterize the bilingual CP that includes codeswitching (meaning morphemes from two or more varieties) and convergence (abstract grammatical structure from two or more varieties).

The emphasis in this chapter is on convergence and attrition without codeswitching; however, in the empirical evidence considered it is not always possible to split these phenomena. Still, as much as possible, convergence with codeswitching (composite codeswitching) is a topic reserved for the next chapter. That chapter deals with inroads into an L1 that seem to lead to bigger steps on the road to language shift. Again, I emphasize that—as I define it—convergence alone does not involve adding morphemes, but rather only abstract structure. I note that in characterizing the state of his Pennsylvania Dutch data from Delaware in the late 1970s as showing convergence, Enninger (1980) refers to convergence of strategies, not of morphemes. Recall that I consider both codeswitching and convergence mechanisms active in other contact phenomena as well as phenomena on their own. Either is at work in language shift. Researchers have referred to codeswitching either as 'the foot in the door' or, more graphically and negatively as 'the worm in the apple' (Bolonyai 1998). When the two occur at once, the chance of shift, or at least a turnover in the Matrix Language if bilingual CPs are maintained, is compounded. Seliger (1996: 612) states that 'code-mixing is a precursor stage for primary language attrition and for eventual death of the L1 within the bilingual community'. And Kuhberg (1992: 149) takes an even harsher stance, arguing that codeswitching is 'developmentally systematic, clearly reflecting deterioration'. It is true that Bolonyai (1999) demonstrates with quantitative evidence that there are more instances of non-target-like Hungarian in the speech of her subjects (young Hungarian/English bilinguals being raised in the United States) than there is when they produce monolingual Hungarian utterances (details are reported in Chapter 6). However, it is also true that in many bilingual communities codeswitching is a part of everyday life with minor instances of convergence as the only effects on the participating languages.

5.1.1. *Examples of convergence*

Examples (1) through (4) illustrate convergence to English and possibly attrition; example (5) shows convergence to Italian. Example (1) represents convergence at the abstract level of lexical-conceptual structure and (2) represents convergence of morphological realization patterns. In (1) a Czech-speaking child who has been living in an English-dominant environment for more than a year neutralizes the two Czech verbs for different types of 'knowing' (along the pattern of English), using *vi:m* 'I know something' for the standard Czech rendition of 'I know someone' (*zna:m*).

(1) **vi:-m** ho, **vi:-m** ji
know/PRES-1S him/ACC know/PRES-1S her/ACC
'I know him, I know her.'

(Saville-Troike, Pan, and Dutkova 1995: 135; morphological glosses from L. Dutkova-Cope)

In (2) a Spanish child from Colombia, but living in the United States, and also fluent in English, produces a compound noun on an English pattern (*manzana jugo* 'apple juice') instead of the Standard Spanish counterpart (*jugo de manzana* 'juice of apple'). Note also the inconsistency in gender in *manzana jugo*. In addition, the child does not observe the pro-drop convention of Spanish; instead, he produces overt first person pronouns as subjects.

(2) Mami, yo quiero, yo quiero
Mommy, 1S/NOM want/1S/PRES 1S/NOM want/1S/PRES
manzana jugo
apple/FEM juice/MASC
'Mommy, I want, I want apple juice.'

(Spanish/English codeswitching data; Milian 1996)

Example (3) shows convergence to English at the level of predicate-argument structure as well as at the level of lexical-conceptual structure. A Hungarian child who is being raised in an English-dominant community in the American Southeast uses the intransitive form of the Hungarian verb *kel* 'wake up' when she intends to produce a verb that takes a Patient argument. In English, the same verb form, *wake up*, can be either transitive or intransitive; the argument structure of the verb phrase makes this clear (i.e. if there is a direct object carrying the thematic role of Patient, the verb is transitive). However, in Hungarian, there are two different verb forms for transitive and intransitive forms. To 'wake somebody up' is conveyed by the causative form of *kel* (this is *kel-t*, with the derivational morpheme *-t*). However, even though the child produces a verb phrase with a Patient argument, she uses the intransitive form that subcategorizes for only one argument, not the target causative form. Her choice indicates convergence at the level of lexical-conceptual structure as well as argument structure because, in effect, the child neutralizes the distinction between causativity and non-causativity of Hungarian.

(3) mert te nem **kel-sz** en-gem fel
Because you not wake/INTRANS PRES/2S 1S-ACC up
'Because you did not rise me up.'
Standard Hungarian: kel-t-esz
wake-TRANS PRES 2S

(Bolonyai 1999: 101)

In (4) a child with Navaho as the L1, but who is receiving limited Navaho-input, uses the wrong aspect marker for 'baby' as an object. In Navaho, different object shapes take different aspect markers. The use of *teeł* in Standard Navaho indicates specifically 'move an animate object in a reclining position' (Saville-Troike, personal communication). In effect, the child is neutralizing lexical-conceptual distinctions that would be made at the level of morphological realization patterns in the target variety. Saville-Troike, Pan, and Dutkova (1995: 142) note that children of a similar age being raised in Navaho-dominant homes produce appropriate verb stems for objects according to shape.

(4) Baby chi'ii doo'**aa**
Baby out FUT take
'He will take out the baby'
Target Navaho: doo'**teeł**

(Saville-Troike, Pan, and Dutkova 1995: 142; morphological glosses supplied by M. Saville-Troike)

In (5) the speaker is a trilingual (French/Italian/Valle d'Aosta patois) living in the Italian region of Valle d'Aosta near the French border. He has been asked to speak his variety of French, even though, like most people in this area, his more dominant language is Italian. Note that all the surface morphemes in this example come from French, but arguably the speaker has the semantics/pragmatics of the Italian verb *prendere* in mind when he produces the French verb *prendre* rather than *recevoir*, the French verb that would be expected in the context of talk about television programs. In Italian, the verb *prendere* is the most frequently used verb for 'receiving' television programs (although Italian also has the verb *ricevere* 'to receive'). He is talking about difficulty in receiving programs on a certain channel from France.

(5) On ne **prend** pas beaucoup ici . . .
One NEG take/PRES/3S NEG much here . . .

Moi j'aime bien, mais on ne **prend** pas beaucoup
1S/EMPH 1S like a lot but one NEG take/PRES/3S NEG much
'... We don't get them here.... I would like to, but we don't get [them].'

(Sarullo 1998: 108)

5.1.2. *Goals of this chapter*

The discussion in this chapter refers largely to attrition, not convergence; however, everything said about the grammatical characteristics of attrition should apply to convergence. My main goal is to consider attrition that affects an L1, although of course attrition of an L2 also happens, and is noted. Certainly, I would argue that the same abstract grammatical processes are involved in the phenomenon, whether it affects an L1 or an L2. The sociolinguistic and psycholinguistic circumstances may well vary. I survey what the contact literature has had to say about L1 attrition, but I devote the most space to proposing alternative theoretical assumptions that predict the grammatical characteristics of a person's language when it shows attrition. That is, I offer scenarios of grammatical processes at work that would explain attrition as a result.

I cite evidence from many sources; unfortunately, however, much of the literature that considers attrition is found in basically sociolinguistic considerations of language shift and language death. Such sources tend to offer general observations about attrition rather than grammatical details. Even studies specifically on grammatical aspects of attrition often are case studies with only a few examples (e.g. Kravin 1992 is a case study of an English/Finnish bilingual six year old; Kuhberg 1992 is a case study of two Turkish girls who returned to Turkey after living in Germany where they acquired German).

De Bot and Weltens noted more than ten years ago that 'research into the consequences of mother tongue language shift for the structure of the language system of individual speakers is not very frequent' (1991: 42). More recently, Håkansson (1995: 154) noted that 'there are very few empirical studies that attempt to describe in detail the grammatical features of the language used by persons involved in language attrition'. The situation has changed little since then. For this reason, much of the data cited here, data including the quantitative grammatical detail necessary to test the proposed assumptions, comes from recent work by my students and a few other recent studies.

5.1.3. *The theoretical frameworks I follow*

The theoretical framework for my scenarios comes from the Abstract Level model and the 4-M model. The basic argument to be developed from the Abstract Level model is that convergence and attrition result when the three levels of abstract grammatical structure in any lemma in the mental lexicon from language X are split and combined with levels in a lemma from language Y. The basic argument to be developed from the 4-M model is that the extent to which attrition first affects an L1 varies with the type of morpheme. An interaction between the two models becomes evident: an argument developed is that splitting and recombining (the main theoretical notion underlying the Abstract Level model) is an earlier attrition feature for conceptually activated morphemes (content morphemes and early system morphemes) than for the structurally assigned late system morphemes. (The most controversial hypothesis for which I offer support predicts that late system morphemes are less susceptible to early attrition than other types of morpheme.) The 4-M model makes the claim that different distributions of morpheme types can be explained in terms of when they become salient in language production.

5.1.4. *Perceptions about convergence*

Before moving on to an overview of attrition research and my own discussion, I want to briefly consider some problems with terminology. Unfortunately, as is well known, many key terms in the literature mean different things to different researchers. This is especially a problem with the term 'convergence'. (For the sake of simplicity, assume the discussion refers to convergence affecting an L1.)

Some researchers emphasize the loss of forms under the influence of another language as a defining feature of convergence. That is, loss, and specifically the loss of forms that are not congruent with another language, seems important. Beniak, Mougeon, and Valois (1984/5: 73) specifically refer to convergence as 'the gradual elimination over time of forms of a language as a result of contact with another language in which corresponding forms are not attested'. Silva-Corvalán (1994*a*) does not use the term 'convergence', but does refer to reduction and simplification in discussing the opposition of indicative vs. subjunctive in Spanish as it is spoken in Los Angeles. She sees the absence of this opposition in English as a possible factor, but emphasizes that 'changes occur rather as a result of reduction of both exposure to and use of a complete variety of a subordinate language in contact with a superordinate one' (p. 269).

Others do not stress loss so much as they stress innovation; for them, the key idea under convergence is the introduction of new forms, with another language as the source. (Note that in its broadest interpretation, this notion of convergence could include lexical borrowing. In fact, borrowing, as defined by Thomason and Kaufman (1988) could include this notion of convergence, if it were restricted to insertions into an L1. They write, 'we will . . . use the term "borrowing" to refer only to the incorporation of foreign elements into the speakers' native language, not to interference in general' (p. 21).)

Writing alone twelve years later, Thomason (2000) has more to say about convergence. She clearly sees convergence differently from me, stating, 'convergence, at its simplest, would be any process through which two or more languages in contact become more like each other' (p. 89), but then she immediately goes on to say this definition is too broad. To narrow the definition, she cites two contexts in which she sees convergence occurring. 'One is a contact situation in which both (or all) languages change in ways that make them more similar. In this context, the point of talking about convergence is to emphasize the fact that the interference is mutual, not unidirectional, and the fact that the resulting convergent structures have no single source' (p. 89). She goes on to write, 'The other main context in which convergence is discussed is in Sprachbund situations, in which the sources of the various areal features are all too often impossible to determine' (p. 90).

Romaine (1995: 72 ff.) contrasts the use of convergence as a term for loss with the use of 'interference' for the introduction of new forms. She recognizes problems with trying to differentiate the common terms in use for externally motivated change (convergence, interference, and borrowing), writing 'part of the problem is that convergence, interference and borrowing all have as their linguistic outcome an increase in the similarity between two or more linguistic systems' (p. 75). Quite correctly, she goes on to point out that 'loss may seldom be absolute' (p. 75). For example, as I show in section 5.5, although the expected form for a slot in a morphosyntactic frame may not occur, the slot is not lost, but often is filled by an alternative form.

Poplack, another linguist whose name is associated with language-contact research, offers a similar definition of convergence, but with a different wrinkle. In Poplack (1997: 289), she makes clear that while convergence obviously implies influence from another language, this need not be overt influence. At first, her view appears similar to my definition of convergence as consisting of influence at an abstract lexical level that results in a composite Matrix Language that frames surface-level clauses. However, it becomes clear that she is referring to the possibility of indirect influence via sociolinguistic factors, not influence at any abstract lexical level—at least in the context of her study of the non-use of French subjunctive by some French speakers in Canada. First, as does Thomason and as do I, she explicitly differentiates convergence from lexical borrowing, stating 'convergence need not involve any visible other-language material' (p. 289). She goes on to stress that convergence results in features resembling both languages (as does Thomason), writing, 'Indeed, convergence may not involve any transfer at all: it may simply consist . . . in the selection and favoring of one of two (or more) already existing native-language forms which coincides with a counterpart in the contact language' (p. 289). She endorses the term 'covert interference' (from Mougeon and Beniak 1991: 11) for such effects as the loss of the subjunctive: 'a minority-language feature undergoes gradual decline and eventual loss because it lacks an interlingual counterpart in the majority of language' (p. 289).

Although the reason I cite Poplack's characterization of convergence is to present an enlarged view on what the term means, it is worth reporting that she concludes that her study actually discounts any notion of convergence as the source of variation in her corpus. Based on her detailed analysis of social-class differences in the use of the subjunctive by French speakers in two Canadian communities and her study of the historical frequency of the subjunctive in Canadian French in supposedly obligatory contexts, Poplack reaches two conclusions. First, professional-class members (who are highly bilingual individuals) favor the subjunctive more than any other class; that is, 'increased proficiency in English shows no evidence of being associated with a loss or even decrease of subjunctive usage' (p. 295). Second, Poplack's study of the historical record on variation in subjunctive use in French 'suggests that there was at least as much variability at earlier periods as is observed today' (p. 306). Thus, neither set of facts supports the notion that extensive use of a superordinate language leads to simplification toward that language under the name of convergence. Poplack does us a service with this cautionary tale; the moral is that convergence does not grow under every bilingual bush and that the term should be used advisedly.

Sharwood Smith and Kellerman (1986: 1) express some frustrations with terminology and suggest that what they refer to as 'the interplay between earlier and later acquired languages' should be referred to as 'cross-linguistic influence' (CLI). They state CLI could cover 'such phenomena as "transfer", "interference", "avoidance", "borrowing" and L2-related aspects of language loss' (p. 1). Note that 'convergence' is not among the phenomena mentioned. They suggest that CLI could be used 'to label the processes involved irrespective of the direction of influence'. But whatever virtues the term CLI may have, I see no evidence that it has caught on in most contact studies; instead, the other terms that Sharwood Smith and Kellerman would like to replace continue to be used. For example, in their influential volume, Thomason and Kaufman (1988) use only two terms to cover all of contact-induced change. For them, 'borrowing' is L2 influence on L1 when the L1 is maintained and refers especially to lexical borrowing, but also to what they call structural borrowing (borrowing of phonological or morphosyntactic features). They go on to use 'interference' for those grammatical features from an L1 that appear in an L2, especially when the L1 speakers may not have acquired the L2 completely (i.e. this includes what is often referred to as substrate influence).

Many researchers, some of whom use the term convergence, while others eschew it entirely, inventing their own terms, seem to have the same theoretical notion in mind captured in my definition of convergence. That is, the asymmetric influence of one language on the other is highlighted. However, they discuss their subject matter in general terms, not introducing the precision that referring to the three levels of abstract grammatical structure that the Abstract Level model affords. For example, in characterizing the Spanish of Spanish immigrants in the industrial part of French-speaking Switzerland, the term that Py (1986) prefers is 'reinterpretation'. Specifically, he speaks of 'reinterpretation of a native language via the host language' (p. 166). He also states that 'modifications may be described as various kinds of restructuring operations' (p. 169). The few examples he gives mirror those cited above as (1) through (5). For example, he reports that the distinction that Spanish makes in verbs of location that take the preposition *a* and those that indicate movement toward a goal and take the preposition *en* is not always made, under the influence of the phonetic similarity of these prepositions to the French prepositions *de* and *à* and the partial overlap in grammatical function. He states that, 'We might say that the French system has exercised an interpretative function on the Spanish system' (p. 167).

5.1.5. *Comparing perceptions of convergence and attrition*

If any of these researchers cited above were asked to differentiate convergence from attrition, they might initially be at a loss. However, they would probably focus on the more sociolinguistic aspects of the two phenomena. That is, convergence is generally considered to show up in an entire community of speakers; in contrast, attrition is thought of more as something characterizing the speech of certain individuals. Also, the received view probably is that convergence is somehow less perceptible than attrition. That is, convergence is felt to be something that happens gradually over several generations and it does not necessarily affect structure in such a dramatic way as attrition does. Also, as it is reported in the literature, attrition happens within an individual lifetime.

These views notwithstanding, I argue that convergence and attrition are more alike than different, both in regard to the grammatical outcomes and the sociolinguistic milieu in which they occur, if not in the time span they take for their effects to be obvious. One difference is that attrition may be less discussed, partly because it is overshadowed by more interest in language shift—although shift may be the end-product of either convergence or attrition and the sociopsycholinguistic circumstances present.

A combination of the two definitions of convergence (as loss and addition under external influence) is somewhat compatible with my own ideas, but not entirely, as becomes clear in section 5.5. Yet, this combination stresses a notion that is lacking in the definition of convergence I give (and that should be there): the notion is that convergence, like other contact phenomena, involves asymmetry in the participation of the languages represented. That is, I consider convergence as largely a one-way phenomenon. Some mutual influence is possible, but in its unmarked realization, convergence involves the grammar and lexicon of a source language, generally one that has more socioeconomic prestige, impinging on another language.[1]

[1] However, having just written above that socio-economic prestige counts in the direction of convergence, let me cite an example where numbers of speakers seems to have counted instead. In a colloquy probably from the 10th century AD, the Latin of the author (a church scholar, Ælfric Bata) shows evidence of convergence to English. Such colloquia were fictionalized conversations. In one conversation, Bata writes, *Sed non babemus forpicem, ut cyninnos nostros quispiam queat secáre foras* (23.7–8) 'But we don't have scissors, so that someone can cut off our hair'. The adverb *foras* is unexpected, meaning 'completely' or 'off' and occurs instead of an expected Latin adverb such as *omino*. In his discussion of Old English influence on the Latin of this period, Gwara (1998: 12–13) argues, 'Bata's speaker's Latin has been influenced by OE *for(e)* ("completely, utterly") an intensifying/perfective prefix in Old English verbs' Here, it is being used as an adverb. Is this a matter of imperfect learning of Latin? It seems very unlikely; instead, it is more likely that the general use of English, especially in what is supposed to be a conversation, just creeps in.

This is not at all the view of convergence of many researchers, such as many historical linguists who think of convergence as a mutual coming together. For example, Hock and Joseph (1996: 395) define convergence as 'the increasing agreement of languages not only in terms of vocabulary (which may in fact remain quite distinct), but especially in aspects of their overall structure'. Further, to cite Thomason from another publication, she refers to convergence as 'one recurrent concept . . . in which structures common to both languages are favored' (1997*d*: 187). I do not dispute these statements as such, but they miss the fact that the source language does not necessarily change at all, belying the notion that mutuality can imply reciprocity.

5.1.6. *How the discussion is organized*

The discussion in the following sections will emphasize several subjects. First, I consider the special use of 'convergence' in the term 'convergence areas', citing details from several such areas. Next, I move on to the main subject, individual attrition. I survey the sociolinguistic settings that seem to promote attrition. I also review existing studies on attrition, considering how it has been studied and the attempts of researchers to explain outcomes in attrition. I briefly consider sociolinguistic explanations, but spend more space on explanations based on claims about the grammatical structuring that attrition shows. Finally, I consider my own theoretical assumptions about the path that attrition takes. I do this in terms of two hierarchies. One ranks levels of abstract lexical structure based on the order in which they show the effects of attrition. The other ranks types of morphemes based on their susceptibility to attrition. Both of these hierarchies are supported with examples and quantitatively based findings from the work of others.

5.2. Convergence areas

The fact that the many linguistic groupings in the world called *Sprachbunde* ('language leagues') are alternatively called convergence areas certainly implies that convergence means the coming together (and therefore the gaining) of features in this context. Present-day results in these areas look like mutual influence was at work in their creation. Without historical records, it is hard to disentangle causes and effects and therefore to know whether structural influence was ever asymmetrical. Could one language have been the main source, with perhaps the identity of that language varying with changing sociopolitical conditions? In a definition that is neutral as to hypotheses of origin, Hock (1988: 302) writes, 'Sprachbünde . . . ideally represent areas set off by a number of geographically coinciding or converging isoglosses'. Thomason and Kaufman (1988: 96) come closer to implying mutual influence as a mechanism in stating, 'What a long-term multilaterial sprachbund seems to promote . . . is the gradual development of isomorphism (equivalence of form) in all areas of structure except the phonological shape of morphemes'. Certainly, most researchers studying convergence areas arrive at the same conclusion that other researchers studying attrition propose. They all suggest that those structures common to the languages involved are what result or remain (in the Sprachbund or in the L1 or L2 undergoing attrition). This notion can be seen as a version of the hypothesis that unmarked structures prevail, with a locally based criterion of markedness. While structural resemblance may sometimes matter, as a major explanation, in section 5.4 I argue that this hypothesis does not take us very far.

The Sprachbund areas often discussed are the Balkans (Joseph 1983), South Asia (Emeneau 1980, Masica 1976), the Pacific Northwest Amerindian area (Sherzer 1976, Beck 2000), the Baltic area, Meso-America (Campbell, Kaufman, and Smith-Stark 1986), pre-modern Europe (Hock 1988), and most recently Northeast China (Slater forthcoming). (The authors cited are only illustrative; there is an extensive literature on almost all of these areas.) The typical characteristic of these convergence areas is commonality—in certain phonological features and in how morphosyntactic patterns are encoded, but not so much in either the forms to encode them or in the lexicon itself. In this way, the languages involved maintain their identities.

The best-known Sprachbund is probably the Balkan area where there are four subgroups of the Indo-European family (Slavic: Bulgarian, Macedonian, Serbian, and Croatian; Romance: Romanian; Albanian; and Modern Greek). There are a number of structural features that many or most of these languages share. Hock (1988: 286–90) lists these 'primary Balkanisms': (i) postposed definite article, (ii) dependent or coordinate clauses replacing infinitival structures, (iii) a marker for future tense based on the verb for 'want, wish', (iv) merger of genitive and dative case, (v) 'doubling' of object clitics, (vi) clitic and postposed possessive pronouns, (vii) retention of a distinct vocative form, (viii) the formation of numerals from 11 to 19, (ix) analytic comparison of adjectives, and (x) deictic particle plus accusative clitic pronouns.

To take another example, some of the morphological similarities that Beck (2000: 159) points out in the Central Northwest Coast Indian languages include: (i) extensive suffixation, (ii) near absence of prefixes, (iii) similarities in the aspectual system, (iv) lack of tense or tense as an optional category, (v) optional distributive plural, (vi) deictic marking absent–present, invisible–visible, (vii) gender in demonstratives, and (viii) numeral classifiers.

5.2.1. *The nature of shared features*

Given such features as those noted in these two areas, one wonders if a thorough study of Sprachbund areas might reveal that a preponderance of shared morphosyntactic features are the type that the 4-M model labels as content morphemes or early system morphemes. Consider some of the features that Campbell, Kaufman, and Smith-Stark (1986) cite as characterizing Meso-America: basic VSO word order, a nominal possession construction, vigesimal numeral system, relational nouns, intimate possession, locatives derived from body parts, special absolutive affixes, and numeral classifiers. In the discussion of attrition below, I argue that similar word order in phrases or clauses, a frequent characteristic of a convergence area in some cases, can be considered an early system morpheme. I refer to the directions for word order in section 5.5. Obviously, word order itself is not an actual surface-level morpheme; it should be clear by now that types of morpheme within the 4-M model are types on two levels, but the abstract, not the surface, level is basic. However, directions regarding word order sent to the Formulator can be regarded as early system morphemes if a particular order is tied to the presence of a specific content morpheme or grammatical structure. For example, word order in the NP depends on the presence of a noun and order reflects the hierarchical relation of other elements to the noun.

Thus, a tentative hypothesis might be that features that are late system morphemes are not as frequent in the list of shared features in a Sprachbund as are content morphemes and early system morphemes. True, some of the shared features may well be considered late system morphemes (e.g. absolutive affixes on nouns that have no other affix in some Meso-American languages, although Campbell, Kaufman, and Smith-Stark (1986: 549) state that this is not a significant areal feature nor equivalent across those languages that have it). In contrast, most of the features in the lists cited for Sprachbund areas are unlikely candidates as late system morphemes. For example, consider such features as locatives derived from body parts or a distinctive nominal possessive construction; these are inherent features of content morphemes, not structurally assigned morphemes that mark relationships across maximal projections (i.e. late system morphemes).

My suggestion is that there is a contrast in the borrowability (and retention) within geographic areas of the means by which conceptual structure in general is encoded vs. the means of indicating relationships in a clause. Recall that late system morphemes are features that depend on their form for co-indexing with heads outside their immediate maximal projection in the larger clause as it is assembled at the level of the Formulator. In fact, one of Beck's major arguments in his discussion of the Northwest Indian Sprachbund is that although Bella Coola shares features with other neighboring languages, it has a number of distinctive features of its own. (He mentions inflectional object–subject agreement markers, typical examples of late system morphemes; however, he seems to favor the argument that the distinctive features resulted from innovations in Bella Coola, not necessarily retentions.)

Even in Kupwar (discussed in the next section), there are apparently few instances of borrowing of actual late system morphemes. Gumperz and Wilson (1971: 161) make this very clear, writing, 'Inflectional morphs forming part of closed paradigmatic sets such as person and gender agreement or tense markers are almost never borrowed'. They give one example of such a borrowing, but go on to make a statement that is very persuasive in the argument I am making: 'Such paradigmatically structured inflectional morphs seem to be at the core of the native speakers [*sic*] perception of what constitute "different languages"' (pp. 161–2).

Not all areas labeled convergence areas are marked by morphosyntactic similarities. In Arnhem Land in northeastern Australia, it is lexical elements, not morphosyntactic features, that are shared (Heath 1981). This grouping shows extreme lexical diffusion (e.g. up to sharing 50 per cent of overall vocabulary in some cases). In arguing against any analogy with either creoles or dialect chains, Heath stresses that the languages in this area have sharp grammatical boundaries including different morphological systems. He states that 'Arnhem Land languages have shown no tendency whatever toward morphological simplification or regularization, nor toward morpheme-by-morpheme intertranslatability' (p. 365).

5.2.2. *Kupwar: a mini-convergence area?*

Kupwar, an Indian village in Maharashtra province where the local varieties of three languages show very similar features, is often cited as the ultimate example in discussions of convergence areas or simply of convergence. The extent to which the grammatical patterns of the three languages are often similar sets Kupwar apart from other convergence areas.

Further, for yet another way of how convergence has been viewed, consider how Gumperz and Wilson (1971) link 'convergence and creolization' in the title of their study of Kupwar. They also comment, 'The most striking result of the various changes the [local] dialects have undergone is the creation of three parallel creole-like local varieties' (p. 164). Their coupling of convergence with creolization may have been more an artlfact of the times (and the fact the paper was originally given at a conference featuring pidgins and creoles), but it implies mutual influences that almost defy analysis and explanation. Simply because the article is well known, this characterization of the Kupwar case arguably has influenced how linguists think of cases when languages share grammatical constructions and therefore how they think of convergence. (Of course, my general argument in this volume is that the same principles and processes shape all contact phenomena, although I argue in Chapter 6 that creoles have a distinctive structural development and outcome because of the social circumstances in which they arose. The result is not the same as with convergence. More important, in neither case do the results truly defy explanation.)

In Kupwar, the varieties involved are Urdu (Indo-Aryan), Marathi (Indo-Aryan, but distant from Urdu), and Kannaḍa (Dravidian). Our only source of data is Gumperz and Wilson (1971), but this study comes up almost always when convergence is mentioned. In their summary of the Kupwar data, Hock and Joseph (1996: 399) state, 'While there are some differences in detail, such as the fact that the "absolutive marker" is an independent (but clitic) word in Urdu and Marathi, but a suffix in Kannada, there is an exact, word-by-word, suffix-by-suffix parallelism in the linear arrangement of the sentences and in the meanings and functions of the morphological elements and words that are used. Put differently, the sentences are exact calques of each other.' An example sentence translated into the three languages illustrates this:

(6)	Urdu	pālā	ĵarā	kāt	kē	lē	kē	ā-	yā
	Ma.	pālā	ĵarā	kāp	un	ghē	un	ā-	lō
	Ka.	tāplā	ĵarā	khōd-	i	tagōnd	- i	ba-	yn
		greens	some	cut	ABS	take	ABS	come	TA

'Having cut some greens, having taken [them], I came.' =
'I cut some greens and brought them.'

(Hock and Joseph 1996: 398, based on Gumperz and Wilson 1971: 159)

In the case of Kupwar, bilingualism in this community is at least three hundred years old, offering the possibility of many ebbs and flows in any dominance competition between the languages. Certainly, at the time of the study of Gumperz and Wilson, there were ample motivations to make Marathi the source of more of the convergent features than the other two languages. (Gumperz and Wilson make clear that a reason the three languages are maintained as distinctive languages is that each set of speakers uses its own language exclusively in the home.) Even though Marathi was the language of a less prestigious group, it was the normal language for intergroup communication. It is considered socially neutral because it is not the home language of the majority nor of either of the more socially dominant groups. The status of Marathi must also be enhanced because, as Gumperz and Wilson note, 'Marathi is and has been for several centuries the dominant regional language' (p. 164).

For these reasons, it is not too surprising that their findings show more convergence toward Marathi than any of the other languages. Their statement is this: Marathi has 'been much more changed toward (where it agrees with one of the other languages) than changed from' (pp. 163–4). They also note that Urdu has undergone the greatest change, with no changes in the list of features considered toward Urdu alone (although there are five toward Urdu and Marathi jointly). Given that Marathi is the language of the untouchable caste, it seems clear that its use in the village depended more on its wider use and possibly the number of its speakers than on its high social status. Admittedly, convergence to Marathi alone does not explain all the shared features in the Kupwar data, but at different points in history, there may have been social conditions making the languages of other language groups more favored, either for actual intergroup communication or as a prestigious source of language features.

5.2.3. *Mechanisms and convergence areas*

As I have already implied, there is a good deal of variety in the type of statements that are made about how convergence areas come about. Of course, the general assumption is that convergence means that new features are added and old ones modified or replaced. But how did this happen? The rationale for not recognizing one source language for a shared feature seems to be that often the factors indicating direction of influence may no longer exist. Further, just because the present landscape is one of a set of shared features, the notion that—over time—the prestige of an individual language rather than consensus could have been responsible for spreading a feature does not seem to be often entertained. That is, with no other evidence than the present state of affairs, most researchers seem to assume convergence areas necessarily implicate mutual influence. This idea of mutuality also seems to carry over to convergence when it only involves two languages. Thomason takes the middle ground in stating that 'convergence may be either one-way or mutual; social factors determine the directionality of the change' (1997*d*: 187).

I argue that convergence areas should not be an exception to the principles characterizing other contact phenomena. In other phenomena, the evidence is unmistakable that the Uniform Structure Principle, which gives preference to maintaining one source variety in bilingual CPs, prevails (this principle is most discussed in Chapter 4). The principle certainly allows for the source variety framing bilingual CPs to change over time. For an example of change, although it does not involve grammar, one need only look at the change in the direction of lexical borrowing between French and English by the late twentieth century as compared with earlier times. At the same time, as I will argue in the next chapter, in succeeding periods whenever one variety replaces another as the dominant source of the morphosyntactic frame, the results may fossilize as a composite with grammatical forms from more than one language. The *appearance* of mutual influence is a possible result.

For example, while at the time they were studied the Kupwar varieties shared many, even most, of their morphosyntactic structures, this does not negate my premise that there is always asymmetry in the source of grammatical features in language contact. Thus, in the case of convergence areas, I would argue that when a specific feature is widespread, it comes from a single source (or a group of closely related sources), not mutual development. Admittedly, in most convergence areas, there is continuing dispute over what those single sources might be. In some cases, sources are more obvious. For example, even though researchers can speak of a Northeast China convergence area, evidence shows that the Gangou dialect of Chinese spoken there organizes a number of grammatical structures along the same lines as neighboring Mongolian languages (Zhu, Chuluu, Slater, and Stuart 1997), not other language groups in the area (even though Gangou dialect does so with Chinese morphemes).

Another fact that adds uncertainty for any argument about sources is that there are no fences around the features defining many Sprachbund areas. That is, many of the features of a given Sprachbund are found elsewhere in the general areas. This certainly is the case with the South Asia grouping and with the Balkan area. For example, Hock (1988: 302–3) asserts that 'of the ten features which are generally considered to define the Balkan Sprachbund, every single one extends beyond that territory, or did so in the past'. Some features extend into the Mediterranean area and Asia. Exactly what this implies is unclear. Does it imply that these features are especially semantically transparent and *therefore would be expected to appear in many places, no matter what?* Also, recall my argument above that most of the features uniting convergence areas are among those that are relatively easily borrowed; they are not inflectional elements (i.e. late system morphemes). In turn, this prompts other questions. There is no question but that certain features are especially thick on the ground in Sprachbund areas; however, does just the fact such areas house many diverse peoples cause researchers to conclude that similarities across their languages are extraordinary? And, in turn, does this cause them to conclude that these similarities represent very unusual cases that only mutual development can explain? I leave this section with such unanswered questions, and turn now to consider convergence involving two languages by discussing evidence on attrition in individuals.

5.3. Individual attrition: a social and psycholinguistic overview

5.3.1. *Relating attrition and shift*

Any discussion of attrition must begin with at least a nod to the social and psychological circumstances in which the phenomenon develops. I recapitulate briefly some of the discussion from Chapter 2. To the extent that it is treated at all in the general literature on contact phenomena, attrition is only a poor relative of shift. In fact, many researchers do not distinguish shift and attrition, but lump the two together under 'loss'. However, shift generally refers to a community phenomenon and a result arising from gradual loss of a language (usually an L1) over time. In contrast, attrition is a phenomenon of individuals, referring to what happens to an individual's production of a language (usually an L1), *and* the state of any loss at a point in time. Seliger (1996: 613) states that 'primary language attrition at the individual speaker level is a precursor condition for language death at the societal level'. De Bot (1996: 579) refers to 'skills' in reference to both phenomena. However, I argue that what the word 'skills' indicates is a further distinction between the two. In the literature on shift, 'skills' means overall degree of proficiency in language X. That is, the shift literature is largely based on large-scale surveys on members of a group in a community who no longer speak language X (or who offer self-reports on speaking it to various degrees of proficiency or who report on the domains in which they use language X). In reference to attrition, 'skills' has more to do with the extent of an individual's command of the lexicon and especially specifics of the grammar of language X. However, in curious support of the folk belief that a language is its words, researchers on attrition often devote more attention to detailing changes in the lexicon than in the grammar.

Of course, individual attrition occurs in the context of group shift, and vice versa. There are two main circumstances favoring the two phenomena. In a bilingual community the relative positions of the competing languages is rarely stable. Given a push by sociopolitical developments, subsequent generations of speakers of minority languages often shift to the dominant language. Even more likely is a shift when a group is a non-indigenous minority—that is, when they are immigrants to a new community. In both cases, the shift begins with individual attrition.

The factors promoting attrition and then shift are both social and psychological. Typically, a loss in the domains in which language X is spoken is the catalyst for individual attrition and then group shift. That is, a language that used to be spoken in many domains (work, school, public discourse, etc.) becomes used only in the home. Official language policies and job and educational requirements are typical motivations for domain shifts. Psychological forces also promote attrition and shift. Speakers of language X begin to see their L1 as not only less useful in the community, but as less valued in both instrumental and sentimental terms not only by out-group members, but also in-group members.

A difference between attrition and shift is that one can generally not speak of shift in the use of language X until a change has occurred across generations of speakers. When there is a generation-based shift, it begins with some attrition in an earlier generation. For example, one scenario could be that as first generation speakers use their L1 less, the model they provide for the second generation may be a different version in some sense from what they acquired. Not surprisingly, some of its structures may show convergence to the dominant language in the community. For example, while they still speak Spanish fluently, first generation Puerto Ricans in New York may begin to use calques from English (English phrases they translate word for word into Spanish words). Or, they may drop certain grammatical constructions (e.g. the subjunctive). When their turn comes, the second generation may not even acquire the version of the L1 of their elders because of domain loss and attitudinal factors. The result is attrition in the second generation and a new version that is transmitted to the next generation. But the reality or details of a second- or third-generation shift away from the L1 is not necessarily due only to having a reduced model to follow—even though this is the scenario many researchers sketch.

5.3.2. *Alternative paths and views*

I offer five qualifications to that scenario. First, any claims that the grammatical models that second-generation children receive are necessarily reduced often seem to be based on more supposition than fact. For example, the work by Boeschoten (1992) on young second-generation Turkish children in the Netherlands has been misinterpreted by some. What his study of twelve children aged four to six actually considers is the non-target-like lexical forms they produced, not grammatical forms. Boeschoten specifically states that the misunderstandings are 'exclusively caused by lexical items [= content morphemes], apart from just one instance of a bound morpheme' (p. 89). Therefore, the study provides no information about deficiency of grammatical models in the home. In all likelihood, generation two's exposure to L1 vocabulary is reduced; further, it stands to reason that some generation-two children *are* exposed to reduced models. But such studies are not empirical support for a blanket assumption about reduced grammars.

Second, under an optimal model, shift is better viewed both theoretically and empirically as not so much reduction as difference/substitution (i.e. a composite Matrix Language structures the morphosyntax). That is, even if there are surface-level omissions, at the abstract level the morphosyntactic frame may show alterations, not gaps. This argument is developed in section 5.5 when quantitative details on L1 attrition in a number of corpora are considered.

Third, how shift is defined makes a difference. For example, Hakuta and D'Andrea discuss two different definitions of shift away from Spanish to English among California Hispanic high school students (N = 308). They speak of shift defined as (i) a change in choice (which is the preferred language) or (ii) as a loss in Spanish proficiency. They state that 'defined as proficiency loss, that loss is best described as occurring most sharply across generations. . . . Defined as a shift in choice, however, this process is observed to begin immediately and in a progressive manner both across and within depth cohorts' (pp. 93–4). (In their study, the 'depth cohort' in which a subject is placed varies with these factors: (i) born in Mexico, (ii) U.S. arrival at what age, and (iii) where parents born.) Hakuta and D'Andrea also found that 'maintenance of proficiency in Spanish is primarily associated with adult language practice in the home, rather than the subject's language attitude or language choice outside the home' (p. 82). As already indicated, shift in choice means less variation in the language use across domains. In fact, the authors conclude, 'Outside the home domain, a subject's language choice shows consistent shift towards English across depths' (p. 84).

Fourth, the extent of shift, at least in some immigrant populations studied, may be exaggerated. Of course, the received view is that the combination of intra-generational attrition and intergenerational shift results in near-complete loss of a migrant language after several generations (as in the often-cited 'cascade' model of Gonzo and Saltarelli 1983). Of course, there is clear support for such a model. For example, Huls and van de Mond (1992: 107), reporting on Turkish families in the Netherlands, state that although Turkish is clearly the dominant language in a family that has lived in the Netherlands for five years, in another family that has been there for fifteen years, 'The dominant language appears to be Dutch'. They also state that the children use Dutch more frequently than their parents.

Similarly, the received view that young second-generation immigrant children typically show a reduced version of their L1 and older immigrants show deep losses is not always accurate. For example, the study in Verhoeven and Boeschoten (1986) is sometimes cited as evidence supporting this view. The results are based on a productive-vocabulary test and sentence-imitation tasks. In regard to grammatical skills, they specifically studied mean length of utterance and number

of non-finite verb forms (verbal nouns, participles, what the
and conditionals) over a hundred utterances. True, these
first-language progress is slower for Turkish children from
age in a Netherlands-based sample in comparison with a sa
cifically, the tests showed significant differences in the co
produced. This is what leads the authors to conclude 'the ac
guage skills by 4- or 8-year-old Turkish children in the Ne
typified as stagnated' (p. 241). Yet, a close reading of the arti
still write, 'typical language deficiencies among the former
not found. These children showed no problems with infle
even incorporated Dutch words seem to follow sound
(pp. 248–9).

Further, de Bot and Clyne (1994) report that the Dutch im
whom they studied largely retained Dutch after many years
jects first studied in the 1970s and then again in 1987.
study, they conclude, 'The data presented here seem to su
not necessarily attrition within generations, at any rate not
of migrants' (p. 27). The only significant results they fou
subjects in 1971 and 1987) were in the type/token ratio of English items (but English types did not increase significantly by 1987) and in adverb placement. While some of their determiners were non-target like, the change across studies was not significant and, more important, the incorrect articles represent substitutions, not losses. Note also that in his study of German immigrants to the United States, forty years or more after their arrival, Gross (2000*a*) found relatively little evidence of attrition in case assignments in determiners or adjectives (cf. section 5.5).

At the same time, other studies do show that when some speakers, especially very young children, no longer use their L1 frequently, the result is extensive loss, not L1 retention or even L1 substitutions. For example, a study by Kaufman and Aronoff (1991) of a single Israeli child who moved to the United States shows a very rapid changeover from Hebrew as the Matrix Language of her bilingual speech to English as the Matrix Language. That is, she may retain some Hebrew content morphemes, but she substitutes English inflections for Hebrew ones. Also, Kuhberg (1992) reports on two Turkish girls (seven and nine years old) who had been fluent in German while living in Germany, but who—upon returning to Turkey and life in a monolingual Turkish society—in the course of fifteen or twenty months moved from being able to carry on monolingual conversations in German to being able to use German only in Turkish/German codeswitching. Also, their speech showed a rapid turnover to Turkish as the Matrix Language of this speech. When asked to speak German, they still produced some German content morphemes, but very few German system morphemes. These cases are discussed again in Chapter 6 when the Matrix Language turnover is dealt with in detail.

However, it is important to note the apparent socio-psychological profile of these cases and to distinguish the route that attrition takes with them from that of speakers who are not so motivated to lose a language as these children. For example, the child losing Hebrew is making no effort to retain her L1. Kaufman and Aronoff (1991: 176), speak of 'the disintegration of the L1 verbal system, accelerated by the child's increasing unwillingess to speak Hebrew'. In the case of the Turkish girls in Kuhberg's study, their only exposure to German is through conversations with the researcher. For these children, attrition means rapid shift and no retention. In contrast, for some other speakers of an attriting language, their goal is not to drop the language. They are simply adding more and more use of the dominant community language and this results in some structural effects on their L1, but the L1 is retained. For example, the Russian boys whom Schmitt studies (cf. section 5.5) still use their Russian skills with their families, even while they are using English more and more in their everyday lives. Perhaps because of this difference, their Russian does not show change in all areas and where it is changing, it shows more substitution than absolute loss.

Fifth, the factors that tip speakers toward attrition and shift in any generation are complex, and their systematic consideration is beyond the scope of this study. To illustrate the types of factors that studies report, consider some findings from Hulsen, de Bot, and Weltens (2002), who studied social network effects in the Dutch community of New Zealand. Their results support the hypothesis that the relative number of L1 contacts in the network in relation to the number of L2 contacts is related to the importance speakers attach to maintenance. However, another hypothesis that the number of L1 contacts in the non-primary network is an indicator of maintenance is not supported; instead, the number of L1 contacts in the primary network seems more influential for language maintenance and shift. Thus, L1 contacts in the neighborhood did not seem to be major factors in maintenance; the authors offer as a possible explanation that this domain seems a less important source of information for second- and third-generation than for first-generation speakers. A hypothesis about the importance of contacts in a home country network (i.e. the Netherlands) is supported. The study also includes a word-retrieval experiment.

Even in a close-knit, homogeneous community, the progression of shift (and therefore attrition) can vary a good deal across speakers in a community from apparently very abrupt to very gradual. Dorian (1973, 1981) has been at the forefront in detailing how not all members of the community have the same grammars. Some members of the East Sutherland Gaelic community she studied persist with the language of their elders relatively intact, but others she can classify only as semi-speakers.

5.3.3. *Motivations promoting attrition and shift*

Speakers generally shift for two reasons. First, they shift languages because of a shift in the balance of the instrumental and sentimental values associated with languages. Of course, language is cited over and over as an ethnic marker of great importance. Witness the grievances in 2001 of the Albanian minority in Macedonia; high on its list of desired changes was the campaign to make Albanian the language of instruction at a self-proclaimed university in Tetovo in Macedonia's northwest. Still, in some cases first languages do lose their ethnic salience. From his extensive studies in small linguistic groups in eastern Africa, Dimmendaal concludes that 'language may not be as important a potential symbol of ethnic identity as some are led to believe' (1989: 28). He cites blacksmiths he met among the Torit people of Sudan who identified themselves as Lopid, despite the fact that several had Tenet as their first language. He also noted that the pastoral Turkana in northern Kenya do not identify themselves with the hunter-gatherers in the area, even though they refer to themselves as Turkana and share with them the Turkana language. Instead, these pastoral Turkana 'feel greater empathy and a historic bond with the Jie and Karimojong across the border in Uganda' (p. 29).

A second reason for speakers to shift languages is more speculative: the model that current speakers use themselves may develop a composite Matrix Language as its frame, based on more and more abstract grammatical input from the dominant language in the picture. At some threshold point, speakers may just drop the composite and shift to the dominant language. This means that shift is not necessarily gradual for many speakers in the final analysis. It may be that speakers reach a point where speaking a variety with much bilingual input in the grammatical frame means too much 'cognitive weight'. This scenario is implied by Haugen (1950*b*) when he writes about the switch of Norwegian immigrants in the United States from Norwegian to English as their main language. Haugen also supports my contention expressed in Chapter 6 that a composite Matrix Language still basically has the morphosyntactic frame of one language. Haugen writes, 'They [bilingual speakers] may switch rapidly from one to the other, but at any given moment they are speaking only one, even when they resort to the other for assistance . . . speakers of e.g. AmN [American Norwegian] continue to speak a recognizably Norwegian language distinct from their English down to the time when they switch to the latter for good' (p. 211).

5.4. An overview of attrition studies

In this section, I review themes in the literature on attrition. Specifically, I discuss the 'Regression Hypothesis' (simplified as 'last in, first out') of Roman Jakobson and earlier researchers. Finally, I go on to discuss critically how the Regression Hypothesis has been reworked or replaced in the current attrition literature. The scope of this discussion is limited to earlier rather than the very late points on the attrition continuum, meaning the grammar of a language near total grammatical demise is not a major topic in this volume.

5.4.1. *Late stages of attrition*

Such a state, language death, may come about in various ways, although I support Denison's view that in general 'languages die, not from loss of rules, but from loss of speakers' (1977: 21). Yet, a case reported for the Albanian-speaking Arvanitika speech community in Greece (cf. Sasse 1991, 1992) seems to argue otherwise. For example, Sasse (1992: 71) offers this characterization: 'Analogy goes in all directions. Suppletive forms are not remembered, irregularities are not observed or are applied to forms where they do not belong. Verb forms are confused. . . . The funniest phenomenon is phantasy morphology (something which sounds like an Aravanitika morpheme being attached to a form) or blends of any sort.' But, as will become clear, my argument is that a language's reaching this extreme state seems unusual. Instead, a language may be marked by extensive analogical leveling and substitutions, but there is always a clear morphosyntactic frame, even if a composite Matrix Language is its source. Polinsky's comment that 'the loss of grammatical system is non-random' (based on the findings from her study of adult speakers of American Russian with severe attrition) supports my view. She states, 'even significant language loss has a principled grammar of its own' (1997: 401).

5.4.2. *A typology of attrition*

How two of the best-known researchers on attrition, de Bot and Weltens, categorize research on language attrition in their 1995 article is a good starting point. First, they divide attrition according to whether it affects an L1 or an L2. Their second basis of classification is the issue of whether the language studied is the dominant variety in the community (i.e. whether what is studied is an L1 or an L2 for most speakers in the community).

De Bot and Weltens then distinguish four types of research. The first type of research is the study of L1 loss in an L1 environment, largely language loss by aging people. Their second type is research on loss of the L1 in an L2 environment. In their scheme, the third type of attrition is loss of a foreign language learned in school (what they mean by loss of an L2 in an L1 environment). Their fourth type is loss of an L2 in an L2 environment; e.g. loss of English by immigrants not speaking English as their L1, but living in an English environment. De Bot and Weltens state there is little evidence of this type of loss. The main interest here—and in most studies—is attrition of an L1 in a largely L2 environment. Note that de Bot and Weltens do not differentiate research on adults from children in their typology. However, one of my main interests in this volume is to compare attrition in the grammars of both children and adults in their L1 when living in a predominantly L2 environment.

5.4.3. *How attrition has been studied*

The literature on attrition has a number of common features. First, even though attrition is normally considered as an individual phenomenon, much of the study has been more sociological than linguistic in nature in the sense it often has consisted of large-scale surveys of communities. Second, if speakers have been dealt with as individuals, often their lexicons have been studied more than their grammars. For example, in a study of the shift from Swedish to Finnish in the Swedish minority group in Finland, Tandefelt (1992) reports that under 'variation in the mode of expression' she studied lexical density, lexical variation, type–token ratio, and verb variation, but not aspects of speakers' grammatical systems. Sometimes the term 'forgetting' is used in the literature, along with the implication that words are the crucial elements that are forgotten.

The third feature follows from the second: there are very few detailed studies of grammatical structure for individuals or groups of speakers undergoing attrition. There are exceptions, such as Dorian's studies of Scottish Gaelic (e.g. 1973, 1978) as well as the cross-linguistic study of Polinsky (1995) and her more specific studies of American Russian attrition (1997, forthcoming). Further, most studies of American Indian languages include a few details on language loss in progress even though they typically refer to loss.

Fourth, related to the lack of specific data sets is the lack of quantitative data on attrition—even when specific data sets are studied. For example, Mithun (1990: 14) reports that 'the speech of even the least fluent Central Pomo speaker abounds with examples of standard case marking, even where the constructions involved are intricate'. However, as support, she only cites two examples, adding 'this speaker used patient case marking appropriately even in contexts where patient arguments would function as subjects in English'.

To take another example, Klintborg (1999) offers a study of very interesting data (audio recordings of Swedish immigrants to the United States who were recorded more than forty years after their time of immigration). However, one must be satisfied with only a few quantitatively based statements about the grammatical system of these speakers, such as this one:

> One might also suspect that American Swedish speech would be colored by the English way of expressing definiteness by means of *the* as against the Swedish clitic article. Still, such traces are very rare: *den kyrka* ('the church') with a separate article replacing the expected *-n* ending, and *den västkusten* ('the west coast') with its double article (both determiner and clitic) are among the few clear cases of such an influence as are the equally few cases where gender, too, is misapplied. (p. 58)

A third example again shows how tantalizing some remarks about the extent of morphosyntactic attrition can be; unfortunately, again, the remarks are not backed up with quantification. In Bavin (1989), Warlpiri, an Australian language spoken in a remote settlement of 800 residents, is the subject. What is of most interest to the discussion here is what is said about Warlpiri morphosyntax. Even though the complex pronominal system has been simplified, individual speakers retain a good deal of Warlpiri morphology. Referring to one young Warlpiri speaker, Bavin states, 'She can and does use complex morphology which includes case markers, focus markers, compound verbs, infinitive constructions, and modal particles' (p. 279). However, no more details are given and the emphasis in this article is on the use of English loanwords. Almost all the examples Bavin cites show how English loans are integrated. She states that English loans 'can take focus markers, case markers and other morphology' (p. 277).

Note that these comments from all three of these studies are arguments against the blanket claim that grammatical loss is an outstanding characteristic of speakers whose L1s are used less often in the face of more use of an L2 that has become dominant in the community. Of special interest is what is said about case marking by Mithun about Central Pomo and by Bavin about Warlpiri. Because they are late system morphemes, such morphemes as case marking are not among the first morphemes lost under attrition. Because they are structurally assigned, they have little conceptual content and it is hypothesized that they are only accessed when larger constitutents are constructed. For these reasons, they seem to be hard to acquire. But once acquired and because they fill slots in the morphosyntactic frame rather than serve to enlarge the lexicon, they do not seem to be easily lost. Again, unfortunately, there are few quantitative studies to offer strong evidence either for or against this assumption. Yet, they seem to remain relatively fixed in more of the data sets in the literature than not. I take up these morphemes again in section 5.5.

Fifth, overviews prevail. These are found in many different places, but few are very recent. There are number of edited volumes, most on language loss in general (e.g. Lambert and Freed 1982, Dorian 1989, Hyltenstam and Obler 1989*a*, Lambert 1989). Some collected works refer specifically to attrition (e.g. Weltens, de Bot, and van Els 1986, Seliger and Vago 1991). Although these works contain individual articles, many of them remain at the overview level. In addition, there are some individual articles outside these volumes that are intended as overviews (e.g. Preston 1982, Sharwood Smith 1983, Clyne 1992, de Bot and Weltens 1995, de Bot 1996, *inter alia*). There are also articles relevant to attrition in edited volumes that focus on other topics, such as language transfer (e.g. Seliger 1996). The articles in a special issue of *Studies in Second Language Acquisition* (1989) are more specific, but do not focus exclusively on grammatical structure nor do they necessarily contain much quantitative data. There is also a special number of *Applied Psycholinguistics* (1986, volume 7) on language loss. Fewer volumes or articles deal with specific topics (e.g. Brenzinger (1992) deals with language loss in East Africa; de Bot (1999) offers a psycholinguistic model of language loss; de Bot and Clyne (1994) provide longitudinal data on attrition in Dutch immigrants in Australia).

5.4.4. *Dealing with the Regression Hypothesis*

Even though I have indicated most studies of attrition are descriptive, there are studies that are more theoretical in nature, with an emphasis on the proposing of hypotheses to explain what happens in attrition. Further, most researchers offer some ideas to explain the data distributions they have found.

Whether what is offered is a set of formal hypotheses or only passing comments, most researchers directly or indirectly indicate awareness of the so-called Regression Hypothesis.

Most researchers who mention the Regression Hypothesis by name attribute it to Roman Jakobson (1941). However, Berko-Gleason (1982: 17) points out that 'speculation about the relationship between acquisition and loss has been in the linguistic literature since the 19th century'. She notes that in the 1880s, Ribot proposed a dictum that has come to be known as 'the rule of Ribot', applying the rule to multilingual aphasics. This dictum holds that the most recently acquired features are the ones most likely to be lost first. According to Berko-Gleason, Freud paid attention to this view and used the term *regression* to refer to a return to the earlier stages of linguistic development. When Jakobson took up this idea, he provided evidence from phonology. In suggesting that there are certain universal mechanisms in language, he links late acquisition with markedness, suggesting that those features that are acquired late are likely to be lost first. De Bot and Weltens (1991) offer a clear overview of the supposed parallels between first language acquisition and what happens in language change (what has been called the Recapitulation Hypothesis) and the supposed links between language acquisition and language loss (the Regression Hypothesis). In their strong forms, both hypotheses are, at best, out of favor.

Many of the overviews on attrition begin with reference to the Regression Hypothesis. If researchers offer their own hypotheses, they typically discount Jakobson. But then, with not a little incongruity, it turns out that many of their hypotheses are really the Regression Hypothesis in new garb.[2] There are some exceptions. For example, the main hypothesis of de Bot and Clyne (1989) that is specific to L2 loss is that such language loss (in long-term immigrants) is not a simple regression phenomenon that occurs the same way across individuals; they argue that the level of retained proficiency in an L2 is critical. Also, Jordens, de Bot, and Trapman (1989) propose two different hypotheses for L1 and L2 speakers who show potential attrition, but their references to 'cognitive factors' remain vague.

5.4.5. *A representative view: Anderson's hypotheses*

Even though at least some of Anderson's hypotheses resemble the Regression Hypothesis, he is arguably the researcher whose hypotheses are still most often cited with approval (Anderson 1982, 1989, *inter alia*). He presented his ideas on attrition, as well as on Interlanguage in second-language acquisition in a number of articles in the 1980s. While I cannot agree with the assumptions behind all of his hypotheses, I can cite one of his premises with approval, his belief in finding answers to what is going on in attrition by looking at other linguistic phenomena.

[2] I thank Steve Gross for suggesting this interpretation to me.

I discuss the particulars of his 1982 article because it is here that Anderson presents his hypotheses in detail. In general, as explanations for attrition, Anderson cites these theoretical notions as explanations: markedness, acquisition order, frequency, transparency, and match to the dominant language.

Altogether, he suggests nine hypotheses, most with several parts. They refer to lexical reduction, phonological reduction, morphological reduction, syntactic reduction, preference for analytic syntax, analogical leveling, paraphrase and circumlocution, lexical borrowing, and morphosyntactic transfer. I am most interested in those referring to morphosyntax, but because there are so many, not even all of them can be discussed in detail. I turn first to the five subhypotheses regarding morphological reduction. They predict (i) the loss of morphologically marked categories, (ii) retention of such categories if they are used frequently by Language Competents, (iii) retention of these categories if they are also marked in the stronger (dominant) language, (iv) retention of morphological distinctions with a high functional load, and (v) retention affected by acquisition order. Not surprisingly, the ones referring to markedness and acquisition order are not very different from the Regression Hypothesis. For example, on acquisition order, Anderson's hypothesis 4e predicts:

> Those grammatical morphemes acquired earliest will be retained the longest by an LA [person whose competence in the relevant language has eroded] and those acquired latest will be lost earliest by the LA. (p. 97)

He states that this hypothesis is a consequence of the other four hypotheses on morphological reduction, linking them all to acquisition: 'The same factors which favor or inhibit acquisition would favor or inhibit retention' (p. 97).

In general, Anderson's hypotheses about both morphology and syntax predict that what will remain will be simplified, streamlined forms (i.e. free forms over bound forms), with semantically transparent patterns prevailing. When there is more than one possible surface structure for one underlying relation, only one surface structure will remain. His hypotheses on analogical leveling also predict that a more regular form or construction will be chosen over an irregular one. Note that these predictions imply markedness at work, too.

Anderson's hypotheses that are specifically about morphosyntactic transfer deserve some comment. His first subhypothesis under this rubric flatly predicts that 'An LA [language attriter] will produce in language X morphological and syntactic constructions based on his stronger language'. The second hypothesis is a version of his 'transfer to somewhere' principle that is well known in the literature of second-language acquisition. This principle assumes that transfer is only possible when there is a structurally receptive slot. His hypothesis regarding attrition states:

> An LA [language attriter] will rely on transfer as a compensatory strategy more often in those cases where forces internal to the language being transferred to (i.e. his weaker

language) would also tend to produce the same construction through overgeneralization. (p. 109)

By way of introduction, Anderson makes an even stronger statement, saying that 'transfer is most likely (and, I am inclined to say, *only possible*) in those forces where both forces internal to the language (overgeneralization) and forces traceable to transfer co-exist' (p. 108). Exactly what forces would have to be present is left open; however, again, something akin to markedness is implied (with the definition of markedness possibly specific to the participating languages).

In addition to his hypotheses, Anderson also offers two general language-use strategies that he assumes LA speakers (language attriters) follow. His first strategy calls for free morphemes whenever possible. The second strategy states that, 'whenever there are different devices to express the same basic meaning, use only one of these devices' (p. 100).

There are a number of attractive elements in Anderson's approach. First, he recognizes that attrition is not an isolated phenomenon. From both an empirical and a theoretical point of view, he is certainly correct to argue that hypotheses 'should be consistent with what we know of other contexts where both LCs [linguistically competent speakers] and LAs [language attriters] acquire and use language' (p. 84). He also states as a basic assumption that language attrition 'can be best studied, described, documented, explained and understood within a framework that includes other phenomena of language acquisition and use' (p. 86). Specifically, he mentions first-language acquisition, pidgin and creole studies, and languages in contact in bilingual communities. I can endorse some of Anderson's hypotheses and especially his views that speakers employ compensatory strategies referring both to discourse strategies and morphosyntax as attritition sets in.

5.4.6. *The lure of markedness*

I stress that Anderson is not the only researcher to rely on markedness for driving his predictions; in fact, this is the explanation most often proposed and often linked with order of acquisition. In the early 1980s, when lists of features characterizing attrition were frequent, many of the items on the list of Preston (1982) refer to markedness by different names (uncommon items, marked items, unique items). Preston's list also includes 'items learned last'. A year later, Sharwood Smith (1983) took up the notion of simplicity; it is no more or no less than another version of markedness. The only difference is that he approaches an explanation from the point of view of processing. For example, one of his hypotheses is this: 'The learner will adopt into either L1 or L2 structures from the other language that will lead to overall processing simplicity. Those subsystems which are relatively easier to process will be less easily lost, more easily acquired, or more likely to remain fossilized in L2' (p. 226).

Markedness figures when attrition is internally motivated, according to Seliger and Vago in their introduction to a volume edited in 1991 on first-language attrition. They point to 'two principal forces bearing on linguistic forms in attriting L1 grammars' (p. 7).

The first force is 'externally induced' and results in such processes as 'variously called transfer, interference, convergence, interlingual effects, or crosslinguistic influences'. What is involved is that 'an element (form, construction, etc.) in L1 is patterned on analogy to L2'. They cite rule generalization as the most common strategy under this force, stating 'an L2 rule is extended to L1'.

The second force refers to leveling of various types, change that they argue is internally induced by either 'universal principles or is related to some fact in the particular grammar of L1' (p. 10). They argue that universal principles have this result: 'in L1 attrition "unmarked" forms are better preserved than and substitute for "marked" ones, but not vice versa' (p. 10). Types of leveling include analogical leveling (an irregular pattern is eliminated), paradigmatic leveling (more uniform paradigms because alternations of morphemes are reduced), category leveling (the domain of one category is extended to another as in tense/aspect systems), and category switch (a category may be maintained, but it is expressed by a different linguistic form).

Curiously, they do not make a clear connection between rule generalization and leveling. Is there no possibility for interaction between the two forces they describe? Can markedness not promote the influence of external influences in any leveling?

In 1996, Seliger still cites markedness as a major reason for changes in an L1 grammar. Sources for this changed grammar are two: (i) the grammar of the L2 and (ii) what remains of UG abilities. Given these sources (and assuming access to non-bilingual native speakers has been cut off), Seliger goes on to say 'changes that take place in the L1 grammar as a result of attrition will reflect (i) transfer from the L2 and (ii) a preference to transfer those elements in L2 that are more in agreement with core universals and therefore less marked' (p. 617). Seliger also proposes a Redundancy Reduction Principle: 'the bilingual creates a new rule for L1 in those areas of grammar where the L2 rule is simpler or less marked in some way' (pp. 617–18).

5.4.7. *What is markedness?*

None of these researchers seems to consider what Thomason and Kaufman (1988) point out about appeals to markedness. Thomason and Kaufman offer a catalogue of the inconsistent array of features that researchers in various areas of linguistics have called marked. They also point out that few, if any, definitions of markedness have an objective basis so that they can be applied consistently across different data sets. Without objective criteria for markedness, at least theory-dependent definitions of markedness are a prerequisite for appeals to it. Any definitions seem to be few and far between, if they exist.

However, whether researchers have theoretical frameworks or not (and more often they do not) and any definitions, they continue to make markedness the favorite explanation for what happens in attrition. We should also note that lack of criteria for markedness also impedes attempts to establish the actual order of acquisition (or loss).

Some researchers do recognize that markedness is not an all-purpose explanation. Even though Clyne (1992) also cites markedness when discussing which features are affected most in attrition, he does recognize that markedness alone is not a sufficient explanation. Clyne states, 'In German, where the gender system is *more marked*, however (three genders, many case-forms), the basic structure remains even in the second and later generations' (p. 22). He compares loss of gender distinctions in determiners among German and Dutch immigrants to Australia and reports that Dutch is moving toward a single unmarked article, but not German. In his data set, Dutch speakers change fifty-two different nouns taking *het* to *de* as their determiner; he reports that comparable German data show only ten gender changes.

As if in an attempt to reconcile his hypothesis mentioning markedness with his findings, Clyne writes, 'The marked features are more likely to be abandoned, except that this more probable in the less complex language than in the more complex one' (p. 24). He recognizes that what his data show is that 'on the whole, for gender in "Australian German", *comparatively* high markedness does not increase syntactic transference and change' (p. 22).

5.4.8. *Sociolinguistic-based explanations for attrition*

In the concluding chapter of her study of Spanish and English in contact in Los Angeles, Silva-Corvalán (1994*a*) sums up her views of what motivates the types of changes that are taking place in Spanish there. In general, she cites sociolinguistic forces as paramount among motivations (e.g. 'Absence of normative pressures on the subordinate language, restriction in the range of communicative uses of the subordinate language, and speakers' positive attitudes towards the superordinate language in contrast to either neutral or negative attitudes toward the subordinate one' (p. 212)). Even specifically in regard to grammatical changes, she argues for language-internal motivations and, again, sociolinguistic considerations. She says that 'postulated direct influence from English is not justified' in regard to tense–modal–aspect morphological changes and goes on to state that 'transfer from English does not appear to play a role in the various patterns of omission of dative, accusative, and reflexive Cls [verbal clitic pronouns]. The complexity of the Spanish system and reduced use and exposure to this language emerge as more adequate reasons for these modifications' (p. 208).

In addition Silva-Corvalán offers a more psycholinguistic explanation of convergence (perhaps related to her comments about certain details of Spanish grammar), followed by a list of the strategies that characterize convergence and that this explanation predicts. Her comments are worth quoting because they are representative of the views of researchers favoring a functional explanation. (In a footnote, she adds that a fifth strategy is codeswitching.)

The general hypothesis investigated is that in language-contact situations bilinguals develop strategies at lightening the cognitive load of having to remember and use two different linguistic systems. In the use of the subordinate language, these strategies include: simplification of grammatical categories and lexical oppositions; overgeneralization of forms, frequently following a regularizing pattern; development of periphrastic constructions, either to achieve paradigmatic regularity or to replace less semantically transparent bound morphemes; and direct and indirect transfer of forms from the superordinate language. (p. 207)

Specifically in reference to contact-induced change (and this may include attrition), Poplack (1997) voices a similar view of the motivations involved. She endorses the view that few would quarrel with and which has been especially forcefully expressed by Thomason and Kaufman (1988) that 'study of the structural properties of language alone can not lead to a predictive theory of linguistic interference' (p. 285). But then she goes on to make a stronger statement: 'This is because the direction and extent of interference, as well as the kinds of features transferred, are socially determined.' While I agree with the notion that studying the social factors involved gives a more complete picture of language contact, I part company with the view that such factors determine the types of features that can be transferred, as is clear in the next section.

5.5. Supporting my own theoretical assumptions

I now present my own assumptions about the morphosyntactic nature of attrition, within the framework of both the Abstract Level model and the 4-M model. My analysis of data from the literature and new data provides empirical support.

5.5.1. *The theoretical framework*

For me, explanations for the form that attrition takes should meet four requirements. First, any hypotheses about attrition should be related to other hypotheses applying to other contact phenomena. If this is the case, then any alternative explanations specifically advanced for attrition data fail to garner support unless they are part of a set of hypotheses that can explain other contact data. That is, simply asserting that explanation X is weak is not convincing unless a researcher can show that all explanations related to explanation X for related data are weak. This first requirement implies the second: any explanation X for attrition should be part of a theoretical framework that can generate explanations for related phenomena. Third, the terms of any explanations should be amenable to objective definitions. Fourth, quantitative data are the preferred source of evidence.

I hope to meet these requirements in the hypotheses I advance here. My views are based on two models already discussed in this volume, the Abstract Level model and the 4-M model. The relevant divisions these models make in their subject matter are open to objective definitions. A reason I am at pains to state the objective ways in which the terms of these models can be defined is that the existence of such criteria contrast with the lack of such objectivity when researchers refer to 'markedness' or even 'simplicity'. Note that the two models motivate the hypotheses that follow, but the hypotheses are not components of the models themselves.

5.5.1.1. The Abstract Level model

Recall the three divisions under the Abstract Level model:

Lexical-conceptual structure (semantic and pragmatic information)
Predicate-argument structure (the mapping of thematic structure onto syntactic relations)
Morphological realization patterns (surface realizations of grammatical structure)

Preverbal intentions in the conceptualizer activate language-specific semantic-pragmatic feature bundles and these are mapped onto lemmas in the mental lexicon as lexical-conceptual structure. Language-specific linking rules based on language universals are the source of predicate-argument structure and morphological realization patterns.

Of course, the details of these three levels are language-specific; however, all lemmas in the mental lexicon include these three levels of abstract grammatical structure. Lemmas underlie surface morphemes and they contain in these three levels all the grammatical information necessary for the surface realization of a lexical entry. The objective basis of how these three levels are defined makes it possible to distinguish one level from another in surface forms in any language.

5.5.1.2. The 4-M model

The 4-M model divides morphemes into four types, content morphemes and three types of system morpheme. The distribution of these morphemes across diverse data sets motivates hypotheses about how the different morpheme types are activated in language production. That is, under this model, the classification of morphemes is not basic; rather, the mechanisms for activating and combining morphemes are basic. In fact, Myers-Scotton and Jake (2000*a*: 1053) claim that 'the interaction between conceptual information and complex grammatical structure in any entry in the mental lexicon and the rules of grammar in the Formulator [in production] are what give any reality to the notion of morpheme'. In combination with content morphemes, 'early' system morphemes contain essential conceptual structure for conveying a speaker's intentions. Together, these morphemes send directions to the Formulator where larger morphosyntactic units are built. When the Formulator receives such directions, another type of system morpheme, late system morphemes, may also be activated. Instead of conveying essential conceptual structure, these late system morphemes are involved in building larger morphosyntactic units because they indicate relationships in the mapping of conceptual structure onto phrase structures.

However, what is relevant in formulating hypotheses based on the 4-M model about attrition is that the four types of morpheme can be identified based on their formal syntactic properties. Myers-Scotton and Jake (e.g. 2001) do not assume that all maximal projections have functional heads. This is an important assumption underlying our definitions of different morpheme type. Recall that the often-cited thematic–functional distinction is not the basis for classifying morphemes in the 4-M model.

Content morphemes are directly elected by intentions; they can occur independently of other elements in any syntactic string.

'Early' system morphemes rely on the heads of their maximal projection (content morphemes) for activation and for information about their form (e.g. whether an article is to express definiteness or not in English).

Late system morphemes satisfy different requirements; they are structurally assigned to indicate relations between elements when a larger constituent is constructed.

'Bridge' late system morphemes occur when the structures of their maximal projections require them. Their form depends on the grammatical configurations that a language-specific grammar requires of a projection. They do not depend on a content morpheme head.

'Outsider' late system morphemes depend on grammatical information outside the immediate maximal projection in which they occur. They are co-indexed with elements outside this projection.

5.5.2. *Attrition hypotheses and the Abstract Level model*

I now state a set of assumptions, offering empirical support where it is available.

Basic assumption. Speakers showing attrition are operating with a morphosyntactic frame just as monolingual speakers do or bilingual speakers producing other forms of contact phenomena. No speakers operate without a grammatical frame. That is, I reject what Seliger (1996: 615) sees as 'the logical problem of primary language attrition'. He contrasts first-language attrition with either L1 or L2 acquisition. His argument is that in acquisition, there is a '*convergence* in the direction of a putative model grammar to which the acquirer, child or adult, is exposed'. But attrition, he claims, 'may be assumed to be *divergent* in the sense that there is no model to be aspired to'. In contrast, I assume that the speaker showing attrition has a model; it is simply a model for which the frame has become a composite, meaning that more than one linguistic system is the source.

Hypotheses 1 and 2 depend on the Abstract Level model. While many researchers recognize changes in the lexicon of speakers undergoing attrition, this model allows us to discuss those changes more precisely and make predictions about the order and degree of change at each of the three levels that the model identifies. Further, the model provides a mechanism for any type of change: in bilingual speech, any level of abstract grammatical structure may be split and recombined with parts of the same level coming from another language.

Overall, a hierarchy in which predicate-argument structure is least susceptible to modification in attrition and lexical-conceptual structure is most susceptible is assumed. These relationships can be expressed in the following general way and then more specifically in the hypotheses that follow:

Predicate-argument structure < morphological realization patterns < lexical-conceptual structure.

5.5.2.1. Lexical-conceptual structure

Hypothesis 1. Of the three levels of abstract lexical structure, the level of lexical-conceptual structure in content morphemes is most susceptible to change through attrition/convergence.

Changes in abstract lexical structure are the most visible signs of convergence or attrition. The only difference between convergence and attrition is that such changes under convergence are not seen as necessarily leading to language loss and shift while changes under attrition are so viewed. Whether convergence or attrition is considered, researchers include many anecdotal examples of how L1 content morphemes show changes in their semantic fields. For example, in a study of the convergence of New York City Spanish to English, Otheguy, Garcia, and Fernández (1989) report that the Spanish verb *jugar* 'play' is used in a way that is new for Spanish. They suggest that the use of this verb in the phrase, *jugar música* 'play music', is based on one of the meanings of English *play.* They state that of the existing (Spanish) senses of *jugar,* 'none . . . have anything to do with the handling of musical instruments' (p. 45).

Whether the topic is convergence or attrition, a more precise way of discussing what happens to the structure of L1 lexical elements in bilingual contexts is to consider them within the Abstract Level model. The model explains resulting structures as evidence that levels of abstract structure from one language can be split and recombined with levels from another language. Note that premises underlying the model are that language production is modular and that lexical entries are complex (Bolonyai (1999: 96) makes a similar comment).

Hypothesis 1 predicts that when an L1 lexical element is used in a non-target-like way, change at the level of lexical-conceptual structure is the most frequent cause. Because the level of lexical-conceptual structure is the level most closely tied to the speaker's intentions, the prediction is that this level is most susceptible to modification because such change can tailor a content morpheme to fit those intentions. Lexical-conceptual structure is modified for two main reasons. (i) In comparison with distinctions made in an L2 lexicon, semantic distinctions that the L1 lexicon makes are no longer important. (ii) New distinctions become important in the message that a speaker wishes to convey. For these reasons, the speaker may remodel an L1 element to reflect new intentions. That is, the speaker combines some L2 structure with L1 structure.

The most prevalent comment in the attrition literature reflects this claim: the lexicon of speakers showing attrition has been reduced or has changed in some way. Unfortunately, most of the literature includes, at best, lists of examples, not quantitative data. However, many examples of lexical change are, in fact, specifically examples of changes in the lexical-conceptual structure of L1 elements. For example, in writing about attrition in Malinche Mexicano (Nahuatl), Hill and Hill include a list of loan translations and blends, reporting only that the number is large (1986: 340–1). One example they cite is the Spanish expression *hacer caso* 'to worry' with *hacer* 'to do' as the source of the new use of Mexicano *chīhua* 'to make'. Mexicano speakers use this verb for 'to make' to express 'worrying', as in *āmo xquinchīhuilī* 'don't worry about them' (p. 340).

Or, to take another example, in his study of the Turkish of Turkish children living in the Netherlands, Boeschoten (1992) finds instances of what he calls 'misinterpetations'. Some examples can be interpreted as the result of a splitting and recombining of lexical-conceptual structure (possibly from Dutch as well as Turkish). For example, one child uses the Turkish verb *likle* 'to button up' for 'to close the door'.

5.5.2.1.1. SCHMITT'S STUDY OF RUSSIAN BOYS IN AN ENGLISH ENVIRONMENT

Fortunately, there is an extensive body of quantitative data to support the assumption that lexical-conceptual structure is most affected in attrition. Schmitt (2000, 2001) studies the Russian spoken by five Russian boys who now live in the United States and for whom English is becoming the dominant language. Their median age for arrival in the United States was four years old. The boys were first recorded five years after arrival (i.e. at about age nine) and then again after two years (i.e. at about age eleven). Since their arrival, they have been going to English-medium schools. They speak some Russian at home with parents and grandparents, but English is their primary language now. The boys were recorded in natural conversations in home environments, but were asked to speak Russian.

Schmitt specifically studies her data in terms of the Abstract Level model and offers quantitative data that show very convincingly that lexical-conceptual structure is the level most affected when attrition sets in. In the first data set, almost 26 per cent (227/878) of the CPs show convergence at any of the three levels under the model. Almost 47 per cent (106/227) of these cases of convergence are at the level of lexical-conceptual structure. In the second data set, 33 per cent of the CPs (399/1,204) show convergence at any level. Close to 60 per cent (239/399) of the cases show convergence at the level of lexical-conceptual structure.

Schmitt interprets this increase in overall convergence as showing that English is doing more than just serving as the Embedded Language in any codeswitching; it is encroaching on the lexical structure of Russian. (Recall that they were asked to speak Russian, so it is no surprise that Russian is the Matrix Language of their conversations, supplying the morphosyntactic frame.) However, the increase in English usage over time affects the conceptual makeup of content morphemes more than it does the mapping of conceptual structure onto syntactic structures. Example (7) from the second data set (about age eleven and after about seven years in the United States) illustrates how the semantic field of the concept of 'thing' in Russian is changing in the direction of English for these boys who have gradually shifted over to English as their dominant language. In Russian there are two nouns that correspond to English *things*. One stands for concrete objects (*shtuki*) and the other (*veschchi*) refers to abstract elements. In this example, the context requires *veshchi*; however, the speaker uses *shtuki*. The indication is that he has neutralized the distinction that Russian makes.

(7)				
oni	zabludi-l-i-s'	i tam	stranny-ije	
3PL/NOM	lost-PST-3PL-REFL	and there	strange-NOM/PL	
shtuk-i	proiskhodj-at			
thing-NOM/PL	happen-3PL/PRES			
Standard Russian:	oni	zabludi-l-i-s',	i tam	stranny-ije
	3PL/NOM	lost-PST-3PL-REFL	and there	strange-NOM/PL
	veshch-i	proiskhodj-at		
	thing-NOM/PL	happen-3PL/PRES		

'They got lost, and strange things were happening there.'

(Schmitt 2001: 172)

Another example shows changes in the lexical-conceptual structure of a Russian verb. Verbs with the meaning of motion are a separate class in Russian. Depending on the prefix and the verb root, a verb may express different types of motion as well as the beginning, progression, and end of motion. One of the results is that the same English verb *go* may be translated into Russian by at least four different verbs. In a number of cases, subjects in Schmitt's study used one Russian verb as if it had the same features as English *go*; that is, they generalize this verb to cover various types of 'going'. This verb, *idti* has the specific meaning of 'to be in the process of going'. In example (8) a form of *idti* occurs instead of the contextually required verb *khodit'* that means 'to move regularly'.

(8)				
eto	van, i on	**idj-ot**	po rel's-am	
DEM	van and it	go-3S/PRES	on rail-DAT/PL	
Standard Russian:	eto	van, i on	**khod-it**	po rel's-am
	DEM	van and it	go-3S/PRES	on rail-DAT/PL

'This van, and it moves on the rails.'

(Schmitt 2001: 180)

5.5.2.1.2. MORE EXAMPLES OF RECOMBINATIONS OF LEXICAL-CONCEPTUAL STRUCTURE

Another study also considers data in terms of the Abstract Level model. This is the study of six Hungarian children, aged seven to nine, who are Hungarian/

English bilinguals living in the United States (Bolonyai 1999). Two arrived in the United States before the age of two and the others were born in the United States. All were born into households with Hungarian as the dominant home language; all the children still speak some Hungarian, even though English is their dominant language today. The children show varying degrees of grammatical competence in Hungarian; for some of them, it is possible their acquisition of Hungarian was never complete.

Bolonyai does not quantify her data in terms of the Abstract Level model, but does provide a number of examples illustrating how abstract lexical structure is split and recombined in the interaction between English and Hungarian examples. Like examples (7) and (8) above, example (9) illustrates neutralization of a contrast. In Hungarian, the verbs involved are *tud* 'know' and *ismer* 'be familiar with'. In (9) *tud* is used along the lines of English *know*. In English, *know* conveys a number of meanings, but certainly both 'know something' and 'be familiar with someone'. It also can occur with either animates or inanimates as thematic role arguments (object NPs). In Hungarian, only *ismer* can occur with animates.

(9) én **tud-om** ez-t a cicá-t
1S know-1S/PRES/OBJ DEM-ACC DEF kitty-ACC
Standard Hungarian: én **ismer-em** ez-t a cicá-t
1S know-1S/PRES/OBJ DEM-ACC DEF kitty-ACC
'I know this kitty.'

(Bolonyai 1999: 100)

Türker's study of codeswitching and convergence in the conversations of young adult Turkish immigrants in Norway (Türker 2000) is another corpus where the Abstract Level model was considered in the data analysis. The subjects were eight young adult Turks who had lived in Norway for at least four years and had gone to Norwegian schools so that all were functionally bilingual. Almost 16 per cent of the CPs studied (771/4,854) included codeswitching with Turkish as the Matrix Language; monolingual Turkish CPs were by far most frequent.

Altogether, the speakers produced twenty-four examples of what Türker refers to as loan translations or semantic triggering. Example (10) illustrates such an example that shows how the lexical-conceptual structure of a Norwegian expression influences the choice of the verb in Turkish. In Norwegian, *å kjøre (på) sykkel* (considered somewhat childish) or just *kjøre sykkel* is used, and means literally 'to drive (on) a bicycle'. The Turkish speaker has used the Turkish verb for 'drive' (*sür*) instead of the expected verb for 'to mount' (*bin*). Also note the omission of Turkish dative case on *bisiklet*; this indicates convergence at the level of morphological realization patterns, too.

(10) Zaten şey-de-ydi-k biz, okul-la şey-e
Anyway thing-LOC-be/PST-1PL we school-POSTPOS thing-DAT

o-r-dan iki-yüz-yetmiş kilometre o-r-dan
that-DERIV-ABL two-hundred-seventy kilometer that-DERIV-ABL
şey-e git-ti-k **bisiklet sür-dü-k**
thing-DAT go-PST-1PL bicycle drive-PST-1PL
'Actually we were on a whatcha call-it, a school whatcha call-it; from there we went there 270 kilometers to the watcha call-it; we rode bicycles (lit., drove bicycles)
Standard Turkish: **bisiklet-e bin-di-k**
bicycle-DAT mount-PST-1PL

(Türker 2000: 172)

5.5.2.2. The remaining two levels of abstract lexical structure

Hypothesis 2. The level of morphological realization patterns is more likely to show modification in attrition than the level of predicate-argument structure.

5.5.2.2.1. MORPHOLOGICAL REALIZATION PATTERNS

Morphological realization patterns include the extent to which grammatical relations are encoded in surface structure and the form that encoding takes. Although Schmitt's data for the Russian boys shows nearly equal percentages of convergence involving predicate argument structure as that involving morphological realization patterns, there is still more evidence of convergence regarding morphological realization patterns. In data set one, 29.5 per cent of the instances of convergence involve morphological realization patterns (67/227) vs. 24.6 per cent (56/227) at the level of predicate argument structure. In her second data set, it is a matter of 18 per cent (72/399) for predicate-argument structure and 22 per cent (87/399) for morphological realization patterns.

Example (11) from Schmitt's data (repeated from Chapter 1) shows an example of a change in morphological realization patterns under the influence of an English counterpart. In Russian, the notion of 'look through' is carried by the Russian verb *pro-smotret'*; yet, in example (11), the speaker adds the preposition *cherez* 'through' to the verb. It is as if the speaker's production is partially directed by the morphological realization pattern in English for this notion; that is, the speaker is treating *pro-smotret'* as if it requires a verb satellite, as its English counterpart, *look through* requires. Note that lexical-conceptual structure is also a composite. Instead of using the required perfective verb form, *pro-smotret'* 'to look through', the speaker uses the imperfective form of the verb *smotret'* 'to look, watch'. Schmitt explains the difference in the surface result in this way: 'In Russian, perfective verbs with prefixes do not only encode the aspect but also express the completion of the action or result. . . . English expresses various nuances of meaning with the help of prepositions' (p. 184).

(11) i on smotre-l cherez knig-u
and 3S/NOM/M look-PST/IMPERF/S/M through book-ACC/S/F

Standard Russian: i on pro-smotre-l ∅ knig-u
and 3S/NOM/M PERF-look-PST/S/M book-ACC/S/F
'And he looked through the book.'

(Schmitt 2001: 188)

In her study of several corpora of German/English codeswitching, Fuller (1997, 2000) finds a number of examples of the influence of English on German structures at the level of morphological realization patterns. Examples (12*a*) and (12*b*) come from her main corpus of Pennsylvania German as spoken in a South Carolina (USA) community. In (12*a*) the English origin noun *sale* selects the preposition *uuf far* 'up for' instead of the Standard German *zu* 'to'. In (12*b*) the English noun *turn* projects a common collocation (*to take turns*). In Standard German this would be expressed with a reflexive and a different verb.

(12) *a* uuf far **sale**
Standard German: zum Verkauf-en
to/NEUT/DAT sell-INF
'up for sale'
b sie nehm-e **turn-s**
they take-3PL turn-PL
Standard German: sie wechsel-n sich ab
they change-3PL REFL up
'They take turns.'

(Fuller 1997: 146)

Another example from Schmitt's corpus of English presence in morphological-realization patterns of CPs otherwise framed by Russian is the decline in the Standard Russian use of the pro-drop parameter. Under this parameter, when the subject is a pronoun, its presence is optional and expected only for emphasis. In general, the boys use overt pronouns where they are not required. Because Schmitt made recordings two years apart, she is able to note that the incidence of overt pronouns goes up sharply over time for her subjects. In the first recording, 69.5 per cent (610/878) of all CPs had overt pronouns. By the second recording, the percentage is up to almost 82 per cent (983/1,204). In her study of the beginnings of attrition in another pro-drop language, Hungarian, Bolonyai (2000) found that overt pronouns were very frequent; thus, 12.8 per cent of all the non-target-like forms in all contexts (64/500) involved the overuse of personal pronouns.

Not surprisingly among the adult subjects of Polinsky (1995: 385), who had not spoken Russian regularly for an average of seven years, overt Russian pronouns are 'used by all the speakers of American Russian'. Polinsky calls these resumptive pronouns (they are co-indexed with the subject of the same clause). One of her suggestions as to how her subjects view the sentence structure seems correct. She writes, 'the resumptive pronoun occurs as a real subject, while the NP with which it is co-indexed is not a subject, but a topic, occupying a much higher position in sentence structure'.

Case marking, of course, is another example of the level of morphological reali-zation patterns. Schmitt included counts for substitutions of one case suffix for another here under English influence on morphological realization patterns; their details are discussed below under Hypothesis 5 when case-marking in general is the subject. Case-marking substitutions did not result in a change in predicate-argument structure. The absence of Russian case marking on English nouns is discussed below under Hypothesis 5 as well; such instances were not counted as part of the numbers reported in this section, although clearly the absence of case marking is a change in morphological realization patterns.

5.5.2.3. Word order

Abstract specifications for word order at all levels of syntax also represent the level of morphological realization patterns. There is little data in the attrition literature on changes in word order, but what there is indicates that change is possible, at least in regard to the alignment of subject (S), object (O), and verb (V) in clauses in some languages. A problem is assessing the status of word order as an indicator of grammatical relations. Whether a language has a rich case system (marking syntactic relations overtly, such as subject vs. object) would seem to influence the potential for unmarked main-clause word order to change under the influence of an L2. Word order in smaller constituents generally seems categorical, especially if their information load regarding any signaling of syntactic relations is low. As mentioned in Chapter 4, Greenberg (1966) found that word order of NPs for a given language is very categorical across his typological classification of thirty languages.

German is one of the few languages for which there has been some systematic study of clausal word order in contact situations. Clyne (1992) reports that the Dutch and German immigrants he studied in Australia show a change in main-clause word order. Although both German and Dutch are Verb-Second languages (with the auxiliary verb in clause-second position and the past participle in clause-final position), immigrants to Australia are generalizing S(Aux)VO order. Clyne describes the change as 'a tendency toward proximity of constituents' (because the change means the past participle will move next to its auxiliary). He notes that the SVO generalization is mainly a second generation phenomenon in German, but it was already 'the dominant type of syntactic change in the first generation of Dutch' (p. 21).

Another German corpus includes data on word-order change in both main and dependent clauses. Gross (2000*a*) studied the German of six German-speaking immigrants (Bavarian dialect) who came to the United States at least forty years ago and who report that English is their dominant (and everyday) language now. He found a difference between word-order change in main clauses and dependent clauses. Word order is a morphological realization pattern; however, in certain cases it can be considered an early system morpheme if one bears in mind that the 4-M model refers to morphemes at two levels, the abstract level and the surface level. Obviously, word order is not a surface-level morpheme, but on the abstract level it can have the characteristics of an early system morpheme (i.e. it can depend on the features of a lexical head for the form it takes). Changes in word order in dependent clauses in Gross's corpus are discussed below under Hypothesis 4 on early system morphemes.

Hlavac (2000) offers a detailed study of the Croatian of second generation young adults living in Australia. Croatian is their L1, while English is their dominant language. Although this publication did not include Hlavac's findings on word order, he makes some general comments on the subject in his email correspondence. Overall, he states that there is 'a general tendency to favour SVO order even where "homeland Croatian" would favour other patterns' (email, 24 April 2001). However, he also points out that even though Croatian allows OVS, OSV, VSO, and even VOS, these are all marked orders. That is, the basic Croatian pattern is SVO like English. In sum, Hlavac's corpus reinforces the notion that word order is susceptible to change, but it is hard to argue conclusively that the change is due exclusively to a splitting and recombining of a morphological realization pattern from English with that of Croatian.

However, in some specific instances the suggestion is there. Hlavac points out that object-final patterns in English may be behind the fact that some Croatian clitic pronouns in his corpus of Croatian/English codeswitching were in CP-final position, disallowed in homeland Croatian (email, 24 April 2001). (Croatian has both full-form and cliticized pronouns; full-form pronouns can occur anywhere, but clitics are usually in second or third position depending on the presence of auxiliary verbs.)

5.5.2.4. Predicate-argument structure

Above, I indicated that close to a quarter of the CPs in Schmitt's Russian corpus showed the effects of a splitting and recombining of abstract lexical structure at the level of predicate-argument structure, but with little change from the first recording to the second recording made two years later. For example, her data show how a missing preposition can make a difference in the case that is assigned to a predicate. In Russian, when the verb *govorju* 'I speak' refers to a language spoken by the speaker, it requires a preposition; this preposition is an early system morpheme, a verb satellite. This verbal complex assigns dative case to its predicate. However, in example (13), the speaker uses the verb *govorju* as if it corresponds to how the English verb *speak* is used in this context (i.e. it assigns prepositional case to its predicate). The speaker also does not mark accusative case on *jazyk* 'language' as is required in Standard Russian. Thus, this example illustrates convergence at two levels. At the level of predicate-argument structure, accusative rather than prepositional case is mapped onto the role of Theme/Patient; at the level of morphological realization patterns, the satellite preposition is missing from the verb complex, following an English pattern, not a Russian one.

(13)

ya	govorj-u	Ø	Russk-iy	jazyk-Ø
1S/NOM	speak-1S/PRES		Russian-ACC/M/S	language
ya	govorj-u	na	Russk-om	jazyk-e
1S/NOM	speak-1S/PRES	in	Russian-PREP/M/S	language-PREP/M/S

'I speak Russian language.'

(Schmitt 2001: 187)

Schmitt reports that some reflexive verbs lose their reflexive suffixes, but she gives no statistics. Both the levels of lexical-conceptual structure and of predicate-argument structure seem to be affected. For example, instead of responding to his mother's question about washing up before getting into bed with a verb showing a reflexive (*umy-l-sya*) 'I washed up', the boy uses its non-reflexive counterpart (*umy-l*) 'I washed'. However, he adds the direct object *litso* 'face'. Schmitt (2001: 187) suggests, 'Such replacement of a reflexive verb with the transitive verb is only possible if the lexical-conceptual structure itself is projected by English. . . . A reflexive verb has quite a different predicate-argument structure than a non-reflexive verb. Namely, a reflexive verb does not subcategorize for a direct object.'

Bolonyai (1999) cites an example of a splitting and recombining of the level of predicate-argument structure (example repeated from 5.1.1). The convergence of English to Hungarian concerns the abstract structure of the English verb *wake up* and its consequences for argument structure. In English, *wake up* can be mapped onto either a transitive or intransitive structure, with the presence or not of an object complement as the only indication of which structure is intended. Note that causativity is also part of the entry for the transitive verb in this case. In Hungarian, the causative is formed by adding the derivational suffix *-t* to the verb *kel* 'wake, rise'. The causative verb (*kel-t*) subcategorizes for a direct object while *kel* does not. In example (14) the child has used *kel* with a causative meaning, but without the Hungarian derivational suffix that is required. In this novel usage, note that not only are the specifications for mapping predicate-argument structure altered for *kel*, but also the other two levels of abstract structure are affected. At the level of lexical-conceptual structure, the distinction between causativity and non-causativity is neutralized, and the morphological realization pattern is missing the causative suffix.

(14)

mert	te	nem	kel-sz	en-gem	fel
because	you	not	wake/INTRANS.PRES/2S	I-ACC	up

Standard Hungarian:

mert	te	nem	kel-t-esz	en-gem	fel
because	you	not	wake-TRANS.PRES/2S	I-ACC	up

'Because you do not wake me up.'

(Bolonyai 1999: 101)

5.5.2.5. Summary: assumptions under the abstract level model

One can find many studies of attrition that focus on change in the lexicon as the clearest sign of attrition. Schmitt's study offers statistics to show that—at least for her corpus—the lexicon is the most affected and that specifically lexical-conceptual structure is most altered in attrition. I expect similar findings for other attrition corpora if they would report quantified data analyzed in terms of the Abstract Level model. Further, I suspect other language-contact phenomena would show similar results. Along those lines, note that I suggest in Chapter 6 that this is so regarding creole structure. (However, note that Polinsky (1995, 1997, forthcoming) suggests that attrition is marked by similarities between the extent to which the lexicon and morphosyntax are affected.)

An analysis in terms of the Abstract Level model rather than one simply in terms of a list of lexical elements affected gives us much more information about the nature of attrition itself. It also indicates that the degree of flexibility that exists in abstract lexical structure varies across the three levels. Recall that by the time of the second recording, the Russian boys in Schmitt's study showed some splitting and recombining of lexical-conceptual structure in more than half of their CPs (60 per cent). Most had been in the United States from five to seven years by this time. I am not surprised that the semantics of content morphemes is easier to alter than the predicate-argument structure for which a verb is subcategorized. However, I am a little surprised that the modifications of predicate-argument structure are as frequent as they are in Schmitt's data. This may have something to do with the fairly extreme differences between the way thematic structure is mapped onto syntactic structure in English in contrast to Russian. English handles as prepositional phrases many roles that surface in Russian as oblique cases. In regard to morphological realization patterns, because English and Russian word order is fairly similar, it is no surprise there is little or no change in word order in the Russian of her subjects.

5.5.3. *Attrition hypotheses and the 4-M model*

I turn now to a set of hypotheses about the actual surface morphemes of a language and the degree to which one type of morpheme is retained relative to other types. The motivation for these hypotheses is the 4-M model. Recall that the hypotheses that can be derived from the model suggest that the level at which different types of morpheme are accessed in language production differs, and these differences, in turn, explain differences in their distribution in various types of corpora (cf. Myers-Scotton and Jake 2000*a*).

In the assumptions that follow, it is important to remember that I refer to attrition within the lifetime of an individual and not changes in the retention of morpheme types in the history of a language. For example, in its history and for a variety of reasons, a language may well have completely lost most suffixes to mark the syntactic relation of case. However, in a speaker's lifetime, even though the trade-off of increasing use of a language dominant in the community is less use of an L1, I argue that types of late outsider system morpheme in that L1 are generally impervious to total loss.

Overall, a hierarchy in which late system morphemes are less likely to show early replacement or loss in attrition is assumed. The relative susceptibility of morphemes can be diagrammed in this way and is explicated under hypotheses 3 through 5:

Late system morphemes < early system morphemes < content morphemes

5.5.3.1. Content morphemes: easy to lose

Hypothesis 3. Content morphemes are not only 'first in' in language acquisition and in contact situations promoting borrowing, but they are also 'first out' in language attrition.

This statement means two things: first, speakers of the waning L1 'forget' content morphemes first. Second, content morphemes from the invading L2 are the first type of morpheme to enter the L1, either to remain as synonyms for L1 content morphemes or eventually to replace them.

There is little or no quantitative data to support this assumption; however, the attrition literature is full of anecdotal evidence that content words dominate as the elements that are 'forgotten' in attrition. For example, Olshtain (1989: 162) cites 'lower accessibility of specific lexical items' as one of two major trends of change in language use. (The other one is, not sursprisingly, 'greater variablity in the application of marked rules'.) Also, Hulsen, de Bot, and Weltens (2002) state that it is generally assumed that the lexicon (= content morphemes) is most susceptible to loss (cf. de Bot 1996) and they cite several studies that confirm that speakers often have word-finding problems. Further, Haugen (1989: 67) states about first- and second-generation Norwegian immigrants in the Upper Midwest, 'The adoption of English loans was my informants' first great step in the direction of English'.

One study that does cite quantitative evidence on content words is Enninger and Raith (1988), an analysis of any convergence/attrition among the Old Order Amish (Pennsylvania German or PG) community in Kent County, Delaware (USA). At least in 1983, 14 per cent (3,985/27,630) of their lexicon consisted of borrowings from American English. In support of my claim that content words are the morphemes most frequently replaced in attrition, Enninger and Raith state, 'Among the lexical importations, the nouns represent almost 70 per cent. Furthermore, their percentage is 19 points higher than that of indigenous nouns' (p. 283).

True, Enninger and Raith go on to indicate that 45 per cent of the imported nouns do fill lexical gaps created when new objects and concepts enter the community. But this leaves more than half of the American English imports as either additions to existing Pennsylvania German nouns or replacements. In an answer to how these other American English imports are employed, Enninger and Raith mention two specific motives for borrowing other American English nouns that are not taken in specifically to fill gaps. These motives are 'economizing' and 'synonym-enrichment'. For example, the Pennsylvania German form *lehrer* is retained to denote 'instructor of religion, preacher' and the American English import *teacher* is added as a synonym, but with the specific meaning of 'school teacher'. We can look at the history of English and see how French borrowings during the Norman conquest sometimes came in to stand alongside native elements (e.g. *cow, beef*).

Almost in anticipation of the claim that the massive lexical borrowing from American English is destabilizing the Amish variety, they demur, writing, 'It is exactly this lexical variability, or rather the lexical flexibility of its users that stabilizes the functionality of the variety, in so far as a growing and changing referential range can be covered in PG speech by exploiting the lexicon of AE [American English]' (p. 285).

A recent source of extensive, quantified information about L2 content words in L1 conversations is Hlavac (2000). Hlavac studies the state of the L1 of young adult Croatian speakers in Australia who also have near-native competence in English. Among lexical inroads from English, 85 per cent are nouns (p. 126). Only 10 per cent of all English-origin words received overt Croatian morphology; however, this percentage may be somewhat misleading since nominative singular is marked with a zero in Croatian. Still, many of the English forms occur where they would be overtly marked for case and plural.

Of special interest here is that Hlavac found that 'transfers do not generally displace their Croatian equivalents' (p. 503). Even within the same conversation, congruent Croatian forms occur alongside their English counterparts. In self-reports on why they 'mix' languages, a large proportion of subjects (75/100) report they use an English word because they 'don't know the word in one language so [they] use a word from the other language' (p. 503). However, sixty-eight subjects report a somewhat different explanation, that they 'mix' 'because the word in the other language comes to [them] faster' (p. 503).

Hlavac also notes that where both the English and Croatian version of a lexical item occur in the same transcript, the English version usually precedes the Croatian one. To Hlavac, this suggests that 'accessibility, and related phenomena such as "lexical attrition" and "recovery" determine when and why transfers and their Croatian equivalents occur' (pp. 503–4).

5.5.3.2. Next in change: early system morphemes

Hypothesis 4. Early system morphemes are less susceptible to replacement or loss in attrition than content morphemes, but more so than late system morphemes. Substitution is more likely than loss.

Bolonyai's data on six Hungarian children show that early system morphemes are treated differently from late system morphemes in the case system. Bolonyai (1999,

2001) suggests that the large set of Hungarian local (mainly locative) case suffixes are early system morphemes in contrast to nominative and accusative, which are late system morphemes. Her subjects, who live in an English-speaking community and show attrition in Hungarian, sometimes replace one locative case with another. Bolonyai (2002) is a reanalysis of her 1999 dissertation data, with a different perspective on what counts to emphasize. I cite some numbers from Bolonyai (2002), but examples entirely from Bolonyai (1999).

The Hungarian case system of these children being raised in an English milieu seems to be relatively intact. In total, 89 per cent (1,216/1,366) of case endings are correct. However, quantitative data of omissions and substitutions of case suffixes show dramatic differences. When the local case markers (early system morphemes) are non-target-like, they show more non-target substitutions to other cases than actual omissions (substitutions: 63 per cent (41/65) vs. omissions: 37 per cent (24/65). Findings for accusative (discussed under assumption 5) show close to total omission when they are non-target-like. At the same time, accusative case in general is very accurate (discussed in section 5.5.3.3.3).

As early system morphemes provide lexical-conceptual structure about conceptualizing spatial relations, it is no surprise that there are many substitutions, not more omissions, in the local cases in Hungarian.

In example (15) the sublative case *-ra* 'onto' (which is called for in Standard Hungarian) is replaced with the illative case *-ba* 'into'. That is, instead of marking Goal and Surface (with sublative case), the child marks Goal and Container (with illative case). Bolonyai suggests that the school classes (P.E., music, and art) are seen more as containers—as they would be in English—than as surfaces, as they would be in Standard Hungarian.

(15) Hogy megy-ünk **P.E.**-be, **music**-ba, **art**-ba.
that go-PRES/1PL P.E.-ILLAT/into music-ILLAT/into art-ILLAT/into
'That we are going to P.E., music, [and] art.'

(Bolonyai 1999: 203)

When there is a substitution, it typically involves one locative suffix for another; that is, it typically involves early system morphemes. Thus, as Bolonyai (1999) points out, 'The Hungarian verb lemma is still projecting a slot for an overt case ending, even though the semantic content of the indirectly elected suffix may not express the same spatial relations as Standard Hungarian would' (p. 200). For example, in stating 'I'm going to Hungary' (*Megy-ek Magyar-ország-ba*), one of Bolonyai's speakers uses the illative case suffix (*-ba*) that encodes 'into a container' when in Standard Hungarian, the case suffix *-ra* that encodes Goal and Surface is expected.

But why are there any omissions at all? Differences in how English expresses (or does not express) spatial relations may explain most of the omissions. The context in which the children showed the most omissions was when the suffix occurred in adjunct or other free-standing phrases that have counterparts in English without prepositions. Out of the twenty-four omissions, twenty-one or 87.5 per cent are in these contexts (Bolonyai 2002: 22). In contrast, as Bolonyai comments (2001: 22), 'children tended to err by substituting one Hungarian case suffix for another where English also offers overt case morphology, in the form of prepositions'.

In a study of another language with an extensive locative case system, Kravin (1992) reports on attrition of Finnish. This is a study of a bilingual boy who lived as an infant in a Finnish-speaking environment in Sweden, but then spent much of his next six years in an English-speaking environment, with short visits with Finns in Sweden. Unfortunately, there are no quantitative data, only a few examples. However, the examples suggest that the speaker employed substitution more than omission of locative cases.

The plural affix on nouns is another example of an early system morpheme in most languages. As such it also is susceptible to change when attrition characterizes the way a language is spoken; however, as a system morpheme, plural is less susceptible than content morphemes. Fuller (2000: 53) states that while German plural-marking patterns are still operating in her Pennsylvania German corpus, the patterns do not generally apply to English-origin nouns. That is, the German plural suffix is replaced by the English plural *-s* on English-origin loans (e.g. *friend-s*). However, what is relevant here is that the speakers have not extended this pattern of replacement to Pennsylvania German nouns. This variety of German has five different plural markers; one of these is *-s*, but it remains a minor allomorph in Fuller's corpus. Only a few of the German nouns in her corpus (6/457) that historically take other markers occur with *-s* instead (e.g. *buch-s* < *bicher*).

In another study involving German, early system morphemes do show a tendency to change. In this study, the subjects are ten native Germans living in the United States for whom German is beginning to lose its dominant language status. Fuller and her co-author (Fuller and Lehnert 2000) show that the speakers' use of German definite articles is undergoing change. German definite articles are multimorphemic, but their role as early system morphemes (the conveying of definiteness) is at issue in this case.

Although both English and German have similar NP structures, constraints on the presence of articles differ. German requires articles in some NPs where they are not used in English (proper nouns, street names, and certain plural nouns). Also, personal status nouns (e.g. occupation) require articles in English, but not in German. In naturally occurring conversations ostensibly in German, speakers followed English patterns 46 per cent of the time (17/37) in contexts with appropriate slots for an article in either language, but not in both. For example, in (16) the prepositional phrase *für defense* follows the English pattern; in monolingual German the phrase would be *für die Verteidigung*. In (16) the German *pattern* is what is being lost, not the article as such (the determiner also signals case, a late system morpheme). Note that the pattern itself depends on the lexical-conceptual structure of its head noun, making the pattern an early system morpheme.

(16) und zwar anstatt die Afrika-Hilfe die wollen
and (EMPH) instead of the/FEM Africa-aid the/FEM want/3PL
das streichen, ich weiss gar nicht wieviel,
that strike I know at all not how much
eine Million, oder . . . und für **defense** geb-en, gel
one/FEM million or and for defense give-INF you know
'And instead of aid to Africa, they want to discontinue that, I don't know how much, a million, or . . . and use it for defense, you know.'

(Fuller and Lehnert 2000: 416)

Another study shows that verb satellites, also early system morphemes, can be lost. Unfortunately, Olshtain (1989) also provides few numbers in writing about second-language attrition (English) in an L1 environment (Hebrew). Her subjects had spent two years in an English-speaking environment before returning to Israel. What is of interest here is that one of the most noticeable losses she reports involves early system morphemes, the satellite particle in English phrasal verbs. Specifically, she notes that the older group (8–14 years old) showed attrition in 'a small number of English structures such as the verb–particle construction' (p. 159). She suggests that typological differences were the main cause for the problems, referring to the verb + particle as 'a rather unique and highly marked feature of English that Hebrew speakers seem to acquire late . . . and lose quite early when attrition sets in' (p. 159). I, of course, would argue that such morphemes are relatively easily affected, not because the construction is so marked in any universal sense, but because of the nature of early system morphemes. They have conceptual content and it is easy to replace their content by use of another verb, or to reanalyze the conceptual content of the main verb (a content morpheme) so that it more closely resembles the Hebrew pattern of how conceptual information is encoded in verbs. (It is also possible that the children had not achieved full proficiency in English during their two-year stay in an English-speaking community.) Beyond three examples, Olstain offers no other data, commenting:

> In spite of the fact that in the initial stages of data collection these children were using all the common verb–particle forms as naturally as any native speaker of the same age, deviations soon started setting in. These deviations were of three types: (a) replacement of a verb–particle form with a single verb such as *close* for *turn off* and *open* for *turn on*; (b) omission of the particle; and (c) replacement with a wrong particle. (p. 159)

To consider a related example, recall example (13) above from Schmitt's study. A similar early system morpheme to that in Olstain's corpus is lost in the speaker's L1, Russian. The Russian boy uses the verb *govor* 'speak' without its satellite particle *na* 'speak in [a language]'. Schmitt explains this example by arguing that the speaker is relying on the predicate-argument structure of English *speak* 'speak [a language]', which does not call for a satellite particle.

5.5.3.2.1. WHEN WORD ORDER IS AN EARLY SYSTEM MORPHEME

As indicated above in the discussion of morphological realization patterns, there are a number of differences between word order in English and German. Perhaps most important, German has different orders for main and subordinate clauses. In main clauses, German places the finite verb in second position and, if there are non-finite verbs, they occur in a cluster in clause-final position. In the varieties of German Gross (2000*a*) studied (Bavarian and Schmiedschau dialects), in addition to main clauses, subordinate clauses with a non-overt complementizer have the verb-second constraint. However, when there is an overt complementizer in these dialects, the finite verb occurs in clause-final position just after the non-finite verb(s). Also, in double-infinitive constructions, the finite verb precedes the infinitive cluster. Thus, these two types of dependent clauses have an SOV order.

The German immigrants to the United States in Gross's sample show variable word order in dependent clauses, sometimes placing the finite verb in clause-final position (as they would in the homeland dialect), but sometimes in immediate post-subject position. If the verb is in post-subject position, the result is an English-like word order.

Gross suggests that the post-subject position word order can be accounted for in two ways. One could say that the grammar 'is simply moving in a direction in which the asymmetry between main clause and subordinate word order is disappearing' (p. 165). As Gross points out, this explanation is a variation on the theme of simplification as the mark of a little-used L1. However, Gross puts his finger on the problem with this explanation, writing, 'Saying that some aspect of the grammar is simplifying does not explain why the target of this change is the subordinate clause' (p. 165). That is, why is the subordinate clause 'simplifying' more than main clauses? Therefore, he goes on to offer a second account. He argues that some complementizers are considered content morphemes in the 4-M model and suggests that 'constituent order in German subordinate clauses may be considered parallel to indirect election of early system morphemes' (p. 168).

Basically, Gross suggests that the conceptual specification of complementizers in German is changing under influence from English and that this change results in a change in word order in the subordinate clauses of his subjects. His argument is that—at the abstract level—word order in subordinate clauses can be considered an early system morpheme with the complementizer as its head. (Recall that the 'morphemes' in the 4-M model are discussed both as abstract forms in lemmas in the mental lexicon and also as surface-level forms; no one is suggesting that word order is a surface-level morpheme. If it helps, think of word order as a morphosyntactic pattern, not a morpheme). Given the argument that conceptually activated morphemes (content morphemes) and early system morphemes are more susceptible to change than late system morphemes, word order in subordinate clauses is more likely to change than word order in main clauses. (He offers a much longer theoretically based argument to support his explanation; cf. Gross 2000*a*: 167ff.)

Gross's hypothesis is this: 'In first language attrition, word order that is indirectly elected at the lemma level will show the greatest degree of L2 influence' (p. 168). Example (17) illustrates a case supporting the hypothesis; the finite verb (*hɔn* 'have') follows the subject *sie* 'they' (for SVO order). In the Bavarian homeland dialect, it would appear in clause-final position in this dependent clause.

(17) i hɔb pɔɔr Kɔrt-en do ge-hɔb-t
I have/PRES/1S pair card-PL here PRT-have-PRT
wɔs **sie hɔn** ge-brɔch-t
what they have PRT-bring-PRT
Bavarian: **wɔs sie ge-brɔch-t hɔn**
what they PRT-bring-PRT have
'I have a few [post]cards here that they brought.'
(Gross 2000*a*: 166)

When quantified, Gross's data support his hypothesis. V-final word order in subordinate clauses with complementizers clearly is on the wane among his subjects. In only 23.2 per cent of the subordinate clauses with an overt complementizer other than *weil* (108/465) do his subjects use V-final word order. He also reports on word order in main clauses, finding evidence of English influence in only 10.5 per cent of all contexts (48/456).

Gross is careful to note that not all German subordinate clauses with complementizers show such change. Those complementizers that still introduce V-final word order are *denn* 'for, because' and also *weil* 'because'. When the complementizer is *weil*, the percentage of V2 dependent clauses is 52.6 per cent (60/114).

When Gross compares his findings with results for three modern Bavarian-dialect speakers (Germans temporarily in the United States on business), he finds that in all other environments except *weil*, they only use V-final word order 3 per cent (3/97) of the time.

5.5.3.3. Last to change: late system morphemes

Hypothesis 5. Of all morpheme types, late system morphemes are least susceptible to absolute omission.

In some data sets—just as is the case for early system morphemes—substitution of one late system morpheme for another may prevail, especially for certain case assignments. However, when this happens, it is important to note that the abstract grammatical frame is still intact; that is, speakers recognize there is a slot in the frame that requires a morpheme. That is, I stress that presenting loss as the prime characteristic of attrition is misleading, if not plain wrong, especially with respect to late system morphemes.

Much of the available data deals with case assignment, and I will concentrate on that in my discussion. If one generalizes on the basis of Schmitt's corpus, actual replacement of the L1 pattern of case assignment with that of the L2 may be more common if the noun is from the L2. However, even then, note that we are still dealing with replacement in a frame, not loss.

5.5.3.3.1. A CASE STUDY OF RETENTION AND SUBSTITUTION

Dorian's study of the last speakers of East Sutherland Gaelic provides a good deal of evidence about the resilience of morphology (e.g. 1973, 1978, 1981, *inter alia*). Looking at Dorian's data in some detail is relevant to this discussion because the speakers show little actual loss in the constructions she considers, and some of them are case markers. Instead of loss, one finds two results: (i) Many constructions are nearly or entirely intact in fluent speakers. (ii) Substitution rather than loss characterizes the other constructions, even for semi-speakers; e.g. one type of consonant mutation may be substituted for the target type. Or, analogical leveling of allomorphs is present in some constructions, especially for semi-speakers. These speakers largely are aware of the ESG grammatical frame; the evidence is that even if they do not provide target forms, they still provide related forms for appropriate frame slots.

The data on ESG that Dorian discusses deal with two different groups of native speakers of ESG who are all bilingual in the dominant language of the community, English. Her pool of ESG speakers numbered about 140 in 1972 (Dorian 1977: 24). These fall into several groups depending on the village. In the two largest villages, fluent speakers are between 70 to 80 years old; but in another village, there are young fluent speakers who are not quite as conservative in their ESG as the older fluent speakers. The other speakers studied are labeled semi-speakers, persons 'who could make themselves understood in imperfect Gaelic but who were very much more at home in English' (1977: 24). Altogether, Dorian (1981) cites quantified data for about thirty-five to forty fluent speakers and about forty semi-speakers, with the numbers much smaller for some reports of results.

I review data especially from her 1973 and 1978 articles where Dorian mainly discusses four constructions. The 1973 article considers retentions or changes in the verbal system and in certain nominal constructions (including what is called 'the passive construction'). The 1987 article considers noun plurals and gerunds.

Understanding of any changes in ESG requires some knowledge of its system of phonological mutuations that generally mark syntactic relations. For example, one mutation is the sole signal of past tense in verbs. The basic system involves lenition and nasalization. Under lenition, in general, the initial obstruent of the root of the relevant word is replaced by a spirant or spirants with other spirants; in most cases, nasalization requires the replacement of an initial voiceless consonant by a voiced consonant (cf. Dorian 1973: 416, or Dorian 1981: 122–4). In reference to fluent speakers of ESG, Dorian (1973: 416) states that 'every speaker has retained an active use of initial consonant mutation as a syntactic device'. In the discussion that follows, I argue that the mutation system affects the status of grammatical morphemes.

Especially the verbal system is very resistant to change, aside from one analogical development in some younger fluent speakers. Otherwise, Dorian notes, 'Even the youngest fluent speakers never fail to lenite in the independent preterit or conditional, or to nasalize in the interrogative positive or the dependent mode' (p. 417). Dorian finds this conservatism 'the more striking' because ESG has borrowed many verbs from English. As noted, all speakers are bilingual in English, and English, of course, is the sole language of most other members of the larger speech community.

All fluent speakers have resisted change almost entirely in one other group of mutational structures. These are lenitions after a small group of high-frequency words including the forms for the adverbs 'very' and 'too', the numeral 'two', and the adjective 'next'.

Dorian (1973) does find some change in the passive construction. Some possessive pronouns modifying a gerund in the so-called passive construction are replaced by an analytic construction (the plurals and third person singular). Except for their use in this construction, only two forms are much used. (As far as I can determine, the pronouns that have been replaced are possessive pronominal adjectives, forms that are early system morphemes.) In the passive construction younger speakers show a change, either by producing a mutation where there is none or by producing a non-target-like mutation. There are two passive constructions in the speech of the oldest fluent speakers, but other speakers show 'analogical remodeling' in regard to mutation patterns. In the youngest group, 'Inappropriate initial consonants become more than twice as common as appropriate ones' (p. 424).

The ESG case system does show substitution, but little outright loss of a system. (i) The genitive case has become something of a relic in general; it does not survive with prepositions. Instead of indicating genitive case, all the speakers prefer a prepositional phrase (e.g. equivalent to 'the father of the lad'). When asked to produce the genitive form, speakers did produce a version showing mutation, but with a good deal of variation across speakers. (ii) The nominative case seems relatively intact, but over time the same grammaticality judgement test showed different results. At first, for a specific group of nouns, speakers used nasalization to mark nominative in almost 100 per cent of the cases. But in a later version of the same set of sentences, younger speakers were inclined to accept a lenited version more than 50 per cent of the time in contexts where the older target is a nasalized version. This weakening of nasalization in the nominative among younger speakers was later confirmed in another test. Still, Dorian also reports that nominative marking in 'two classes of nouns, one defined by phonology and one by grammatical gender, show no mutation change at all' (Dorian 1973: 473). However, she also notes 'a movement toward a caseless nasalized definite masculine noun' (Dorian 1973: 434). (iii) Articles and nouns after all simple prepositions must be marked with the dative case in standard ESG. Again, mutation marks the case, with lenition part of the target form. Even though all speakers used a lenited dative as their commonest response, Dorian (1973: 430) does comment that the number of nasalized nominative forms (non-target when dative is intended) was 'striking'. (One other case exists, vocative. Dorian (1981: 134–5) reports that three semi-speakers do not use vocative at all, but eight show some use. Older fluent speakers used it in 95 per cent of possible environments and younger fluent speakers used it 75 per cent of the time.)

Dorian (1978) shows that the fluent ESG speakers, who use Gaelic almost exclusively as a home language, show little or no attrition of the plural and gerund forms under study. This is in the face of analogical leveling to simple suffixes by semi-speakers. These semi-speakers favor one allomorph for plural (*-ən*) and one for gerund formation (*-al*). 'That is, the sense of plurality in nouns, and gerund formation in verbs, resides for s.s. [semi-speakers] increasingly in one strongly productive allomorph' (p. 601). This finding supports hypotheses put forth by various researchers (including Anderson) that analogical leveling prevails as attrition sets in. However, note that this leveling applies to early system morphemes, ones that I suggest are more likely to change than late system morphemes. Dorian compares several speakers individually. Where a semi-speaker forms plurals by simple suffixation 67 per cent of the time (53/79), an older fluent speaker forms them in this way only 48 per cent (38/79) of the time. Dorian comments,

> simple suffixation, which is clearly attractive to the s.s. [semi-speakers] as a device, could easily be extended to account for all noun plurals and gerunds. Y.f.s. [young fluent speakers], who do show departures from the o.f.s. [old fluent speakers'] norm in other aspects of ESG structure, seem almost entirely impervious to the possibilities for simplification in these complex morphological structures. (1978: 606)

How do the morphemes comprising these constructions fare in terms of the 4-M model and the assumptions framing this section? The assumptions imply that content morphemes and early system morphemes are replaced or lost more frequently than late system morphemes. Dorian (1973) indicates that the paradigm of possessive pronouns (equivalents for 'my' etc.) is one of the features of ESG most sharply reduced; such forms, of course, are early system morphemes. The other ESG morphemes under study (e.g. plural and gerund marking) also are early system morphemes and are largely retained in their target-like forms by fluent speakers. However, semi-speakers level the set of allomorphs for both forms, using mainly suffixes, not allomorphs involving mutation. Other morphemes studied, such as case, are late system morphemes. As discussed above, the case system is certainly weakening among young fluent speakers and semi-speakers. Still, the nominative–dative distinction is strongly maintained by older fluent speakers (98 per cent in two villages, 77 per cent in another), and even by 56 per cent of the semi-speakers in the two villages and 32 per cent in another village (Dorian 1981: 147). Further, remember that even when they produce non-target forms, they mark them with mutation, even if it is the wrong mutation.

Thus, again, the general finding is either maintenance or substitution, not loss. Also, when she comments on the dominant use by semi-speakers of simple plural suffixes instead of mutation, Dorian (1978: 606) stresses that they still maintain a highly complex morphology in other ways. 'Final mutation, vowel alternation, suppletion, quantity change, subtraction, zero formation—all are still in use among s.s. [semi-speakers] although to a lesser extent than among fluent speakers.'

How does one explain the similar very high retention by all fluent speakers of early system morphemes (plural marking and gerund form) and verbal morphology (including tense as well as mode and negation), as well as case (a late system morpheme) in general? Perhaps more to the point in any discussion of attrition, how does one explain the fairly high retention of target mutations by semi-speakers, for example, the dative–nominative distinction?

The key to retention may be that the form of all of these morphemes depends on mutation. One can argue that these forms *become* late system morphemes. That is, they are examples of the 'pull down principle' (cf. Gross 2000*b*, Myers-Scotton and Jake 2000*a*). The morphosyntactic information as to whether nasalization or lenition is required for mutation to take its proper form is only available when larger constituents are assembled.[3]

5.5.3.3.2. LATE SYSTEM MORPHEMES IN OTHER ADULT DATA SETS

Unfortunately, many data sets in which attrition is discussed do not offer quantitative data. For example, Rayfield (1970) discusses a community of Yiddish speakers who came to the United States from eastern Europe forty or fifty years before the date of the study. Rayfield studies more than a hundred members of a number of social organizations in Venice, California (a part of Los Angeles along the coast). The main languages of 'the Beach' are Yiddish and English, with Yiddish predominating in everyday conversations.

As is the case with many studies of attrition, this study offers only anecdotal evidence relevant to the assumptions based on the 4-M model about morpheme retention in the L1. However, Rayfield's general comments and her examples are supportive of the assumptions, especially the claim that content morphemes are most susceptible to change. Rayfield speaks of 'a very large number of English loanwords' in Yiddish speech. She states (1970: 58), 'A sample count from *Forverts*, the most popular Yiddish daily newspaper and the one whose style most closely resembles the speech of the *bilingual majority*, gives about ten per cent of English words'. Note that she adds 'of which only a small fraction, perhaps one-fifth, is necessary in the sense that there is no convenient Yiddish equivalent'.

[3] I thank Janice Jake for this observation.

In regard to structural interference, Rayfield states that the borrowing of 'function words' into both Yiddish and English is 'strong'. However, a close examination of the forms in question shows that she refers to content morphemes, not system morphemes. She cites Yiddish *ober* 'but', *un* 'and', *oder* 'or' and English *but, because, so*. Further, Rayfield states, 'On the whole, there is little interference from English in the major patterns of Yiddish structure' (p. 66). The few examples of structural changes to Yiddish that she cites are relatively minor, such as (18). The future tense is modeled on the pattern of English 'going to'. The inflected verb is in second position, according to the Yiddish model, but the adverb *bald*, which precedes *kumen* in homeland Yiddish, is placed after it, as in an English construction.

(18) **All right**, ge ikh kum-en bald
go 1S come-INF soon
'All right, I'm going to come in a minute.'

(Rayfield 1970: 69)

A perusal of anecdotal examples in the attrition literature and a set of recent quantitative studies shows that Dorian's ESG data is not exceptional. That is, the notion held by some that attrition is best characterized as loss of inflectional morphology is simplistic, if not simply wrong. Instead, the state of morphology in attrition is better seen in terms of the extent to which the abstract morphosyntactic frame of the attriting language is maintained. The results are best interpreted as sometimes showing retention of L1 target forms, sometimes substitution of one L1 form for another, sometimes substitution of an L2 form, and then, but only then, sometimes outright loss. But the crucial point is that most of the time, the abstract morphosyntactic frame of the L1 is retained; that is, the need to fill its slots is observed.

To support this claim, I discuss in some detail results for several recent studies with quantitative data for case assignment, considering children separately from adults. Hlavac (2000) offers the most extensive discussion of case with the largest sample. Recall that his subjects are young adult Croatians living in Australia. The sample of one hundred had equal numbers of males and females, with an average age of 21.38 years. The majority (eighty-eight) were born in Australia; all not born in Australia arrived at a pre-school age. The majority still live with relatives whose dominant language is Croatian and about 90 percent reported they speak Croatian or Croatian and English with their parents, but 64 per cent reported they speak English with their siblings. While all these second generation subjects probably speak Croatian frequently, they are English-dominant.

Hlavac's statistics show conclusively that target-like case retention is the order of the day in his corpus. In a series of tables, he shows that 91 per cent of all Croatian NPs (8,444/9,318) receive target-like case assignments (e.g. p. 485). Further, there is little statistical variation between singular and plural in this regard. However, both masculine singular nominatives and masculine singular accusative inanimates are realized by zero. If the nominative forms are discarded, then 15 per cent of the remaining forms are non-target-like; if both nominative and accusative are not considered, then 25 per cent are non-target-like (p. 484). Still, for singular forms only, 82 per cent (913/1,116) of genitives are target-like, 86 per cent (320/370) of instrumentals, 84 per cent (74/89) and 74 per cent of locatives are (896/1,207). Percentages for plural forms are not too different.

The most telling finding regarding non-target-like forms is that they often are instances of substitution, not loss. 'Nearly one third (287 of 874) of the non-target realisations are accusative forms replacing locative case' (p. 489).

Various structural factors may affect whether case marking is target-like or not. (i) The percentage of non-target plural forms is lower than that for singular forms, but there are more competing suffixes for singulars than plural. (ii) Yet, locative, instrumental, and dative plural forms have a higher number of non-target forms even though all these cases (in the plural) are collapsed and have the same suffix (*-ima*). (iii) Croatian prepositions govern a particular case. In relative terms, NPs with non-target case marking are more likely than not to be preceded by a preposition that itself shows the case marking. Altogether, 171 NPs that should have accusative marking do not have it. Of these, 65 per cent (112) occur with prepositions that are case-marked. (iv) Further, nearly one third (287/874) of non-target realizations are accusative forms replacing locative. This is also happening in some homeland, less prestigious varieties. This finding of the accusative as the default replacement for locative is also found in Ďurovič's study of Croatian immigrant children in Sweden (1983). In fact, in general, Hlavac's findings match those of the implicational scale of case replacement of Ďurovič. Example (19) shows locative replacement by accusative on the noun following a preposition in the locative (*život* 'life'), the most common replacement.

(19) . . . što ću ja radit u život, onda sam . . .
what will/1S 1S do/INF in/LOC life M/ACC/S then be/1S
'. . . what will I do in life, and then I . . .'

(Hlavac 2000: 489)

In sum, in Hlavac's study there were far more intact case assignments than substitutions. And where there are non-target forms, there is substitution, not loss. In fact, 92 per cent of the non-target forms are replaced by substitutions, not loss (p. 492). That is, slots are hardly left empty, meaning the frame itself is recognized and maintained. Hlavac himself comments, 'Non-target case-marking is not prevalent statistically. Where it occurs it amounts to "reduction" or "levelling" of the case system' (p. 492).

A further point that Hlavac now makes is this: the system under attrition is actually more complex than without. The 'reduced' case-marking system (with substitutions) applies to NPs containing nouns, but never to those with pronouns.

That is, pronouns retain the original homeland Croatian case system. 'This results in a more complex system with case-marking also depending on the grammatical category of the head of NP' (email, 24 April 2001).

To predict which cases will undergo substitution, Ďurovič invokes a hierarchy that is at least reminiscent of a markedness hierarchy, with the idea that the less common cases are more likely to undergo substitution. However, Gross (2000*a*) shows that any argument based on markedness or simplicity alone is not an optimal explanation for what happens to grammatical structure in attrition situations.

Based on implications from the 4-M model, Gross develops a hypothesis that predicts that late system morphemes will be 'the last morpheme type to show effects from the L2' (p. 152). He is able to support his hypothesis with case-marking data from German determiners and adjectives, but he also shows that simplicity is not necessarily part of the explanation. Bear in mind that his subjects were even more distant from their home communities than Hlavac's subjects. (Gross's subjects were six German immigrants who had been living in the United States for at least forty years when they were interviewed in informal conversations conducted in the participants' native German dialect. English is the main language they had used for these forty years.)

In German, predicate adjectives are not inflected for case and gender; however, prenominal adjectives are. For example, see (20) from Gross's data.

(20) des wɔr-en gut-e Russ-en
those be/PST-3PL good-NOM/PL Russian-PL
'Those were good Russians.'

(Gross 2000*a*: 156)

Out of all the contexts for prenominal adjectives in his corpus, almost 90 per cent of contexts show the target case marking. Inaccurate forms occurred only 5.1 per cent of the time (18/354) and there were fifteen cases where there was no case-marker at all in the slot for an adjectival suffix. Thus, a total of 9.3 per cent of slots for an adjectival case-marker show non-target-like realizations.

Gross's results for determiners show even stronger support for the hypothesis that late system morphemes are not easily susceptible to loss or even change. Only 2.8 per cent of determiners were inaccurate (54/1,917). Further, when taken together, inaccurate forms for determiners and adjectives amount to only 3.2 per cent (72/2,271). Gross notes that this number contrasts sharply with results that he reports for content morphemes in his corpus. Gross examined production for idioms and various collocations and found that 29.7 per cent of the total showed some inaccuracies. Obviously, this finding supports hypothesis 3 (content morphemes are the morpheme type most susceptible to change in attrition).

When Gross sums inaccurate case marking for both determiners and adjectives, he finds that the results do not support a simple markedness hypothesis. In order to show that markedness or simplification is an adequate explanation of the data, one must show that dative case marking is being abandoned at a higher rate than, for example, accusative. Instead, Gross's data show a different state of affairs. His results show that there are more incorrect accusative forms (N = 12, all masculine singular, all indefinites) than dative forms (N = 15, all plural definites) in determiners. Further, if determiner data are summed with adjective data, the results are even more dramatic. Now 6.1 per cent (43/717) of accusative contexts show inaccurate forms vs. only 2.9 per cent (19/645) of dative contexts.

Still, even though Gross reminds the reader that nearly 97 per cent of all case/gender assigning contexts in his corpus obey L1 constraints, he suggests that his results indicate that the German NPs are converging to English. He writes, 'German late system morphemes are beginning to be used in an English-like manner: although the numbers are small, determiners are starting to mark only definiteness as in English' (p. 159).[4]

Gross notes that various studies of the sequence of first-language acquisition of case assignment indicate that the consistent, accurate production of nominative and accusative case precedes the acquisition of dative case. Thus, something other than supposed markedness must be at work in attrition in order to explain the retention of dative case in his corpus. In another study of thirty-five elderly L1 speakers of German who have lived in anglophone countries since the 1930s, the prediction was for the case system to be first reduced to a two-case one, with dative lost (Schmid 2001). However, the author states, 'The prediction that it will be the dative which is most vulnerable has not been borne out for any of the emigration groups' (p. 21). Furthermore, the case usage of one (N = 7) of the three emigration groups that Schmid studied does not differ from that of a control group for any of the cases. The other two emigration groups overuse the nominative, but no other details are reported.

Other studies of attrition in adults do not support assumption 5 as conclusively as Hlavac's and Gross's studies; yet, some of them definitely support the theoretical notion of substitution rather than loss and the division between the loss of content morphemes and system morphemes in general. For example, Maandi (1989) reports changes in the case-marking system of Estonian as spoken in a Swedish-dominant society, but she finds substitutions, not loss. Maandi studied three generations of speakers in the Estonian community of Sweden (N = approximately 75). She comments, 'all three generations are fully fluent speakers and as such are well aware of the conservative case-marking system'. However, she adds there is a 'clear tendency toward a new system' (p. 235). Based on an acceptability test, Maandi found changes in the distinction between the genitive and the

[4] Retention of a robust L1 case system does not necessarily correspond with regular exposure to the L1. For example, Gross reports that his subjects, who have been away from a German-dominant milieu for about forty years, have the opportunity to speak German only in social gatherings with non-family members, possibly once a month (email, 5 October 2001). Two of his subjects are married to each other, but they said that they almost exclusively spoke English with each other.

partitive as markers of the direct object. 'In the context traditionally calling for the Genitive, the third generation in particular claims to be using the Partitive and, to a somewhat lesser degree, the Nominative' (p. 236).

Another example of a new system comes from Fredsted's study (2001) from the multilingual northern German city of Flensburg. Fredsted sees her results as showing leveling of the system, but at the same time producing a new system. A two-case system has become usual (nominative–accusative) instead of the Standard German (nominative, accusative, genitive, and dative). Accusative frequently replaces dative (as in *Ich wollte* ***sie*** *ja erst'n Klied kaufen, aber dann schenkte ich* ***sie ein*** *Gutschein* 'At first I would have bought her a dress, but then I gave her a gift token'.[5] Note the use of *sie* 'her' instead of the dative *ihr.* (The speaker also uses nominative *ein* 'a' instead of the target accusative *einen*, but this is not a typical occurrence.) Accusative as a replacement for dative is also very frequent after certain prepositions that govern dative in Standard German. However, the dative still occurs in various idioms and collocations (e.g. *auf dem Markt* 'on the market'). In addition, various analytic expressions replace the Standard German postposed genitives; however, again, in collocations, the genitive still occurs.

The data reported in other studies without quantitative data do not seem all that different from that cited above; however, the researchers seem to view their findings more in terms of loss rather than retention or substitution. For example, Campbell and Muntzel (1989) is often cited as a typology of the change-processes in dying languages. In regard to changes outside of phonology, the authors speak largely in terms of loss. They write of morphological reduction, citing a tendency for case endings on adjectives to be lost in American Finnish. They also discuss syntactic reduction, citing loss in Pipil (spoken in Central America) of certain suffixes marking 'future' and the loss of its original morphological passives. They also mention certain changes in American Finnish, including some changes in word order, that may be an 'act of syntactic reception' (p. 194) with English as the influence.

Polinsky also speaks of loss, but at the same time shows evidence of substitution. She has studied attrition extensively in Russian immigrants to the United States (e.g. 1995, 1997, forthcoming). Polinsky (1995) offers the most detailed results. For this corpus, she 'chose to focus on those subjects who showed the most severe attrition . . . because I believe they simply show how far you can stretch the loss' (email, 24 September 2001). Polinsky studied twenty speakers of American Russian. She defines American Russian as the first language of speakers for whom it is a secondary language. (Emigré Russians are those for whom Russian is first and primary.) For her subjects the average age of leaving the L1 Russian environment was nine and the average time outside the L1 community was seventeen

[5] This example comes from a study by Eike Ketelsen and was recorded in a natural conversation in 1959.

years, with an 'average lapse period' of seven years. Clearly, her subjects are at the far end of attrition and differ from the boys whom Schmitt studied.

Polinsky's results cover a number of grammatical constructions; here, I continue to focus on case assignment. Clearly, Polinsky's subjects have leveled the six-case Russian system and Polinsky writes of it in these terms: 'American Russian abandons this case system' (p. 375). At the same time, she states that the loss of the case system is systematic, as is its replacement by a two-case system. Dative is replaced by accusative and accusative is replaced by nominative. Polinsky states, 'While the nominative becomes the multifunctional case, the accusative is specialized as the case of the indirect object and in some cases is used to encode the direct object' (p. 381).

Interestingly, in Schmid's study of attrition in German, it is the control group that shows substitution in the case system; they substitute accusative for dative or vice versa. (The control group consists of speakers of a northwestern variety of German who are sixty years old or older). In contrast, the immigrant groups, who were expected to show attrition, show over-generalization of nominative case as their main error. Schmid reports that the immigration groups 'use nominative infelicitously in about one-third of the cases' (p. 10). She reports no information on their other uses of cases. Thus, although the number of errors in the control group and the immigrant groups shows little or no difference, the types of error they make and the reported data indicate that the control group is retaining more of a case system than are the immigrant groups.

Two brief articles, Preston and Turner (1984) and Preston (1986) compare how case is realized in American Polish with case in homeland Polish. Unfortunately, the authors only study the frequency with which various cases appear in the data studied, not the extent of their target-like production. Still, some of the findings are instructive. Clearly, there are differences across the data sets. For example, Preston (1986: 1015) states that the two varieties of Modern Polish considered show more divergence in their relative frequencies of case realizations than the Polish speakers in Upstate New York show. For example, accusative is much more frequent in the New York data than the homeland data. Also, the use of instrumental to make predicate nominals is significantly lower in the New York varieties than the homeland varieties. Yet, Preston and Turner (1984: 136) see the New York data as forming a system. They write, 'We try to show . . . how the AmerP [American Polish] case system operates as a system (rather than as a depleted or altered sub-system of some standard) in one area of the United States where Polish is widely used'.

Polinsky (1995: 382 ff.) also discusses changes in verb forms in her Russian subjects. Subject–verb agreement, of course, is a prototypical example of the late outsider system morpheme since the morpheme only receives its form from information outside the VP (i.e. from the subject). In Polinsky's view 'subject–verb agreement is consistently disappearing' in her subjects. Still, although she states that one speaker produces only 30 per cent correct agreement, the most proficient speakers do have 66 per cent correct agreement. Recall that the average subject in her study has an 'average lapse period' of seven years and has been outside the L1 Russian environment for seventeen years. Against this background, the extent of loss of subject–verb agreement does not look so extreme—although at the same time it is hard to deny that the system of conjugation is weak. In contrast, Schmitt's Russian boys, who have been in an English-dominant milieu for about seven years, but who can be considered around the supposed critical age for ease of language acquisition, largely maintain subject–verb agreement. As noted above in section 5.5.2.2.1, the only real change they show in the verbal system is also using full pronouns in Russian, a pro-drop language.

5.5.3.3.3. LATE SYSTEM MORPHEMES IN CHILD DATA SETS

The findings reported for adults in the previous section show different results. In some cases (Hlavac 2000, Gross 2000*a*), case systems are clearly robust. And even in Polinsky's Russian data, there is a case system, albeit a reduced one.

Data relevant to attrition from child bilinguals show a different picture from that reported in some of the literature for adults. Most important, there is more evidence of both retention and substitution of L1 case assignments than of outright loss. In this way, these corpora are not very different from those of Dorian, Hlavac, and Gross. Note all these corpora supporting retention or substitution report extensive quantified data, stating target-like realizations in relation to overall possible contexts.

For example, in a number of publications, Pfaff (1991, 1994*a*, 1994*b*, *inter alia*) shows that the case system for Turkish is relatively intact in the Turkish children whom she studies in Berlin. Pfaff studies several different populations. In Pfaff (1991) she reports on case marking by three children (four- and five-year olds) in her KITA study. She states, 'The percentage of nonstandard case marking is low for all children, but considerably higher for inflected cases than for uninflected nominatives' (p. 113). Her statistics indicate that non-standard nominative marking (zero in Standard Turkish) ranges from 3.7 to 40 per cent across the children. For cases with overt realizations, the percentage of non-target forms ranged from 2.17 to 10.74 per cent across the children. For example, a child who produced 318 inflected forms had only 6.6 per cent non-target-like forms. Pfaff goes on to conclude about case:

> This indicates that there is little or no tendency to *lose* the inflectional system in favor of some more analytic means of expressing case relations, but rather that some nonstandard substitutions occur. In fact, analysis of the type of substitution errors provides more support for our finding that case marking is essentially intact in these young bilinguals. Erorrs are limited to peripheral semantic frames rather than representing prototypical case relations . . . and are paralleled by errors make by Turkish monolingual children. (pp. 113–14)

Elsewhere, Pfaff (1994*a*, 1994*b*) considers both Turkish-dominant and German-dominant children in Berlin, stating, 'the bilingual children make relatively few errors in Turkish morphology. This is particularly striking for the suffixes which express case, subject–verb agreement and tense–mood–aspect' (1994*b*: 44). When there are not target-like forms, she does not find loss in the case systems, but substitutions. For example, she notes, 'While the errors of Turkish-dominant children tend to involve overmarking of lexically irregular nouns in the genitive . . . the errors of German-dominant children involve undermarking of genitives and substitutions of one suffix for another' (1994*b*: 45).

Also, Schmitt (2000, 2001) finds that the five Russian boys she studied retain case assignments according to the Standard Russian pattern at a very high percentage for nominative and accusative and less so for the other cases, but still well above half for all cases but one. When there are replacements, they are most often from nominative and accusative. There are no absolute losses at all. That is, some form is always assigned to the slot for case realization. Recall that the second recording was made seven to nine years after immigration and it shows the case system is still largely intact. These findings seem to contrast with those of Polinsky for Russian adults cited above; however, Polinsky did find substitution, not outright loss, in the case system and therefore still finds a system.

In the Russian boys' first recording, nominative was target-like 99.5 per cent (401/403) in most cases and in the second recording this finding hardly changed: 98 per cent (558/564). Accusative case was target-like in 90 per cent of the cases (153/170) in the first recording and in 84 per cent of the cases (168/199) in the second recording.

The other cases show lower target-like findings. While genitive was target-like 85 per cent of the time (79/93) in the first recording, in the second recording the percentage was only 68 per cent (102/151). The dative case also showed a drop, but a smaller one: 82 per cent (36/44) in the first recording and 73 per cent (37/51) in the second recording. Prepositional case was 75 per cent target-like in the first recording (35/47) and 67 per cent (27/41) in the second recording. Only the instrumental case fell below 50 per cent. Target-like instrumental forms occur 42 per cent of the time (10/24) in the first recording and 45 per cent of the time (16/35) in the second recording.

Example (21) illustrates the replacement of instrumental by nominative case. Certain prepositions require instrumental case when used in the past or future tenses in Standard Russian. However, Schmitt's subjects consistently replace instrumental with nominative in these contexts.

(21) Ona budj-et uchitel'nits-**a**
3S/NOM be-3/FUT teacher-NOM/S/FEM
Standard Russian: uchitel'nits-**ej**
teacher-INSTR/S/FEM
'She will be a teacher.'
(Schmitt 2000: 208)

In sum, it is important to remember that there are no absolute losses at all in the case system for these boys. And for the contexts requiring most cases, target-like forms appear much of the time. Except for the instrumental case, at the very least, two-thirds of the case realizations are correct. One can argue that the case system is changing (with nominative and accusative replacing some other cases), but there still is a robust case system signaled by overt late outsider system morphemes.

Finally, more quantitative evidence about how case assignment as one example of a late system morpheme is retained or not in the context of child language attrition comes from the Hungarian/English corpus of Bolonyai (1999, 2000, 2002). In Hungarian, while nominative (assigned to subject) and accusative (assigned to direct object) are late outsider system morphemes, the other cases are largely early system morphemes, identifying thematic roles largely having to do with location in space or time.

Bolonyai specifically studied retention of the accusative case. Accusative is a late system morpheme because it is structurally assigned, expressing the grammatical relation of direct object through overt morphology in Hungarian. It is the most common case in Standard Hungarian and is also the most common one in Bolonyai's corpus.

Clearly, the Hungarian case system is largely intact; after all, the majority of all case endings are correct (89 per cent or 1,216/1,355). And the accusative is the most accurate case (91.8 per cent or 719/783). At the same time, the accusative is also the case showing the most omissions. In contrast, most of the errors in the local cases are errors of substitution (98 per cent). The majority of all omissions (72.4 per cent or 63/87) do reflect absence of the Hungarian accusative form. Still, keep in mind the overall numbers: even though the accusative case is missing more than any other case, it still is more accurately produced than any other type of morpheme (91.8 per cent of the time or 719/783).

Also, a look at the total errors in the corpus is enlightening (Bolonyai 2002, table 4). Out of this total, those for the accusative represent 42.7 per cent (64/150) while those for local cases are 43.3 per cent (65/150) and those for other cases are 14 per cent (21.150).

These two pieces of data—(i) that the accusative case is largely accurate over the largest number of tokens for any one case, and (ii) that the accusative case does not contribute a greater percentage of errors than the local cases—support the hypothesis that late system morphemes are not the most easily lost morpheme type.

Of course a compelling question is why does the accusative case show omission when the other cases largely show substitution? Nothing appears in sixty-three out of the sixty-four non-target-like accusative cases. Bolonyai (1999) offers an extensive discussion of what happens to the slot that would be projected by Hungarian for accusative. Bolonyai (2002) continues this discussion with more explicit evidence. Bolonyai predicts that 'breakdowns in mapping the direct object function onto surface level were expected to arise due to typological influence from English, where the object is not marked morphologically in spell-out' (2002: 26). This prediction is supported: forty-six out of the sixty-three accusative case omissions clearly reflected convergence to English. Some of the instances with no marking involve English nouns; but some of them are Hungarian nouns. (English nouns are bare in Schmitt's Russian/English corpus; they and other bare nouns are discussed in the next section.)

In her 1999 dissertation, Bolonyai hypothesizes that there are more instances of accusative loss when word order matches English SVO order than when it is SOV or OSV. She also suggests that the accusative will be omitted in one-word responses (without the subcategorizing verb overtly expressed). She finds that of the contexts where the accusative suffix is omitted, these two hypotheses explain the most omissions. Accusative is most omitted in sentences with (S)VO order (almost 48 per cent (30/63)) and second most often in one-word responses (30 per cent (19/63)). Finally, it is also omitted in sentences with (S)OV or O(S)V order (22 per cent (14/63)). Example (22) shows an omission in a one-word response.

(22) Édes burgonyá-t kér-sz vagy rizs-t?
sweet potato-ACC want-PRES/2S/SUBJ or rice-ACC
'Would you like sweet potato or rice?'
Response: **rizs-Ø**
'Rice.'

(Bolonyai 1999: 196)

Further, recall section 5.5.3.2 where local cases were discussed; this high rate of accusative omission contrasts with what happens when target-like forms do not occur for the local cases. Overall, the locative cases involve more substitution (63 per cent or 41/65) than omission (36.9 per cent or 24/65) (Bolonyai 2002, table 5). Clearly, this contrast of substitution for locative cases with omission for accusative represents a contrast in what happens to early system morphemes vs. late system morphemes—at least when English is the encroaching language. With other languages with more overt case systems, the results might be different, but the contrast is worth noting.

In sum, Bolonyai's results suggest several conclusions directly relevant to this discussion of case assignment. (i) Hungarian case assigment is more robust than moribund among her subjects, who are English-dominant and some of whom may not have completely acquired Hungarian before becoming immersed in an English-language community. (ii) Oblique cases (mainly locatives) that are early system morphemes are more prone to substitution than accusative (a late outsider system morpheme). Accusative differs from the oblique cases not only in being a late system morpheme, but also in not being a case that English projects overtly. Thus, if the children's Hungarian is converging to English, it is no surprise that some Hungarian accusative forms are beginning to be realized as zeros (omissions). (iii) Because English and Hungarian are incongruent in encoding spatial relations, it also is no surprise that non-target-like use of the Hungarian oblique suffixes does occur (supporting Hypothesis 6 in Bolonyai 1999: 189). English does realize (most of) the conceptual relations that Hungarian local suffixes project, but it often realizes them in other ways than case assignment. Still, even if the Hungarian of these children is converging to English, because these Hungarian locative suffixes convey conceptual information, one would predict this information must be overtly realized in some way (i.e. substitution, not zeroes).

Overall, then, Bolonyai's data support two other points about attrition that are worth stressing. First, in young children, at least, the inflectional system of the L1 remains relatively robust even while the L2 of the environment is increasingly becoming their dominant language. Second, changes in the system indicate that a composite Matrix Language is developing, with abstract lexical input from the L2 (English) as well as the L1, even while the L1 is the main source of input.

5.5.3.3.4. BARE ENGLISH NOUNS

What is most interesting about case assignment in several data sets is what happens to English nouns when they occur in a sentence otherwise largely or entirely framed by the L1 of these speakers. First, consider how Schmitt's Russian boys treat English nouns. They consistently access them as bare forms; that is, the English nouns show no case marking at all. In the first data set, 96 per cent of the English nouns (98/102) are bare forms and in the second data set 97.8 per cent (137/140) are bare. They are missing suffixes which assign case. Of course these suffixes are multimorphemic, also encoding gender and number. Of note is that the clause in which the bare English noun appears otherwise almost always follows the morphosyntactic requirements of Standard Russian. Thus, what we have is a clause entirely 'in Russian' except for the English noun that shows no Russian case assignment. (However, the clause may show convergence at the levels of abstract lexical structure as discussed above.) Bear in mind the results reported above for Russian nouns; they almost always either receive a target-like case marking or another case marking appears as a substitution. The net result is that Russian nouns and English nouns receive radically different treatment.

Schmitt (2001) explains this result as evidence that a composite Matrix Language frame is in effect, with English governing realization of the English noun at all levels of abstract lexical structure. That is, at the level of morphological realization patterns, English does not project a slot for case assignment and therefore there is no overt case assignment on the English noun.

Example (23) illustrates the use of a bare English noun.

(23) odin byl **pitcher-∅**
one was pitcher
Standard Russian: pitcher-**om**
INSTR/M/SG
'One was [a] pitcher.'

(Schmitt 2001: 226)

Other researchers view their data sets in similar terms. Recall that Bolonyai's results in her study of Hungarian children show that zero marking with accusative often involves an English noun. She (1999: 216–17) interprets the English nouns with no overt case marking in this way:

data analyses have indicated that much of what appears to be 'loss' of surface morphemes in L1 attrition is, indeed, replacement of abstract features in the L1 by corresponding features in the L2, at different levels of production. *The restructuring mechanisms in L1 attriton and convergence are systematic and reflect ways in which children attempt to keep their linguistic systems internally consistent.* (Italics added)

In addition, Halmari (1997: 145) reports 162 instances of non-target-like English forms in her corpus of American Finnish/English codeswitching for which most of the speakers were adults, but also included two children. All of these English forms were 'associated with clear non-fluencies' (p. 147). This is not surprising because Halmari points out that not all of her subjects were equally proficient in Finnish. Further, 39 per cent of these non-fluencies (63/162) were produced by one speaker. Halmari comments, 'Her Finnish was characterized by word searches and frequent switching to English' (p. 152). In general, the bare English forms lack proper Finnish morphology. Although Halmari does not offer statistics that specifically identify problems with case suffixes, this was the source of many non-target-like forms. Halmari makes a similar suggestion to that of Schmitt and Bolonyai; that is, she agrees that the likely explanation for English forms lacking target-like case assignments is that the speakers producing such forms are following English, not Finnish, abstract directions for realizing case (email, 10 April 2001). 'What I find interesting is that the switch into an English noun without an overt and expected Finnish case is most often preceded by . . . [a] repair, which indicates there is a "problem" in processing', Halmari comments.

5.5.3.3.5. ATTRITION IN MORPHEME TYPES

Admittedly, there is little quantitative data to support all aspects of the proposed hierarchy of susceptibility of morpheme types to attrition. Further, the evidence from adults is sometimes different from that for children, or it is intepreted differently. Yet, what evidence there is generally supports a ranking of this nature and the notion of system. When there is change in a language due to attrition, content morphemes are affected first, followed by early system morphemes, including word order when it is dependent on content morphemes, with late system morphemes least affected initially—and when affected—with a new system in place.

Late system morphemes < early system morphemes < content morphemes

Relatively new quantitative data offer strong support for this hierarchy, especially in reference to the late system morpheme of case. In some data sets, the results show that target-like case assignment is very robust. These are the findings, even in the face of the dominant use of another language by speakers (e.g. Croatians in Australia, Russian and Hungarian children in the United States). Even after a lengthy period of only infrequent use (German immigrants in the United States), the case system is largely intact. This is not to deny that in some instances, case systems are restructured via substitutions of one case for another; admittedly, in some data sets, this is the main outcome. However, even when this happens, the point is that in all instances an abstract system is still in place, albeit a modified system.

5.6. Conclusion

This chapter covers a number of issues relevant to convergence and attrition, sometimes arguing for different responses than those favored by some other researchers.

First, the relation of convergence and attrition is discussed. The suggested conclusion is that the two phenomena may differ in certain ways in how they are perceived, but that they are very similar from the grammatical point of view. Both show clauses with all surface-level morphemes from one language, but part of the abstract lexical structure from another source. That is, both are framed by composite Matrix Languages. The examples cited in section 5.5 show how abstract lexical structure from one language can be combined with structure from another language. When this happens, the semantics and pragmatics of lexical elements may change. Perhaps more important, which grammatical relations are encoded, and/or how they are encoded, may change. Thus, the result of such splitting and recombining is a restructuring of the morphosyntactic frame, the Matrix Language.

One structural difference is that convergence may be thought of as both a mechanism promoting other language contact phenomena and also an outcome itself, while attrition is largely only more of an outcome. As a mechanism, convergence is, in fact, the restructuring of a language's frame, resulting from a combining of that language with abstract grammatical structure from another language.

Even though they are structurally similar, convergence and attrition may be viewed differently in a sociolinguistic sense. Convergence is often seen as a gradually developing phenomenon, affecting large parts of an entire speech community, while attrition is viewed more as a phenomenon resulting from lack of use by an individual of a language, usually the L1, often coupled with lack of sufficient input. Both convergence and attrition may result in language death, but attrition is seen as a surer road to language death. Languages 'die', as Denison (1977: 21) put it, when 'there is nothing left for them appropriately to be used about'. Attrition (and language death) can and does affect different members of a community differently. As long as speakers use a language regularly, its structure can remain largely intact, as Dorian's studies of fluent speakers of East Sutherland Gaelic show (e.g. Dorian 1981).

Second, the definition of convergence as an outcome is considered, along with the nature of 'mutual influence' as a mechanism of convergence. I argue that influence is largely asymmetrical, with the variety of the more powerful and prestigious group influencing the structure of the other variety. I also question convergence areas in terms of the true mutuality in their development. I make two arguments: (i) I suggest that such areas result from past instances of asymmetrical relationships. That is, there is little mutuality, but instead succeeding times in which one variety was dominant and influenced other varieties. (ii) I raise the issue of whether convergence areas are so unusual as is sometimes thought. That is, I suggest that the type of features that distinguish them generally involve conceptual structure, not structurally assigned grammatical relations. Within the terms of the 4-M model, features showing conceptual structure are content morphemes and early system morphemes, and they are rather easily acquired. Therefore, they spread rather easily from one variety to another, making the rise of convergence areas very likely. Under the model, the reason for this is that both types of morpheme encode speaker's intentions; content morphemes are directly elected by speaker intentions and, in turn, they point to the early system morphemes that add specifity to the intended meaning. The hypothesis is that they are salient at the level of the mental lexicon and are the elements sending directions to the Formulator for further production. Because of their relation with conceptual structure, they are the types of morphemes that are prime candidates to spread from one language to another, with some type of prestige (or possibly practicality as in the Kupwar case in section 5.2.2) as the impetus for spread.

Third, I devote most attention in the chapter to attrition. I begin by surveying the main ideas in the existing literature on attrition, paying special attention to notions about markedness and simplicity, as well as analogical leveling in relation to these two. I then discuss my own views about attrition.

The problem with many studies of attrition is that they are based on two ill-defined constructs, markedness and simplicity. True, it may well be that structures that are marked by not being shared by the languages involved are more easily lost than others. Certainly, many researchers argue that when a particular structure is similar across the waning language and a more widely used language, this may make it even more likely that there will be a change in the direction of the more dominant variety. Further, evidence reported here does seem to show that when there is substitution of one form for others—for example in a paradigm of case affixes—the more frequently used ones (the more unmarked ones, often nominative and accusative) take the place of others.

However, frequency or markedness may be relatively unimportant. Instead, surface-level change may be more a reflection of a restructuring of more abstract conceptual relations. For example, the restructured case system may encode figure and ground relations more than syntactic relations (what may be happening in the Hungarian locative case system of the Hungarian children in Bolonyai (1999, 2001)). No matter what, the basic problem with employing markedness and simplicity as explanatory constructs is that there is no definition of either one that is universally applicable. Given this situation, researchers invoking these constructs ought to provide definitions of their own that are integrated into a particular theoretical framework. Based on a study of Serbo-Croatian immigrants who came to Norway as adults, Skaaden (1999) suggests that distinguishing between central and periphery positions in the system helps explain structures found in a language undergoing attrition. She argues that 'marginal members of the [grammatical] system are more vulnerable to attrition than central members' (p. 289). Again, however, we have the problem of definitions.

For these reasons among others, I suggest that a set of assumptions based on the Abstract Level model and the 4-M model can better explain which elements are more susceptible to change than others under attrition. Both models offer definitions of the terms they employ.

5.6.1. *Abstract lexical structure and susceptibility to change in attrition*

The following hierarchy of susceptibility of alteration under attrition is predicted with the three levels of abstract grammatical structure in the Abstract Level model:

Predicate-argument structure < morphological realization patterns < lexical-conceptual structure

5.6.2. *Morpheme type and susceptibility to change in attrition*

The hypotheses of the 4-M model regarding differential access of different types of morphemes in language production support the following hierarchy:

Late system morphemes < early system morphemes < content morphemes

5.6.3. *The evidence and its interpretation*

Note that the predicted hierarchies complement each other. In both, elements showing conceptual structure are considered to be more susceptible to modification or loss. And in both, those elements that encode grammatical relations within the clause are considered to be least susceptible to modification or loss. Predicted loss or modification is not so much a matter of 'tight organization' as it is a matter of the type of abstract structure that morphemes encode.

Where there are quantitative studies, they offer a good deal of support for these hierarchies, although not every study is supportive to the same extent. Details and examples in much of the non-quantified attrition literature also offer some anecdotal support—even though the same studies may contain the received view that more complex, more marked structures are more susceptible to loss early in attrition. Because the hypothesis of the 4-M model is that late system morphemes are not salient until late in language production, one can assume they would be called marked or complex. In addition, late system morphemes generally are not accurately acquired until relatively late in either first- or second-language acquisition. Still, the hypotheses in this chapter predict they are not the most susceptible to early loss.

Section 5.5 details a number of quantitative studies of attrition in both adults and children, all supporting the assumption that, among morpheme types, late system morphemes are least susceptible to absolute loss when attrition takes place. Data on case assignment exemplifies the argument about late system morphemes. These studies show that case systems remain more intact than not, although admittedly in some corpora more than others (more in the corpora of Gross 2000*a* and Hlavac 2000, less in Polinksy 1995). Further, even when a specific case is not retained, it is replaced by a related form through substitution. The net result is that a frame remains in place. Given these findings, I suggest that it is a mistake to characterize attrition as wholesale loss.

The value of presenting explanations for the route that attrition takes in terms of these two models is that it is possible to make more precise predictions about the nature of attrition than those generally found in the literature. Further, the differences that the models predict for different levels of abstract lexical structure and morpheme type are also reflected in other contact phenomena. For example, we have seen in earlier chapters how the requirements for some types of morpheme are different in classic codeswitching than those for other morphemes. In the next chapter, we see how lexical-conceptual structure makes content morphemes the major catalyst in creole formation, while the late system morphemes of creoles largely depend on reconfigured content morphemes for their surface forms. We will also see how recognizing a division between content morphemes and system morphemes helps explain the form of many mixed languages.

6

Lexical Borrowing, Split (Mixed) Languages, and Creole Formation

6.1. Introduction

Although the title of this chapter may make this look like a rag-tag bag, it is not. There is a thread that relates all three of these contact phenomena, and it is the special role of the lexicon (content morphemes) as it contrasts with that of grammatical relations. This matter is considered in relation to lexical borrowing, mixed languages, and creole formation. None of these phenomena is considered in as much detail as codeswitching receives in Chapters 3 and 4 and convergence and attrition have in Chapter 5. The reason for the less complete treatment is simply the need to keep the scope of the volume manageable. However, I hope that the following treatment of each phenomenon captures the central nature of its structuring. As Leonard Talmy (1985, 2000: 21) has written about the relationship between the lexicon and grammar:

> A fundamental design feature of language is that it has two subsystems, which can be designated as the *grammatical* and the *lexical*. . . . Why is there this universal bifurcation when, in principle, a language could be conceived having only a single system, the lexical? The explanation . . . is that the two subsystems have distinct semantic functions, ones that are indispensable and complementary. To develop this account further, we must first note that we take a sentence (or other portion of discourse) to evoke in the listener a particular kind of experiential complex, here termed a cognitive representation or CR. The grammatical and lexical subsystems in a sentence seem generally to specify different portions of a CR. . . . The grammatical specifications in a sentence . . . provide a conceptual framework or, imagistically, a skeletal structure or scaffolding for the conceptual material that is lexically specified.

I begin by discussing lexical borrowing, a subject already raised earlier in relation to codeswitching. In addition, the sociolinguistic conditions favoring borrowing are discussed in Chapter 2. Next we will see how lexical elements figure in the formation of some mixed languages and how their nature figures very prominently in the grammatical structure of creoles.

6.2. Lexical borrowing

Almost all languages include lexical elements that have come from another language. As Haugen (1989: 197) puts it simply, but clearly, the term '"borrowing" is the general and traditional word used to describe the adoption into a language of a linguistic feature previously used in another'. He goes on to note that the term was a byproduct of early nineteenth-century studies of sound change. 'Borrowing was essentially that which remained unaccounted for by the sound laws, and could be explained by outside influence' (p. 197). Borrowings were recognized as mostly lexical items and came to be known as loanwords. Haugen wryly notes that the term itself is a loanword, calqued on the German term *Lehnwort.*

6.2.1. *The background on borrowing*

Linguistics depends largely on Haugen for its understanding of how the term 'borrowing' has been used. Weinreich (1967), who was more or less Haugen's contemporary, was perhaps even more influential in the early study of the effects of one language on another, but he uses the term 'interference' much more than 'borrowing' and has less to say about lexical borrowing. For Weinreich, interference is the general term for contact phenomena, and thus when he writes about effects on the lexicon, he speaks of 'one vocabulary interfering with another' (1967: 47).

In his classic study of borrowing, also published more than fifty years ago, Haugen (1950*b*: 211 ff.) introduces borrowing with something of a backward compliment for the expression, stating, 'The real advantage of the term "borrowing" is the fact that it is not applied to language by laymen. It has therefore remained comparatively unambiguous in linguistic discussion, and no apter term has yet been invented' (p. 211).

He goes on to emphasize borrowing as process in his definition, referring to how a speaker deals with something new from a new language:

> If he [the speaker] reproduces the new linguistic pattern, NOT IN THE CONTEXT OF THE LANGUAGE IN WHICH HE LEARNED THEM, but in the context of another, he may be said to have 'borrowed' them from one language to another. The heart of our definition of borrowing is then THE ATTEMPTED REPRODUCTION IN ONE LANGUAGE OF PATTERNS PREVIOUSLY FOUND IN ANOTHER. (p. 212)

By 'pattern' Haugen means largely lexical elements, not grammatical patterns. This is clear because in the ensuing discussion he only offers a classification of loanwords and what happens to them in the process of reproduction. Even while insisting that borrowing is 'strictly a process and not a state' (p. 213), he acknowledges that 'most of the terms used in discussing it are ordinarily descriptive of its results rather than of the process itself' (p. 213). And Haugen himself continues this tradition, devoting most of his efforts in this work and elsewhere to devising terminology and then to cataloguing types of borrowings. He is well known for illustrating his classifications with examples of how Norwegian immigrants to the

Upper Midwest of the United States treated English words in their American Norwegian (e.g. Haugen 1953).

In Haugen (1950*b*), he begins his discussion of types of new words by emphasizing that 'imports' differ from 'substitutions'. Imports are loanwords that are 'similar enough to the model so that a native speaker would accept them as his own. . . . But insofar as he [the speaker] has reproduced the model inadequately, he has normally SUBSTITUTED a similar pattern from his own language' (p. 212). This is an important distinction (between imports as not phonologically integrated and substitutions, which are) because too many writers erroneously assume that most lexical borrowings are necessarily phonologically integrated. He goes on to set up three terms to cover the outcomes of the borrowing process: loanword, loanblend, and loanshift. The most general term 'loanword' refers to elements showing no morphological substitutions, but they do show degrees of phonological substitutions. For example, the speech of Norwegian immigrants in the United States showed various substitutions. The English word *field* received its phonological form from the unrelated Norwegian word *fil* 'file'. Or, two contemporary examples that are imports in many languages are *salsa* 'sauce' from Spanish and *sushi* 'cakes of cold rice with various wrappings' from Japanese. Loanblends are combinations of L1 material with L2 material; Haugen also used the term 'hybrids' for such borrowings. As an example he cites *bockabuch* 'pocket book' from Pennsylvania German speakers (with substitution of Pennsylvania German *buch* for English *book*). Loanshifts do not actually include surface-level alien morphemes but instead influence L1 material; the category includes loan translations (calques) and semantic borrowings. English *it goes without saying* is based on French *ça va sans dire*. A contemporary example of a semantic borrowing is *latte* 'milk' (Italian) for a drink of coffee with steamed milk.

Haugen's divisions are not often observed today; instead, most discussions refer only interchangeably to either 'borrowings' or 'loanwords', although loan translations or calques are recognized. What Haugen called semantic borrowings are generally subsumed under the rubric of convergence.

Up until the publication in 1988 of Thomason and Kaufman's influential study of what they refer to as 'contact-induced change', there was little further discussion in the literature of the nature of borrowing. Presumably, because the emphasis had been on classification and description, the topic was not deemed theoretically interesting. Of course, in the meantime there were many descriptive case studies and mentions of borrowings in various overviews of specific languages. The Thomason and Kaufman volume is very valuable because it reawakened interest in the process of borrowing, at least in circles interested in language change or language contact. Their volume is an impressive compendium of examples showing that much language change can be attributed to contacts with other languages.

Borrowing received new attention under Thomason and Kanfman as one of the 'two basic types of interference' (1988: 37). They call the other type 'interference', but sometimes 'interference through shift' or 'shift-induced interference'. They define borrowing in a usual way as 'the incorporation of foreign features into a group's native language by speakers of that language: the native language is maintained but is changed by the addition of the incorporated features' (p. 37). They go on to predict, 'Invariably, in a borrowing situation, the first foreign elements to enter the borrowing language are words' (p. 37). Earlier, Weinreich (1967: 56) identified borrowing even more closely with the lexicon, writing, 'The vocabulary of a language, considerably more loosely structured than its phonemics and its grammar, is beyond question the domain of borrowing *par excellence*', referencing Meillet (1921).

What makes the Thomason and Kaufman treatment innovative is that they emphasize three features about borrowing that imply process: (i) Borrowing is differentiated from interference in that speakers who borrow elements still retain their L1. (ii) The extent of borrowing and, more important, the types of elements borrowed depend on the degree of cultural contact. Terms such as 'long-term' and 'intensive' are used to characterize contact that results in more than lexical borrowing into an L1. (iii) While most studies of borrowing are content to consider lexical items, Thomason and Kaufman include prominently what they call structural borrowing, i.e. incursions into the phonology, morphology, or syntax of the recipient language.

The other basic type of interference is shift-induced interference, occurring when an L1 is not retained. This term refers to the influence of one language on another in a shifting situation; specifically, the L1 of the shifting speakers affects the target language (TL). The major differences between borrowing and interference seem to be the following: (i) 'Unlike borrowing, interference does not begin with vocabulary: it begins with sounds and syntax, and sometimes includes morphology as well before words from the shifting group's original language appear in the TL [target language]' (p. 39). (ii) As noted above, the L1 is maintained in borrowing and it is not in interference. (iii) Interference seems to require a more specific set of sociological conditions to occur than does borrowing, although both happen when there is some bilingualism and cultural contact between groups.

While the distinctions Thomason and Kaufman make between borrowing and interference certainly aid researchers in describing contact-induced change, the problem is that the proposed distinctions do not hold up very well, either practically or theoretically. First, for them, borrowing starts out as largely lexical, but, then, it also can involve phonology, syntax, and morphology when the cultural contact with the donor language is long and intense. Further, borrowing can accompany interference. Thus, the structural boundaries between borrowing and interference are blurred. Can either one include the same material? The only clear difference is a sociolinguistic one (i.e. under borrowing, the L1 is maintained). Second, although interference is distinguished from borrowing by happening in a shifting situation, both borrowing and shifting have the same general motivations: cultural contacts. Labeling 'cultural contacts' by degrees still does not define the degrees, and so we have no real way to differentiate those that promote structural borrowing from those promoting only lexical borrowing. Then, distinguishing the cultural contacts that promote borrowing from those that promote shift is no easier.

To be fair, Thomason and Kaufman do describe a set of cultural contact conditions that seem necessary for interference to occur. For example, intensity of contact matters: 'where the shifting group is very small relative to the TL [target language] speaker group, there will be little or no interference to the TL [target language] as a whole' (p. 47). Also, if the shift occurs after the shifting group is 'fully bilingual and well integrated into the TL [target language] community', there is little interference. In fact, interference only seems to occur under the special conditions of a rapid shift and a shifting group that is 'so large numerically that the TL [target language] model is not fully available to all its members [so that] imperfect learning is a probability, and the learners' errors are more likely to spread throughout the TL [target language] speech community' (1988: 47).

More important for this chapter, the mechanisms that generate either borrowing or interference are not self-evident in Thomason and Kaufman's portrayals. Thomason and Kaufman seem to refer to borrowing and interference as mechanisms themselves. They write, 'Now that we have carefully distinguished the two basic mechanisms of contact-induced change, we must emphasize that there is unfortunately no reason to expect these two types of interference to take place in mutually exclusive contexts' (1988: 45). Also, the implication of their set of types of borrowing is that the intensity of cultural contacts is a mechanism promoting more or less structural borrowing. Degree of contact (from 'casual' to 'intense') characterizes the five categories of borrowing that they set out.

I can agree with them that cultural contact, the sociolinguistic history of the speakers, is a starting point in any discussion of language contact. But, as I explain below, I cannot agree that 'both the direction of interference and the extent of interference are socially determined; so, to a considerable degree, are the kinds of features transferred from one language to another' (1988: 35). I do agree with them that all the proposed structural constraints that they discuss from the extant literature do fail, but I do not agree that they fail 'because linguistic interference is conditioned in the first instance by social factors, not linguistic ones' (1988: 35). Rather, they fail because they are ill-defined (e.g. markedness) or simply the wrong sorts of constraints to be mechanisms in language contact.

Treffers-Daller (1999) sets out to test Thomason and Kaufman's notions about the role of social factors in borrowing. Her results indicate to her that the structure of the languages, not differences in the sociohistory of the speakers, plays a more prominent role in setting the nature of borrowing and shift-induced interference. Based on a comparative study of borrowing and shift-induced interference in Brussels and Strasbourg, she argues that despite important differences in the sociolinguistic profiles of the two cities, 'the overall contact patterns are very similar, both from a quantitative and from a qualitative point of view' (p. 1). Treffers-Daller's careful study largely just presents comparative data from the two cities, although she does point out there are basic asymmetries in the type of influence, as is noted below. However, she does not offer her own ideas to explain the similarities in outcome. Below, I discuss my own views on mechanisms of lexical borrowing.

6.2.2. *Motivations for borrowing*

It is obvious that some members of community X have to be bilingual enough to produce some words or phrases in language Y if words from Y are ever to be incorporated into language X. But these individuals are not enough. There have always been certain bilingual individuals in any society—travelers, diplomats, merchants, academics, and traders, among others. Still, although they may enrich their conversations with alien words, their novel choices rarely have permanent effect. That is, individual bilinguals are rarely the main sources of new words in a recipient language unless they are extraordinarily celebrated (heads of state, media stars?). Thus, when one considers why borrowed elements appear in a language, the distinction between personal and communal bilingualism probably makes a difference. Innovators may bring in new lexical elements, but adoption does not necessarily follow. Serious lexical borrowing requires a critical mass: it happens when persons who are well connected in the society adopt the new words. In addition, borrowing is helped along when large numbers of persons in the same society have some measure of bilingualism, because if speakers care about being understood, other societal members have to be bilingual enough to understand the imported words when they are first used. Of course, later—once they are coming into general usage—monolinguals use the lexical borrowings, too. (Note that the degree of bilingualism required to promote lexical borrowing is much lower than that needed to engage in codeswitching or for the L2 to effect many changes in the L1 at the levels of abstract lexical structure—at least in my experience and how I read relevant studies.)

In the modern world, the necessary degree of group bilingualism for lexical borrowing to occur widely turns out to be rather easy to achieve. In large segments of a community's population, such bilingualism even can result from the general availability of the mass media across linguistic borders. Also, the degree of available education today often means studies include access to an international language. And of course, whatever is the local language of the computer (often English) promotes borrowings from that language, albeit not always words very useful in other aspects of one's life (e.g. one does not have to be a medical doctor to perform an illegal operation on the computer).

Psychologically, the source of borrowings generally is a society that commands more prestige than the recipient society. That is, borrowing is typically an asymmetrical process—like other language-contact processes. Of course, there are a number of kinds of prestige. A society with socioeconomic prestige is often the source of borrowings in today's society; however, a society with prestige in regard to undefinable aspects of 'culture' and 'style' may also be the source of borrowings. Relationships between societies change over time: certainly during the Norman Conquest, French was the source of many borrowings into English. Because French was long considered the best language of diplomacy until very recently, it continues to be the source of some borrowings. However, with the rise of English-speaking cultures in the twentieth century in the area of international business and technology, English is now the source of many borrowings into even French, as well as in other societies. The main point—however the French government views the phenomenon—is that there and elsewhere, borrowing is rarely reciprocal.

Treffers-Daller (1999) finds quantitative evidence of such asymmetries in lexical borrowing in her study of two European cities. Each setting studied includes a Germanic variety and French: Strasbourg (French and Alsatian) and Brussels (French and Brussels Dutch). In both cases, French has the higher socioeconomic prestige, and it is the source of most borrowings. She writes, 'The Brussels and Strasbourg data show exactly the same asymmetry, in that French words are easily borrowed in the Germanic varieties, whereas the lexical influence of the Germanic varieties on French is very limited' (p. 9).

6.2.3. *Types of lexical borrowings*

A division between types of borrowings that is useful in relation to discussions of other contact phenomena is the division between cultural and core lexical borrowings. (i) Cultural borrowed forms are words for objects new to the culture (e.g. *CD* or *compact disk*, *espresso*), but also for new concepts (e.g. *overtime*). (ii) Core borrowed forms are words that more or less duplicate already existing words in the L1 (e.g. words for 'brother' or 'home' or words for time references such as *le weekend* in French). Cultural borrowed forms usually appear abruptly in a language when influential individuals or groups begin using them. These cultural borrowed forms may appear frequently in two outcomes: (i) in the monolingual speech of either bilinguals or monolinguals (speaking the recipient language), or (ii) in the codeswitching of bilinguals. They have an obvious immediate utility (they fill lexical gaps in a language); this is why speakers are motivated to make them a part of their repertoire as soon as they learn them. While core borrowed forms eventually may appear in the speech of monolinguals in a recipient community, I suggest that core borrowed forms usually begin life in the recipient language when bilinguals introduce them as singly occurring codeswitching forms in the mixed constituents of their codeswitching (cf. Myers-Scotton 1993*a* [1997]: 163 ff.).

Core borrowed forms, especially discourse markers, from English into Canadian French are studied by Mougeon and Beniak (1991). They conclude that the French speakers who use English *so* the most were persons who use French and English about equally in their private domains; that is, it is not infrequent users of French who pepper their French with English loans. Instead, it is speakers who are actively bilingual—speakers who do not compartmentalize their languages in their private lives. Mougeon and Beniak call this 'unpatterned bilingualism'. Interestingly, they conclude that 'the gratuitous nature of core lexical borrowing [e.g. *so*] is reminiscent of the phenomenon of code-switching, which is also especially characteristic of speakers who exhibit unpatterned bilingualism. . . . In fact, that sentence connectors and other kinds of discourse organizers like *so* are so often reported in lists of core lexical borrowings may not be a coincidence, since these items all occur at prime switch points' (1991: 211). They advance a hypothesis that agrees with the position taken here: that core lexical B-forms start out as code switches (cf. Myers-Scotton (1993*a* [1997]: 174 ff.).

6.2.4. *What lexical categories are borrowed*

The most obvious statistic about borrowing is that more nouns are borrowed than any other category. For example, Haugen (1950*b*: 224) reported that 75.5 per cent of the loanwords in his American Norwegian corpus were nouns. The dominance of nouns is also evident in a number of recent studies, such as two studies of French–English contact in eastern Canada (Poplack, Sankoff, and Miller 1988 and Mougeon and Beniak 1991). Treffers-Daller (1999: 9) found that more than half of the borrowings were nouns in her study of French loans in two corpora, into Brussels Dutch in Brussels and into Alsatian in Strasbourg. She found that 58.4 per cent (2329/3988) of the loans in Brussels were nouns and 65.9 per cent (297/452) of those in Strasbourg were nouns.

This statistic is no surprise because almost all borrowed elements are content morphemes, and nouns, along with verbs, are the prototypical content morphemes. Recall content morphemes are defined as elements that assign or receive thematic roles within a CP. They are mainly nouns, verbs, adjectives, and some adverbs and some prepositions. I suggest that nouns are borrowed more frequently than any other category because they receive, not assign, thematic roles. That is, their insertion into the frame of another language is less disruptive of predicate-argument structure than insertions of any content morphemes assigning thematic roles (i.e. verbs, but also prepositions and predicate adjectives). I propose that nouns are rarely borrowed to satisfy thematic roles that they do not satisfy in their source language. Their semantic or pragmatic import is open to change (i.e. specifications at the level of lexical-conceptual structure), but it is less likely their thematic roles will change (i.e. their specifications at the level of predicate-argument structure). Thus, for example, nouns that are Agents are borrowed into syntactic slots that Agents can occupy in the recipient language.

Also frequently borrowed are discourse markers and some subordinators, as are conjunctions. The Turkologist Lars Johanson (1999: 252) notes that 'throughout Turkic language history, conjunctors [conjunctions], but also some discourse markers] are amazingly often global copies of foreign originals, e.g. Persian, Arabic and Slavic words for "and", "but", "for", etc.' (Recall that my associates and

I argue that discourse markers assign discourse-level thematic roles in the sense that they restrict the interpretation of the CP of which they are a part (cf. Myers-Scotton and Jake 2001: 95–6).) We are careful to distinguish discourse markers as content morphemes from content morphemes that participate in the thematic grid of the CP. (Those content morphemes within the CP's grid assign and receive such thematic roles as Agent, Patient, and the like.) In contrast, Topic and Focus or Consequence exemplify the discourse thematic roles that discourse markers assign. Blakemore (1992: 137) discusses discourse markers as 'discourse connectives', writing that 'they can be regarded as effective means for constraining the interpretation of utterances in accordance with the principle of relevance'. Discourse markers indicate various interpretations, but they often assign a Contrastive Focus to the following IP proposition. For this reason, in codeswitching data sets, such markers often come from the Embedded Language and a 'double contrast' is achieved. For example, consider *but* in example (1).

(1) [$_{CP}$ **but** [$_{IP}$ si-on-i kama tu-na Ø-kazi ny-ingi these days$_{IP}$] $_{CP}$]
1S/NEG-see-NEG as 1PL-have CL9-work CL9-much these days
'But I don't see [him] as we have much work these days.'

(Swahili/English; Myers-Scotton Nairobi corpus 1988)

Pronouns that often appear in initial position in a CP are similar to discourse markers in that they assign the discourse-relevant role of Topic. However, only pronouns meeting the definition of content morphemes in the CP (they receive thematic roles) occur in these discourse-thematic positions. Compare the occurrence of French *moi* to assign topic with **je*, which cannot assign roles at any level (cf. Jake 1994). In some codeswitching corpora, there is apparent 'doubling' of pronouns when one appears in topic position. In fact, there is no doubling at all; rather two different types of pronominal elements appear, for example an Embedded Language pronominal discourse marker (a content morpheme) followed by a Matrix Language pronominal element (cf. Myers-Scotton, Jake, and Okasha 1996).

In contrast to content morphemes, system morphemes generally are not easily borrowed, especially late system morphemes. In various ways, this fact has been recognized many times in the earlier literature on contact situations. Haugen (1950*b*) comments that 'the instances of new inflections actually introduced into wide use in the language are few, cf. the uncertain fate of classical plurals in E [English] words like *phenomena, indices*, etc.' (p. 225). Writing about borrowings in the history of Turkish, Johanson (1999: 253) states, 'Relators that are practically never copied include case markers and simple adpositions'. Also, more than sixty years ago in writing about 'the problem of hybrid languages', Roberts (1939: 36–7) makes this pithy statement: 'Grammar is one; it must stand or fall as a unit.' As Thomason and Kaufman (1988) correctly point out, such comments are too extreme; however, I argue that system morphemes do not enter a language in the same way or via the same mechanism as content morphemes; therefore, I resist calling them borrowings. My scenario for them is different, as I point out below.

In some cases, early system morphemes have been borrowed along with their content morpheme heads. For example, Haugen (1950*b*: 218) points out that English plural *-s* is borrowed into American Norwegian 'with its stem and treated as if it were part of a singular noun'. He goes on to say, 'This becomes such a common thing that the N [Norwegian] suffixed article may be adding to it, producing a hybrid inflection *-s* + *-a* "the", e.g. *kisa* "the keys"' (p. 218). There are examples in other data sets of the plural suffix being borrowed into a language, with that language putting its own plural suffix on the borrowed form. The result is similar to the double morphology in codeswitching discussed in Chapter 3.

6.2.5. *When structurally assigned morphemes are involved*

In Thomason and Kaufman's borrowing scale of five levels, increased cultural contact correlates with increased borrowing. At the first level, there is only lexical borrowing, but at the fifth level there is 'heavy structural borrowing' of 'major structural features that cause significant typological disruption' (pp. 74–5). The catalogue of features that they list as characterizing each level and the accompanying examples are very useful in outlining the elements that can enter a language in a contact situation. However, employing the 4-M model, I classify the elements differently and argue that different mechanisms are involved from those they consider.

I argue that the incorporation into a recipient language of surface-level system morphemes, and most especially late system morphemes, is a different contact phenomenon from lexical borrowing because of the major mechanism involved. I argue that late system morphemes only come into a language when its morphosyntactic frame undergoes a reconfiguration. The mechanism promoting such a change is convergence. This happens when what I have referred to as a Matrix Language turnover is underway. Of course, the mechanism of codeswitching may also be involved, as I have argued elsewhere (Myers-Scotton 1998*a*), but I now think that it is convergence that makes the difference between lexical borrowing and new grammatical outcomes. Instead, codeswitching is a major mechanism in promoting convergence; it also is more of a mechanism in lexical borrowing, and especially the borrowing of core borrowed forms.

Consider how this can be so, beginning with lexical borrowing. In classic codeswitching, what we largely have are integrations of lexical elements that are content morphemes; there also are Embedded Language islands. At the abstract level, producing Embedded Language forms (that can become lexical borrowed forms) in codeswitching involves a matching of those forms with Matrix Language counterparts for 'sufficient congruence'. The Embedded Language forms need not be identical to the Matrix Language forms to pass the congruence filter. It is especially at the level of lexical-conceptual structure that they can be somewhat different—as long as they are congruent enough in regard to predicate-argument structure and, secondly, morphological realization patterns to fit into the morphosyntactic frame projected by the Matrix Language. In fact, we would expect them to be somewhat different at the level of lexical-conceptual structure; otherwise, a major motive for calling them up at all is lacking (they often have a somewhat different semantic field or pragmatic reading from the Matrix Language counterpart, adding 'something' the Matrix Language counterpart cannot supply).

But the point is that codeswitching provides an easy avenue for core borrowed forms to come into the recipient language (the Matrix Language). I do not suggest details, but it is very likely this entry is gradual. That is, a potential borrowed form must first appear as a codeswitching form a number of times. From there, they can move—as borrowed forms—into even monolingual speech in the recipient language. Thus, codeswitching is a mechanism.

Of course much lexical borrowing occurs *without* codeswitching; I want to be very clear on this point. As noted above, simply the need for cultural B-forms to fill gaps (words for new items and concepts) is important. I claim these forms enter the recipient language abruptly—figuratively and literally by word of mouth—because they have an immediate use and no really competing forms. (Of course, there is nothing to stop them from entering through codeswitching, too.) In addition, there is the fascination with power (the speech of the powerful always attracts other speakers who would copy it). Finally, there is the lure of novelty. Both power and novelty promote imitators and therefore lexical borrowing.

Note that although codeswitching can and does accompany new grammatical outcomes (Thomason and Kaufman's structural borrowings), it is not the major mechanism in these types of intervention. A piece of negative evidence is the fact that much codeswitching occurs in clauses that show no new grammatical outcomes. This is classic codeswitching. Instead, I argue that such outcomes must be preceded by convergence as a mechanism. Why convergence? As I argued and demonstrated in Chapter 5, convergence is the process that involves changes in the abstract lexical structure underlying semantic and grammatical relations. *In fact, convergence is the restructuring of a language's frame.* This happens in bilingual speech because one language—usually the more powerful and prestigious language—impinges on another. The Abstract Level model refers to this as splitting and recombining at the abstract level. When these changes are accomplished, the frame of a CP changes. Johanson (1999, *inter alia*) makes this same argument. He writes:

> The basic code may change considerably through global copying. Lexical copying may be extensive, without leading to a shift of the basic code. But what interests us here are factors that modify the basic code and change the very frame for insertion of copies. As a matter of fact, both global and selective, notably combinational, copies take [an] active part in morphosyntactic change. (p. 250)

With the frame altered in the direction of language X, actual surface-level grammatical forms from Language X to fill slots on that frame can follow. In this way, convergence is the major mechanism that brings in grammatical outcomes from another language.

Evidence to support the split between what promotes lexical borrowing as different from what promotes new grammatical outcomes (Thomason and Kaufman's structural borrowing) is readily available. First, the study by Treffers-Daller (1999) referred to above provides quantitative evidence. She shows the asymmetry between the direction of lexical borrowing, pointing out, for example that in the Brussels Dutch corpus, a total of 3,988 single French words appear (corpus word total N = 160,000), but only 118 single Dutch words appear in French texts (corpus word total N = 40,000) (p. 9). However, in the face of all these French lexical loans into Brussels Dutch, Treffers-Daller found very little morphological influence. She writes, 'There are only a few examples in which the inflection morphology of local Dutch varieties seems to have been influenced by French' (p. 14). As one of the few examples, she cites the possibility that some plural forms are influenced by French; plural, of course, is an early SM, conceptually activated, not structurally assigned. She also notes that in texts in which Dutch is the dominant language (presumably the Matrix Language), 'adjective inflection is Dutch, on native vocabulary as well as on borrowed vocabulary' (p. 16). Finally, she says the word order of the main clause and the subordinate clause in Dutch-based texts 'has hardly been influenced by French syntax' (p. 16). Her reports on Alsatian-based texts in Strasbourg are similar. Second, as is evident from a casual perusal of texts from many languages (and as Thomason and Kaufman recognize in its borrowing scale), lexical borrowing can appear on its own, with no new grammatical outcomes (structural borrowing). The opposite is not true; when there is grammatical borrowing, there may well be lexical borrowing. Still, having one without the other (i.e. lexical borrowed forms on their own) implies the same mechanism is not paramount for both types of outcomes.

It is important to note that I do not need to alter my definition of convergence in making this argument. Convergence involves only outside influence at the abstract level; no surface-level morphemes change. However, once the abstract level is changed, the morphosyntactic frame is affected, and surface-level changes can follow. Abstract changes at the level of abstract predicate-argument structure and morphological realization patterns make the language in question receptive to incursions of actual structurally assigned morphemes (i.e. late system morphemes, either bridges or outsiders). The presence of such morphemes is the sign of the beginning of a Matrix Language turnover. This is discussed at length in the next section. I discuss mixed languages as the result of a Matrix Language turnover, generally a turnover that fossilizes without going to completion. Here, I argue that when we see system morphemes in a language, they are not the result of the same mechanisms that result in lexical borrowed forms, just with more cultural contact added. Rather, these system morphemes are the result of a Matrix Language turnover that was arrested. In my view, the results of arrested turnovers form a continuum from only a handful of alien system morphemes in a language to an entire morphosyntactic frame (as in the case in Ma'a discussed in section 6.6). Where there are only a few alien system morphemes, they are the remnants of a turnover that was arrested very early. In other cases, the turnover is much greater and we have what is called a mixed language.

6.2.6. *The borrowing scale of Thomason and Kaufman*

We return now to Thomason and Kaufman's borrowing scale and examine the examples cited in terms of the 4-M model. Thomason and Kaufman cite rather general examples to illustrate the types of effects at each level. Bear in mind that not all items in a lexical category must be the same type of morpheme under the 4-M model. Further, morphemes can and do differ cross-linguistically in their morpheme type under the model. With these points considered, it still appears as if until Thomason and Kaufman's levels 4 and 5, most of their structural borrowings are either content morphemes (e.g. pronouns, discourse markers, etc.) or early system morphemes. For example, derivational affixes are early system morphemes (they are conceptually activated and add specific meaning to their head elements). Even word-order change is an early system morpheme *if* there is a content morpheme as the head of the syntactic structure (e.g. Complementizers heading subordinate clauses). Borrowed adpositions generally are either content morphemes or early system morphemes; a few may be late system morphemes. When one arrives at Thomason and Kaufman's levels 4 and 5, the examples they cite definitely do include some late system morphemes, although content and early system morphemes still seem to prevail. For example, under their level 4, they discuss the Kupwar situation (described in this volume in Chapter 5). However, most of the structural incursions in Kupwar's languages are syntactic rules (a noun-modifier agreement rule), not actual morphemes. These syntactic rules represent changes in the four languages involved, but changes at the level of abstract structure (morphological realization patterns). Under level 5, Thomason and Kaufman discuss cases that do show actual importation of late system morphemes. This is so in some dialects of Asia Minor Greek (according to Dawkins's 1916 study). In their case study of this variety (1988: 215 ff.), Thomason and Kaufman note, for example, that some dialects involved use Turkish inflectional suffixes—borrowed personal suffixes—with Greek verbs. Clearly, these are late system morphemes. In my terminology, then, certainly the types of external influences at Thomason and Kaufman's level 5 (and perhaps level 4) do result in more than just lexical borrowed forms and a few early system morphemes. As I have already indicated, my explanation for such changes is that they are the result of a Matrix Language turnover that did not go to completion. I suggest that the argument and evidence presented in the next section about turnovers and mixed languages can bring system to an explanation for how alien system morphemes, and especially late system morphemes, can enter a language.

6.3. Mixed languages > split languages

In this section, the division between the lexicon and the grammatical system of language continues to be very relevant. Mixed languages are the subject. Because of the negative connotations of 'mixed', especially in a volume that emphasizes systematicity, I propose a new name for such languages and will refer to them as split languages. Dimmendaal (1998: 105), following the lead of Hill and Hill (1986) regarding languages showing much borrowing, suggests the term 'syncretic languages'. I prefer 'split languages' as more transparent and hope others will use it too. Another possible choice is 'merged languages'.[1]

6.3.1. *Split languages, past and present*

Split languages are based on input from two other varieties (possibly more, but generally two). In and of themselves, multiple inputs are not unusual in the history of any language. But these split languages do not just show some influence from other languages; rather, they typically show a split in their basic organization. This split is of interest here because it is prototypically right along the line between the lexicon and the grammatical system. The prime example of this split is Ma'a, an East African language with its morphosyntactic frame and its basic system morphemes from Bantu sources, but its lexicon largely from other sources, with notable Cushitic input. Even this split is not entirely neat; note that not all the vocabulary comes from sources other than the source of the morphosyntax. Other split languages do not show such a major division between their morphosyntax and lexicon; instead, they may show fissures within their grammatical system, with some types of morphology and phrase structures coming from one of the contributing languages and other structures from the other contributor. These divisions often seem to depend on typological differences—incongruencies between the contributing languages regarding salient semantically based features and how they are encoded in morphosyntactic structures. For example, Michif, derived largely from Cree and French, includes many French NPs, but largely only Cree-based VPs.

At least in language-contact circles, there is a good deal of interest in split languages today. Almost ironically, the very existence of such languages has only been accepted in the modern history of linguistics. Even so, just thirty years ago, the title of one of the first (or the first?) comprehensive studies of a split language implies the then received view of such varieties. The article is titled 'The strange case of Mbugu'. Written by Goodman (1971), this article introduced Ma'a (also called Mbugu) to a general audience. It was published in a volume largely dealing with pidgins and creoles (Hymes 1971). A decade earlier Whiteley (1960) had mentioned Ma'a in a short article titled 'hybrid languages' in an Africanist journal, and

[1] Matras (2000*b*) also uses *split* (but more as a verb) extensively to characterize the development in what he calls mixed languages.

there are references in the Africanist archives to Ma'a under various names going back to an 1885 word list. However, following Goodman's article, there was little general interest in split languages until 1994. In the meantime, both the study of pidgins and creoles and of codeswitching was generating a good deal of interest in language contact in some circles, as was Thomason and Kaufman's 1988 volume on contact-induced change. Inevitably, this enthusiasm spilled over to split languages. In 1994, Bakker and Mous edited a volume titled *Mixed Languages, 15 Case Studies of Language Intertwining.* A volume titled *Contact Languages*, including some split languages, came out in 1997 under Thomason's editorship. Since then, several workshops on mixed languages have been held in Europe, with an edited volume in preparation based on the most recent workshop held at Manchester in 2000. Most of an issue of the journal, *Bilingualism, Language and Cognition* is devoted to a keynote article (Matras 2000*a*) on mixed languages followed by peer commentaries. Today, split languages also are topics of papers at many conferences organized around bilingual themes.

6.3.2. *The Matrix Language Turnover Hypothesis*

I argue that such split languages arise when there is a Matrix Language turnover underway. Recall earlier discussions of the Matrix Language in this volume. The Matrix Language is a theoretical construct, encapsulating the notion that all CPs in any language are structured at the abstract level by a morphosyntactic frame. This frame is called the Matrix Language. In bilingual speech that involves classic codeswitching, the frame is synonymous with the morphosyntactic frame of one of the source languages. (That language may also be called the Matrix Language, as a convenience.) However, in bilingual speech that involves convergence (or that involving composite codeswitching, which includes both codeswitching and convergence) the source of the Matrix Language is not a single source language. Rather, abstract structure from more than one participating language makes up the frame. The resulting abstract frame is called a composite Matrix Language.

Arguably, there would not be a composite Matrix Language without convergence, with codeswitching a likely factor, too. Codeswitching is a phenomenon in its own right, but it is also the main structural mechanism promoting convergence. In turn, convergence is also a phenomenon that at the same time is the main mechanism promoting modifications of the abstract lexical structure of a language. Thus, convergence is represented by the splitting and recombining of abstract lexical structure across two (or more) varieties, as discussed in earlier chapters.

Now, split languages also have a composite Matrix Language, but one that generally goes a step further than one including only abstract structure from more than one source. At least in the languages meeting the strong definition for split languages, not all the surface-level late system morphemes come from the same language as the morphosyntactic frame, as they often do under convergence or composite codeswitching. Instead, some of the (surface-level) late system morphemes come from the 'other language' involved in the compound. (If codeswitching is involved, this 'other language' is the 'old' Embedded Language.) The late system morphemes are of special interest because they are structurally assigned, called by the grammar rather than accessed to convey speaker intentions. Of the late system morphemes, the outsider system morphemes are most important as the cement holding the clause together because they are co-indexed with elements outside their immediate maximal projection. When some of these system morphemes come from the Embedded Language, it is implicational evidence that the morphosyntactic frame structuring the language has changed. Based on the splitting and recombining of abstract grammatical structure that marks convergence, the frame changes and becomes amenable to taking in system morphemes from that second language. Thus, a chain of events, beginning with convergence, results in new grammatical outcomes on both abstract and surface levels. (This is a recap of my remarks in section 6.1 where I outline how the language production process underlying lexical borrowing differs from that of grammatical borrowing.)

Early system morphemes may have the same source as either late system morphemes or content morphemes, or both, depending on the specific split language. In some split languages, such as Michif, the only system morphemes from a source outside the original frame are early system morphemes; I discuss this in the next section. More study is needed to decide if there is a patterning to the distribution of early system morphemes in general across split languages.

When the frame initially begins to change, only a very few late system morphemes may come from the other language, and the influx may never go any further than that. There are many cases in the world of languages with some alien system morphemes; at least a few of these may be late system morphemes (if we had details on how they function, we could decide if they qualify as late ones). For example, Brendemoen (1999: 370) lists some possible candidates for late system morphemes that are due to Greek influence in Black Sea Turkish dialects. However, in a classic split language, all (or all in a major paradigm or conjugation) of its late system morphemes come from a second source in the relevant structure (e.g. in Mednyj Aleut all the verbal inflections come from Russian). When this happens, several outcomes are possible: (i) fossilization at some point, and therefore an arrested shift, (ii) a gradual shift to a new morphosyntactic frame—a complete turnover of all the late system morphemes with or without a turnover in at least some of the lexicon, (iii) a simple shift to the invading language in a wholesale fashion, i.e. an abandonment of split language in mid-stream and a turnover to one of the participating languages or another language entirely. I have always argued that Ma'a is an example of scenario (ii). We have some evidence of scenario (iii) apparently happening in northeast Africa (Dimmendaal 1998). I suspect that this is the way a turnover happens in more cases of language shift than we realize, and it may be rather abrupt. Unfortunately, because the progressive grammars of earlier stages of languages that were left behind in a shift situation are not typically available, we have no direct evidence that one route to shift is through a Matrix Language turnover. Thus, I readily admit the Matrix Language Turnover Hypothesis has not been tested (cf. Myers-Scotton 1998*a*). But the hypothesis is testable, if longitudinal data of the relevant sort were collected. Scenario (iii), an abrupt shift, would be preceded by some evidence of a composite Matrix Language. Such a shift would imply that at some point the cognitive weight of maintaining a composite Matrix Language becomes too great, or it is not worth the social capital it brings in.

Thus, I argue that split languages represent turnovers that do not go to completion, but stop 'along the way'. Where they stop partly determines the form they show today. For this reason, the varieties that are called mixed languages are, indeed, a mixed bag. In different split languages, splits are found in different places within the grammar. For example, in some of the more celebrated cases, significant parts of the morphosyntactic frame and its system morphemes—but not all—come from a language other than the main lexifier. I discuss Mednyj Aleut as such a split language.

6.3.3. *What counts as a split language*

I suggest two definitions of a split language, a strong definition and a less stringent one to accommodate uncertain cases. The strong definition is this:

> A split language shows all—or almost all—of its morphosyntactic frame from a different source language from large portions of its lexicon; this frame includes all—or almost all—of its late system morphemes from the language of the morphosyntactic frame.

A less stringent definition is this:

> A split language shows a major constituent with its system morphemes and major parts of the morphosyntactic frame from a different source language from that of most of the lexicon and the morphosyntactic frame of other constituents.

Obviously, the distinction between the definitions that matters is the extent to which the entire morphosyntax, and specifically its late system morphemes, come from a language different from the main source of the lexicon. Even though the definitions are hedged, the overall basis of differentiating a split language from other languages is principled in the sense that it refers to splits in systems of features, not just features. That is, system morphemes are a system and late system morphemes are a subsystem. These are included in the morphosyntactic frame itself (realizing predicate-argument structure and morphological realization patterns), which is also a system. These definitions contrast with the lists of lexical and grammatical elements that other researchers generally have offered to define mixed languages. The motivation for including elements in the lists seems to be recurrence in mixed languages. In contrast, specifying late system morphemes as part of the 'strong' definition has a principled basis (i.e. the 4-M model and the Differential Access Hypothesis stating that late system morphemes are accessed differently in language production from those morphemes that are conceptually activated). Specifying system morphemes as a general category in the less stringent definition also has a principled basis. This is the distinction between content and system morphemes (in terms of thematic role assignment properties) in the MLF model and also in the 4-M model.

While I do not claim that these definitions draw the firm line around the set of legitimate split languages, still, the definitions can rule out certain languages. Certainly, under the definitions, any variety that shows only extensive lexical borrowing is not a split language. (Some of the non-starter languages may have a few early system morphemes pulled along with their content morpheme heads, but unless this phenomenon is systematic, as it is in Michif in the NP constituent, the variety is not a split language, even under the less stringent definition.)

For example, neither Nahuatl (Mexicano) nor Maltese is a split language. True, Nahuatl has many lexical borrowings from Spanish, but it has, at best, only a few Spanish system morphemes. In fact, Hill and Hill (1986: 194) write, 'In spite of the breadth of borrowing from Spanish into Mexicano, few Spanish affixes have been incorporated into Mexicano speech except in borrowed fixed phrases . . . we have found only three borrowed Spanish affixes'. Not surprisingly, under the 4-M model, all three of these affixes are early system morphemes. They are two derivational affixes (diminutive and agentive) and one inflectional one, the plural suffix. Many Spanish discourse markers are borrowed, but they are content morphemes at the discourse level, as I argue in section 6.1.

Or, to take another example, Maltese is not a mixed language even though it is one of the fifteen languages discussed under that rubric in Bakker and Mous (1994). The examples cited by Drewes, the author of the chapter on Maltese in that volume, make it clear that many Italian- and English-content morphemes may have been borrowed into Maltese, but not system morphemes. Maltese is a Semitic variety, a Western Arabic dialect akin to North African Arabic dialects. It is spoken on the Maltese islands of Malta and Gozo south of Sicily. Perhaps 50 per cent of its vocabulary or more comes from Romance sources (largely Italian). Drewes himself states, 'the morphology of Maltese is predominantly Semitic. Verbs of English or Italian origin are conjugated with the Arabic prefixes and suffixes' (p. 87).

6.3.4. *Matrix Language turnovers at work elsewhere*

Evidence that the Matrix Language Turnover Hypothesis is not an explanation created on the spot to rationalize the existence of split languages comes from case studies showing attrition that illustrate actual turnovers near completion. (These studies are mentioned in Chapter 5 as illustrations of abrupt, rather than gradual, attrition.) In the first case, two Turkish girls turn from German as the Matrix Language of their composite Matrix Language to Turkish (Kuhberg 1992). The girls (seven and nine years old) had previously acquired German (in all probability, a non-standard dialect) as an L2 while living in Germany. Kuhberg studied them longitudinally after their families moved back to Turkey. Except for their test conversations with the researcher, both girls received exposure only to Turkish in Turkey. Over the time of the study, they not only spoke less and less German, but the source of their late system morphemes changed from German to Turkish. Example (2) shows one of the girls marking tense in both German (*hab*) 'have' and in Turkish (*-im* in *geht-im* 'go-past') with German word order. Example (3) shows that German verbs are becoming less available and Turkish verbs are taking over. Note as well in (3) that German *löwen* receives Turkish case assignment. In this final stage, the *macht* form of the German verb *machen* 'make' is frequently used as an auxiliary. Here it is used with a Turkish verb (*bin*).

(2) ich *hab* in die Schule *geht*-**im**
I have in DET/F/S school go-1S/PST
'I went to school.'

(3) Löwen-**le** Katz duru-yor belk-iyor-lar
lion-COMIT cat stand-PRES.PROG wait-PRES.PROG-3PL
'The cat is standing with the lion, they are waiting'
Und da *macht* die Löwen und Katz bin-iyor-lar
and there make DET/F/S lion and cat get on-PRES.PROG-3PL
'And there the lion and the cat are getting on'

(Kuhberg 1992: 146)

The second case, a child's loss of a first language, shows a similar Matrix Language turnover pattern when the child studied moved from a Hebrew-speaking environment in Israel to an English-speaking milieu in the United States (Kaufman and Aronoff 1991). On entry to the United States at age two and six months, the child is a fluent speaker of Hebrew, similar to her peers. She attends an English-speaking nursery school, but Hebrew is the exclusive language used at home. Kaufman and Aronoff (1991: 180) next report she 'exhibits native-like fluency in both languages' at age three and one or two months. She now shows intersentential codeswitching and some intrasentential codeswitching, the latter consisting of L2 words inserted into an L1 frame. However, the child becomes unwilling to speak the L1, so this period of relatively balanced use of both languages is short. The Hebrew verb forms she produces are defective, modeled on a canonical triliteral root (third person singular masculine PAST). Example (4) illustrates her use of one of these deviant L1 verbs with both Hebrew and English inflections, but clearly in an English morphosyntactic frame at age three years and six months:

(4) I'm *me-nagev-ing* myself. I want to *i-nagev* myself.
I'm PRES-dry-ing myself. I want to IMPERF-dry myself.
'I'm drying myself. I want to dry myself.'

(Kaufman and Aronoff 1991: 182)

Example (5) at four years and four months shows that her Matrix Language has turned over to English, with only a single holistic form for all of her Hebrew verbs which then receive English inflections. Here, English provides the suffix for third person, present tense.

(5) When it **i-calcel**-*z* I will turn it off
VERB FORMATIVE-ring-3S/PRES
'When it rings, I will turn it off.'

(Kaufman and Aronoff 1991: 187)

Kaufman and Aronoff stress the child's creativity. However, the argument of this volume is that the steps the child goes through illustrate not so much creativity, as universally present strategies. While the child may be creative in her formation of Hebrew verbs, she is otherwise acting out the Matrix Language turnover in very predictable ways.

The corpora showing attrition exemplified in Chapter 5 offer other examples of a composite Matrix Language less developed, but nevertheless developing and therefore movement toward Matrix Language turnovers. Recall, for example, that Bolonyai's suggestion about missing accusative affixes in Hungarian is that English is directing how accusative is overtly realized (Bolonyai 1999, 2002). Also, Schmitt (2001) suggests that the bare English nouns (with no case marking) in her Russian/English corpus reflect English morphological realization patterns, not Russian ones. Also recall the view of Gross (2000*a*) that his German subjects are beginning to use German determiners to signal only definiteness (as in English) with German requirements to specify number, gender, and case becoming less salient.

6.3.5. *What promotes the move from convergence to split languages?*

What makes the difference between a composite Matrix Language that is a composite by virtue of abstract structure from more than one source and a split language? This is not a question I can answer completely. Clearly, two related abstract constructs are involved in making the distinction. The constructs are (i) the notion of a composite Matrix Language that includes *both* abstract lexical structure and a split of the source for *grammatically crucial surface-level system morphemes* and the main source for content morphemes, and (ii) the notion that this state of affairs begins a Matrix Language turnover, but a turnover that is arrested at some point.

Just as clearly, such a split only arises under dramatic sociopolitical conditions. The way that languages are grammatically structured determines the shape of split languages, but certain sociolinguistic factors promote their formation. These conditions have to involve such severe changes that the language of a new order can do more than just introduce new lexical elements into the language(s) of the less powerful; it can figuratively storm the gates of that language.

The problem with this scenario is that it offers no objective definition of what would count as a power shakeup that is extensive enough to accomplish this feat and what would not. I can only suggest a short list of conditions that should constitute a sufficiently disruptive power shakeup: (i) invasion and subsequent subjugation of an indigenous group and its colonization by a foreign power; (ii) migration and a new life that requires regular use of a dominant L2; (iii) long term employment in an alien culture, using the L1 of that culture; and (iv) indigenous, but minority, status under totalitarian rule. But I am quick to admit that these same conditions can promote the more common outcome in contact situations, a shift to the dominant language.

One more socio-psychological condition is necessary for a split language to develop, one that almost all researchers who write about split languages stress. The speakers of the beseiged language must perceive their language as an essential part of their ethnic identity and they must insist on maintaining that identity, if only as a remnant. Thus, in case after case of split languages, the argument is that speakers of such languages see themselves as unique in a sea of 'others' (and generally unfriendly others) and want a linguistic means to signal their insistence on an identity of their own. For example, Bakker (1992: 2) makes this comment about Michif: 'The impetus for its emergence was the fact that the bilingual Métis were no longer accepted as Indians or French and they formulated their own ethnic identity, which was mixed and where a mixed "language of our own" was considered part of their ethnicity.'

Some researchers persist in arguing that split language speakers even have gone so far as to construct (invent?) at least parts of the lexicon. For example, Mous seems to continue to prefer this explanation for the source of the lexicon of Ma'a, and Golovko (2000) hints at overt efforts on the part of Mednyj Aleut speakers to make their language 'different'. I return to this point at the conclusion of this section. I do not accept the notion that speakers can reinvent a lost lexicon (i.e. the Cushitic element in Ma'a) any more than they can consciously decide which parts of their grammatical constituents need replacing. Any serious reshaping of a language conforms to innately based principles that are universally evident in the structuring of other contact phenomena, and these principles are not part of a speaker's conscious knowledge. For example, how could diverse speakers decide consciously to exercise the constraints of the MLF model, constraints that are followed all over the world when speakers engage in codeswitching? How could they recognize the divisions of morphemes into four types that the 4-M model shows make a difference in distribution patterns in various types of data sets? However, I do agree that speakers can consciously decide they want to change the way they speak, but this is not the same thing as deciding *how* to change it.

6.3.6. *Representative split languages*

In the next three sections, I detail views about the structural facts of the genesis of three of the main languages that are recognized as mixed languages (as split languages), Ma'a (also called Mbugu), Michif, and Mednyj Aleut (also called

Copper Island Aleut). I discuss how the main researchers studying these varieties have characterized them, and then I give my own views, based on the Matrix Language Turnover Hypothesis. I also give some details about other split languages.

6.4. Michif

Michif is a split language spoken by fewer than a thousand people in North Dakota and Montana in the United States and in the areas of Canada immediately to the north. In general, one can think of Michif as showing a largely Cree grammar and a lexicon in which between 83 and 94 per cent of the nouns are French (Bakker 1992). Cree is an Amerindian language in the Agonquian family. Michif is spoken by Métis, largely descendants of fur traders and their Cree-speaking wives.

The major sources for information about Michif are Rhodes (1977), Bakker (1992, 1994, 1997), and Bakker and Papen (1997). In addition, Bakker and Muysken (1995) offer a short description and Dimmendaal (1998) and Myers-Scotton (1998*a*) suggest brief interpretations of Michif's structural basis. Obviously, Peter Bakker has had the most to say about Michif. In his 1992 dissertation, he speaks of the problems that Michif presents. Of course, he is right in stating that Michif is a problem for the family tree model of genetic relations; of course, all the split languages are. However, he also states it is a problem both for theories of language contact and for theoretical models of language. Because 'it is a language with two completely different components with separate sound systems, morphological endings and syntactic rules' (p. 1), he sees it as a problem for both psycholinguistic models of language production and models of grammatical structure. I argue here that Michif is not such an insurmountable problem. However, one must remember that Bakker put down these views before any systematic study of split languages was really begun, and other early researchers also held similar views. In 1992, Michif *did* appear to be very exotic.

Example (6) shows Bakker's morph-by-morph transcription of part of a Cree text (from which he has taken out the false starts):

(6)						
	un	**vieux**	opahikê-t	ê-nôhcihcikê-t		
	an/M	old	trap-he/CONJ	COMP-trap-he/CONJ		
	êkwa	**un**	**matin**	ê-waniskâ-t	ahkosi-w	
	and	an/M	morning	COMP-wake up-he	be sick-he	
	but	kêyapit	ana	wî-nitawi-wâpaht-am	**ses**	**pièges**
	but	still	this	one want-go-see/it-he/it	his/P	trap

(Bakker 1992: 3; from story by Modeste Gosselin in Saskatchewan)

Bakker also gives this version that Gosselin told in English. Note that it includes material not found in the Michif version:

That old trapper, way up north, he was old, the old bugger. He was trapping up there in a cabin. He took sick, you see. And when he got up in the morning he was sick, but still he had a little bit to eat and then he had to go and see, visit his traps.

Bakker states that the story (seventeen lines in its entirety) is a representative example of Michif in the 1980s. He points out several structural facts about it: (i) Cree and French words are used in fairly equivalent numbers; (ii) all of the verbs are Cree; (iii) all of the nouns are French; (iv) the only words that are not French or Cree are two English words (*but, through*). In addition, (i) French articles, both definite and indefinite are used and they agree with their nouns in gender; (ii) French possessive adjectives are also used, agreeing in gender and number (e.g. *son bras* 'his arm'); French prepositions are also used; (iii) there also are a few French adjectives that also agree in gender and number (*un gros arbre* 'a big tree'), but French adjectives apparently only appear in totally French NPs; (iv) however, the demonstratives are Cree and there are different demonstratives for animate and inanimate nouns.

Other texts show that both French and Cree can be the source of some other lexical elements. Adverbs as well as quantifiers come from both French and Cree. Prepositions also can come from both languages. Numerals are always French. English words are used, too, because English is the language most used by Michif speakers. Discourse markers can come from Cree, French, or English. Of course, the most interesting parts of Michif are its VPs and why they seemingly must come from Cree.

6.4.1. *Why Cree dominates in the Michif VP*

Bakker and others make clear that the VP is basically that of Plains Cree. As with other split languages, extensive language contact seems to be the necessary ingredient in Michif formation. Bakker and Papen specifically state that multilingualism and codeswitching have been considerable in the Métis nation. They note that although today most Michif speakers do not know either French or Cree (they know English), 'wherever Michif exists, Cree and French are spoken too, or were spoken until recently' (1997: 353). Not surprisingly, I argue that codeswitching and convergence between Cree and French are the basis for the development of Michif. Again, not surprisingly, I argue that Cree was the Matrix Language, with French as the EL.

Bakker introduces his notion of 'language intertwining' as a characterization of mixed languages; its main purpose seems to be to recognize that two languages are involved in any split language (1992: 204). Basically, this notion says that a mixed language consists of the lexicon of one language and the grammatical system of another. As a parsimonious description, 'language intertwining' is useful, but it is has no explanatory value.

6.4.2. *Head-marking in Michif and the VP*

Given this scenario, Dimmendaal (1998: 103) argues that 'the observed structure is not a matter of accidental "mixing", but a departure from a Cree-type (matrix) language through massive relexification and regrammaticalization, following the head-marking structure of Cree as a syntactic parameter'. His argument has several parts. First, he endorses the principles from the MLF model for codeswitching: (i) morpheme order comes from one of the participating languages labeled the Matrix Language in mixed constituents; and (ii) certain types of system morphemes (now called late outsider system morphemes under the 4-M model) must come from that same Matrix Language. Second, he adds the implications arising from the fact that Michif, like Cree, is a head-marking language.

Drawing on Nichols's (e.g. 1992) typology of languages as either head-marking or dependent-marking, Dimmendaal points out that in a typical head-marking language, the verb provides the important information about the argument structure of a clause. In contrast, in a dependent-marking language, the syntactic roles of arguments are often expressed by inflections in the NP (i.e. the thematic arguments of predicates). Not only does the verb potentially constitute a complete utterance, but its constituents express all the basic relations that must be overtly signaled in the language. He writes, 'Cree sets the frame of matrix language plus embedded language constituents not only by governing the morpheme order, or by supplying system morphemes active in signaling relations, but also in the direction of government' (p. 103).

Because Cree gives Michif its head-marking status, its Matrix Language in mixed constituents, and its typology, it is easy to see why verbs in Michif must necessarily follow a Cree-like pattern—even though, as content morphemes, French verbs are potential insertions in a codeswitching mixed constituent. First, as heads in a head-marking language, Cree verbs encode many grammatical relationships. These include references to many semantic distinctions not made in French or other European languages. If these distinctions depend on grammatical elements that are co-indexed with elements outside the verb, then the grammatical elements are outsider late system morphemes and must come from the Matrix Language. (This prediction of the MLF model as the source of such elements in codeswitching holds elsewhere and there is no reason to expect it not to hold in Michif.)

To take only a few examples, (i) there is a system of gender marking based on animacy/inanimacy that must be expressed in the verb; the stem of the verb often changes and there are also different suffixes depending on this feature. (ii) Also, there is a person hierarchy that means that whenever two or more person affixes are present in one verbal complex, a certain hierarchy of the order in which the persons are expressed is observed, and it includes the obviative. There are also a number of derivational suffixes which indicate changes in valency (number of arguments of the verb). (iii) As Bakker (1994: 21) observes and as Dimmendaal (1998: 103) repeats in his own words, 'the polysynthetic structure of Cree and frequently blurred morpheme boundaries in the Cree verb, make it less easy to combine a Cree verb system with French lexical roots'. With all of this structure favoring Cree verbs and their affixes, it is not hard to imagine why so few French verbs appear in Michif. Examples (7*a*) and (7*b*) illustrate the animacy distinction that is apparent in the verb suffixes. Note the French NPs in both sentences. French *laržã* is animate because its Cree counterpart *šu:nija:w* is animate. In contrast, *la pɛj* is inanimate, following related Cree nominalized verbals.

(7) *a* ki:-mičɪmɪn-**e:w** a:tɪht **laržã**
PST-hold-TRANS AFFIX 3>3′ some money
b ki:-mičɪmɪn-**am** a:tɪht **la pɛj**
PST-hold-TI.3>4 some the payment
'He kept part of the money/payment.'

(Bakker and Papen 1997: 316)

6.4.3. *Other than French Verbs in the Michif VP*

What does happen to the few French verbs in Michif is in line with what one would expect from a verbal system that is hard to crack. Bakker and Papen (1997: 317–18) illustrate the few French and English verbs that take the full set of Cree verbal inflectional affixes. The alien verbs are treated as grammaticalized nouns. This is evident from the fact that a non-finite form, the French infinitive, is used. English bare verbs even receive the French infinitive suffix *-er*. Further evidence is the fact that the French masculine definite article (*le*) stands as a prefix. (As in most codeswitching, the French or English verb retains its original phonological structure.) Example (8) illustrates an English verb *rab* 'rob'integrated into a Michif verb frame (with what appears to be a French infinitival suffix).

(8) nu ki:-kɪške:ht-am **la** **bãk**
NEG PAST-know/TI-TI.3>4 DET/F/S bank
e:-ki: -**lɨ**- -**rab**-**i**-hk
COMP-PST-DET/M/S- -rob-INF-IMPERS
'He didn't know about the bank being robbed.'

(Bakker and Papen 1997: 318)

Given this nominalization of French and English verbs before they can serve as Michif verb stems, it is no surprise to find out that there is also a productive process to combine French nouns or adjectives (in addition to verbs) with Cree verbal affixes. Most are derived by means of the Cree suffix *-ɪwɪ* 'to be'.

6.4.4. *Codeswitching as the promoter of French Noun Phrases in Michif*

Finally, if we accept the idea that codeswitching was a mechanism resulting in Michif, we can understand why the French elements in Michif are only either content morphemes or French NPs. Under codeswitching in which Cree is the Matrix Language, these NPs can come in as EL islands, consisting of nouns and their modifiers. As long as they are well-formed in the EL, such islands are entirely acceptable under the MLF model of codeswitching. The nouns are preceded by articles that are early system morphemes (not the late system morphemes that come from Cree in Michif and fill slots for such morphemes, as the MLF model predicts they will). Outside of considering these French NPs as having arisen in this way, there is no other structurally based explanation either for (i) how they appear in Michif or (ii) the precise form they take. Simply arguing that they appear spontaneously or through bilingualism does not provide a mechanism to explain them.

6.4.5. *Michif as a split language?*

If there were only French NPs in Michif and no Cree nouns, then one could argue that Michif simply is a case of fossilized codeswitching, and no more. However, because there are also a few Cree nouns in Michif and because they 'behave as if they were French nouns' (Bakker and Papen 1997: 324), the codeswitching argument alone becomes difficult to support. One reason is that these Cree nouns are pluralized by French articles instead of Cree suffixes. For this reason, I prefer to argue that Michif, indeed, does represent a split language, one showing the effects of convergence as well as codeswitching.

Its structures can be explained if one considers that Michif may have originated as a form of codeswitching with Cree as the Matrix Language. Michif is not a language that meets the strong definition of a split language because it does not have surface-level late system morphemes from a language other than the main language of its lexicon or the morphosyntactic frame of its VPs. However, it does meet the less stringent definition for a split language because it has constituents (NPs) from an outside source (French), with early system morphemes and portions of the morphosyntax of those NPs frames from that outside source. The fact that those early system morphemes appear *outside* of the French islands (Determiner + N) is evidence that the basic morphosyntactic Michif frame itself is no longer just based on Cree. That is, convergence has figured in an abstract restructuring that has had the surface-level effect of allowing French early system morphemes (basically French determiners) to appear.

6.5. Mednyj Aleut

A surface look at Michif and Mednyj Aleut tells us that they are almost mirror images of each other. In most ways, the main processes that led to Mednyj Aleut are identical to those resulting in Michif, although there is a crucial difference. The difference is that there definitely was a Matrix Language turnover in Mednyj Aleut, but there is no need to postulate anything beyond the superficial beginnings of a turnover for Michif. (I use 'superficial' because even any beginnings in Michif involved only early system morphemes in NPs.)

What do I mean when I say they are mirror images? First, there is no question but that the surface results look like opposites of each other: in Michif it is the 'outside' language (French) that supplies most of the NPs and in Mednyj Aleut it is the 'inside' language (Aleut) that does this, while the other two languages (Cree in Michif and Russian in Mednyj Aleut) are responsible for many or all verbal inflections. Second, in both cases, codeswitching is the original mechanism involved, but then convergence also enters the picture. One can easily identify implicational evidence of a Matrix Language and an Embedded Language in both.

Only in Mednyj Aleut do we need to postulate extensive convergence as a second mechanism at work, resulting in an arrested Matrix Language turnover from Russian as the Matrix Language to Aleut. I develop this argument below along the lines of the detailed argument of Golovko (2000) and the much briefer analysis of Dimmendaal (1998).

6.5.1. *The historical background of Mednyj Aleut (CIA)*

Mednyj (Mednij in some studies) Aleut is the language of the Copper Island (Russian *mednyj* 'copper'). Hereafter it is referred to as CIA, as is a general practice in the literature. Copper Island is one of the Commander Islands, a small group of islands ninety kilometres off the eastern coast of Kamchatka and about one hundred and fifty kilometres from Attu, the westernmost of the Aleutian islands (Vakhtin 1998).

CIA may now have no active speakers; in his 1994 article, Golovko reports no more than ten to twelve active CIA speakers. The few studies of CIA have all been based on two possibly slightly different data sets. Field work by Menovščikov in the 1960s is the basis for Menovščikov (1969) and various publications by Thomason. The main Thomason references are Thomason and Kaufman (1988) and Thomason (1997*c*). Publications and papers by Golovko and Vakhtin are based on their field work some twenty years later in 1982 and 1985. Golovko also conducted field work alone in 1988. Their publications include a number of joint publications in Russian as well as several solo works in English (e.g. Golovko 1994, 1996, 2000, Vakhtin 1998).

As is the case with most split languages, little is known about the origin of CIA. One view is that it emerged at the end of the nineteenth century around the time of the decay of a joint Russian–American company. Copper Island was populated in the nineteenth century through a series of resettlements, including Russian seal hunters and fur traders, with the largest group consisting of Aleuts. So-called creoles also were included. They were children of Russian men and Aleut women.

6.5.2. *How CIA arose*

All researchers seem to agree that codeswitching was a feature of the community in which CIA emerged. All also agree that the social motivations are the key to why CIA arose as a unique language in the community. (However, as we will see, Thomason also seems to think that socio-psycholinguistic motivations (i.e. linguistic creativity and ease of learning) also determine the structure that CIA has taken.) All researchers also seem to agree that the creole population was instrumental in forming CIA, although Thomason also brings in the Russians who intermarried with Aleuts. Vakhtin (1998) points out that in Golovko and Vakhtin

(1990) he and his colleague argued that the creoles are the candidate for a group who would need a means of communication with both the Aleut-speaking population and the Russians.

6.5.3. *Pertinent structural facts about CIA*

The morphological facts of CIA that need to be explained are clear enough. There is a basic split with the finite verb morphology and its accompanying pronouns on one side; they are all Russian. On the other side is almost all the rest of the grammar and the lexicon; they come from Aleut. Even so, there are many Russian words in the language and some Russian phonemes, but only in morphemes of Russian origin.

Thomason (1997*c*: 457) gives some additional details that are relevant to the basic divisions. There are some Aleut features in the finite verb complex, such as the special topic–number agreement pattern, the preposed Aleut pronouns with unaccusatives, and the Aleut agglutinative tense + number + person/number pattern in one of the two alternative past-tense formations. However, it is important to realize that the suffixes in this agglutinative pattern are Russian; only the patterns are Aleut. (I comment that the crucial morphemes signaling grammatical relations in the verb, therefore, all seem to be Russian. Pronouns are content morphemes. In the scenario of a turnover that I sketched above as well as the definitions given in section 6.3.2, I made it clear that 'old' Matrix Language grammatical patterns are filled with some 'new' late system morphemes from the invading language—just what seemed to have happened with CIA verbs.) The result is an arrested turnover (beginning with the verb) from a variety of Aleut to a variety of Russian. This turnover according to Golovko is sketched in detail in section 6.5.6.

6.5.4. *Codeswitching and CIA: modern parallels*

Vakhtin (1998) implies that cross-generational differences in language-use patterns, notably codeswitching in the younger generations, figure in the origin of CIA, not a pidgin. He uses a contemporary example to illustrate what he surmises took place years earlier when CIA was formed. He recorded the example of a five-year-old girl who was trying to talk to her mother 'in the mother's tongue' in a Yupik Eskimo village in 1985. What the daughter said is illustrated in example (9):

(9) **Mam** **ya** **èto** quuv-**a-yu?** **Ya** **èto** niv-**a-yu?**
Mother, I this pour out-SV-1S I this pour into-SV-1S
'Mom, shall I pour this out? Shall I pour this [into something]?'

(Yupik/Russian; Vakhtin 1998: 324)

Vakhtin comments, 'Out of seven morphemes, five are Russian [those in bold]. But the two verb stems are Yupik.' He reports that the mother reacted to the question as if it were the usual way for the daughter to speak. Vakhtin comments that if one compares the verb forms in this example with a CIA verb, 'we shall see that they look very much alike' (p. 324).

6.5.5. *A social shift and a Matrix Language turnover*

Vakhtin goes on to say that what would be needed to explain the social history that produced CIA would be a favorable shift in the social status of the Aleut language at some time in history so that 'the children may have found themselves in a situation where they felt the need for a different language as the means of ensuring their identity. Russian, their native language, could no longer serve this purpose' (p. 324).

He hypothesizes that these children (who formed CIA) did not speak Aleut, but their grandparents did. 'The children could have constructed a jargon using Russian as the grammatical and lexical basis and filling in Aleut stems they knew.' He goes on to argue that the grandparents would have supported attempts to speak this new variety. Further, if there were restored contact with Atkan (Aleut proper), then (under Vakhtin's scenario) 'The extensive influence of Atkan Aleut brought in derivational morphology and was responsible for the considerable expansion of the Aleut lexicon. After several generations, CIA emerged' (p. 325).

In his unpublished paper, Golovko (2000) seconds the general drift of Vakhtin's scenario, but is more definite in the grammatical details. It is worth noting that he does not bring in the Atkan Aleut nor mention the possibility that Russian was the primary language of children. Instead, it is important to recognize that the main feature of his scenario is a Matrix Language turnover. He also sees not only bilingualism, but also codeswitching as necessary conditions for any split language to arise. He writes, 'Of course code-switching is not the reason for the emergence of a mixed-language, but a mixed-language cannot start without it' (p. 2). He goes on to endorse the notion of a Matrix Language turnover which he says 'is the dynamic component which many previous constructs were lacking'.

In fact, Golovko implies there were two turnovers. The first one is a turnover from Aleut to Russian that was arrested, but a turnover *while codeswitching was still the main medium of communication.* He posits Aleut/Russian codeswitching as common, but with Aleut first as the Matrix Language and then a turnover to Russian as the Matrix Language in this codeswitching. 'This turnover was promoted due to external circumstances of [a] sociopolitical character' (p. 2). He argues that the islanders were proficient enough in Russian for this to happen. Their Russian may well have been a very non-standard Russian, as is the case in other settlements today in areas of Siberia colonized by the Russians that he discusses as similar situations as far as acquiring Russian is concerned. He also cites archival records in St Petersburg that indicate 'it is obvious that all Aleuts on the Russian territory could speak and write Russian'. Finally, he asserts there is archival evidence that 'at the turn of the century the first language was, no doubt, Aleut' (p. 4).

6.5.6. *The turnover fossilizes and the Russian VP*

What happened next was that the start of the turnover to Russian (as the Matrix Language within codeswitching) stopped. The language fossilized where it was. Golovko (2000) writes, 'The reason for the fossilization of the code-mixing product in the middle of the way to complete shift is search for group identity'(p. 4). He points out that when Menovščikov visited the island in 1963, he could not find any traces of 'pure' Aleut, even though the speakers claimed their Aleut was just like that of their grandparents. 'The assumption could be made that [pure] Aleut passed away so quickly because it involved a negative evaluation of the identity associated with it' (p. 4).

Still, the version of Aleut that the Creoles spoke did not go away. Instead, the Creoles stopped the progression of Russian in their Aleut. In effect, this represents *a second turnover*—in the sense that the turnover to Russian was arrested and there was a turn now to accept what became CIA, meaning accepting the extensive Aleut component. Why did the shift to Russian not go to completion? Why did it stop with the VP? The answer Golovko gives is the search for a symbol of unique identity. There seems to be general agreement among researchers that 'The creole population of the colonies was set apart both from the Russian employees of the company and from the Aleuts during the 19th century' (Thomason 1997c: 453). Golovko (2000) states that the term 'creole' was readily accepted by the population and they used it for self-nomination. He writes, 'In terms of language, unmarked code-switching was the only thing which could separate them from both Russians and Aleuts. . . . As the conditions for fossilization were perfect, fossilization took place' (p. 5). Example [10] illustrates a sentence from CIA. Note that the Russian counterpart is not entirely parallel (the CIA version has an inflection for third person singular, but the Russian version has an inflection for third person plural).

(10) **oni** taanga-x̂ su-la-**jut**
they spirit-s take-MULT-PRES/3/S
Russian: **oni** spirit-noe pokupa-**jut**
they spirit-PL buy-3PL/PRES
'They are buying spirits.'

(Golovko 1996: 67)

6.5.6.1. An Aleut frame with Russian input

It is no surprise that Golovko (1996: 66) notes that elements of the argument structure of the VP are 'surprisingly Aleut-like'. That is, basic parts of the morphosyntactic frame still have Aleut as their source. So do the early system morphemes to express valency changes (e.g. causation). This does not change the fact that the late system morphemes in that frame that mark person and tense are 'completely Russianized'. The absence of person marking in the Russian past is compensated for by the use of Russian pronouns. Russian third person accusative pronouns are also used in the present instead of the original set of endings in Aleut. In (11) the case-marked pronoun, *ego* 'he/accusative', comes from Russian. Note also the Russian complementizer *čto* 'that' as well as the verbal suffix *-it*. Only the verb stem, *ilaxta* 'love' (a content morpheme, of course), comes from Aleut.

(11) ... čto ona ego ilax̂ta-it
COMP she-NOM he-ACCUS love-3S/PRES
Russian: ... čto ona ego ljub-it
COMP she-NOM he-ACCUS love-3S/PRES
'... that she loves him'

(Golovko 1996: 71)

6.5.6.2. Another grammatically based view

Arguing from a more typological basis, Dimmendaal (1998: 104) basically agrees with Golovko's structural assessment. However, my interpretation of his argument assumes that he begins with the first turnover in progress (to Russian). He suggests that initial borrowing from CIA into Russian (at the point while Russian was in the process of becoming the Matrix Language) best explains the facts, not Russian borrowing into CIA or Aleut. He bases his interpretation on the fact that what the 4-M model calls late system morphemes are from Russian (the finite suffixes of the verb), adding that other ways of constructing verb forms involving tense, number, and person marking are from Russian. He argues, 'In other words, the verbal predicate, as the main constituent determining the syntactic frame, is provided by Russian'. These would have been the structurally assigned morphemes that invaded the Aleut frame, signaling the beginning of the turnover to Russian under Golovko's scenario (and mine). He goes on to point out other Russian features in CIA. CIA word order is relatively free, like Russian order, but unlike Aleut order. Finally, he states that Russian Complementizers and conjunctions figure in complex sentence constructions.

In contrasting the Russian features with Aleut ones, Dimmendaal notes that the nominal morphology of CIA not only comes from Aleut, and (agreeing with Golovko's comment above) that elements of the overall morphosyntactic frame itself are from Aleut. He mentions gender and case specifically. In CIA there is no gender and only two case distinctions; in contrast, Russian has both gender and six case distinctions.

6.5.6.3. A more functional approach

Thomason (1997*c*) takes a more functional approach to explaining CIA. She begins by addressing the question of mechanisms and the relative role of codeswitching. She says, 'There are more mechanisms of interference than have generally been recognized—specifically ... not all contact-induced language change comes about through code-switching' (p. 464). The other mechanisms she mentions are: 'code alternation (the use by the same speaker of two different languages, but in different settings), passive knowledge of another dialect or language, 'negotiation', second-language acquisition strategies, and changes brought about by speakers' deliberate decisions. It seems likely that both code-switching and deliberate decisions by speakers—individual creativity—were operative' (p. 464).

A moment's reflection indicates that these strategies and states of affairs that Thomason lists as other mechanisms (outside of codeswitching) are not mechanisms in the same sense as codeswitching and convergence are. In and of itself, this is not a problem. But the problem is that, because they themselves have unconstrained natures, they neither constrain nor specifically promote or predict anything; therefore, it is difficult to say when they are salient or not or whether any effects can be definitely attributed to them and not to other factors. In contrast, codeswitching (under the MLF model at least) is a set of constraints that in effect, predict what morphosyntactic configurations can occur when codeswitching exists. Likewise, convergence, as a mechanism, specifically promotes observable effects (changes in the three levels of abstract lexical structure that in turn can mean a restructuring of a language's morphosyntactic frame). Convergence also predicts that splitting and recombining with abstract levels from another language occurs in bilingual speech, and it predicts the order in which the levels will show the effects.

Thomason goes on to consider the direction of formation in CIA, first suggesting that Aleut elements may have been brought into Russian, not the other way around. At the same time, she indicates that if Russian were 'first', this would explain why Russian is the source of verb inflection. The explanation would be 'the relative ease with which lexical items are code-switched (and borrowed) by comparison to inflectional affixes'. She adds, 'If code-switching went in the other direction, taking only the finite verb inflection from Russian, then we need to explain that surprising choice'. Thomason does go on to say that if what seems to be her favored scenario holds (bringing Aleut stems into a Russian base), 'We need to explain why the result of the language's structure . . . is Aleut and not Russian' (p. 464).

Thomason also tries to answer the question of why CIA includes the finite verb morphology from Russian, but not other constituents. Her answer seems to be based on the strategy of taking the lesser of two evils and the notion of ease of learning. She argues that the Russian and Aleut systems of noun inflection fit together 'fairly well', but notes the two verb systems differ greatly. Because of this, she suggests that Russians who knew Aleut would find the noun 'more manageable than the verb; and that in turn makes it more likely that the speakers . . . might have used the Russian endings as one means of lessening the learning burden for Russian semi-Bilinguals who wanted to use it (notably the Russians who intermarried with Aleuts, and then, later, the Russians who intermarried with creoles)' (p. 465).

Of course, Thomason's view about which language was the original base language is quite different from that of Golovko (and to some extent Dimendaal); they see Russian inflections already present when Aleut becomes ascendant (but for the second time). Also, their scenario depends on having the creoles, not the Russians, as most instrumental in shaping CIA. These are the views that I endorse because they fit with how a Matrix Language turnover would be accomplished, as I indicate below.

6.5.7. *Explaining CIA structure*

In summary, CIA represents the prototypical example of the scenario proposed by the Matrix Language Turnover Hypothesis that ends in an arrested shift. Although the motives to develop such a language no doubt have a psychological basis—a desire for an ethnic symbol—the grammatical organization of CIA can be explained entirely in terms of structural mechanisms:

1. Relatively unmarked codeswitching had to be available as the major medium of communication in the community, based on fluency in Aleutian, as the Matrix Language, with some (increasing?) fluency in Russian.
2. Within this codeswitching, Aleut had to start out as the Matrix Language in order to explain how Aleut eventually remains the source of frame elements outside of verb inflection.
3. Convergence at the levels of abstract lexical structure had to have occurred so that the 'old' Matrix Language of this codeswitching (Aleut) would have been sufficiently altered so that 'new' late system morphemes from the 'old' Embedded Language (Russian) could take over slots in the frame.
4. In order to explain the Russian inflections that end up in CIA, Russian had to begin to take over as the Matrix Language in codeswitching.
5. Still, in order for codeswitching to fossilize with Aleut largely in place (as it was in the final analysis), the original turnover to Russian had to be arrested, and a second turnover to Aleut (or, at the least a revitalized Aleut) had to take place.
6. Of course the arrest of the shift where it stopped is not motivated by structure, but social considerations. Still, structural mechanisms and constraints establish the possible outcomes on which social motivations can operate.

6.6. Ma'a (Mbugu)

Ma'a may well be the best-known split language (mixed language), the one that has been discussed the most in recent years, but it is also one on which there is little agreement about the details of its origin. As I indicated earlier, Ma'a (Mbugu) was introduced to modern linguistic circles in 1971 by Goodman. Then, Thomason published a paper (1983) on Ma'a in an Africanist journal and when Thomason and Kauffman wrote their major work on language contact (1988), Ma'a was among the languages that rated its own case study. Since then, Thomason included a chapter about Ma'a in the volume she edited on contact languages (1997*a*). In the meantime, a specialist on East African Bantu languages, Maarten

Mous, did field work in the Usambara mountains of northeastern Tanzania where Ma'a is spoken. He has since written several articles on the language (Mous 1994, 2001, forthcoming). I discuss Ma'a in Myers-Scotton (1992, 1993*a* [1997]) and again in terms of a Matrix Language turnover in Myers-Scotton (1998*a*). I consider other approaches here, but I largely conclude that my earlier arguments fit the theoretical frameworks that can accommodate the facts, those that I espouse in this volume.

Ma'a has always been referred to as a language with a Bantu grammar and a lexicon coming largely from Cushitic. Mous's recent field work shows that, in fact, two overlapping varieties exist in the community. He refers to them as registers, and Thomason (1997*b*: 476) seems to agree that they are registers, at least from a sociolinguistic standpoint, although she sees what she calls Ma'a (Inner Ma'a / Inner Mbugu, I assume) as 'linguistically a separate language'. I would be inclined to say the two varieties together are one language, but are different register/styles of that language used for different purposes. When I refer to Ma'a alone, I mean inner Ma'a.

6.6.1. *The grammar of Ma'a*

There is little disagreement about the structure of Ma'a. It is a language with a morphosyntactic system that almost entirely corresponds to the system of neighboring Bantu languages (e.g. especially Pare, but also Shamba(l)a). Mous calls one variety of Ma'a Inner Mbugu (Inner Ma'a), after local usage. The other variety is called Normal Mbugu (Normal Ma'a). Both 'registers' have the same grammatical system; what differs is the lexicon. 'When people choose to speak Ma'a they maximise the use of Ma'a lexemes and these make up to over ninety percent of an average stretch of speech' (Mous, forthcoming: 3). Like other languages, Ma'a is acquired in childhood and is not threatened by extinction, as are some other split languages. Mous (forthcoming) makes the point that Ma'a is stable. He writes, 'In 1934, Copland published a text in Ma'a which could in every respect pass for present-day Ma'a' (p. 4). Mous notes that there are Ma'a people who do not speak the Inner Ma'a register; they apparently arrived late in the area, but they are still considered ethnically as Ma'a.

Example (12) comes from Mous's field notes of Inner Ma'a / Inner Mbugu:

(12) va-mbughu va-ngi va-tek-i-a he
CL2-Mbugu CL2-many CL2-loose-APPL-FV LOC16
ichi kishamba
CL7.DEM CL7-shambaa
'Many Mbugu get lost in Shambaa [a place].'

(Mous 1993, Mboko and Mzee Ishika, 10/10/93 I, line 20)

Example (13) compares the same sentence in Inner Ma'a (13*a*) and Normal Ma'a (13*b*):

(13) *a* áa-pú-ndaté kú'u
3S-PST-break stick/his
'He broke his stick'

b áa-baha ndatá y-akwé
3S-PST break CL9-his
'He broke his stick'

(Mous 1993 field notes)

Almost everything about Ma'a grammar fits the Bantu pattern. Not only do all the late system morphemes of verbal morphology fit the Bantu mold, even most of the derivational suffixes do, and these are early system morphemes, after all. (Only two, whose origin is unclear, do not resemble Bantu forms, the unproductive causatives *-ti* and *-ri*.) Ma'a has a Bantu noun-class system in all respects; that is, there is agreement on adjectives, and subject and object marking in the verb. Its noun-class system is identical with that of Pare except for one class.

Like the general Eastern Bantu pattern, the Inner Ma'a demonstratives distinguish three degrees of deixis. In contrast, in the southern Cushitic languages of Iraqw and Burunge (both spoken in Tanzania, too), there is a four-way distinction. The origin of the surface forms in Ma'a is difficult to establish. The possessives again show a Bantu system although it is not easy to establish the source language for the actual forms; note these are early system morphemes. Many of the forms include a /k/ that may be related to the masculine-gender marker in many Cushitic languages. However, Mous says, 'It is most probable that Inner Mbugu took words rather than suffixes from the Cushitic source; and the fact that these words already contain gender markers might explain why the Inner Mbugu possessives have no noun class agreement' (1994: 192).

6.6.2. *The origins of Ma'a*

Any disagreements about Ma'a have to do with how its lexicon originated. To a lesser extent, there is also not a consensus regarding whether the shift to a Bantu morphosyntax was abrupt or gradual. Mous (1994: 197) makes these generalizations about the lexicon:

> Single entries have a Bantu origin, often Shambaa or Swahili. If a word is from Pare, it belongs to the Normal Mbugu register. If a word can be shown to be Cushitic (Southern or Eastern Cushitic) or Masai, it is Inner Mbugu, excluding Cushitic loanwords in Pare. It should be noted that for many Inner Mbugu forms, the origin is not clear. Words containing *hl*, *x*, or ' are restricted to Inner Mubugu.

There are various views about the mechanics of the shift to Bantu in Ma'a. Goodman (1971: 252) implies a gradual shift to a Bantu system ('The Bantu and the non-Bantu language may have gradually become ever more alike until they were little more than stylistic variants, depending on who was speaking to whom'). In 1983 and again in later publications, Thomason argues that Ma'a was originally a Cushitic language and that its original grammar was replaced 'by Bantu grammar and lexicon over several centuries as bilingual Ma'a speakers incorporated more and more Bantu features into their speech' (1997*b*: 478). She cites 'intense cultural pressure from their Bantu neighbors', 'but resistance to assimilation led them to maintain at least vestiges of their language' (p. 478). While some others challenge this view, I think the notion of gradual Bantuization is a reasonable hypothesis, a view I have always supported in my writings. However, on its own, this scenario 'needs legs'; it needs more specifics and in particular a structural mechanism.

6.6.3. *Ma'a as a Matrix Language turnover*

I argue that a Matrix Language turnover, both stimulated and accompanied by codeswitching and convergence, is the mechanism. I discuss Ma'a as the prime example of a turnover of the Matrix Language frame, the language best conforming to the strong definition of a split language. At the same time my notion of a Matrix Language turnover has never meant an abrupt turnover; that is why it is discussed as a series of stages in Myers-Scotton (1998*a*) and here as well.

Here are my hypotheses for the stages expressed in terms of the theoretical frameworks framing this chapter:

1. Cushitic-speaking peoples (the Ma'a), having moved into Tanzania from the north (where Cushitic languages are more common in northern Kenya, Somalia, and Ethiopia), find themselves surrounded by speakers of Bantu languages.
2. Practical purposes lead them to become bilingual in at least one of these closely related Bantu languages.
3. Yet, the Ma'a do not want to give up their own language. But it is hard to avoid communication with neighbors, and this promotes a period of codeswitching as a compromise strategy, with codeswitching perhaps even becoming their unmarked mode of communication for in-group talk.
4. Extensive codeswitching encourages convergence to the Bantu languages at the levels of abstract lexical structure. Convergence eventually means non-target-like forms, but codeswitching itself is a mechanism promoting convergence. (In Bolonyai (1999), discussed in Chapter 5, the author reports that her six Hungarian subjects (aged seven to nine) produced more non-target forms in Hungarian when they engaged in Hungarian/English codeswitching than when they spoke monolingual Hungarian. Almost 19 per cent (577/3,087) of the all-Hungarian CPs had non-target-like forms, but 31 per cent (175/558) of the CPs showing Hungarian/English codeswitching included non-target-like forms (p. 149).)
5. The Ma'a develop their 'normal' style or register as their dominant variety, just because they have many more opportunities to use it (at a minimum, they use it in all out-group activities).
6. They preserve Inner Ma'a for in-group talk; however, with convergence, first the abstract grammatical frame of Inner Ma'a is modified and then—with these modifications affecting the morphosyntactic frame itself—surface-level Bantu system morphemes begin to come in.

7. Gradual Bantuization follows, crucially among the late system morphemes, but finally in the entire grammatical system. The lexicon moves toward Bantu, too, but largely remains intact.

There may be those who consider these stages and the very idea of a Matrix Language turnover as ad hoc explanations. My response is this: although these stages refer specifically to how Ma'a developed, they are grounded in theoretical frameworks that correctly predict outcomes in other contact phenomena. For example, the theoretical notion of the modularity of conceptually activated morphemes and the structurally assigned morphemes that relate elements in larger constituents is not unique to split languages. (The split between how content morphemes and system morphemes are distributed, and then again a split within system morphemes, have been demonstrated in earlier chapters in other contact phenomena.) Thus, it behooves anyone who discounts the turnover hypothesis and other hypotheses based on such theoretical constructs to offer not only competing hypotheses to explain Ma'a, *but also* a theoretical framework with interrelated constructs to replace the frameworks underlying the turnover hypothesis. These competing hypotheses and theoretical constructs should also be able to offer reasonable explanations of not just Ma'a, but also of the other phenomena explained by the frameworks I favor.

6.6.4. *Other views about origins*

In his 1994 article, Mous endorses the notion that codeswitching could be involved in the rise of the new Ma'a, but he expresses three problems with my scenarios.

1. The first stage(s) cannot be shown. I see this as no problem; Mous is asking for more than *anyone* can produce. All the evidence for any hypothesis about any stages up to recorded history has to be inferred; direct evidence is not available.

2. If I am right about Ma'a, Mous cannot understand why other cases of codeswitching did not lead to a mixed language. I stress that, in and of itself, codeswitching is not the road to a Matrix Language turnover, a point I have tried to make many times. Yes, I can outline the structural characteristics of such a turnover and the grammatical mechanisms involved. However, this does not mean that I can predict when classic codeswitching (with a single source for the Matrix Language) will lead first to composite codeswitching (with more than one source for the Matrix Language) and second to a Matrix Language turnover. As I argue above, social conditions are what set the mechanisms in motion, and only the most radical situations promote more than the beginnings of a turnover. In fact, there are few turnovers that go only so far and not to completion (as one explanation for language shift); if there were, we would have more split languages.

3. Mous states that people who engage in codeswitching have a positive attitude towards the languages they use. I imagine he would also argue that a turnover requires a positive attitude. I disagree; emotional reactions to group relations are more complex than that. First, an initial positive attitude always could have existed and later changed. Second, although we know nothing of the economic power of the neighboring Bantus in relation to the Ma'a, because of their sheer numbers,

the Bantu peoples were relatively more powerful. And, as Roberts (1939) observes, power has its charms. I quote him on this point in Chapter 2. He invites the reader to consider that prestige is derived from the Latin *praestigae* 'tricks' by way of the French word for 'illusion'. Consider the use of English in today's world; do all L2 users of English have nothing but positive attitudes about the language and its native speakers?

6.6.5. *Re-inventing a lexicon*

Earlier, I indicated that many researchers studying various split languages make a point of arguing that the lexicon in such languages depends on deliberate partial relexification. This is a theme in many of the case studies in Bakker and Mous (1994), and it is repeated today. For example, Mous (forthcoming) favors such a scenario for Ma'a, involving picking and choosing from non-Bantu sources in the broader East African area. Mous writes, 'Lexical manipulation is the "conscious" creation of lexical forms that are parallel in semantic and morphosyntactic properties to an existing lexical item in the language and is in essence what Matras (2000*a*: 93) calls "lexical re-orientation"' (p. 1). It becomes clear that what Mous has in mind is the creation of lexical forms in Inner Ma'a that are parallel to those in Normal Ma'a (Mbugu) as a means to distinguish Inner Ma'a.

In Myers-Scotton (1998*a*) I argue against conscious grammatical creation except in ritual languages and linguistic games of limited use. My position has not changed. Obviously, I am sympathetic with the notion that the abstract structures underlying lexical elements can be split and assembled in bilingual speech, resulting in new combinations. This is the basic argument of the Abstract Level model. The types of changes that model predicts happen regularly in monolingual speech (e.g. *stonewall* becomes a verb meaning 'engage in delaying tactics'); they also happen in language-contact phenomena. All creolists know that such strategies of convergence are essential in creole formation, as I argue in the next section, and they are illustrated in Chapter 5 where attrition is discussed. However, attributing to humans the ability to initiate a lexicon based on a 'search and replace' command is something else. Applied outside of the special areas of rituals and games, the idea of such manipulation has many flaws, not the least of which is that it requires conscious efforts and a group consensus. Again, however, I do not deny that a community can consciously or unconsciously 'decide' to make changes in the variety it speaks; communities (often official agencies) do decide to rid their languages of alien words, for example, and sometimes they are successful. But a community cannot decide to invent new words (without existing models) or invent the form grammatical structures will take. Rather, universal structuring principles constrain them.

6.7. Summary: mixed/split languages

Obviously, a discussion of only three split languages does not provide much of a sense of the extent or characteristics of all split languages. Instead, my main purpose here is to describe and analyze three example languages that offer dramatic evidence that a split can be made—even at different places—between the lexicon and the morphosyntactic frame. It is precisely because these two systems are complementary (but within a unified whole) that such splits are possible. However, this is only the beginning of explanation. Without a theoretical model with constructs that also apply elsewhere, split languages would remain only as 'strange cases' (Goodman 1971 on Ma'a) that have 'peculiar structural features' (Bakker and Papen 1997: 306 on Michif).

All three split languages discussed can be viewed as the result of a Matrix Language turnover that fossilizes at different points in the three languages. In none of the three does the turnover go to absolute completion, although in Ma'a the turnover is almost complete for the morphosyntactic frame and its surface-level morphemes, and the frame is the normal referent of the term Matrix Language. Although known split languages are not many, the only thing that clearly unites all the 'received' ones is that they show some split between the source of some system morphemes and their frame, and much of the lexicon. The split does not always go in the same direction. For example, in Romani dialects, the 'outsider' language is the source of much of the morphosyntax (as it is in Ma'a). But in Media Lengua, the 'insider' language (Quechua) supplies the morphosyntax and the outsider language (Spanish) is the source of the lexicon (Muysken 1997). In another case, Gangou dialect of Chinese (spoken in northeastern China where there are neighboring Mongolian languages), there may only be one actual surface-level system morpheme that comes from Mongolian, even though many of the details of the morphosyntactic frame clearly come from Mongolian (Zhu *et al.* 1997). Is this a mixed language? I would like to argue it is, but it does not fit if the requirement is that there must be a split between the source of a substantial number of surface-level late system morphemes and much of the lexicon. Clearly, more discussion is needed. Still, I cannot agree with those researchers who see the category of split language as less than a coherent type. (Part of the problem is that—as I have indicated above—cases of simple heavy lexical borrowing have been included under the mixed-language rubric.)

Whatever developments happen, what is most important in split languages is not that they are composed largely of material from two different source languages or that, because of this, they do not fit normal family-tree models. The point is that they do 'fit' with other linguistic phenomena from speech errors in monolingual speech to Interlanguage in second-language acquisition that show similar differential distributions between content morphemes and system morphemes.

6.8. Creole formation

Traditionally, creoles have been considered as the language varieties that developed during the seventeenth through the early twentieth centuries through contacts between speakers of colonial varieties of a European language on the one side and speakers of a number of non-European languages on the other side. However, today other varieties that developed largely from contacts between groups who all spoke non-European languages in such places as Africa (e.g. Sango in the Central African Republic) are also referred to as creoles.

Note that I do not differentiate pidgins and creoles. The general view probably still is that creoles develop from pidgins. For example, Muysken and Smith (1995: 3) write, 'One vital difference from pidgins is that pidgins do not have native speakers, while creoles do'. However, they go on to point out that varieties that some call extended pidgins (e.g. Tok Pisin, Nigerian Pidgin English, and Sango) are beginning to acquire native speakers. Whether they have native speakers or not, it seems difficult to draw the line between such varieties and creoles on a structural basis. Others question the basis for arguing that pidgins necessarily precede creoles. Thomason and Kaufman (1988: 149) rightly point out, 'the evidence for the traditional view that a full-fledged pidgin language, relexified or not, was the major direct source for every plantation creole . . . strikes us, as it has struck others, as thin'. Further, there is a lack of evidence of pidgins preceding creoles in most Caribbean settings and there also is increasing support for the notion of creolization as a gradual process (Mather 2001).

6.8.1. *The sociohistorical background*

As in the other contact phenomena discussed in this chapter, creoles show a division between the development and organization of the lexicon and the morphosyntactic frame and its morphemes. Still, the structural outcomes in creoles definitely set them apart from other contact phenomena. To a large extent, what makes them different must be the social and psycholinguistic milieux in which they were formed. In general, we can say this about these milieux:

1. Speakers of different languages, mostly not mutually intelligible, were brought together in a plantation setting.
2. With an obvious need for some communication with each other, they needed a lingua franca.
3. In almost every case, no L1 from among the slaves/workers had numerous enough or powerful enough advocates to make any one L1 a choice for this role.
4. Another language, whatever variety the overseers/owners spoke, was another candidate; just because it was their language and therefore had a utilitarian value in the setting, it had the measure of prestige to make it an attractive candidate.
5. At the same time, the slaves/workers did not necessarily spend much time in earshot of these overseers/owners; therefore, they had few opportunities to acquire this language.

6.8.2. *A preliminary statement: how the creole developed*

Yet, even under what must have been turbulent and bewildering social conditions, the framers of a creole had the same abstract linguistic-structuring means available to them that are evident in the structure of other contact phenomena and language in general. My argument is that they applied these principles and processes to two targets to create a language of wider communication. At the same time, feasibility limited what they could do; therefore, the language of the overseers/owners was a target for lexical elements and their own first languages were the target for a composite morphosyntactic frame.[2]

6.8.3. *The study of creoles*

Offering anything like an overview of research on creoles in this volume is beyond my intentions. My thinking is that, with all the attention creoles draw today, fulfilling such an objective need not be a high priority in this already lengthy volume. I can keep the discussion within reasonable bounds by continuing to focus on the bifurcation between the lexicon and the grammatical system and how it figures in creole development. Further, many creolists have already done a good job of describing outcomes; my goal is rather to detail mechanisms for outcomes.

A large body of literature exists to cover the other aspects of pidgins and creoles, and it continues to grow rapidly. I do offer a short listing of that literature. Like many students of split languages, many creolists do not concentrate their attentions on the linguistic structures themselves. Rather, most creolists are more interested in probing historical records to arrive at conclusions about the genetic relationships and sociohistorical factors relating to creole origin (e.g. Baker 1983, McWhorter 1992, 1995, *inter alia*), or the lack of existing languages as antecedents (Bickerton 1981, 1999). Related to this goal is interest in uncovering new information about the ethnic groups present during creole formation and changes in these populations (e.g. Arends 1995, Singler 1996). Some creolists do offer grammatical descriptions of specific creoles (e.g. Rickford 1987 on the Guyanese creole continuum, Faraclas 1996 on Nigerian Pidgin English). Others are concerned with establishing sources for specific lexical elements (e.g. Baker and Huber 2000). Some also seek sources for specific grammatical constructions (e.g. LeFebvre 1998, Lumsden 1999*a*, Siegel 1999, 2000). Others make close studies of certain typological features across creoles. Favorite topics are serial verbs (Sebba 1987, McWhorter 1992, 1995) or the tense–mood–aspect systems (e.g. a volume edited by Singler 1990, Winford 1993) or other special features (e.g. Bruyn, Muysken, and Verrips 1999 on double-object constructions). The links between creolization, language change, and language acquisition, from the point of view of I(nternalized)-language is the subject of contributors to DeGraff (1999*a*).

Sociolinguists, especially those within the Labovian variationist tradition, continue to look for correlations between various factors, typically demographic variables, and variation in structures across a given creole community. The model of LePage and Tabouret-Keller (1985) relating language and social identity in creole communities continues to be influential. The authors explain inter- and intragroup variation by arguing that 'linguistic behavior [is] . . . a series of *acts of identity*' (p. 14) by which people negotiate their social group memberships. LePage and

[2] My discussion here is a revised version of Myers-Scotton (2001*b*).

Tabouret-Keller argue that the creole communities themselves differ in the extent to which they are linguistically *focused* (i.e. the extent to which little variation in the grammar exists) and to the extent that they are *diffuse*, with greater grammatical variation. These ideas, of course, fit in with the notion that creolization was a gradual process and that to speak of a creole continuum best describes the community repertoire in at least some cases. Such a continuum is thought of as including the creole at one end of a spectrum as the basilect, followed by intermediate forms (mesolectal varieties), and then the lexifier language (the acrolect).

In addition, there has been a steady stream of overview/textbooks on pidgins/creoles since the late 1980s (e.g. Mühlhäusler 1986, Romaine 1988, Holm 1988, Arends, Muysken, and Smith 1995). DeGraff (1999*a*) was just mentioned and Holm (2000) is a new introduction to pidgins and creoles.

Much of the flurry of activity of the last twenty years has been a reaction to Bickerton's publication in 1981 of his 'bioprogram hypothesis' for creole development. In addition to much discussion and other publications, this impetus initially stimulated Muysken and Smith (1986), an edited volume emphasizing comparisons of universalist vs. substratist hypotheses. The momentum has not yet been lost and has been given a new life with new controversies. Although creolists have long agreed that creoles are different from other languages at least on the basis of their social histories, they find much to disagree about. For example, McWhorter (1998) and its claims that creoles can be distinguished from non-creole languages, based on rather general structural grounds, is a current lightning rod for some controversies.

Holm (2000: 64) notes, 'Sociolinguistics continues to shape the theoretical perspectives of those working on pidgin and creole languages'. I take this to mean that he sees little emphasis on theories to explain the constraints on creole formation that are other than socially motivated theories; this is my reading of current research. In terms of priorities, Holm himself probably represents many creolists in this statement: 'Perhaps the most basic challenge for creolists in the twenty-first century is to write exhaustive linguistic and sociohistorical descriptions of all the known pidgin and creole languages and their various dialects' (2000: 67). Rather than by means of more descriptions, I see more emphasis on developing theories of the grammatical structuring as a way to better understand creole structure.

6.8.4. *Three main views about creole structuring*

Even so, three main types of hypotheses about creole origin that have to do with structure do exist. The argument I present here differs from all three of the main positions on this subject, but somewhat paradoxically supports all of them, but not for the usual reasons given for these positions. The superstrate is defined as the variety spoken by overseers/owners; it is also called the lexifier. The substrate languages are those varieties that are known to be, or supposed to be, languages spoken by the slaves/workers.

1. The superstratist position is largely discounted today, although it is not dead. This hypothesis assumes that slaves (or indentured laborers) looked to the language of their overseers/owners as a target for a lingua franca to use in the multilingual plantation population. Under this position, the main speakers of the creoles themselves had a very passive role; the superstrate speakers were the active ones, simplifying their language in speaking to the workers. Alleyne (1980) was one of the first creolists making a comprehensive statement that disagrees with this position to emphasize instead the role of the African substrate in the formation of specific creoles.
2. The substratist position is that, as much as they could, slaves maintained their own languages; thus, present-day creoles reflect the basic structures of these languages. This position is very alive and well; its proponents continue to offer many examples of likely substrate influence in current creoles. Much of the discussion of the phonology and syntax in Holm (2000) is a case in point. However, substratists still do not offer theoretical frameworks that can explain why certain structures/features come from the substrate languages, but not others.
3. Bickerton (1981, 1986, 1999, *inter alia*) is the main figure when universalist positions are mentioned. His basic argument is that creoles only resulted when the children of first generation slaves/workers developed a language by applying the universal innate principles (Universal Grammar) that are especially available to young children. In contrast, existing pidgins were seen as chaotic and not the basis for today's creoles. There are variant UG positions today, but nothing yet with a theoretical framework so fully developed as that of Bickerton.

There are clear problems with Bickerton's hypothesis. What records there are indicate mortality rate was very high among slaves and that there were very few children. Further, it is counterintuitive to assume that children paid no attention to the language of the parents (their L1s and the pidgin that may have been in use). However, it is hard to deny that Bickerton's view (that creoles are based on universal principles) offers an answer that pure substratist hypotheses cannot provide to the question, why do creoles around the world have many key structural features that show so many resemblances? At the same time, Bickerton cannot explain similarities between creoles supposedly formed by children and such creoles as Cameroon Pidgin whose expansion does not seem to have involved restructuring by children.

Most creolists today probably subscribe to no single hypothesis for creole development. Mufwene (1986) expresses well what seem to be the views of many: both universals and substrate features were necessary ingredients. However, a framework spelling out their relationship is still missing. Here, I present my own views and a framework in a set of hypotheses. While my arguments recognize input from all the same sources as superstratist, substratist, and universalist hypotheses, my arguments are different. I argue that there is input from all three sources, but cognitively based constraints restrict the type of input the different sources can have.

6.8.5. *Questions in need of answers*

For me, the following are key questions that most creolists do not address:

1. Why do many creoles 'look like' the languages of the superstrate where they were formed?
2. Given such resemblances, why are most creoles not more mutually intelligible with these superstrates?
3. Of the elements that clearly come from the superstrate, why are some more intelligible than others to superstrate speakers? Why are there some types of superstrate elements (nouns and verbs) and not others (certain types of grammatical elements)?
4. A question directed at substratists: if substrate languages are so important, why do creoles not look more like them?

6.8.6. *Organizing principles motivating theoretical claims*

1. A specific universally present principle of language is relevant to creole development. This principle states that different morpheme types do not simply serve different functions, but they are accessed differently in language production. This principle is captured as the Differential Access Hypothesis in the 4-M model and has been discussed often enough already in this volume. A related and important notion, not part of the model itself, is this: although late system morphemes, not conceptually activated content morphemes, primarily convey grammatical relations, the lemmas underlying content morphemes are the critical part of an interface between conceptual structure and phrase structure. In this sense, phrase structure is not so autonomous as many syntacticians argue it is. I follow Jackendoff in this view. He writes, 'the formal role of lexical items is not that they are "inserted" into syntactic derivations, but rather that they license the correspondence of certain (near)-terminal symbols of syntactic structure with phonological and conceptual structures. There is no operation of insertion, only the satisfaction of constraints' (1997: 89–90).

2. The theoretical notions behind the Abstract Level model are also relevant to creole formation. The key observations in the model have been discussed in earlier chapters and in section 6.7.

3. In any linguistic production, there are always underlying, uniform specifications about what type of surface forms can be projected, how they can be structured or arranged, and the like. This is a variation on the Uniform Structure Principle discussed especially in Chapter 4. The principle simply states that all structures in any constituent in a given language will observe that language's constraints for that constituent. (Note that the principle operates not just in phrase-structure rules but also in various interfaces, such as argument structure in relation to syntactic structure; e.g. can a Locative or a Dative Experiencer element appear in subject position and control verb agreement?)

In bilingual speech, such as creole development, the Uniform Structure Principle has to deal with competing structures. It often does this by favoring the structures of one participant; this preferential treatment is the source of pervasive asymmetry in bilingual speech. However, the modularity that already exists across subsystems may solve some potential clashes. Of course, I have in mind modularity regarding the lexicon and the morphosyntactic frame.

These principles apply in all linguistic phenomena, even though surface outcomes in various phenomena differ. As DeGraff (1999*b*: 477) writes, 'creoles are no more and no less than the result of extraordinary external factors coupled with ordinary internal factors'. This point has been made over and over in this volume, but it needs to be repeated in this discussion of creole formation. The reason is that the social and psycholinguistic conditions under which pidgins/creoles arise are so distinctive that some creolists, either openly or in their heart of hearts, assert that creoles are unique.

4. There always is a morphosyntactic frame supporting the Uniform Structure Principle. This frame is called the Matrix Language. In monolingual data the source of the frame goes without saying. Also, in some forms of bilingual speech (lexical borrowing and classic codeswitching) the source of the frame is easily identified under the principles of the MLF model as only one of the participating languages. However, in other contact phenomena, the frame is a composite of abstract features from more than one source.

The creole frame is a composite of elements from two or more substrate languages (except in unusual cases, such as Berbice Dutch where the frame largely comes from one substrate source, Eastern Ijɔ.) Even though any speaker's own L1 could provide a frame, this does not happen for reasons familiar to creolists. First, there are typically competing substrate languages involved. Second, not all speakers of the emerging creole are proficient enough in the same single variety so that its frame could serve as the Matrix Language in forming a lingua franca for the multilingual group. Third, which substrates are major contributors of frame elements depends on a host of factors, including demographics, and power relations, but also how numbers waxed and waned and even which group was numerous at the outset (cf. Mufwene's (1996) Founders' Principle). Fourth, from a structural standpoint, features that are unmarked in the specific sense that they are shared by participating speakers should end up in the creole. However, the makeup of any one actual composite Matrix Language for any creole is not considered here; I limit discussion to theoretical motivations and the hypotheses derived from them that are meant to apply in all creoles.

6.8.7. *Predictions based on the organizing principles*

Five hypotheses to account for creole structuring follow. The discussion also illustrates the predictive power and robustness of each hypothesis.

6.8.7.1. Hypothesis 1

Hypothesis 1. The substrate varieties contribute to creole formation by supplying the 'invisible' morphosyntactic frame of the creole.

Language users typically think of speech production as 'words'. This preoccupation with 'language as words' is even reflected in the names that linguists gave to creoles in the past, such as 'English-based' or 'French-based' creole. These names refer to the lexicon of a creole, but they leave out the fact that all languages are multilevel edifices, with only the words 'visible'. What is out of sight is the scaffolding that gives the visible surface its form.

Persons forming a creole could recognize early on that what was required in their multilingual circumstance was a means of communication other than each one's L1. It was simply impractical to expect others to speak one's L1. This, along with their role in plantation life, was the major reason for workers to turn to words in the language of overseers/owners to convey their intentions. Because content morphemes carry meanings, and substrate speakers could intuit that certain superstrate content morphemes match the semantics of their L1 lexical items and constructions sufficiently to communicate their intended meanings, they incorporated these morphemes into the developing creole.

But the grammatical frame of the superstrate variety was not so easily worked out for two reasons. First, abstract elements are not available for introspection to the same extent that the semantics of content morphemes are. The directions that go to the Formulator in language production indicate how to incorporate content morphemes in larger constituents. Such directions are abstract; they are not available for speakers to verbalize—even directions in their own L1. Second, with limited access to the superstrate, the best substrate speakers could do was work out some of those morphemes that seemed to carry meanings. For this reason, substrate speakers had to fall back on their L1s for the morphosyntactic frame in creole formation; the frame from the superstrate was simply not available.

Still, because such frames are abstract specifications for well-formedness (i.e. slots to be filled and not specific morphemes), this has two advantageous effects. First, frames can be retained longer than substrate-content morphemes. Cases of attrition discussed in Chapter 5 show that while the abstract lexical structure of L1 content morphemes may change under the influence of an L2, the L1 frame can remain largely intact. Second, features of a frame are not tied to specific morphemes; frames can accept morphemes from another language (the superstrate), provided their specifications are sufficiently congruent (codeswitching demonstrates this).

6.8.7.1.1. A LIKELY SUBSTRATE-BASED FRAME AND SCOPE WITHIN THE NP

For example, consider a feature of Caribbean creoles that is familiar to most creolists: the scope of the determiner in NPs in these creoles is similar to that of likely West African substrates. Of course, such a feature is an abstract specification of the morphosyntactic frame. Example (14) illustrates how such scope operates in Yoruba, one of the West African languages that Holm (1988) identifies as 'relevant' in Caribbean creoles. Note the determiner *náà* has scope over the entire NP. This contrasts with the scope of determiners in English or French, two of the main lexifier languages in the Caribbean. In (15) from Haitian Creole we see that even with a relative clause intervening (as in (14)), the scope of the determiner is the entire NP.

(14) owó [tí nwón fún mi] **náà**
lit. 'money (which they gave me) the'

(Yoruba; Rowlands 1969: 197, cited in Holm 1988: 190)

(15) M' te achte liv [m te pou li] **a**
I ANT buy book I ANT SUBJUNC read DET
'I bought **a** book [that I had to read].'

(Haitian Creole; Lefebvre 1998: 190)
French: **le** livre qui . . .

In another discussion, Lefebvre states that '[i]n both Haitian and Fongbe, for some speakers, the plural marker may occur within the same noun phrase as the determiner' (1998: 84). The plural marker follows the determiner, as in example (16). Again, then, its scope is the entire NP. The Haitian element for plural is *yo*, and Lefebvre (1998: 86) notes that Sylvain (1936) and Goodman (1964) have suggested that its source in Haitian Creole is the French third person pronoun *eux*.[3]

(16) krab **la** **yo** (Haitian)
àsɔn ɔ lɛ (Fongbe)
crab DET PL

(Haitian and Fongbe; Lefebvre 1998: 85)

In sum, scope in NP is a feature of the frame of Haitian Creole that follows along the same lines as that of likely substrate languages. Such examples support Hypothesis 1, that the creole frame comes from the substrates, not the superstrate nor likely universal principles.

6.8.7.1.2. SLOTS IN THE SUBSTRATE VERBAL FRAME

Another example indicates how the Tok Pisin frame shows the same requirement for an overt transitive marker that is evident in Austronesian languages. While Tok Pisin may well have resulted from input from a number of substrate languages (Baker 1983), Austronesian languages were certainly among the substrate varieties involved at some point, if not initially. In Tok Pisin, the verbal suffix (*-im*) is employed as a transitive marker, probably from *him* (an English personal pronoun and a content morpheme). Example (17) shows how Tigak, a typical Austronesian language (spoken on New Ireland), marks transitivity similarly, with the verbal suffix (*-i*).

[3] Elsewhere, Jake (1994) and Myers-Scotton and Jake (2000*a*) discuss French pronouns as both content morphemes (such as *eux* and the other 'strong' forms) and as late system morphemes (the clitics).

(17)

em	i	pait-**im**	mi	gi	vis-**i**	ri	tang	anu
3S	PREDM	hit-TRANS	me	3S/SUB	hit-TRANS	3PL/OBJ	ART	men
'He hit/hits me'				'He hit the men'				

(Tok Pisin; Jenkins 2000: 133) (Tigak; Jenkins 2000: 133)

6.8.7.1.3. TMA MARKERS AND SERIAL VERBS

Probably the two best-known features of creole morphosyntactic frames are the slots for tense–mode–aspect markers (especially those in the Caribbean creoles) and the provisions for serial verbs. Verbs in the Caribbean creoles differ from their superstrate counterparts; for example, they have no verbal suffixes to mark tense or aspect. Instead, they generally have a set of preverbal particles indicating at least tense (when an action occurred) and aspect. The TMA system is discussed further in section 6.8.7.3.2.

Creolists often have noted the resemblances between serial verbs in creole languages and their putative substrate languages. (Serial verbs consist of a series of minimally two verbs with the same subject, but not joined by conjunctions or complementizers. See (18*a*) and (18*b*).) Bickerton argues that serial verbs are found in creoles only because they are part of the set of universally based features. Because serial verbs are found elsewhere in non-creole languages as well as in creoles, it is hard to dispute the possibility that a universally based strategy could be at work. Still, within creoles, serial verbs are especially a feature of those creoles that have likely substrates also showing serial verbs. These include the Caribbean creoles, with Kwa languages as likely substrates, and Tok Pisin, with Austronesian substrates. Further, as Holm (2000: 211) notes, not all creoles with likely African substrates have serial verbs: 'A broader survey reveals that they are largely absent in creoles such as Cape Verdean and Guiné-Bissau CP [Creole Portuguese] and Palenquero codeswitching [Creole Spanish], which were less influenced by Kwa languages.' Holm (1998, 2000) discusses serial verbs in general extensively; another recent exposition is McWhorter (1992) on serial verbs in Saramaccan compared with likely Kwa counterparts.

Jenkins (2000) points out that not only do Austronesian languages have serial verbs similar to those in Tok Pisin, but they all use the same semantic model to express the actions of 'bring' and 'take' by combining the verb 'get' with 'come' and 'go' respectively. Examples (18*a*) and (18*b*) show counterparts from Tok Pisin and Tigak.

(18) *a*

man	i	**kis**-im	pik	i	**kam**
man	PREDM	get-TRANS	pig	PREDM	come

(Tok Pisin)

b

tang anu	gi	SUK	IMA	tang	vogo
ART man	3S/SUBJ	get	come	ART	pig

(Tigak)

'The man is bringing/brought the pig.'

(Jenkins 2000: 135)

6.8.7.1.4. DISCOURSE FOCUS

It is also clear that the focus discourse structure in various Caribbean creoles, whether with English as the lexifier (as in Jamaican Creole) or Spanish as the lexifier (as in Papiamentu) has counterparts in West African languages. Hagège (1993) cites counterpart examples from these creoles and Twi and Yoruba. Example (19) illustrates how focus operates in Jamaican. The preposed verbal copy (*tiif*) is negated to show scope over the entire proposition.

(19) **A** **no** **tiif** kofi tiif de mango
FOC NEG steal Kofi steal the mango
'Kofi did not steal the mango' (he bought it)

(Jamaican Creole; Bailey 1966: 95, cited in Hagège 1993: 137)

6.8.7.1.5. SUMMARY: EVIDENCE OF A SUBSTRATE FRAME

In sum, examples (14) through (19) support Hypothesis 1 about a composite of substrate languages as the source of the morphosyntactic frames of creoles. Note that I do not claim that these examples are more than an indication of the type of evidence that is available. However, I do not think that systematically identifying the exact counterparts of current creole structures is possible. There simply is not enough historical evidence now, and I doubt there ever will be, given the complex of factors that would have to be assembled to support the claim that the features of one substrate were more salient than those of another at the time of creole formation. Instead, what I claim *can* be supported is the theoretical notion of a composite Matrix Language as the basis for the creole frame and therefore as a partial explanation for the morphosyntactic frame found in creoles today. Of course not all frame features in present day creoles can be attributed categorically to substrate sources. Certainly, convergence with the superstrate(s) at some point in creole history, as well as universal processes that may or may not be innately based, may account for some frame features. Semantic transparency and such considerations as hierarchies of grammatical relations (i.e. what relations are most likely to be overtly expressed) are examples of such universal features.

6.8.7.2. Hypothesis 2

Hypothesis 2 and 2*a* refer to the lexical elements that can appear in developing creoles.
Hypothesis 2. Both substrate- and superstrate-content morphemes can be the target of surface forms that are also content morphemes in the creole.
Hypothesis 2*a*. Superstrate-content morphemes are much more frequent in the creole than substrate ones.

Because their role is to realize speaker intentions to communicate a specific proposition, it is no surprise that content morphemes are readily turned to when speakers are developing a creole. What *is* surprising is that few *substrate* content morphemes make it into the creole. A moment's thought indicates that most content morphemes will come from the superstrate unless substrates share many lexical elements. Also, superstrate-content morphemes, even with limited access to superstrate speakers, are still more accessible to more substrate speakers speaking diverse L1s.

6.8.7.2.1. EXAMPLES OF CONTENT MORPHEMES IN THE CREOLE

There are a few words that can be attributed to substrate varieties, such as *bukra* 'white man' in Gullah texts, as well as in other Caribbean creoles. (Gullah is spoken on the off-shore islands of South Carolina and Georgia.) A possible source for */bʌkrə/* is *mbakara* 'white man', lit. 'he who surrounds or governs'. It is found at least in the Nigerian languages of Ibibio and Efik. (Jones-Jackson (1978: 425–6) lists twenty-two forms in the Turner texts of Gullah that are still used in the Wadamalaw community in coastal South Carolina.)

(20) *Substrate content morpheme in Gullah*
de ha no **bʌkrə**
'They have no white man.'

(Turner 1949 [1969]: 260–1)

Thus, as I argue, the superstrate becomes the main target for the lexicon of the developing creole. Which content morphemes appear depends on some match between what speakers perceive as the lexical-conceptual structure of the content morpheme candidates and the abstract lexical structure that the abstract creole morphosyntactic frame requires. Requirements refer to available slots, but more importantly, match speaker intentions with the semantic relations that the frame specifies for overt encoding.

In many cases, the content morphemes from the superstrate are very recognizable in today's version of any creole. For example, it is not hard to figure out that *liv* in Haitian Creoles comes from French *livre* 'book' or that *sitor* in Tok Pisin is from English *store.* In some cases, a content morpheme may change its lexical category. For example, in Gullah *soldier* became a verb meaning 'fight'. See example (21).

(21) wɛl, ʃɪʤə wʌn **soljə** ɒn əs tʊde
'Well, such a one soldier on us today' (*soldier* = *fight*)

(Gullah; Turner, 1969: 286–7)

6.8.7.2.2. SPLITTING AND RECOMBINING OF ABSTRACT LEXICAL STRUCTURE

Recall the Abstract Level model. Under this model, all three levels of abstract lexical structure can be split in any one lemma supporting a content morpheme; one or more levels can come from other sources, typically the language that provides the grammatical frame in bilingual speech. How much from the levels of predicate-argument structure and morphological realization patterns is retained depends on the morphosyntactic frame of the creole and its substrate origins. For example, does the frame allow for adjective phrases of the order that English has? Many West African languages employ stative verbs instead of adjectives to convey similar argument structures to those of English adjectives (cf. Faraclas 1996: 62). When English adjectives occur in certain creoles they can receive the same TMA markers as verbs do. Bakker, Smith, and Veenstra (1995: 172) cite this clause from Saramacan, *dí mitíi tá-bígi* 'the child is getting big', with *tá* presumably as an aspect marker.

To take an example showing a change in morphological realization patterns, consider what happens to French NPs in Haitian Creole. Not only do Haitian Creole determiners come from a different source from French determiners (they come from French *là*, the directional adverb), but they follow nouns, not precede them as they do in French (compare French *le livre* with *liv la* 'the book').

On this view, what others have called reanalysis (e.g. Lumsden 1999*a*, Lefebvre 1998) is defined as realignments in the abstract lexical structure of the lemma that supports the surface-level content morpheme. Of course, some superstrate-content morphemes are integrated into the creole with approximately the same specifications for the three levels of abstract lexical structure that they have in the superstrate.

Other content morphemes, especially those that surface as system morphemes, are more radically changed, as is the point of Hypothesis 3. The argument of this hypothesis is that content morphemes are reconfigured, not as content morphemes, but to fill structural gaps in the creole morphosyntactic frame.

6.8.7.3. Hypothesis 3

Hypothesis 3. Content morphemes from the superstrate can be reconfigured as system morphemes to satisfy the requirements of the abstract morphosyntactic creole frame that is based on a composite Matrix Language from the substrates.

As support for this hypothesis, consider Baker's (1994) discussion of the diminutive prefix *ti-* in Mauritian Creole. This prefix seems clearly to be derived from the French adjective *petit.* What is relevant here is not simply that the French adjective is reconfigured; after all, creolists have long recognized that superstrate words are reconfigured in creoles. Rather, what is important to note is that the French adjective is pressed into service as a prefix on nouns. That is, a content morpheme (*petit*) has been reconfigured as an early system morpheme.

If one puts this structural fact together with the social fact that many of the slaves on Mauritius were speakers of Bantu languages, one can make an argument that *petit* was reconfigured as a prefix to meet the requirements of a composite Matrix Language with Bantu-language input. In Bantu languages, nouns typically show an overt prefix that indicates the class of the noun. Some of these classes are based on semantic similarities. Thus, in some Bantu languages, small objects occur in class 13 (compare Luganda *akabuzi* 'small kid/goat' (class 13) vs. *embuzi* 'goat' (class 9)). That is, as Baker (1994: 81) notes, '*ti-* behaves in essentially the same way as the diminutive class prefix which is a feature of all Bantu languages'. Richardson (1963) reaches similar conclusions. These noun-class prefixes are early system morphemes; that is, they are conceptually activated to flesh out the meaning of their nominal heads.

6.8.7.3.1. WHY CONTENT MORPHEMES ARE PRESSED INTO SERVICE

Gaps for structurally assigned morphemes (late system morphemes) may be more difficult to fill than those for content morphemes. These late system morphemes indicate relationships between content morphemes. Even though structurally assigned late system morphemes are what are required, such morphemes from the superstrate are not available because their level of activation is low until larger constituents are assembled by the Formulator. This makes them hard to acquire (as evidence from first-language acquisition and Interlanguage in second-language acquistion shows).

Given this situation, again, speakers turn to content morphemes from the superstrate because they do not depend on other morphemes or any construction to make them salient. They are especially available if their meanings have a 'family resemblance' to the relationship to be conveyed. Even so, these content morphemes generally require extensive reconfiguration on one or more of the levels of abstract lexical structure if they are to fill gaps in the frame for structurally assigned morphemes.

For example, consider what happens with *by and by*, a collocation that serves as an adverbial adjunct in English. When it is introduced into Tok Pisin, its lexical-conceptual structure can be retained (with modifications), but how it functions in regard to the level of morphological-realization patterns changes. It becomes a system morpheme signaling future tense as in example (22) below. Note that, at least in Tok Pisin spoken on New Ireland, *bai* occurs in sentence-initial position; this is where the irrealis marker (*vo*) occurs in Tigak, an Austronesian language on New Ireland. In some varieties of Tok Pisin it has moved to a position immediately before the verb (where future markers occur in English).

Examples already cited show how content morphemes are reconfigured to fill slots for system morphemes in creoles. These additional examples are included just to indicate the scope of this procedure. In example (22), *along* has been reconfigured as *long*, a case marker for Goal in this example; it also occurs elsewhere in Tok Pisin as something of an all-purpose preposition. This example also shows how *he* has been reanalyzed as *-i*, a predicate marker, and *him* has been reanalyzed as *em*. Both English pronouns are content morphemes. Both *long* and *-i* function as late system morphemes. In example (23*a*) and (23*b*) *de* (probably from English locative adverb *there*) functions as an existential copula.

(22) **bai** em i go long situa
FUT 3S PM go to store
he will go to the store.'

(Tok Pisin; Jenkins 2000: 138)

(23) *a* dì mòni **de**
ART money COP/TA
'There is money.'

(Nigerian Pidgin; Faraclas 1996: 222)

b A **de** fòr haws.
1SG COP/TA PREP house
'I am at/on/in front of/ the house.'

(Nigerian Pidgin; Faraclas 1996: 60)

6.8.7.3.2. CONTENT MORPHEMES AS TMA MARKERS

Recognizing that only content morphemes may be reanalyzed to serve as system morphemes clarifies some puzzles in creoles. One of these puzzles is that almost all creoles with English as the main lexifier employ the same English-based morphemes to mark TMA, but almost none of these morphemes encode TMA in the superstrate. Why is this? In many cases, many of the TMA features are marked in the superstrate with late system morphemes. In accord with Hypothesis 5 below, late system morphemes are not available for use in the creole. Instead, what are employed? It is no surprise the answer is 'content morphemes' from the superstrate, and content morphemes that occur before the main verb in some English verb forms (e.g. *been* in *I have been working*). One of the most common content morphemes employed is the past participle (*been* > *ben, bina*), which is actually composed of a content morpheme and a system morpheme that together signal a completed or affected event. (Non-finite verb forms are discussed in Chapter 3 as holistic units even at the level of the mental lexicon.) Another point to bear in mind is that the superstrates do not typically encode the same TMA features as the substrates.

Holm (1989: 407, 2000: 174 ff.) provides tables showing TMA verbal markers in Caribbean varieties. For those in Holm (1989) with English as the superstrate, thirteen out of twenty-three employ a phonetic variation of *been* to mark what he calls unmarked anterior. Another past participle, *done*, is a frequent marker of anterior habitual aspect (fourteen out of twenty-three). For those that mark anterior completive aspect, ten out of ten use a variant of *done*. Another non-finite verb form that is also a content morpheme, the verb stem for *go*, is a common marker for future in irrealis aspect (nineteen out of twenty have a variant of *go*). A frequent marker of anterior in progressive aspect is *de*. Its origin is in some dispute, but the most common suggestion is another content morpheme, deictic adverbial location *there*.

6.8.7.4. Hypothesis 4

Hypothesis 4. Early system morphemes from the superstrate are only available to satisfy creole requirements when they are accessed along with their heads.

Early system morphemes largely are only accessible as a consequence of their content morphemes being accessible. That is, early system morphemes are only satellites of content morphemes. But just because they are satellites of content morphemes, they may well be accessed in creole formation along with their content morphemes. This happens irregularly, although more frequently with some superstrate languages.

In creoles, there is not necessarily a doubling of early system morphemes (as there is in classic codeswitching with plural markers in cases discussed in Chapter 3). However, there are numerous examples of superstrate content morphemes that appear in the creole with an early system morpheme attached. Many creolists have noted this phenomenon, referring to such results as containing an agglutinated determiner, but they have not explained it. Examples include units in the creole that in French are phrases (i.e. units derived from French nouns preceded by their definite articles or a form of the partitive, e.g. French partitive *de la, du*). Any data set of monolingual French data makes it clear that French nouns do not occur categorically with either definite articles or partitives. This is evidence that the nouns and these early system morphemes do not share a single lemma in the mental lexicon, but rather are in separate lemmas. Yet, it is a content morpheme and its early system morpheme that are inserted as one unit in a creole frame. See examples (24*a–d*).

(24) *a* ban Siven pa mahz **lavyan**
'Siven's family don't eat meat.' (Siven = given name),
compare *lavyan* with Fr. *la* + *viande*

(Mauritian Kreol; Baker 1972: 78)

b ban Midlenz abitye ar **lapli**
'The inhabitants of Midlands are used to rain'
compare *lapli* with Fr. *la* + *pluie*

(Mauritian Kreol; Baker 1972: 78)

c **delo** 'water' (compare with Fr. *de l'eau*)

(Seychelles Creole; Corne 1977: 22)

d mo lav antye mo **lekor**
'I wash my whole body.' (compare *lekor* with Fr. *le corps*)

(Mauritian Creole; Corne 1988: 74)

Note that these cases occur with a relatively high frequency when Bantu languages are likely to be numerically dominant in the substrate. This is recognized by Baker and Corne (1986: 172), who point out that there is 'evidence for a link between a high proportion of agglutinated forms [det + noun] and a high level of Bantu immigration from the Portuguese-based Creoles of Africa'. They go on to say that 'while such forms are not found in areas without Bantu immigration (the Creole of the Cape Verde islands or of Guinea-Bissau and Casamance—areas without Bantu immigration) they abound in the Gulf of Guinea Creoles of São Tomē, Príncipe and Annobon, islands in which a larger part of the population is of Bantu descent'. Such forms are also found in the Ile de France and Reunion creoles, of course, as well as in Haitian Creole. Baker and Corne comment on the Bantu element of the slave population in the Indian Ocean creoles and Singler (1996) comments on the Bantu presence in the Haitian situation. In fact, Singler states that 'the total number of speakers of Bantu languages over the entire period of slave importation into Haiti is probably more than double the number of speakers of Gbe dialects' (p. 216).

The connection between these [det + noun] forms in creoles and a Bantu population of slaves is that Bantu languages are characterized by a set of noun classes, most marked with overt class prefixes that obviously resemble the French determiners in their prenominal position. Of course, the 4-M model adds the theoretical motivation that both the French determiners and the Bantu noun-class prefixes (on nouns) are early system morphemes.

This state of affairs supports the claim of the 4-M model that early system morphemes are conceptually linked to their heads, depending on the heads of their maximal projection for directions about their form. This characteristic distinguishes early system morphemes from late system morphemes and can explain, too, why the creole speaker perceives them as part of a unit with their heads.

Conversely, another prediction derived from the 4-M model is that late system morphemes will not be perceived in creoles as units with their heads with such regularity. The prediction is that such examples are possible, but definitely exceptional.[4]

6.8.7.5. Hypothesis 5

Even though other superstrate morphemes appear with regularity in creoles, Hypothesis 5 limits the role of superstrate late system morphemes.

Hypothesis 5. Late system morphemes from the superstrate are not available to satisfy the requirements of the creole morphosyntactic frame.

[4] There are three examples of the same late system morpheme from English (present third person singular *-s*) in Turner's (1969) Gullah texts. The same speaker produced all three as non-standard inflections (*I believe-s* and *we enjoy-s*).

I follow many creolists in making an argument in this chapter that the superstrate was the most viable source of surface forms for speakers who were developing a creole. Yet, Hypothesis 5 now predicts that late system morphemes from the superstrate were not available. Why? Late system morphemes are hardly accessible at all for two reasons. First, they offer the would-be creole builder very little to work with in regard to conveying semantics/pragmatics. However, much more important is this: the lemmas underlying late system morphemes are not salient at the level of the mental lexicon when the linking of intentions to lemmas is being made. Recall the model of language production sketched in Chapter 1. In that model, intentions activate semantic-pragmatic feature bundles that point to language-specific lemmas in the mental lexicon. Late system morphemes are not on the scene until they are activated at the level of the Formulator. Thus, metaphorically, they are not positioned at the loading dock when the semantic/pragmatic feature bundles that convey intentions are electing their vehicles in the mental lexicon. What are available are superstrate content morphemes, and because their levels of abstract structure can be reconfigured, they can appear as late system morphemes in the creole.

In earlier chapters, I cite evidence that distinguishes late system morphemes from other morphemes in a variety of types of data. The evidence from creoles supports this claim, too; that is, it supports Hypothesis 5. An excellent example is a comparison of how English existential *there* (as in *there's a fly in my soup*) functions in contrast to English locative adverbial *there* (*I live over there*). Existential *there* is a late system morpheme, and, as is predicted by Hypothesis 5, it does not appear at all in creoles. That is, it is not available for reconfiguration. However, adverbial *there* is a content morpheme and it does appear in creoles, reconfigured as a marker of progressive aspect (*de*) in many creoles with English as the superstrate (Holm 2000: 181).

Where a slot in the creole frame would call for a late system morpheme, it is either filled with a content morpheme or a null. Earlier examples support this observation. To take a new example, we can see in (25) how a content morpheme (*get*) is reconfigured to fill the slot for a existential late system morpheme in Hawaiian Creole English. This is a well-known example, cited by Siegel (2000), but originally cited by Bickerton (1981: 67). *Get* also has other uses in Hawaiian Creole English. Here it conveys the type of possession in the notion of 'have'. (See Talmy (1985) for a comparison of possession and existence.)

(25) **Get** wan wahine shi **get** wan data
'There is a woman who has a daughter.'

(Hawaiian Creole English; Bickerton 1981: 67, cited in Siegel 2000: 212).

Examples under (26) show how either content morphemes (in (26*a*) and (26*b*)) or nulls (in (26*c*)) in other creoles fill a slot that would be filled by the existential *it* or its equivalent in the superstrate. All examples come from Holm (1988: 88) and all translate in English as 'it's raining'.

(26) *a* **ren** a faal
English 'Rain is falling' ('It's raining')
(Jamaican Creole)

b **lapli** ap tonbe
'La pluie est tombé
French 'Il pleut'
(Haitian Creole)

c ∅ awa ta kai
Spanish: ∅ está lloviendo [*sic*]
(Papiamentu)

The content-morpheme preposition *après* 'before' becomes a TMA marker in many creoles with French as the lexifier. For example, Lefebvre cites an example in which *après* is the basis of the definite future marker in Haitian Creole (see example (27)).

(27) Mari ap prepare pat
Mary DEF/FUT prepare dough
'Mary will prepare dough'
(Haitian Creole; Lefebvre 1998: 241)

Again, this example supports Hypothesis 5; that is, the frame calls for a late system morpheme, but such morphemes are not available from the superstrate. What are available are content morphemes that can be reconfigured to satisfy the requirements of the frame.

6.8.7.6. Summarizing the examples

In summary, I stress that many of the examples cited here have been cited by others and, even taken together, they are not sufficient evidence on their own to support conclusively the hypotheses. They are cited as suggestive of the evidence that is available. However, what is important now is that this set of five hypotheses seems to predict the major details of the story of creole formation.

6.8.8. *Comparing these hypotheses with relexification*

At first glance, the hypotheses proposed here seem to mirror the relexification hypothesis of Lefebvre (1996, 1998, 2001, *inter alia*, and Lumsden 1999*a*, *b*). There *are* similarities, and for this reason I am naturally sympathetic to their arguments.

For example, although she does not discuss in any detail how it would be an ingredient in the formation of Haitian Creole, Lefebvre (1998) refers to dialect leveling. In many ways, dialect leveling could have a similar result to my claims about the formation of a composite Matrix Language; a composite may have both abstract and surface structural input from more than one source. However, from Lefebvre (2001), it appears this is not so. She refers to dialect leveling as 'a social process' (p. 372) and also writes, 'leveling is hypothesized to operate on the output of relexification, thus reducing the variation produced by the relexification of several lexicons' (p. 373). Thus, leveling seems more a way to consolidate than to build, and a composite Matrix Language is definitely the result of building based on multiple inputs.

Once more, the goal, the model, and the explanations of Lefebvre and Lumsden are not the same as mine. First, their goal is more specific; they propose specifically to account for the formation of Haitian Creole and argue for specific roles in this formation for Fongbe and for French. Lefebvre (1998: 16) writes, 'Relexification is thus a mental process that builds new lexical entries by copying the lexical entries of an already established lexicon and replacing their phonological representations with representations derived from another language'. (I note in Myers-Scotton (2001*b*) that their views underplay the role of the semantics of superstrate morphemes in their selection for the creole; they are not primarily selected for their phonological shapes.)

Second, it is not clear how Lefebvre and Lumsden motivate their arguments. There are many references to 'mental processes' (e.g. Lefebvre 1998: 16–18, Lumsden 1999*a*: 129, 1999*b*: 225), but they give no specifics. In contrast, the mental processes that motivate my hypotheses should be clear. The abstract architecture of language competence and production—how the lemmas underlying morphemes are differentially accessed, how their levels of abstract lexical structure may be split and recombined, and their differential distribution in other data sets—is the motivation I offer. This explains how it is that superstrate-content morphemes can participate in the developing creole, and in what ways, and how it is that late system morphemes that are present in either the substrate or the superstrate cannot. (To motivate their use of the term 'relexification', Lefebvre and Lumsden do cite Muysken's (1981) use of the term in reference to Media Lengua, a mixed or split language spoken in the Central Andes; however, there is no parallel between its use there and creole formation, as I argue in Myers-Scotton (2001*b*).)

Lefebvre and Lumdsen do generally recognize that what I call content morphemes from the superstrate are involved in producing what they call functional forms (system morphemes). For example, Lefebvre states that 'the speakers assign a phonological form to the function words for the copied lexicon on the basis of the phonetic form of superstratum *lexical* category items' (italics in the original) (1996: 296–7). Elsewhere, Lefebvre argues that certain functional elements from the superstrate are relexified in Haitian Creole nominal structure (1998: 78 ff.). However, the elements she cites are a mixed bag, either content morphemes (French *là*, a locative adverb, French third person emphatic pronoun *eux*) or early system morphemes under the 4-M model (French deictic demonstratives, *ce*, *ces*, *cette*, *celui*, *ceux*, *celle*(*s*)). Whether one accepts the 4-M model's classification is not the issue. Rather, the problem is that in neither case does Lefebvre offer a theoretical motivation why lexical category items (e.g. nouns) in most cases, but in other cases certain functional-category items (ones that, like nouns, are also content morphemes) from French should appear signaling grammatical relations in Haitian Creole. In Lefebvre (1996: 297), she makes this comment: 'Lexical, as opposed to functional, items are more salient (Mufwene (1996)), and therefore easier to identify.' (In Lefebvre 2001: 375, she does divide functional elements that are involved in relexification into two categories (those 'with some semantic content' and those that 'have no semantic content') and indicates they are copied differently in creole formation. Those with no semantic content are said to be realized as nulls.)

No matter what the differences in our approaches, many of the arguments of Lefebvre and Lumsden at least about Fongbe as one of the substrates for Haitian Creole are very convincing. Also, Lefebvre (1998) offers an admirably detailed exposition of the dialect of Haitian Creole she studies.

6.8.9. *Conclusion: creole development*

In all likelihood, creole developers' initial attempts at devising an intergroup language support scenarios offered by many creolists that emphasize the use of 'words'. For example, Baker states, 'My working assumption is that, when such inter-ethnolinguistic contacts arose, all parties used morphologically reduced versions of their own languages together with gestures until intercommunication was achieved' (2000: 48–9). However, my argument is that Baker's 'morphologically reduced versions' were not just *any* words, but only content morphemes (i.e. nouns and verbs, but also other content morphemes, such as pronouns, some prepositions, and deictic demonstratives and adverbs) and possibly early system morphemes). They were morphologically reduced because the constituents were surely stripped of superstrate late system morphemes, and possibly also lacking early system morphemes, for reasons I have discussed.

Yet, even at this stage, creoles had grammatical frames. There is no such thing as speech taking place without a grammatical frame—unless it is the speech of persons with brain pathologies. Speakers of the early pidgin/creole were using content morphemes—no matter what their source—in versions of the abstract grammatical frame of their own language. And, as speakers learned a few content morphemes from other languages, they maintained the frame of their own languages as much as they could as the Matrix Language of any bilingual utterances. (Many expatriates today follow this same pattern: they pick up content morphemes from local languages and insert them into the frame of their own language; they need not learn any of the grammatical frame of local languages to do this.)

Gradually, however, creole developers converged regarding the aspects of their own first languages that became the frame of the developing creole. That is, the frame becomes a composite of the participating substrate languages. As the creole develops, speakers incorporate more and more content morphemes from the superstrate language. Some of these serve as content morphemes in the creole, but others serve as system morphemes, filling the gaps in the grammatical frame for system morphemes that the composite Matrix Language projects. However, this is an incomplete picture of creole development because it leaves unanswered several basic questions.

First, how could the superstrate content morphemes fit the composite frame? If one accepts the premises of the 4-M and Abstract Level models and the model of language competence and production they imply, as well as the empirical evidence from other contact phenomena, the answer is clear. Speakers may have had limited access to the superstrate language, but they could learn content morphemes with some lexical-conceptual resemblance to content morphemes in their own languages.

Second, why not incorporate superstrate system morphemes and the superstrate frame? That is, why not a composite including the superstrate frame(s)? Typological relatedness counts, but more important is the claim that the structurally assigned morphemes that realize the frame are accessed differently from conceptually activated morphemes. And of course I have argued that limited access to superstrate speakers made a difference, too. Thus, while substrate speakers might have been able easily to adopt features of the frame of languages related to their L1s, it was simply more difficult for them to work out the frame of the superstrate language. Because content morphemes are first salient as having 'meanings' (the level of lexical-conceptual structure), substrate speakers could acquire superstrate content morphemes, even if one assumes limited contact. This argument holds even if superstrate speakers addressed slaves/workers only in a pidgin because a pidgin would consist largely of content morphemes. What this argument adds to these well-known views about the social conditions arguing against access to superstrate grammar is a theoretical argument that allows speakers to separate input to the grammatical system from input to the lexical system.

The net result is that the creole appears on the surface to be a simplified and modified version of the superstrate. This, of course, is a misleading, simplistic view of the roles of *both* superstrate(s) and substrates in creole formation. Of course, the most important input from the substrates, the underlying grammatical scaffolding, is largely imperceptible. Just as misleading, however, is the view that the range of linguistic material present in the superstrate, or the community in general, is equally viable as input.

6.9. Conclusion: from lexical borrowing to creole formation

In this chapter I have discussed three types of language contact phenomena that are not as different from each other as they first appear to be. The reason for discussing them in the same chapter is that if they are examined from the right perspective, they all do show—in surprisingly obvious ways—the same basic division in language in general, elements in the lexicon on one side and those signaling grammatical relations on the other.

This division is evident in the most ordinary of contact phenomena, lexical borrowing: Although content morphemes from the lexicon can be readily borrowed from one language to another, morphemes signaling grammatical relations cannot.

This division is also what lies below in determining potentials for redistributions in linguistic subsystems or modules in the development of split or mixed languages. Such languages typically show a split between the source of large parts of their lexicons and parts of their morphosyntax. One reason such languages are relatively scarce is that upheavals in the morphosyntax cannot be explained as simply structural borrowing. A chain of structural events is required that is quite different from that motivating lexical borrowing. At the same time, certain social conditions prevail; typically, the ethnic identity of a group of people is threatened in some way.

Linguistically, the development of a split language begins with bilingualism and some codeswitching that motivates convergence. In turn, enough convergence that affects the levels of predicate-argument structure and of morphological-realization patterns can open the door for alien structurally assigned system morphemes. When this happens, parts (or all) of the morphosyntax may end up coming from the alien language while much of the original lexicon is maintained. (Or, the divisions may be the other way around: the original ethnic language supplies the morphosyntax, as in the case of Media Lengua, but this may be less usual.) Either way, the result: a split language.

Different types of changes, ones even more dramatic, are required for creole formation. I argue that speakers who formed creoles operate with two targets. Content morphemes from the superstrate language are their targets to provide a lexicon and—when they are reconfigured—to fill slots in the morphosyntactic frame. However, the target for this frame is a composite of frames from the substrate languages of the slaves/workers. Given the social and psycholinguistic conditions and the nature of the morphosyntactic frame and structurally assigned system morphemes, neither the superstrate or the substrate can provide total input for both the lexicon and the grammar.

Thus, the overall claim is that there are common threads in how the form of these different contact phenomena is constrained. True, even universally present linguistic blueprinting can result in different surface-level edifices when social conditions are not the same. Still, how subsystems vary, how linguistic elements are organized at abstract levels, how they become available in language production, and the differential roles they serve in language can offer far-reaching explanations of specificity not offered elsewhere.

7

Concluding Remarks: The Out of Sight in Contact Linguistics

7.1. Concluding remarks

A main theme in this volume is the theoretical notion that the same principles and processes underlie all language contact phenomena. Although I have not stressed a second notion as much, I have tried to indicate along the way that these principles and processes are not basically different from what structures language in a general sense. That is, what happens to languages when their speakers know and use two or more languages is not really unusual if one considers the larger linguistic picture. The fact that we are dealing with bilingual speech does mean certain other provisions need to be made, but they are not all that remarkable and certainly not curious and never bizarre. It is for these very reasons that I suggest that the discussions in this volume have relevance beyond contact phenomena to general linguistic theory. I have stressed that we can see how the division, as well as the interface, between the basic roles of the lexicon and structurally assigned grammatical specifications is apparent in contact phenomena.

I do not claim to cover all language-contact phenomena in my discussions, but I hope I have covered the main ones. Some that I do not consider at all, such as child bilingual acquisition or language death/endangered languages, have large literatures of their own. Further, it is easy to see how the processes that I have covered can be applied to any contact phenomena that lack coverage here. For example, many researchers find that the constraints that the MLF model formulates for classic codeswitching largely are useful in discussing child bilingual acquisition (cf. Lanza 1997, Paradis, Nicoladis, and Genesee 2000, *inter alia*). Also, what is said here about convergence and attrition certainly applies to language death and the structural fate of endangered languages.

The contact phenomena singled out for attention here include codeswitching (Chapters 3 and 4), convergence and attrition (Chapter 5), and lexical borrowing, split (mixed) languages, and creole development (Chapter 6). The emphasis in all treatments is on grammatical structures, not the social and psycholinguistic factors that motivate or affect the structural outcomes. For this reason, the treatment in Chapter 2, which does cover these factors, is relatively brief. I want to be clear that I do not intend to offer a comprehensive coverage of these non-grammatical factors in this volume.

A second major theme of the volume is that contact phenomena covered and their structures can be explained within the theoretical frameworks of three models. First comes the Matrix Language Frame model that was explicated at length in Myers-Scotton (1993*a* and the Afterword in the second edition, 1997). In this current volume, the MLF model is discussed again at length in Chapter 3 in an attempt to clarify my own thinking and to clear up misunderstandings; however, the model has changed very little from the 1993 version. Second, two new supporting models are introduced, although they both have been discussed in print in Myers-Scotton and Jake (2000*a*, *b*, 2001); they also figure in a number of recent dissertations. These are the 4-M model and the Abstract Level model. These models add new precision to how codeswitching is to be accounted for under the MLF model. Perhaps even more important, while some of the provisions of the MLF model certainly apply beyond classic codeswitching to other contact phenomena, the provisions of the two new models are very relevant to a wide range of contact data other than codeswitching, as well as monolingual data. They are only applied to contact data in this volume. Also, I have tried to indicate at least the gist, and sometimes the details, of other approaches to the contact phenomena discussed, but this is not a critical review of the literature.

7.2. Hypotheses for further testing

I conclude this volume with a set of hypotheses derived from the MLF model, the 4-M model, and the Abstract Level model. The notions they contain are at least implicit—sometimes clearly explicit—in the discussions throughout the volume. Here, I try to state them more formally. Some are stated in testable forms, but others are not. I try to indicate those that are more assumptions for discussion rather than hypotheses for testing.

Two theoretical themes orchestrate the hypotheses: (i) The participating varieties in bilingual speech do not participate equally, with one of them achieving dominance in the grammatical subsystems in some contact phenomena and pressing forward for this dominance in other phenomena. (ii) Different types of morphemes have different types of connections to abstract grammatical structure. The ways in which they contrast affect the ways in which contact situations impact on their realizations in bilingual speech.

In offering these hypotheses my aim is to go beyond producing a list of the types of outcomes that can happen to lexical elements or grammatical structures when speakers bring languages into contact. I also wish to avoid generalizations about outcomes that have no obvious motivation or connection with other generalizations. For example, to say that mismatches between languages result in influence of one language on another may be superficially accurate, but it is only superficially explanatory. One reason is that it is not tied into a set of related premises and principles—a theoretical framework.

The hypotheses express two themes from the frameworks or models shaping this volume. The themes embody the principles that are played out as processes or outcomes in contact linguistics. They are evident at times in the structure of monolingual speech, but their effects are magnified when two languages come together, especially within the same CP.

1. One theme is the asymmetry between participating languages in contact phenomena and the press forward of the abstract frame of one language to prevail. My argument is that asymmetry is an expression of structural pressure within the system of language in general toward a single unified source of abstract lexical structure. Is it putting it too strongly to say that nature abhors the structural variation that bilingual speech introduces? The push is toward a unified source of the abstract grammatical frame, and in bilingual speech; that means a Matrix Language. Of course this ideal of a single source does not necessarily manage to prevail always. There is a tension between or among competing systems.

2. A second theme is the inherent lack of parity between different types of morphemes within the abstract frame of all languages in terms of their patterns of distribution. Of course the basic lack of equivalence is between content and system morphemes, but then again—as the 4-M model tell us—there is also disproportion between the distribution—and arguably the importance—of late system morphemes over early ones.

7.2.1. *Preliminaries to the hypotheses*

I begin with a summary of the three sources for bilingual CPs, even though they should be more than familiar by now.

1. *Classic codeswitching.* The CP is bilingual because there are surface-level morphemes from both participating languages. Grammatical structure is derived from only one of the participating languages; this is the source language of the Matrix Language of the CP.

2. *Composite codeswitching.* The CP is bilingual because there are both surface-level morphemes from both participating languages and also abstract grammatical structure from both languages. That is, composite codeswitching entails the presence of convergence. This means there is a composite Matrix Language as the grammatical frame of the CP.

3. *Convergence.* The CP is bilingual but all the surface level morphemes come from one language. The source of bilingualism in such CPs is abstract grammatical structure from more than one language. Again, there is a composite Matrix Language framing the CP.

Note an important difference between these two forms of codeswitching: composite codeswitching occurs simultaneously with convergence at some level of abstract structure, but classic codeswitching does not. The reason is that convergence necessarily entails abstract structure from more than one participating language; in contrast, in classic codeswitching, all structure in bilingual CPs is derived from one participating language, augmented by some compromise strategies, such as bare forms and Embedded Language islands.

However, also note that composite codeswitching is different from convergence without codeswitching. Composite codeswitching must include surface morphemes from both participating languages. Convergence includes surface-level morphemes from only one language, but abstract grammatical structure from both languages. However, as I argued in relation to attrition, the waning language does not easily give up 'control' of the most crucial elements in the morphosyntactic frame (late system morphemes). Further, at any point in the development of the composite Matrix Language, one language does dominate in supplying the frame. The result is that not anything goes.

7.2.2. *Basic assumptions about the roles of codeswitching and convergence*

Assumption 1. Either codeswitching or convergence, or both, are the contact phenomena that are entailed by other forms of contact phenomena.

Assumption 2. There is not a categorical link between the presence of classic codeswitching in a community and language shift. That is, structural contact developments resulting in language shift are not necessary outcomes of classic codeswitching. What is more certain is that classic codeswitching frequently leads to increased lexical borrowing and often leads to convergence.

Assumption 3. Neither is shift a necessary outcome of convergence. However, convergence is more likely than classic codeswitching to lead to further structural contact developments resulting in language shift.

Assumption 4. Composite codeswitching need not lead to shift. However, it more frequently leads to shift than either classic codeswitching or convergence. The rationale is that composite codeswitching includes two ways in which the putative Matrix Language is compromised. First, if codeswitching includes many Embedded Language islands, this means more switches in the activation level of the participating languages. Second, convergence means incursions from a putative Embedded Language into any or all of the three levels of abstract grammatical structure of the morphosyntactic frame. Example (1*a*) is included to illustrate composite codeswitching, just in case it is difficult to visualize. The example comes from the speech of a young adult Croatian/English bilingual living in Australia for whom English is probably his dominant language. This example shows convergence to English structure at a number of levels.

(1) *a*

to	je	možda	najbolje	što	sam	ja
that	is	perhaps	best/NEUT/S/NOM	COMP/NOM	be/1S	I

što	ja	**rememba-∅**	ya
COMP/NOM	I	remember	AFFIRM

b Homeland Croatian:

. . . to	je	možda	najbolje	što	sam	(ja)
that	is	perhaps	bestNEUT/S/NOM	COMP/NOM	be/1S	I

(doživio)	čega	se	sjećam
experience/3S/M/PAST PART	COMP/GEN	REFL/ACC	remember/1S/PRES

'. . . that is perhaps the best thing that I have, that I remember . . . ya'

(Croatian/English; Hlavac 2000: 58)

This example illustrates composite codeswitching because it both shows codeswitching (the English verb *remember* is part of the CP) and a grammatical frame incorporating English abstract structure in various ways. First, Croatian is a pro-drop language, meaning that self-standing subject pronouns are marked and generally only used for emphasis. Yet, in (1*a*) *ja* 'I' occurs. Second, English *remember* is a transitive verb with the Experiencer in subject position and the Theme in object position. This is the syntactic structure of (1*a*). However, in Croatian, the equivalent for *remember* (*sjećati se*) calls for a reflexive in object position while the Theme appears as a genitive object, with genitive (marked on the complementizer *čega*). Instead of *čega*, the speaker produced *što* in the nominative case and there is no reflexive.

7.2.3. *Summary for basic assumptions*

If there is language shift, the mechanisms involved follow this hierarchy:

Classic codeswitching < convergence < composite codeswitching (i.e. shift most likely with composite codeswitching)

7.3. Lexical borrowing and codeswitching

Hypothesis 1. Core borrowings gradually enter the recipient language as a result of their initial appearance as singly occurring Embedded Language content morphemes in codeswitching. In contrast, cultural borrowings can be abrupt borrowings; they need not go through a codeswitching stage.

7.4. Content morphemes

Hypothesis 2. Content morphemes are 'first in' in a number of contact phenomena and perhaps in all.

The motivation for this hypothesis is the following: Keep in mind that the main goal of speakers is to satisfy their intentions to convey specific meanings, including pragmatic inferences. This is the work of content morphemes (and sometimes early system morphemes along with their content morpheme heads). When words in a second language convey such intentions better than those that the speakers already know in their L1, semantic/pragmatic 'bootstrapping' kicks in. That is, speakers incorporate content morphemes from an L2 into their speech. Eventually, if these morphemes are used again and again, they are included in a reconfiguring of the speakers' competence.

Supporting evidence for the hypothesis: Empirical evidence discussed in Chapter 6 shows that content morphemes (especially nouns) are the first and most frequent category appearing as lexical borrowings. They also are the singly occurring form most often appearing in mixed constituents in classic codeswitching. In addition, evidence not discussed here shows they are the first elements to be produced in first language acquisition and in second language acquisition. Pidgins are largely composed of content morphemes and nothing else.

Hypothesis 3. In comparison with system morphemes, content morphemes are also 'first out' or 'first challenged' in situations of attrition and shift in the sense that L1 content morphemes are duplicated or replaced by L2 content morphemes that are close counterparts.

Note that this hypothesis does not predict that all L1 content morphemes are replaced at an early stage by L2 content morphemes. Rather, it predicts that L2 content morphemes are brought into bilingual CPs *to compete with L1 content morphemes* before L2 system morphemes are involved. Example (2) shows the type of data that support this hypothesis. A lexical borrowing (*boss*) from English is used for a common referent in Pennsylvania German. A possible German counterpart *Meister* or *Hauptman* has different connotations, probably a reason why *boss* is chosen.

(2) In die Firma, ja, da war ich der **boss**
in the firm yes there be/PST I DEF/M boss
'In the company, yes, there I was the boss.'

(Pennsylvania German; Fuller 2000: 47)

7.5. Early system morphemes

Hypothesis 4. Because of their link to content morphemes, early system morphemes may 'move' with them in various contact phenomena in contrast with late system morphemes.

The motivation for this hypothesis is the following. Recall that early system morphemes share the feature of [+conceptually activated] with content morphemes. Also recall that early system morphemes only occur because they are indirectly elected by their head-content morphemes. For these reasons, there is a strong link between a content morpheme and the early system morpheme that it elects. This hypothesis applies to all forms of language contact.

The type of evidence supporting this hypothesis includes a number of lexical borrowings in many European languages from Arabic that include an Arabic definite article along with a content morpheme. A well-known example is *algebra* in example (3). Also, in Michif, discussed in Chapter 6, we see that French nouns are incorporated into a Cree-based frame, along with their determiners (early system morphemes).

(3) algebra < Arabic *al-jabr* 'the science of reuniting'

Hypothesis 4*a*. When Embedded Language content morphemes are inserted into Matrix Language frames in either classic codeswitching or composite codeswitching, they sometimes show 'double morphology'. When this happens does not seem to be predictable. However, the early system morpheme hypothesis discussed in Chapter 3 predicts that in codeswitching, only early system morphemes can double (not late ones).

What happens is this: a singly occurring Embedded Language content morpheme is not accessed alone in codeswitching, but rather carries along an early system morpheme. Example (4) shows the type of example supporting this hypothesis, the most common form of such double morphology, doubling of the plural affix. This example comes from Shona/English codeswitching. The English content morpheme *day* receives the plural prefix (*ma-*) from the Matrix Language in this example, Shona, but it also retains the English plural suffix.

(4) **But** ma-**day-s** a-no a-ya- handisi ku-mu-on-a
but CL6/PL-day-PL CL6/PL-DEM CL6/DEM 1S/NEG/do INF-OBJ-see-FV
'But these days I don't see him much.'

(Shona/English; Crawhall 1990 cited in Myers-Scotton 1993*a* [1997]: 111)

7.6. Late system morphemes

Hypothesis 5. Because late system morphemes are the most basic features of the morphosyntactic frame in any CP, in bilingual CPs they are subject to different restrictions on their occurrence than either early system morphemes or content morphemes.

The motivation for this hypothesis is the implicational evidence that late system morphemes are accessed at a different point in the production process from either content morphemes or early system morphemes. This evidence is the distribution of morpheme types across diverse data sets; such distributions are mentioned in Chapter 3 (also, some distributions are the subject of Myers-Scotton and Jake 2000*a*). Recall from the discussion in Chapters 1 and 3 that the hypothesis is that late system morphemes are only accessed when the lemmas underlying content morphemes send directions to the Formulator about how larger constituents are to be assembled. Thus, while content morphemes and early system morphemes are conceptually activated, late system morphemes are structurally assigned.

This generalization is captured in the Differential Access Hypothesis introduced in Chapter 1 and repeated here:

The different types of morpheme under the 4-M model are differently accessed in the abstract levels of the production process. Specifically, content morphemes and early system morphemes are accessed at the level of the mental lexicon, but late system morphemes do not become salient until the level of the Formulator.

Based on this hypothesis, the following hierarchy is predicted for the sequence in which different morpheme types will be affected when a composite Matrix Language forms and/or when attrition takes place:

Late system morphemes < early system morphemes < content morphemes

This hierarchy is discussed in Chapter 5 in relation to attrition, with data presented to support the hierarchy.

Hypothesis 5*a*. In acquisition scenarios, late system morphemes are 'last in' regarding either presence or accuracy. That is, late system morphemes are more difficult to acquire, and to acquire accurately, in any type of language acquisition (e.g. child acquisition, second-language acquisition, language shift, creole formation, etc.).

Such studies of Second Language Acqusition as Wei (1996, 2000*a*) support this hypothesis. Example (5) illustrates the type of quantitative data Wei reports, evidence that supports this hypothesis. It is an utterance by a Japanese speaker who is learning English. Note that he does not produce the third person present tense singular form of the verb accurately; however, he does produce accurately many other aspects of English structure. The problem verb forms (*go, study, make*) should contain the suffix *-s*, a late outsider system morpheme marking subject–verb agreement. Its form is not available until a constituent larger than the VP is assembled. Note that the speaker has no trouble producing the early system morpheme plural marker (*-s*) on *chemicals*.

(5) My brother go-∅ to university in Japan. He study-∅ physics, and my father make-∅ chemicals at company, his company.

(Wei 1996: 162)

Hypothesis 5*b*. Compared to bridge late system morphemes, outsider late system morphemes are more difficult to acquire because outsider late system morphemes must look outside their immediate maximal projection for their form. I leave it to other researchers to test this hypothesis.

Hypothesis 5*c*. In classic codeswitching, the System Morpheme Principle applies. That is, in mixed constituents, all the outsider late system morphemes must come from the language whose morphosyntax is isomorphic with the Matrix Language frame.

Data supporting this hypothesis are discussed in Chapter 3 and are found in other publications, too. Example (6) illustrates the type of data that support this hypothesis; the example includes three late outsider system morphemes. Two of these are in the verbal assembly (the subject prefix and the tense prefix (*si-ku-come*). The third is the noun class prefix on *z-angu* 'my'. *Zangu* is an AdjP, a maximal projection; however, it must look to the noun *books* for information about the form of its prefix. Even though *books* is an English noun, it is treated as falling in Swahili noun class 10, a class that has zero as one of the possible realizations of its subject prefix. The possessive adjective *zangu* shows the prefix of this class (*zi* + *angu* > *zangu*). Note that the plural suffix *-s* comes from English, but it is an early system morpheme and therefore is not a counterexample to this hypothesis. (On the argument that *books* has a zero prefix (discussed in Chapter 4), it is an example of double morphology; see Hypothesis 4*b*.)

(6) Leo si- -ku-**come** na **ø-book-s** z-angu
today 1S/NEG-PST/NEG-come with CL10/PL-book-PL CL10-my
'Today I didn't come with my books.'

(Swahili/English; Myers-Scotton 1993*a* [1997]: 80)

The prediction is that this principle also applies in composite codeswitching, but—at some point and especially if a language shift is going to completion—late system morphemes from the L2 (the 'old' Embedded Language) start to fill slots in the frame. Unfortunately, there is little evidence to test this prediction; shift from a longitudinal and structural viewpoint is hardly studied. However, Fuller (2000) does provide a test with data from Pennsylvania German, a language showing a good deal of convergence toward English. Even with this convergence, the late system morphemes still come from the Germanic sources of the frame, not from English.

Hypothesis 5*d.* At least in the initial stages of attrition (and often much longer), late system morphemes, especially outsider late system morphemes, are 'last out'. They are the last morphemes to show convergence toward a new target language.

Although many conceptually activated morphemes are also retained, many of them are replaced by counterparts from the more dominant language in the context. The prediction about late system morphemes is supported by data on late middle-aged Germans who have lived in the United States for forty years or more (Gross 2000*a*). Under Gross's analysis, of a total of 2,271 contexts for late system morphemes (determiners and adjectives with case marking), only seventy-two receive non-target-like case/gender morphology (2000*a*: 150 ff.). Also, the majority of target case markers are maintained in Hlavac's corpus for second-generation speakers of Croatian in Australia (2000: 483). Even when both nominative and accusative types are excluded (because zero is the case marker for masculine nominative singular and masculine accusative singular for inanimate objects) 75 per cent of the instances for the remaining four cases are target-like.

Examples (7*a*) and (7*b*) illustrate the type of data that support the hypothesis. In this case, elements integral to the abstract grammatical frame are still maintained in an L1 of a speaker who left the L1 environment forty years ago and who speaks the L1 now only occasionally. The examples come from Gross's study of speakers of a non-standard German dialect who live now in the United States. The examples illustrate one speaker's target-like use of a late system morpheme when it is appropriate and no late system morpheme when it is not called for. The same speaker projects a slot (and fills it with the target form) for a late system morpheme, marking case and number on the predicate adjective (*gut-e*) in (7*a*).

However, in (7*b*) the slot is not projected and the speaker produces a target-like bare adjective (*gut*).

(7) *a*

des	wɔr-en	gut-e	Russ-en
those	be/PAST-3PL	good-NOM/PL	Russian-PL

'Those were good Russians.'

b

i hɔb	net sehr	gut	aus-k-scha-t	domɔɪs
I have/PRES/1SG	not very	good	out-PRT-look-PRT	then

'I didn't look very good at that time.'

(Gross 2000*b*: 156)

Hypothesis 5*e*. This is a rider to Hypothesis 5*d*. When attrition takes place, the target late system morpheme for a slot may be replaced by another late system morpheme from the same paradigm. In effect, the slot, not the target morpheme for the slot, is the real 'last out' element.

This hypothesis predicts that the slot for the late system morpheme is often maintained in the grammatical frame, but the target late system morpheme for the slot, making a well-formed construction, is typically replaced by another late system morpheme. That is, substitution, not loss, characterizes much of the attrition data. Data from many sources, the study of Australian Croatian/English bilinguals (Hlavac 2000), and a study of Russian children for whom English is becoming a dominant language (Schmitt 2000) support this hypothesis. Example (8) illustrates the type of susbstitution of case markers that is frequent in this corpus.

(8)

ona	idj-ot	v	podrug-u
she-NOM/SG/3	go-3S/PRES	to	friend-ACCUS/FEM/SG

Standard Russian:

ona	idj-ot	k	podrug-e
she-NOM/SG/3	go-3S/PRES	to	friend-DAT/FEM/SG

(Schmitt 2001: 209)

The speaker produces two non-target-like forms. First, he uses the preposition *v* instead of the target *k*. Second, instead of the appropriate dative case suffix, he uses the accusative suffix.

Hypothesis 5*f*. Generally, bridge late system morphemes also must come from the Matrix Language source language in classic codeswitching or from the dominant language in the frame in early versions of composite codeswitching.

Like outsider late system morphemes, bridge system morphemes are structurally assigned. Because the prediction is that their access in production occurs only when larger constituents are assembled at the level of the Formulator, they are more a part of the grammatical frame itself than conceptually activated morphemes.

The Uniform Structure Principle offers special motivation for this hypothesis (but also for the others). This principle, introduced in Chapter 1, but discussed at several other points, is restated here:

A given constituent type in any language has a uniform abstract structure and the requirements of well-formedness for this constituent type must be observed whenever the constituent appears. In bilingual speech, the structures of the Matrix Language are always preferred.

In codeswitching, this means maintaining the Matrix Language whenever possible, especially in regard to parts of the morphosyntactic frame. Example (9) illustrates the type of example that supports this hypothesis. It is an example of CL with the bridge system morpheme from the Matrix Language. In this example, Shaba Swahili (spoken in Congo) is the Matrix Language and French is the Embedded Language. Note that even though the nouns in this [NP [NP]] construction (*enterrement* and *grand chef*) are from French, the bridge system morpheme (*ya*) is from Shaba Swahili.[1] The translation of the [NP [NP]] is 'burial of [the] big chiefs'.

(9) ku-ri-kuwa fashi moya (h)ivi **reservé** juu
CL17-TMA-COP place DET like that reserve/PP for
enterrement ya ba-**grand chef**
burial CONN/ASSOC CL2/PL big chief
'There was a place reserved for the burial of the big chiefs.'
(Shaba Swahili/French; de Rooij 1996: 112)

In contrast to Hypothesis 5*c* (the System Morpheme Principle) where no counterexamples are predicted, a few exceptions to this hypothesis do occur in the literature. Although all late system morphemes are structurally assigned, the two types (bridges and late outsiders) respond to different types of syntactic restrictions, and this may make the difference.

7.7. Multimorphemic elements

Hypothesis 6. In multimorphemic elements (consisting of two or more system morphemes and including a late system morpheme), the late system morpheme takes precedence. This means that the entire element shows distribution patterns as if it were a late system morpheme. This is the 'pull down' or 'drag down' principle.

[1] In Standard Swahili, the associative element in this construction would be considered multimorphemic. That is, part of its form would be a late system morpheme co-indexed with the noun class of the possessed item and therefore its form would vary with the class involved. The late system morpheme would combine with the invariant bridge system morpheme (i.e. -*a* as the bridge). However, it is more likely that in Shaba Swahili the entire element (*ya*) is an invariant bridge system morpheme (i.e. not co-indexed with specific noun classes).

Evidence supporting this hypothesis is not discussed in this volume; however, Myers-Scotton and Jake (2000*a*) discuss such elements and Myers-Scotton and Jake (2001*a*: 113–14) provide strong implicational evidence from a corpus including German as one of the participating languages. The rationale is that—in German—the morpheme for case, which is part of the determiner, is a late system morpheme, and it is not fully assigned until constituents larger than the NP are assembled. In German, verbs and prepositions assign a determiner's case even though the determiner occurs in an NP.

7.8. Insufficient congruence

Assumption. Bare forms and Embedded Language islands occur in classic codeswitching as compromise strategies when there are problems regarding 'sufficient congruence' at any of the three levels of abstract grammatical structure (i.e. lexical-conceptual structure, predicate-argument structure, or morphological realization patterns).

The best example of a bare form is the combination of a 'do' verb from the Matrix Language, generally with all the necessary inflections the context requires, plus a non-finite verb form from the Embedded Language that conveys the intended content for a verb in the relevant context. That is, the Embedded Language verb is bare in the sense that it does not receive the requisite Matrix Language inflections. Such 'do' constructions are discussed in Chapter 4.

Different motivations for Embedded Language islands are also discussed in Chapter 4. Some such islands are collocations and they seem to occur because they satisfy pragmatic considerations that a Matrix Language counterpart does not quite meet. However, others are structurally motivated, and especially the extent to which islands are structurally motivated deserves more study.

7.9. Change in frame requirements

Assumption. When there is sufficient convergence between a waxing language (an 'old' Embedded Language) and a waning language (an 'old' Matrix Language) undergoing attrition, abstract grammatical structure from the waxing language may assign features to slots in the CP frame that were previously under control from the waning language.

In Chapter 5, data on case assignment from Bolonyai (1999, 2002) and Schmitt (2001) are discussed in these terms. Specifically, English is the waxing language. In the Hungarian corpus, the argument is that English, not Hungarian, controls accusative case assignment. English assigns a zero to the slot for accusative case assignment in Bolonyai's analysis. In the Russian corpus, English nouns occurring in a Russian frame do not receive Russian case assignment; the nouns are not overtly case-marked at all (they appear as they would in English). The argument for both corpora is that the language undergoing attrition has lost control of assigning overt case, but case itself is not 'lost'. The other participating language (English) takes over case assignment, and there are no overt case morphemes.

7.10. Levels of abstract lexical structure

Hypothesis 7. There is a hierarchy of susceptibility to change for the three levels of abstract lexical structure. Lexical-conceptual structure is most susceptible to change, followed by morphological realization patterns and predicate-argument structure.

'Change' refers to splitting and recombining of abstract grammatical structure within a language or involving two or more languages. That is, under the Abstract Level model, any of these levels can be split from the lemma underlying one surface form and combined with levels in a lemma underlying another surface form. In creoles, splitting and recombining often occurs within content morphemes of one language, the superstrate. In Gullah, a creole spoken on the South Carolina and Georgia coast, *rebel time* [rɛbəl tɒim] is reconfigured to mean 'slavery'.[2]

This hierarchy is predicted:

Predicate-argument structure < morphological-realization patterns < lexical-conceptual structure

This hierarchy is discussed in Chapter 5 in relation to attrition and relevant data supporting the hierarchy are presented.

7.11. Split (mixed) languages

Assumption A. A split language shows a morphosyntactic frame from a different source from large portions of its lexicon and includes minimally late system morphemes from the language of that frame.

Assumption B. A split language shows at least one major constituent that systematically has system morphemes, possibly with major parts of the morphosyntactic frame of that constituent, from a different source language from that of most of the lexicon.

Languages show the types of structures found in split languages when convergence to another language at abstract grammatical levels promotes a restructuring of the morphosyntactic frame, making it a composite of elements from both languages (discussed in Chapter 6). This restructuring allows alien structurally assigned morphemes to fill slots in the composite frame. What differentiates a split language from a language that has undergone convergence resulting in incorporation of some structurally assigned morphemes (late system morphemes)

[2] The same speaker uses [rɛbəl tɒim] again later on in the same narrative (p. 264). In both cases, Turner translates this compound as 'slavery'.

from an outside source is the notion of systematicity. By my definitions, a split language must show systematic inroads into at least one major constituent. This may well mean that not all languages others call mixed (split) languages are included under my definitions.

The assumptions are briefer paraphrases of definitions introduced in Chapter 6. Assumption A is a stronger definition of split (mixed) languages. Few languages seem to meet this assumption entirely, although Ma'a, spoken in Tanzania, is an example of such a language. Example (10) illustrates the less stringent definition in Assumption B with an utterance from Mednyj Aleut. Although this language has input from both Aleut and Russian, verbal inflections always come from Russian. Note that in this example, the self-standing pronouns (content morphemes) are also from Russian, as is the present tense suffix on the verb. However, the overall morphosyntactic frame of the CP seems to come from Aleut, the language of much of the lexicon.

(10) Mednyj Aleut:	ty menja	hamayaaxta-iš
	you me	ask-2S/PRES
Russian:	ty menja	sprašiva-eš
	you me	ask-2S/PRES

'you ask me.'

(Golovko 1996: 71)

A tentative hypothesis about constituent structure in a split (mixed) language is this: within any constituent, all the late system morphemes come from the same language.

7.12. Creole formation

Assumption. The different types of morpheme under the 4-M model have different potentials for occurrence in creole formation. This is a major subject in Chapter 6. Examples are cited in that chapter to support the following hypotheses; some supporting examples are repeated here.

Hypothesis 8*a*. Of all morpheme types, content morphemes from the superstrate and substrate languages are most available in creole formation.

Hypothesis 8*b*. Content morphemes serve as content morphemes (i.e. participants in the thematic grid). Or, they are reconfigured to fill slots in the morphosyntactic frame for system morphemes. The slots are projected by lemmas from a composite substrate.

Example (11) from Tok Pisin, a Papua New Guinea pidgin/creole illustrates how some English content morphemes are retained as content morphemes (*em* < *him*, *go*, *sitor* < *store*). It also shows how other content morphemes are reconfigured as system morphemes. The English content morpheme *along* is reconfigured as a case marker for Goal. Also, *by* is reconfigured as a future marker. And finally, *he* is reconfigured as a predicate marker.

(11) **bai** em **i** go **long** sitor
FUT 3S PREDM go to store
'He will go to the store.'

(Jenkins 2000: 138)

Hypothesis 8*c*. Early system morphemes sometimes are accessed in creole formation along with their content morpheme heads.

This hypothesis duplicates an earlier hypothesis about early system morphemes and their general tendency to be accessed along with their heads. Examples are discussed in Chapter 6. Note this hypothesis does not make any categorical predictions, but only refers to a potential. Example (12) illustrates such a form (*lavyan* 'the meat') in a creole.

(12) ban Siven pa mahz **lavyan.**
'Siven's family don't eat meat.'
(lavyan < la viande French)

(Baker 1972: 78)

Hypothesis 8*d*. No late system morphemes from any of the participating languages may appear in the creole.

Instead, as noted under Hypothesis 8*a*, content morphemes are reconfigured to fill needed slots or slots are left unfilled. For example, example (27) in Chapter 6 shows how *après* (French) 'after' becomes a future marker *ap* in Haitian Creole.

In example (11) above, English *bai* 'by' is reconfigured as a future marker. Example (13), also in Chapter 6, shows the content morpheme *get* reconfigured for the slot of the existential late system morpheme. The creole is Hawaiian Creole English.

(13) **Get** wan wahine shi get wan data.
'There is a woman who has a daughter.'

(Bickerton 1981: 67, cited in Siegel 2000: 212)

7.13. Conclusion

The assumptions and hypotheses presented here often refer to 'the out of sight' in contact phenomena. In this volume, the general argument has been that abstract principles—necessarily out of sight—but as integrated and empirically motivated parts of a theoretical framework, best explain the form that contact data take. In the earlier chapters, these assumptions and hypotheses are supported by discussion and examples (and often quantified data). Here, the hypotheses are restated and encapsulated to give readers a sense of the entire volume. I hope readers will consider research to test the hypotheses further.

In closing, I would like to think that my discussions in this volume are part of what Talmy (2000: 2) has called the 'conceptual approach' to language study. He states that this approach 'is concerned with the patterns in which and the processes by which conceptual content is organized in language'. In this regard, I have stressed that we can see how the division, as well as the important interface, between the basic roles of the lexicon and structurally assigned grammatical specifications is apparent in contact phenomena.

More specifically, I also see my work as recognizing that explanations lie in linking a theory of language with a theory of language processing in a manner similar to the views expressed in Jackendoff (2002). Jackendoff stresses the need to consider what aspects of an utterance are in long-term memory (content morphemes in my frameworks) and what aspects can be constructed online with working memory. One of his conclusions is this: 'By taking very seriously the question of what is stored and what is computed online, we have managed to justify a major reorganization of the theory of grammar. If this is letting the theory of performance intrude on the theory of competence, so be it. For my own taste, such interaction between the two theories is the proper way for linguistic research to proceed in the future' (p. 424). My arguments in this volume show that I couldn't agree more.

References

ABDULAZIZ, MOHAMMED, and OSINDE, KEN (1997), 'Sheng and Engsh (sic): Development of Mixed Codes among the Urban Youth in Kenya', *International Journal of the Sociology of Language*, 125: 43–63.

ABNEY, STEPHEN (1987), 'The English Noun Phrase in Its Sentential Aspect'. Ph.D., Cambridge, MA: MIT.

ALLARD, RÉAL, and LANDRY, RODRIGUE (1992), 'Ethnolinguistic Vitality Beliefs and Language Maintenance and Loss', in Willem Fase, Koen Jaspaert, and Sjaak Kroon (eds.), *Maintenance and Loss of Minority Languages*, 171–95. Amsterdam: Benjamins.

ALLEYNE, MERVYN (1980), *Comparative Afro-American.* Ann Arbor: Karoma.

AMUZU, EVERSHED (1998), 'Aspects of Grammatical Structure in Ewe–English Codeswitching', MA thesis, Oslo: Univ. of Oslo.

ANDERSON, ROGER (1982), 'Determining the Linguistic Attributes of Language Attrition', in Lambert and Freed (1982), 83–118.

—— (1989), 'The "Up" and "Down" Staircase in Second Language Development', in Dorian (1989), 385–94.

ANNAMALAI, E. (1989), 'The Language Factor in Code Mixing', *International Journal of the Sociology of Language*, 75: 47–54.

ARENDS, JACQUES (ed.) (1995), *The Early Stages of Creolization.* Amsterdam: Benjamins.

——, MUYSKEN, PIETER, and SMITH, NORVAL (eds.) (1995), *Pidgins and Creoles, An Introduction.* Amsterdam: Benjamins.

ARONOFF, MARK (2000), 'Morphology Between Lexicon and Grammar', in Geert Booij, C. Kemann, and J. Mugdan (eds.), *Morphologie/Morphology I*, 344–9. Berlin: Mouton de Gruyter.

AUER, PETER (1998*a*), 'Introduction: Bilingual Conversation Revisited', in Auer (1998*b*), 1–24.

—— (ed.) (1998*b*), *Code-Switching in Conversation.* London: Routledge.

AZUMA, SHOJI (1991), 'Two Levels Processing Hypothesis in Speech Production: Evidence from Intrasentential Code-Switching', paper presented at the 27th Chicago Linguistic Society Meeting, May.

—— (2001), 'Functional Categories and Codeswitching in Japanese/English', in Rodolfo Jacobson (ed.), *Codeswitching Worldwide II*, 91–103. Berlin: Mouton de Gruyter.

BACKUS, AD (1992), *Patterns of Language Mixing: A Study of Turkish–Dutch Bilingualism.* Wiesbaden: Harrassowitz.

—— (1996), *Two in One: Bilingual Speech of Turkish Immigrants in the Netherlands.* Tilburg, The Netherlands: Tilburg Univ. Press.

—— (1999*a*), 'The Intergenerational Codeswitching Continuum in an Immigrant Community', in Extra and Verhoeven (1999), 261–79.

—— (1999*b*), 'Evidence for Lexical Chunks in Insertional Codeswitching', in Bernt Brendenmoen, Elizabeth Lanza, and Else Ryen (eds.), *Language Encounters across Time and Space*, 93–109. Oslo: Novus Forlag.

BAILEY, BERYL (1966), *Jamaican Creole Syntax.* New York: Cambridge Univ. Press.

Baker, Philip (1972), *Kreol: A Description of Mauritian Creole.* London: C. Hurst and Company.

——(1983), 'Australian Influence on Melanesian Pidgin English', *Te Reo*, 36: 3–67.

——(1994), 'Creativity in Creole Genesis', in Dany Adone and Ingo Plag (eds.), *Creolization and Language Change*, 65–84. Tübingen: Max Niemeyer Verlag.

——(2000), 'Theories of Creolization and the Degree and Nature of Restructuring', in Ingrid Neumann-Holzschuh and Edgar Schneider (eds.), *Degrees of Restructuring in Creole Languages*, 41–63. Amsterdam: Benjamins.

—— and Corne, Chris (1986), 'Universals, Substrata and the Indian Ocean Creoles', in Muysken and Smith (1986), 163–83.

—— and Huber, Magnus (2000), 'Atlantic, Pacific and World-Wide Features in English-Lexicon Contact Languages', paper presented at Annual meeting, Society for Pidgin and Creole Linguistics, Chicago, 1/2000.

Bakker, Peter (1992), 'A Language of Our Own: The Genesis of Michif—the Mixed Cree-French Language of the Canadian Métis'. Ph.D., Amsterdam: University of Amsterdam.

——(1994), 'Michif, the Cree-French Mixed Language of the Métis Buffalo Hunters in Canada', in Bakker and Mous (1994), 13–33.

——(1997), *'A Language or Our Own'. The Genesis of Michif—the Mixed Cree-French Language of the Canadian Métis.* Oxford: Oxford Univ. Press. (Revised version of Bakker 1992.)

—— and Mous, Maarten (eds.) (1994), *Mixed Languages: 15 Case Studies in Language Intertwining.* Amsterdam: IFOTT.

—— and Muysken, Pieter (1995), 'Mixed Languages and Language Intertwining', in Arends, Muysken, and Smith (1995), 41–52.

—— and Papen, Robert A. (1997), 'Michif: a Mixed Language Based on Cree and French', in Thomason (1997*a*), 295–363.

——, Smith, Norval, and Veenstra, Tonjes (1995), 'Saramaccan', in Arends, Muysken, and Smith (1995), 165–78.

Barkhuizen, Gary, and de Klerk, Vivian (2000), 'Language Contact and Ethnolinguistic Identity in an Eastern Cape Army Camp', *International Journal of the Sociology of Language*, 144: 95–117.

Barth, Frederick (1972), 'Ethnic Processes on the Pathan–Baluch Boundary', in Gumperz and Hymes (1972), 454–64.

Bavin, Edith L. (1989), 'Some Lexical and Morphological Changes in Warlpiri', in Dorian (1989), 267–86.

Beck, David (2000), 'Grammatical Convergence and the Genesis of Diversity in the Northwest Coast Sprachbund', *Anthropological Linguistics*, 42/2: 147–213.

Belazi, H. M., Rubin, E. J., and Toribio, A. J. (1994), 'Code-Switching and X-Bar Theory: The Functional Head Constraint', *Linguistic Inquiry*, 25: 221–37.

Bell, Alan (1984), 'Language Style as Audience Design', *Language in Society*, 13: 145–204.

Beniak, Edouard, Mougeon, Raymond, and Valois, Daniel (1984/5), 'Sociolinguistic Evidence of a Possible Case of Syntactic Convergence in Ontarian French', *Journal of the Atlantic Provinces Linguistic Association*, 6/7: 73–88.

Bentahila, Addelâli, and Davies, Eirlys E. (1992), 'Code-Switching and Language Dominance', in Richard J. Harris (ed.), *Cognitive Processing in Bilinguals*, 443–7. Amsterdam: Elsevier.

————(1998), 'Codeswitching: An Unequal Partnership?', in Rodolfo Jacobson (ed.), *Codeswitching Worldwide*, 25–49. Berlin: Mouton de Gruyter.

BERG, THOMAS (1987), 'The Case against Accommodation: Evidence from German Speech Error Data', *Journal of Memory and Language*, 26: 277–99.

BERK-SELIGSON, SUSAN (1986), 'Linguistic Constraints on Intrasentential Code-Switching: A Study of Spanish–Hebrew Bilingualism', *Language in Society*, 15: 313–48.

BERKO-GLEASON, JEAN (1982), 'Theoretical Aspects of Psycholinguistics and Sociolinguistics with Special Relevance to Language Loss', in Lambert and Freed (1982), 13–23.

BERMAN, RUTH A., and OLSHTAIN, ELITE (1983), 'Features of First Language Transfer in Second Language Attrition', *Applied Linguistics*, 4/3: 222–34.

BERNSTEN, JANICE (1990), 'The Integration of English Loans in Shona: Social Correlates and Linguistic Consequences'. Ph.D., East Lansing, MI: Michigan State Univ.

——(2000), 'Creative Construction: Shona/English Codeswitches'. Paper presented at First International Conference on Linguistics in Southern Africa, Cape Town, 1/2000.

—— and MYERS-SCOTTON, CAROL (1988), Shona/English corpus.

BHATIA, TEJ K., and RITCHIE, WILLIAM C. (1996), 'Bilingual Language Mixing, Universal Grammar, and Second Language Acquisition', in William C. Ritchie and Tej K. Bhatia (eds.), *Handbook of Second Language Acquisition*, 627–88. San Diego: Academic Press.

BICKERTON, DEREK (1981), *Roots of Language*. Ann Arbor, MI: Karoma.

——(1986), 'Beyond *Roots*: The Five-Year Test', *Journal of Pidgin and Creole Languages*, 1/2: 225–32.

——(1999), 'How to Acquire Language without Positive Evidence: What Acquisitionists Can Learn from Creoles', in Michel DeGraff (ed.), *Language Creation and Language Change, Creolization, Diachrony, and Development*, 49–74. Cambridge, MA: MIT Press.

BICKMORE, LEE S. (1985), 'Hausa–English Code-Switching'. MA thesis, Univ. of California at Los Angeles.

BLAKEMORE, DIANE (1992), *Understanding Utterances: An Introduction to Pragmatics*. Oxford: Blackwell.

BLOM, JAN-PETER, and GUMPERZ, JOHN (1972), 'Social Meaning in Structure: Code-Switching in Norway', in Gumperz and Hymes (1972), 407–34.

BOCK, KATHRYN, and LEVELT, WILLEM (1994), 'Language Production: Grammatical Encoding', in Morton A. Gernsbacher (ed.), *Handbook of Psycholinguistics*, 945–84. New York: Academic Press.

BOESCHOTEN, HENDRIK (1992), 'On Misunderstanding in a Non-Stabilised Bilingual Situation', in Willem Fase, Koen Jaspaert, and Sjaak Kroon (eds.), *Maintenance and Loss of Minority Languages*, 84–97. Amsterdam: Benjamins.

BOKAMBA, EYAMBA (1988), 'Code-Mixing, Language Variation, and Linguistic Theory: Evidence from Bantu Languages', *Lingua*, 76: 21–62.

BOLINGER, DWIGHT (1968), *Aspects of Language*. New York: Holt, Rinehart, and Winston.

BOLONYAI, AGNES (1998), 'In-between Languages: Language Shift/Maintenance in Childhood Bilingualism', *International Journal of Bilingualism*, 2/1: 21–43.

——(1999), 'The Hidden Dimensions of Language Contact: the Case of Hungarian–English Bilingual Children'. Ph.D., Columbia, SC: Univ. of South Carolina.

——(2000), '"Elective Affinities": Language Contact in the Abstract Lexicon and Its Structural Consequences', *International Journal of Bilingualism*, 4/1: 81–106.

——(2002), 'Case Systems in Contact: Syntactic and Lexical Case in Bilingual Child Language', to appear in *Southwestern Journal of Linguistics*.

Booij, Geert (1996), 'Inherent versus Contextual Inflection and the Split Morphology Hypothesis', in G. Booij and J. van Marle (eds.), *Yearbook of Morphology* 1995, 1–16. Dordrecht: Kluwer.

Boretzky, Norbert, and Igla, Birgit (1994), 'Romani Mixed Dialects', in Bakker and Mous (1994), 36–68.

Boumans, Louis (1998), *The Syntax of Codeswitching: Analysing Moroccan Arabic/Dutch Conversations.* Tilburg, The Netherlands: Tilburg Univ. Press.

——(1999), 'Codeswitching and the Organisation of the Mental Lexicon', in Extra and Verhoeven (1999), 281–99.

—— and Caubet, Dominique (2000), 'Modelling Intrasentential Codeswitching: a Comparative Study of Algerian/French in Algeria and Moroccan/Dutch in the Netherlands', in Jonathan Owens (ed.), *Arabic as a Minority Language*, 113–80. Berlin: Mouton de Gruyter.

Bourdieu, Pierre (1991), *Language and Symbolic Power.* Cambridge, MA: Harvard Univ. Press. (Translation of parts of earlier works from 1977 onwards.)

Bourhis, Richard, Giles, Howard, and Rosenthal, D. (1981), 'Notes on the Construction of a Subjective Vitality Questionnaire for Ethnolinguistic Groups', *Journal of Multilingual and Multicultural Development*, 2: 145–66.

Boyd, Sally (1997), 'Patterns of Incorporation of Lexemes in Language Contact: Language Typology or Sociolinguistics?', in Gregory Guy, Crawford Feagin, Deborah Schriffrin, and John Baugh (eds.), *Towards a Social Science of Language*, vol. II, 259–83. Amsterdam: Benjamins.

Brendemoen, Bernt (1999), 'Greek and Turkish Language Encounters in Anatolia', in Bernt Brendemoen, Elizabeth Lanza, and Else Ryen (eds.), *Language Encounters across Time and Space*, 353–78. Oslo: Novus forlag.

Brenzinger, Matthias (ed.) (1992), *Language Death, Factual and Theoretical Explorations with Special Reference to East Africa.* Berlin: Mouton de Gruyter.

Bruyn, Adrienne, Muysken, Pieter, and Verrips, M. (1999), 'Double-Object Constructions in the Creole Languages: Development and Acquisition', in Michel DeGraff (1999*a*), 329–73.

Budzhak-Jones, Svitlana (1998), 'Against Word-Internal Codeswitching: Evidence from Ukrainian–English Bilingualism', *International Journal of Bilingualism*, 2/2: 161–82.

Callahan, Laura (2001), 'Spanish/English Codeswitching in Fiction: A Grammatical and Discourse Function Analysis', Ph.D., Berkeley: Univ. of California.

Campbell, Lyle (1987), 'Syntactic Change in Pipil', *International Journal of American Linguistics*, 53: 253–80.

——, Kaufman, Terrence, and Smith-Stark, Thomas C. (1986), 'Meso-America as a Linguistic Area', *Language*, 62/3: 530–70.

—— and Muntzel, Martha C. (1989), 'The Structural Consequences of Language Death', in Dorian (1989), 181–96.

Canfield, K. (1980), 'A Note on Navajo–English Code Mixing', *Anthropological Linguistics*, 22: 218–22.

Caubet, Dominique (1977), Moroccan Arabic/French corpus.

Chomsky, Noam (1965), *Aspects of the Theory of Syntax.* Cambridge, MA: MIT Press.

——(1986), *Barriers.* Cambridge, MA: MIT Press.

——(1995), *The Minimalist Program.* Cambridge, MA: MIT Press.

CLYNE, MICHAEL (1967), *Transference and Triggering.* The Hague: Nijhoff.
——(1992), 'Linguistic and Sociolinguistic Aspects of Language Contact, Maintenance and Loss: towards a Multifacet Theory', in Willem Fase, Koen Jaspaert, and Sjaak Kroon (eds.), *Maintenance and Loss of Minority Languages*, 17–36. Amsterdam: Benjamins.
——(1997), 'Multilingualism', in Florian Coulmas (ed.), *Handbook of Sociolinguistics*, 301–14. Oxford: Blackwell.
CORNE, CHRIS (1977), *Seychelles Creole Grammar.* Tübingen: TBL Verlag Gunter Narr.
——(1988), 'Mauritian Creole Reflexives', *Journal of Pidgin and Creole Languages*, 3: 69–94.
COULMAS, FLORIAN (1992), *Language and Economy.* Oxford: Blackwell.
CRAWHALL, NIGEL (1990), Shona/English corpus. Unpublished.
DAWKINS, R. M. (1916), *Modern Greek in Asia Minor.* Cambridge: Cambridge Univ. Pres.
DE BOT, KEES (1989), 'Language Reversion Revisited', *Studies in Second Language Acquisition*, 11: 167–77.
——(1996), 'Language Loss', in Goebl *et al.* (1996), 579–85.
——(1999), 'The Psycholinguistics of Language Loss', in Extra and Verhoeven (1999), 345–61.
—— and CLYNE, MICHAEL (1989), 'Language Reversion Revisited', *Studies in Second Language Acquisition*, 11: 167–77.
————(1994), 'A 16-year Longitudinal Study of Language Attrition in Dutch Immigrants in Australia', *Journal of Multilingual and Multicultural Development*, 15/1: 17–28.
——and WELTENS, BERT (1991), 'Recapitulation, Regression, and Language Loss', in Seliger and Vago (1991), 31–51.
————(1995), 'Foreign Language Attrition', *Annual Review of Applied Linguistics*, 15: 151–64.
DEGRAFF, MICHEL (ed.) (1999*a*), *Language Creation and Language Change, Creolization, Diachrony, and Development.* Cambridge, MA: MIT Press.
——(1999*b*), 'Creolization, Language Change, and Language Acquisition: An Epilogue', in DeGraff (1999*a*), 473–543.
DE ROOIJ, VINCENT (1996), *Cohesion through Contrast: Discourse Structure in Shaba Swahili/French Conversation.* Amsterdam: IFOTT.
DENISON, NORMAN (1977), 'Language Death or Language Suicide?', *International Journal of the Sociology of Language*, 12: 13–22.
DIMMENDAAL, GERRIT (1989), 'On Language Death in Eastern Africa', in Dorian (1989), 13–32.
——(1998), 'Language Contraction versus Other Types of Contact-Induced Change', in Matthias Brenzinger (ed.), *Endangered Languages in Africa*, 71–117. Cologne: Köppe.
DISCIULLO, ANNE-MARIE, MUYSKEN, PIETER, and SINGH, RAJENDRA (1986), 'Government and Code-Mixing', *Journal of Linguistics*, 22: 1–24.
DORIAN, NANCY C. (1973), 'Grammatical Change in a Dying Dialect', *Language*, 49/2: 413–38.
——(1977), 'The Problem of the Semi-Speaker in Language Death', *International Journal of the Sociology of Language*, 12: 23–32.
——(1978), 'The Fate of Morphological Complexity in Language Death: Evidence from East Sutherland Gaelic', *Language*, 54/3: 590–609.
——(1981), *Language Death: The Life Cycle of a Scottish Gaelic Dialect.* Philadelphia: Univ. of Pennsylvania Press.

Dorian, Nancy C. (1986), 'Making Do with Less: Some Surprises along the Language Death Proficiency Continuum', *Applied Psycholinguistics*, 7: 257–76.

——(1988), 'Western Language Ideologies and Small-Language Prospects', in L. Grenoble and L. Whaley (eds.), *Endangered Languages*, 3–21. Cambridge: Cambridge Univ. Press.

——(ed.) (1989), *Investigating Obsolescence.* Cambridge: Cambridge Univ. Press.

Dowty, David (1979), *Word Meaning and Montague Grammar.* Dordrecht: Reidel.

Drewes, A. J. (1994), 'Borrowing in Maltese', *Mixed Languages*, P. Bakker and M. Mous (eds.), 83–111. Amsterdam: IFOTT.

Ďurovič, Ludmila (1983), 'The Core Systems of Diaspora Children', *Slavica Lundensia*, 9: 21–94.

Dussias, Paola E. (1997), 'Sentence Matching and the Functional Head Constraint in Spanish/English Codeswitching', *Spanish Applied Linguistics*, 1/1: 114–50.

Edwards, John (1985), *Language, Society and Identity.* Oxford: Blackwell.

——(1994*a*), *Multilingualism.* London: Routledge.

——(1994*b*), 'Ethnolinguistic Pluralism and Its Discontents: A Canadian Study, and Some General Observations', *International Journal of the Sociology of Language*, 110: 5–85.

El Aissati, Abderrahman (1996), 'Language Loss among Native Speakers of Moroccan Arabic in the Netherlands'. Ph.D., Nijmegen, The Netherlands: Katholieke Universiteit Nijmegen.

Emeneau, Murray B. (1980), *Language and Linguistic Area: Essays by Murray B. Emeneau.* Stanford, CA: Stanford Univ. Press.

Enninger, Werner (1980), 'Syntactic Convergence in a Stable Triglossia Plus Trilingualism Situation in Kent County, Delaware, U.S.', in Peter Nelde (ed.), *Sprachkontakt und Sprachkonflikt*, 343–50. Wiesbaden: Steiner.

—— and Raith, Joachim (1988), 'Varieties, Variation, and Convergence in the Linguistic Repertoire of the Old Order Amish in Kent County, Delaware', in Peter Auer and Aldo di Luzio (eds.), *Variation and Convergence*, 260–93. Berlin: de Gruyter.

Essien, Okon (1995), 'The English Language and Code-Mixing: A Case Study of the Phenomenon in Ibibio', in Ayo Bambose, A. Banjo, and A. Thomas (eds.), *New Englishes, A Western African perspective*, 269–83. Ibadan, Nigeria: Mosuro.

Extra, Guus, and Verhoeven, Ludo (eds.) (1999), *Bilingualism and Migration.* Berlin: Monton de Gruyter.

Eze, Ejike (1998), 'Lending Credence to a Borrowing Analysis: Lone English-Origin Incorporations in Igbo Discourse', *International Journal of Bilingualism*, 2: 183–201.

Faraclas, Nicolas G. (1996), *Nigerian Pidgin.* London: Routledge.

Fase, Willem, Jaspaert, Koen, and Kroon, Sjaak (1992), 'Maintenance and Loss of Minority Languages: Introductory Remarks', in W. Fase, K. Jaspaert, and S. Kroon (eds.), *Maintenace and Loss of Minority Languages*, 3–13. Amsterdam: Benjamins.

Fay, David (1980), 'Transformational Errors', in Victoria Fromkin (ed.), *Errors in Linguistic Performance: Slips of the Tongue, Ear, Pen, and Hand*, 111–22. New York: Academic Press.

Ferguson, Charles A. (1959), 'Diglossia', *Word*, 15: 325–40.

Finlayson, Rosalie, Calteaux, Karen, and Myers-Scotton, Carol (1998), 'Orderly Mixing and Accommodation in South African Codeswitching', *Journal of Sociolinguistics* 2: 395–420.

FISHMAN, JOSHUA A. (1972), *The Sociology of Language*. Rowley, MA: Newbury House.

FORSON, BARNABAS (1979), 'Code-Switching in Akan–English Bilingualism'. Ph.D., Univ. of California at Los Angeles.

FREDSTED, ELIN (2001), Flensburger Stadsprache: alles Deutsch oder was? Inaugural address, Universität Flensburg, Germany.

FULLER, JANET (1996), German/English codeswitching corpus. Unpublished.

——(1997), '"Pennsylvania Dutch with a Southern Touch": A Theoretical Model of Language Contact and Change'. Ph.D., Columbia, SC: Univ. of South Carolina.

——(2000), 'Morpheme Types in a Matrix Language Turnover: The Introduction of System Morphemes from English into Pennsylvania Germans', *International Journal of Bilingualism*, 4/1: 45–58.

—— and LEHNERT, HEIKE (2000), 'Noun Phrase Structure in German–English Codeswitching: Variation in Gender Assignment and Article Use', *International Journal of Bilingualism*, 4/3: 399–420.

GAL, SUSAN (1996), 'Language Shift', in Goebl *et al.* (1996), 586–93.

GARRETT, MERRILL (1982), 'Production of Speech: Observation from Normal and Pathological Language Use', in A. W. Ellis (ed.), *Normality and Pathology in Cognitive Functions*, 19–76. London: Academic Press.

——(1988), 'Process in Sentence Production', in Frederick Newmeyer (ed.), *The Cambridge Linguistics Survey III*, 69–96. Cambridge: Cambridge Univ. Press.

GASS, SUSAN (1996), 'Transference and Interference', in Goebl *et al.* (1996), 558–67.

GAZDAR, GERALD, KLEIN, EWAN, PULLUM, GEOFFREY, and SAG, IVAN (1985), *Generalized Phrase Structure Grammar*. Cambridge, MA: Harvard Univ. Press

GILES, HOWARD, BOURHIS, RICHARD Y., and TAYLOR, DONALD M. (1977), 'Towards a Theory of Language in Ethnic Group Relations', in H. Giles (ed.), *Language, Ethnicity and Intergroup Relations*, 307–48. London: Academic Press.

'VON' GOEBL, HANS, NELDE, PETER, STARY, ZDENÊK, and WÖLCK, WOLFGANG (eds.) (1996), *Kontaktlinguistik: Ein internationales Handbuch zeitgenössischer Forschung*. Berlin: Walter de Gryuter.

GOLOVKO, EVGENIJ V. (1994), 'Mednyj Aleut or Copper Island Aleut: An Aleut-Russian Mixed Language', in Bakker and Mous (1994), 113–21.

——(1996), 'A Case of Nongenetic Development in the Arctic Area: The Contribution of Aleut and Russian to the Formation of Copper Island Aleut', in Ernst H. Jahr and Ingvild Broch (eds.), *Language Contact in the Arctic: Northern Pidgins and Contact Languages*, 63–77. Berlin: Mouton de Gruyter.

——(2000), 'Language and Ethnic Identity: Sociolinguistic Conditions for the Emergence of Mixed Languages', Paper presented at the Workshop on Mixed Languages, Univ. of Manchester, 12/2000.

—— and VAKHTIN, NIKOLAI B. (1990), 'Aleut in Contact: The CIA Enigma', *Acta Linguistica Hafniensia*, 72: 97–125.

GONZO, SUSAN, and SALTARELLI, MARIO (1983), 'Pidginization and Linguistic Change in Emigrant Languages', in Roger W. Anderson (ed.), *Pidginization and Creolization as Language Acquisition*, 181–97. Rowley, MA: Newbury House.

GOODMAN, MORRIS (1964), *A Comparative Study of Creole French Dialects*. The Hague: Mouton.

——(1971), 'The Strange Case of Mbugu', in Hymes (1971), 243–54.

GREENBERG, JOSEPH (1971), 'Urbanism, Migration, and Language,' in J. H. Greenberg, *Language, Culture, and Communication*, 198–211. Stanford, CA: Stanford Univ. Press. (Originally published in 1965.)

——(1963 [1966]), 'Some Universals of Grammar with Particular Reference to the Order of Meaningful Elements', in J. Greenberg (ed.), *Universals of Language* (2nd edition), 73–113. Cambridge, MA: MIT Press.

GROSJEAN, FRANCOIS (1982), *Life with Two Languages: An Introduction to Bilingualism*. Cambridge, MA: Harvard Univ. Press.

——, and MILLER, J. L. (1994), 'Going in and out of Languages: An Example of Bilingual Flexibility', *Psychological Science*, 5: 201–6.

GROSS, STEVEN (2000*a*), 'The Role of Abstract Lexical Structure in First Language Attrition: Germans in America'. Ph.D., Columbia, SC: Univ. of South Carolina.

——(2000*b*), 'When Two Becomes One: Creating a Composite Grammar in Creole Formation', *International Journal of Bilingualism*, 4/1: 59–80.

GUMPERZ, JOHN. J. (1982), 'Conversational Code-Switching', in J. J. Gumperz (ed.), *Discourse Strategies*, 55–99. Cambridge: Cambridge Univ. Press.

—— and HYMES, DELL (eds.) (1972), *Directions in Sociolinguistics*. New York: Holt, Rinehart, and Winston.

—— and WILSON, ROBERT (1971), 'Convergence and Creolization: A Case from the Indo-Aryan/Dravidian Border in India', in Hymes (1971), 151–67. (Republished in J. Gumperz, *Language in Social Groups*, 251–73. Stanford, Calif.: Stanford Univ. Press, 1971.)

GUPTA, ANTHEA F., and YEOK, SIEW PUI (1995), 'Language Shift in a Singapore Family', *Journal of Multilingual and Multicultural Development*, 16: 301–14.

GWARA, SCOTT (1998), 'Second Language Acquisition and Anglo-Saxon Bilingualism: Negative Transfer and Avoidance in Ælfric Bata's Latin *Colloquia*, *ca.* A.D. 1000, *Viator*, 29: 1–24.

HAGÈGE, CLAUDE (1993), *The Language Builder*. Amsterdam: Benjamins.

HAKUTA, KENJI, and D'ANDREA, DANIEL (1992), 'Some Properties of Bilingual Maintenance and Loss in Mexican Background High-School Students', *Applied Linguistics*, 13/1: 72–99.

HÅKANSSON, GISELA (1995), 'Syntax and Morphology in Language Attrition: A Study of Five Bilingual Expatriate Swedes', *International Journal of Applied Linguistics*, 5/2: 153–71.

HALMARI, HELENA (1997), *Government and Codeswitching: Explaining American Finnish*. Amsterdam: Benjamins.

HARWOOD, JAKE, GILES, HOWARD, and BOURHIS, RICHARD (1994), 'The Genesis of Vitality Theory: Historical Patterns and Discoursal Dimensions', *International Journal of the Sociology of Language*, 108: 167–206.

HASSELMO, NILS (1970), 'Codeswitching and Modes of Speaking', in G. Gilbert (ed.), *Texas Studies in Bilingualism*, 179–210. Berlin: de Gruyter.

——(1972), 'Code-Switching as Ordered Selection', in E. Finchow, K. Guinstad, N. Hasselmo, and W. O'Neil (eds.), *Studies for Einar Haugen*, 261–80. The Hague: Mouton.

HAUGEN, EINAR (1950*a*), 'Problems of Bilingualism', *Lingua*, 2: 271–90.

——(1950*b*), 'The Analysis of Linguistic Borrowing', *Language*, 26: 210–31.

——(1953), *The Norwegian Language in America: A Study in Bilingual Behavior*. Philadelphia: Univ. of Pennsylvania Press.

——(1989), 'The Rise and Fall of an Immigrant Language: Norwegian in America', in Dorian (1989), 61–73.

——(1992), 'Borrowing: An Overview', in William Bright (ed.), *International Encyclopedia of Linguistics*, 197–200. Oxford: Oxford Univ. Press.

HEATH, JEFFREY (1981), 'A Case of Intensive Lexical Diffusion: Arnhem Land, Australia', *Language*, 57: 335–67.

——(1989), *From Code-Switching to Borrowing: Foreign and Diglossic Mixing in Moroccan Arabic*. London and New York: Kegan Paul International.

HELLER, MONICA, and PFAFF, CAROL (1996), 'Code-Switching', in Goebl *et al.* (1996), 594–609.

HILL, JANE, and HILL, KENNETH (1977), 'Language Death and Relexification in Tlaxcalan Nahuatl', *International Journal of the Sociology of Language*, 12: 55–69.

—— ——(1986), *Speaking Mexicano*. Tucson: Univ. of Arizona Press.

HLAVAC, JIM (2000), 'Croatian in Melbourne: Lexicon, Switching and Morphosyntactic Features in the Speech of Second-Generation Bilinguals'. Ph.D., Melbourne: Monash Univ.

HOCK, HANS HENRICH (1988), 'Historical Implications of a Dialectological Approach to Convergence', in Jacek Fisiak (ed.), *Trends in Linguistics, Historical Dialectology*, 283–327. Berlin: Mouton de Gruyter.

—— and JOSEPH, BRIAN (1996), *Language History, Language Change, and Language Relationship*. Berlin: Mouton de Gruyter.

HOEKSTRA, TEUN, VAN DER HULST, HARRY, and MOORTGAT, MICHAEL (1980), 'Introduction', in T. Hoekstra, H. van der Hulst, and M. Morrtgat (eds.), *Lexical grammar*, 1–48. Dordrecht: Foris.

HOLM, JOHN (1988 and 1989), *Pidgins and Creoles* (vols. I and II). Cambridge: Cambridge Univ. Press.

——(2000), *An Introduction to Pidgins and Creoles*. Cambridge: Cambridge Univ. Press.

HORROCKS, GEOFFREY (1987), *Generative Grammar*. London: Longman.

HULS, ERICA, and VAN DE MOND, ANNEKE (1992), 'Some Aspects of Language Attrition in Turkish Families in the Netherlands', in Willem Fase, Koen Jaspaert, and Sjaak Kroon (eds.), *Maintenance and Loss of Minority Languages*, 99–115. Amsterdam: Benjamins.

HULSEN, MADELEINE, DE BOT, KEES, and WELTENS, BERT (2002), 'Between Two Worlds: Social Networks, Language Shift and Language Processing in Three Generations of Dutch Migrants in New Zealand'. To appear in *International Journal of the Sociology of Language*, 153: 27–52.

HYLTENSTAM, KENNETH, and OBLER, LORAINE K. (eds.) (1989*a*), *Bilingualism across the Lifespan*. Cambridge: Cambridge Univ. Press.

—— ——(1989*b*), 'Bilingualism across the Lifespan: An Introduction', in Hyltenstam and Obler (1989*a*), 1–12.

—— and STROUD, CHRISTOPHER (1996), 'Language Maintenance', in Goebl *et al.* (1996), 567–78. Berlin: Walter de Gruyter.

HYMES, DELL (ed.) (1971), *Pidginization and Creolization of Languages*. Cambridge: Cambridge Univ. Press.

JACKENDOFF, RAY (1990), *Semantic Structures*. Cambridge, MA: MIT Press.

——(1997), *The Architecture of the Language Faculty*. Cambridge, MA: MIT Press.

——(2002), *Foundations of Language: Brain, Meaning, Grammar, Evolution*. Oxford: Oxford University Press.

JAKE, JANICE L. (1994), 'Intrasentential Codeswitching and Pronouns: On the Categorial Status of Functional Elements', *Linguistics*, 32: 271–98.

JAKE, JANICE L. (1998), 'Constructing Interlanguage: Building a Composite Matrix Language', *Linguistics*, 36: 333–82.

—— and MYERS-SCOTTON, CAROL (1997*a*), 'Codeswitching and Compromise Strategies: Implications for Lexical Structure', *International Journal of Bilingualism*, 1: 25–39.

—— —— (1997*b*), 'Relating Interlanguage to Codeswitching: The Composite Matrix Language', *Proceedings of Boston University Conference on Language Development*, 21: 319–30.

—— —— (2001), 'Constraints in Bilingual Speech: You Can't Just Say What You Want to Say', Paper presented NWAV30 (New Ways of analyzing Variation) annual conference, Raleigh NC, 10/01.

—— —— and GROSS, STEVEN (2002), 'Making a Minimalist Approach to Codeswitching Work: Adding the Matrix Language', *Bilingualism, Language and Cognition* 5, 1: 69–91.

JAKOBSON, ROMAN (1941), *Kindersprache, Aphasie und allgemeine Lautgesetze*. Uppsala: Almqvist & Wiksell.

JENKINS, REBECCA SUE (2000), 'Language Contact Phenomena in New Ireland'. Ph.D., Columbia, SC: Univ. of South Carolina.

JOHANSON, LARS (1999), 'Frame-Changing Code-Copying in Immigrant Varieties', in Extra and Verhoeven (1999), 247–60.

JONES-JACKSON, PATRICIA A. (1978), 'Gullah: on the Question of Afro-American Language', *Anthropological Linguistics*, 20: 422–9.

JORDENS, PETER, DE BOT, KEES, and TRAPMAN, HENK (1989), 'Linguistic Aspects of Regression in German Case Marking', *Studies in Second Language Acquisition*, 11: 179–204.

JOSEPH, BRIAN D. (1983), *The Synchrony and Diachrony of the Balkan Infinitive. A Study in Areal, General, and Historical Linguistics*. Cambridge: Cambridge Univ. Press.

JOSHI, ARAVIND (1985), 'Processing of Sentences with Intrasentential Code Switching', in D. R. Dowty, L. Karttunen, and A. Zwicky (eds.), *Natural Language Parsing*, 190–205. Cambridge: Cambridge Univ. Press.

KAMWANGAMALU, NKONKO M. (1987), 'French/Vernacular Code Mixing in Zaire: Implications for Syntactic Constraints on Code Mixing', in *Chicago Linguistic Society Proceedings* 22, B. Need, E. Schiller, and A. Bosh (eds.), 166–80. Chicago: University of Chicago Linguistics Department.

—— (1989), 'Theory and Method of Code-Mixing: A Cross-Linguistic Study'. Ph.D., Univ. of Illinois, Urbana.

KAUFMAN, DORIT, and ARONOFF, MARK (1991), 'Morphological Disintegration and Reconstruction in First Language Attrition', in Seliger and Vago (1991), 175–88.

KLAVANS, JUDITH L. (1983), 'The Syntax of Code-Switching: Spanish and English'. *Selected Papers from the 13th Linguistic Symposium on Romance Language* 14, 213–32. Amsterdam: Benjamins.

KLEIN, WOLFGANG (1993), 'The Acquisition of Temporality', in Clive Perdue (ed.), *Adult Language Acquisition: Cross-Linguistic Perspectives II*, 73–118. Cambridge: Cambridge University Press.

KLINTBORG, STAFFAN (1999), *The Transience of American Swedish*. Lund: Lund Univ. Press.

KOUWENBERG, SYLVIA (1994), *A Grammar of Berbice Dutch*. Berlin: Mouton.

KRAVIN, HANNE (1992), 'Erosion of a Language in Bilingual Development', *Journal of Multilingual and Multicultural Development*, 13: 307–25.

KUHBERG, HEINZ (1992), 'Longitudinal L2-Attrition versus L2-Acquisition, in Three Turkish Children—Empirical Findings', *Second Language Research*, 8/2: 138–54.

Kulick, Don (1992), *Language Shift and Cultural Reproduction: Socialization, Syncretism and Self in a Papua New Guinean Village.* Cambridge: Cambridge Univ. Press.

Lahlou, Moncef (1991), 'A Morpho-Syntactic Study of Code Switching between Moroccan Arabic and French'. Ph.D., Austin: University of Texas-Austin.

Lambert, Richard D. (1989), 'Language Attrition', *Review of Applied Linguistics*, 83–4: 1–18.

—— and Freed, Barbara F. (eds.) (1982), *The Loss of Language Skills.* Rowley, MA: Newbury House.

Lambert, Wallace (1967), 'A Social Psychology of Bilingualism', *Journal of Social Issues*, 23: 91–109.

Lambert, William E. (1975), 'Measurement of the Linguistic Dominance of Bilinguals', *Journal of Abnormal and Social Psychology*, 50: 197–200.

Landry, Rodrigue, and Allard, Réal (1992), 'Ethnolinguistic Vitality and the Bilingual Development of Minority and Majority Group Students', in W. Fase, K. Jaspaert, and S. Kroon (eds.), *Maintenance and Loss of Minority Languages*, 223–51. Amsterdam: Benjamins.

———— (1994), 'Ethnolinguistic Vitality: A Viable Construct', *International Journal of the Sociology of Language*, 108: 5–13.

Langacker, Ronald W. (1987), *Foundations of Cognitive Grammar*, vol. I, *Theoretical Prerequisites.* Stanford, CA: Stanford Univ. Press.

Lanza, Elizabeth (1997), *Language Mixing in Infant Bilingualism.* Oxford: Oxford Univ. Press.

Lefebvre, Claire (1996), 'The Tense, Mood, and Aspect System of Haitian Creole and the Problem of Transmission of Grammar in Creole Genesis', *Journal of Pidgin and Creole Languages*, 12: 231–312.

—— (1998), *Creole Genesis and the Acquistion of Grammar.* Cambridge: Cambridge Univ. Press.

—— (2001), 'The Interplay of Relexification and Leveling in Creole Genesis and Development', *Linguistics*, 39: 371–408.

LePage, Robert, and Tabouret-Keller, Andrée (1985), *Acts of Identity: Creole-Based Approaches to Language and Ethnicity.* Cambridge: Cambridge Univ. Press.

Levelt, Willem J. M. (1989), *Speaking: From Intention to Articulation.* Cambridge, MA: MIT Press.

Li, Wei (1998), 'The "Why" and "How" Questions in the Analysis of Conversational Code-Switching', in P. Auer (1998*b*), 76–98.

—— (ed.) (2000), *The Bilingualism Reader.* London: Routledge.

Lieberson, Stanley (1982), 'Forces Affecting Language Spread: Some Basic Propositions', in Robert L. Cooper (ed.), *Language Spread: Studies in Diffusion and Social Change*, 37–62. Bloomington: Indiana Univ. Press.

Lipski, John (1987), 'Language Contact Phenomena in Louisiana Isleño Spanish', *American Speech*, 62: 320–31.

Lumsden, John (1999*a*), 'Language Acquisition and Creolization', in DeGraff (1999*a*), 129–58.

—— (1999*b*), 'The Role of Relexification in Creole Genesis', *Journal of Pidgin and Creole Languages*, 14: 225–58.

Maandi, Katrin (1989), 'Estonian among Immigrants in Sweden', in Dorian (1989), 227–42. Cambridge: Cambridge Univ. Press.

MACKEY, WILLIAM (2003), 'Bilingualism and Multilingualism', to appear in Ulrich Ammon, Norbert Dittmar, and Klaus J. Mattheier (eds.), *Sociolinguistics/Soziolinguistik* (second edition). Berlin: Walter de Gruyter.

MACSWAN, JEFF (1999), *A Minimalist Approach to Intrasentential Code Switching: Spanish–Nahuatl Bilingualism in Central Mexico.* New York: Garland.

——(2000), 'The Architecture of the Bilingual Language Faculty: Evidence from Intrasentential Code Switching. *Bilingualism, Language and Cognition*, 3: 37–54.

MAHOOTIAN, SHAHRZAD (1993), 'A Null Theory of Codeswitching'. Ph.D., Evanston, IL: Northwestern University.

—— and SANTORINI, BEATRICE (1996), 'Remarks on the Functional Head Constraint', *Linguistic Inquiry*, 27/3: 464–79.

MASICA, COLIN P. (1976), *Defining a Linguistic Area: South Asia.* Chicago: The Univ. of Chicago Press.

MATHER, PATRICK-ANDRE (2001), 'Review of John Holm (2000), *An Introduction to Pidgins and Creoles.* Cambridge Univ. Press'. Published on Linguist List, April 2001.

MATRAS, YARON (2000*a*), 'Mixed Languages: A Functional-Communicative Approach', *Bilingualism, Language and Cognition*, 3: 79–99.

——(2000*b*), 'Re-examining the Structural Prototype', paper presented at Workshop on Mixed Languages, University of Manchester, 12/2000.

MCWHORTER, JOHN H. (1992), 'Substratal Influence in Saramaccan Serial Verb Constructions', *Journal of Pidgin and Creole Languages*, 7: 1–53.

——(1995), 'Sisters under the Skin: A Case for Genetic Relationship between the Atlantic English-Based Creoles', *Journal of Pidgin and Creole Languages*, 10: 289–333.

——(1998), 'Identifying the Creole Prototype: Vindicating a Typological Class', *Language*, 74: 788–818.

MEECHAN, MARJORY, and POPLACK, SHANA (1995), 'Orphan Categories in Bilingual Discourse: Adjectivization Strategies in Wolof-French and Fongbe-French', *Language Variation and Change*, 7: 169–94.

MEEUWIS, MICHAEL, and BLOMMAERT, JAN (1998), 'A Monolectal View of Code-Switching: Layered Code-Switching among Zairians in Belgium', in Auer (1998*b*), *Code-Switching in Conversation*, 76–98. London: Routledge.

MEILLET, ANTOINE (1921), *Linguistique historique et linguistique générale.* Paris: Collection linguistique publiée par la Société de Linguistique de Paris, 8.

MENOVŠČIKOV, GEORGIJ A. (1969), 'O nekotoryx social'nyx aspektax évoljucii jazyka'. *Voprosy social'noj lingvistiki*, 110–34. Leningrad: Nauka.

MILIAN, SILVIA (1996), Spanish/English codeswitching data.

MITHUN, MARIANNE (1990), 'Language Obsolescence and Grammatical Description', *International Journal of American Linguistics*, 56: 1–26.

MORAIS, ELAINE (1998), 'Language Choice in a Malaysian Car-Assembly Plant', *International Journal of the Sociology of Language*, 130: 89–105.

MORALES, AMPARAO (2000), '¿Simplificación o interferencia?: el español de Puerto Rico', *International Journal of the Sociology of Language*, 142: 35–62.

MOUGEON, RAYMOND, and BENIAK, ÉDOUARD (1991), *Linguistic Consequences of Language Contact and Restriction.* Oxford: Clarendon Press.

MOUS, MAARTEN (1993), field notes.

——(1994), 'Ma'a or Mbugu', in Bakker and Mous (1994), 175–200.
——(2001), 'Ma'a as an Ethno-Register of Mbugu', *Sprache und Geschichte in Afrika* (SUGIA), 16/17: 253–320.
——(forthcoming), 'The Linguistic Properties of Lexical Manipulation and Its Relevance for Ma'a and for Mixed Languages in General', to appear in Peter Bakker and Yaron Matras (eds.), *The Mixed Languages Debate*. Berlin: Mouton de Gruyter.
MUFWENE, SALIKOKO (1986), 'The Universal and Substrate Hypotheses Complement One Another', in Muysken and Smith (1986), 129–62.
——(1996), 'The Founder Principle in Creole Genesis', *Diachronica*, 13: 83–134.
MÜHLHÄUSLER, PETER (1986), *Pidgin and Creole Linguistics*. Oxford: Blackwell.
MUSTAFA, ZAHRA, and AL-KHATIB, MAHMOUD (1994), 'Code-Mixing of Arabic and English in Teaching Science', *World Englishes*, 13: 215–24.
MUYSKEN, PIETER (1981), 'Halfway between Quechua and Spanish: The Case for Relexification', in Arnold Highfield and Albert Valdman (eds.), *Historicity and Variation in Creole Studies*, 52–78. Ann Arbor: Karoma.
——(1994), 'Media Lengua', in Bakker and Mous (1994), 207–11.
——(1995), 'Code-Switching and Grammatical Theory', in Lesley Milroy and Pieter Muysken (eds.), *One Speaker, Two Languages*, 177–98. Cambridge: Cambridge Univ. Press.
——(1996), 'Syntax', in Goebl *et al.* (1996), 117–24.
——(1997), 'Code-Switching Processes: Alternation, Insertion, Congruent Lexicalization', in Martin Pütz (ed.), *Language Choices, Conditions, Constraints, and Consequences*, 361–80. Amsterdam: Benjamins.
——(1998), 'How to Slice the Cake?', *Bilingualism, Language and Cognition*, 1: 31.
——(2000), *Bilingual Speech: A Typology of Code-Mixing*. Cambridge Univ. Press.
——, and SMITH, NORVAL (eds.) (1986), *Substrata versus Universals in Creole Genesis*. Amsterdam: Benjamins.
——(1995), 'The Study of Pidgin and Creole Languages', in Arends, Muysken, and Smith (1995), 3–14.
MYERS-SCOTTON, CAROL (1976), 'Strategies of Neutrality: Language Choice in Uncertain Situations', *Language*, 52: 919–41.
——(1988), Swahili/English Nairobi corpus.
——(1992), 'Codeswitching as a Mechanism in Deep Borrowing, Language Shift, and Language Death', in Matthias Brenzinger (ed.), *Language Death, Factual and Theoretical Explorations with Special Reference to East Africa*, 31–58. Berlin: Mouton de Gruyter.
——(1993*a* [1997]), *Duelling Languages: Grammatical Structure in Codeswitching* (1997 edition with a new Afterword). Oxford: Clarendon Press.
——(1993*b*), 'Elite Closure as a Powerful Language Strategy: The African Case', *International Journal of the Sociology of Language*, 103: 149–63.
——(1993*c*), *Social Motivation for Codeswitching: Evidence from Africa*. Oxford: Clarendon Press.
——(1997): see Myers-Scotton (1993*a*).
——(1998*a*), 'A Way to Dusty Death: The Matrix Language Turnover Hypothesis', in Lenore Grenoble and Lindsay Whaley (eds.), *Endangered Languages: Language Loss and Community Response*, 289–316. Cambridge: Cambridge Univ. Press.

MYERS-SCOTTON, CAROL (1998*b*), 'A Theoretical Introduction to the Markedness Model', in Carol Myers-Scotton (ed.), *Codes and Consequences, Choosing Linguistic Varieties*, 18–38. New York: Oxford Univ. Press.

——(2001*a*), 'The Matrix Language Frame Model: Developments and Responses', in Rodolfo Jacobson (ed.), *Codeswitching Worldwide II*, 23–58. Berlin: Mouton de Gruyter.

——(2001*b*), 'Implications of Abstract Grammatical Structure: Two Targets in Creole Formation', *Journal of Pidgin and Creole Languages*, 16.

—— and BERNSTEN, JANICE (1995), Acholi/English corpus.

—— and BOLONYAI, AGNES (2001), 'Calculating Speakers: Codeswitching in a Rational Choice Model', *Language in Society*, 31/1: 1–28.

—— and JAKE, JANICE (1995), 'Matching Lemmas in a Bilingual Language Production Model: Evidence from Intrasentential Codeswitcing', *Linguistics*, 33: 981–1024.

————(1999*a*), 'Chichewa/English Codeswitching: The "do" Verb Construction', in Rosalie Finlayson (ed.), *African Mosaic*, 406–17. Pretoria: Univ. of South Africa Press.

————(1999*b*), 'Giving Structure to Creoles', paper presented at Annual Conference on Pidgin and Creole Language, Los Angeles, Jan. 8–9.

————(2000*a*), 'Four Types of Morpheme: Evidence from Aphasia, Codeswitching, and Second Language Acquisition', *Linguistics*, 38: 6, 1053–100.

————(eds.) (2000*b*), 'Testing a Model of Morpheme Classification with Language Contact Data', *International Journal of Bilingualism*, 4/1 (special issue).

————(2001), 'Explaining Aspects of Codeswitching and Their Implications', in Janet Nicol (ed.), *One Mind, Two Languages: Bilingual Language Processing*, 84–116. Oxford: Blackwell.

———— and OKASHA, MAHA (1996), 'Arabic and Constraints on Codeswitching', in Mushira Eid and Dilworth Parkinson (eds.), *Perspectives on Arabic Linguistics IX*, 9–43. Amsterdam: Benjamins.

(MYERS)-SCOTTON, CAROL, and URY, WILLIAM (1977), 'Bilingual Strategies: the Social Function of Code-Switching', *International Journal of the Sociology of Language*, 13: 5–20.

NARTEY, JONAS (1982), 'Code-Switching, Interference or Faddism? Language Use among Educated Ghanaians', *Anthropological Linguistics*, 24/2: 183–92.

NELDE, PETER (1997), 'Language Conflict', in Florian Coulmas (ed.), *Handbook of Sociolinguistics*, 285–300. Oxford: Blackwell.

NICHOLS, JOHANNA (1992), *Linguistic Diversity in Space and Time*. Chicago: Chicago Univ. Press.

NOONAN, MICHAEL (1992), *A Grammar of Lango*. Berlin: Mouton de Gruyter.

NORTIER, JACOMINE (1990), *Dutch–Moroccan Arabic Codeswitching among Moroccans in the Netherlands*. Dordrecht: Foris.

——(1995), 'Code Switching in Moroccan Arabic/Dutch vs. Moroccan/Arabic/French Language Contact', *International Journal of the Sociology of Language*, 112: 81–95.

OBONDO, MARGARET AKINYI (1996), *From Trilinguals to Bilinguals?* Stockholm: Stockholm Univ. Center for Research on Bilingualism.

OKASHA, MAHA (1995), Arabic/English codeswitching corpus. Unpublished.

——(1999), 'Structural Constraints on Arabic–English Codeswitching: Two Generations'. Ph.D., Columbia, SC: University of South Carolina.

OLSHTAIN, ELITE (1989), 'Is Second Language Attrition the Reverse of Second Language Acquisition?', *Studies in Second Language Acquisition*, 11: 151–65.

Otheguy, Ricardo, Garcia, Ofelia, and Fernandez, Mariela (1989), 'Transferring, Switching, and Modeling in West New York Spanish: An Intergenerational Study', *International Journal of the Sociology of Language*, 79: 41–52.

Pan, Barbara Alexander, and Berko-Gleason, Jean (1986), 'The Study of Language Loss: Models and Hypotheses for an Emerging Discipline', *Applied Psycholinguistics*, 7: 193–206.

Paradis, Johanne, Nicoladis, Elena, and Genesee, Fred (2000), 'Early Emergence of Structural Constraints on Code-Mixing: Evidence from French–English Bilingual Children', *Bilingualism, Language and Cognition*, 3: 245–61.

Park, K. S. (2000), 'Korean–Swedish Code-Switching: Theoretical Models and Linguistic Reality'. Ph.D., Uppsala Universitet: Institutionen för Nordiska Språk.

Paulston, Christina Bratt (1994), *Linguistic Minorities in Multilingual Settings.* Amsterdam: Benjamins.

Pfaff, Carol (1979), 'Constraints on Language Mixing: Intrasentential Code-Switching and Borrowing in Spanish/English', *Language*, 55: 291–318.

——(1991), 'Turkish in Contact with German: Language Maintenance and Loss among Immigrant Children in Berlin (West)', *International Journal of the Sociology of Language*, 90: 97–129.

——(1994*a*), 'Toward an Integrated Approach to the Development of Morphosyntactic and Communicative Competence: The Turkish of Bilingual Children in Germany, Part 1', *Dil Dergisi / Language Journal*, 20: 22–9.

——(1994*b*), 'Toward an Integrated Approach to the Development of Morphosyntactic and Communicative Competence: The Turkish of Bilingual Children in Germany, Part 2', *Dil Dergisi / Language Journal*, 21: 43–56.

Pinker, Steven (1989), *Learnability and Cognition: The Acquisition of Argument Structure.* Cambridge, MA: MIT Press.

Polinsky, Maria (1995), 'Cross-Linguistic Parallels in Language Loss', *Southwest Journal of Linguistics*, 14/1 and 2: 87–123.

——(1997), 'American Russian: Language Loss Meets Language Acquisition', in Wayles Browne, Ewa Dornisch, Natatsha Khondrashova, and Draga Zec (eds.), *Annual Workshop on Formal Approaches to Slavic Linguistics*, 370–406.

——(forthcoming), 'American Russian: An Endangered Language?', to appear in Eugene Golovko (ed.), *Russian in Contact with Other Languages.* Amsterdam: Benjamins.

Poplack, Shana (1980), 'Sometimes I'll Start a Sentence in Spanish y termino español: Toward a Typology of Code-Switching', *Linguistics*, 18: 581–618.

——(1987), 'Contrasting Patterns of Code-switching in Two Communities', in Erling Wande, Jan Anward, Bengt Nordberg, Lars Steensland and Mats Thelander (eds.), *Aspects of Multilingualism*, 51–77. Upsala, Sweden: Bortströms.

——(1988), 'Language Status and Language Accommodation along a Linguistic Border', in Peter H. Lowenberg (ed.), *Language Spread and Language Policy*, 90–118. Washington, DC: Georgetown Univ. Press.

——(1997), 'The Social Linguistic Dynamics of Apparent Convergence', in G. Guy, C. Feagin, D. Schriffrin, and J. Baugh (eds.), *Towards a Social Science of Language*, vol. II, 285–309. Amsterdam: Benjamins.

—— and Meechan, Marjory (1998), 'How Languages Fit Together in Codemixing', *International Journal of Bilingualism*, 2: 127–38.

POPLACK, SHANA, SANKOFF, DAVID, and MILLER, CHRISTOPHER (1988), 'The Social Correlates and Linguistic Processes of Lexical Borrowing and Assimilation', *Linguistics*, 26: 47–104.

PRESTON, DENNIS (1982), 'How to Lose a Language', *Interlanguage Studies Bulletin*, 6/2: 64–87.

——(1986), 'The Case of American Polish', in Dieter Kastovsky and Aleksander Szwedek (eds.), *Linguistics across Historical and Geographical Boundaries (vol. 2: Descriptive, Contrastive and Applied Linguistics)*, 1015–23. Berlin: Mouton de Gruyter.

—— and TURNER, MICHAEL (1984), 'The Polish of Western New York: Case', *Melbourne Slavic Studies*, 18: 135–54.

PY, BERNARD (1986), 'Native Language Attrition amongst Migrant Workers: Towards an Extension of the Concept of Interlanguage', in M. Sharwood Smith and E. Kellerman (eds.), *Crosslinguistic Influence in Second Language Acquisition*, 163–72. New York and Oxford: Pergamon Press.

RAPPAPORT, MALKA, and LEVIN, BETH (1988), 'What to Do with Ø Roles', in W. Wilkins (ed.), *Syntax and Semantics: Thematic Relations*, 7–36. New York: Academic Press.

RAYFIELD, JOAN RACHEL (1970), *The Language of a Bilingual Community*. The Hague: Mouton.

RHODES, RICHARD (1977), 'French Cree—A Case of Borrowing', in William Cowan (ed.), *Actes du 8ème Congrès des Algonquistes*, 6–25. Ottawa: Carleton University.

RICHARDSON, IRVINE (1963), 'Evolutionary Factors in Mauritian Creole', *Journal of African Languages*, 2, part 1: 2–14.

RICKFORD, JOHN R. (1987), *Dimensions of a Creole Continuum*. Stanford, CA: Stanford Univ. Press.

RITCHIE, WILLIAM, and BHATIA, TEJ (1999), 'Codeswitching, Grammar and Sentence Production: The Problem of Light Verbs', in *The Development of Second Language Grammars*, Elaine. C. Klein and G. Martoharjono (eds.), 269–87.

ROBERTS, MURAT H. (1939), 'The Problem of the Hybrid Language', *Journal of English and German Philosophy*, 38: 23–41.

ROEPER, THOMAS (1999), 'Universal Bilingualism', *Bilingualism, Language and Cognition*, 2/3: 169–86.

ROMAINE, SUZANNE (1988), *Pidgin and Creole Languages*. New York: Longman.

——(1989 [1995]), *Bilingualism* (second edition). Oxford: Blackwell.

ROWLANDS, E. C. (1969), *Teach Yourself Yoruba*. London: English Univ. Press.

RYAN, ELEN B., and GILES, HOWARD (1982), 'An Integrative Perspective for the Study of Attitudes toward Language Variation', in E. Ryan and H. Giles (eds.), *Attitudes toward Language Variation*, 1–19. London: Arnold.

SANKOFF, DAVID (1998), 'A Formal Production-Based Explanation of the Facts of Code-Switching', *Bilingualism, Language and Cognition*, 1: 39–50.

——, POPLACK, SHANA, and VANNIARAJAN, S. (1990), 'The Case of the Nonce Loan in Tamil', *Language Variation and Change*, 2: 71–101.

SANTORINI, BEATRICE, and MAHOOTIAN, SHAHRZAD (1995), 'Code-Switching and the Syntactic Status of Adnominal Adjectives', *Lingua*, 96: 1–27.

SARULLO, PAOLA RUSTICI (1998), ' The Linguistic Situation in Valle D'Aosta: A Study on the Function and the Structure of Codeswitching and Convergence between Italian and French'. Ph.D., Columbia, SC: Univ. of South Carolina.

SASSE, HANS-JÜRGEN (1991), *Arvanitika. Die alganischen Sprachreste in Griechenland*. Part 1. Wiesbaden: Harrassowitz.

——(1992), 'Theory of Language Death', in Brenzinger (1992), 7–30.

SAVIČ, JELENA (1995), 'Structural Convergence and Language Change: Evidence from Serbian/English Code-Switching', *Language in Society*, 24: 475–92.

SAVILLE-TROIKE, MURIEL, PAN, JUNLIN, and DUTKOVA, LUDMILA (1995), 'Differential Effects of L2 on Children's L1 Development/Attrition', *Southwest Journal of Linguistics*, 14: 125–49.

SCHMID, MONIKA S. (2001), 'First Language Attrition: The Methodology Revised', submitted for publication.

SCHMITT, ELENA (2000), 'Overt and Covert Codeswitching in Immigrant Children from Russia', *International Journal of Bilingualism*, 4: 9–28.

——(2001), 'Beneath the Surface: Signs of Language Attrition in Immigrant Children from Russia'. Ph.D., Columbia, SC: Univ. of South Carolina.

SEBBA, MARK (1987), *The Syntax of Serial Verbs*. Amsterdam: Benjamins.

SELIGER, HERBERT W. (1996), 'Primary Language Attrition in the Context of Bilingualism', in William C. Ritchie and Tej K. Bhatia (eds.), *Handbook of Second Language Acquisition*, 605–26. San Diego: Academic Press.

—— and VAGO, ROBERT M. (eds.) (1991), *First Language Attrition*. Cambridge: Cambridge Univ. Press.

SHARWOOD SMITH, MICHAEL (1983), 'On First Language Loss in the Second Language Acquirer: Problems of Transfer', in Susan Gass and Larry Selinker (eds.), *Language Transfer in Language Learning*, 222–31. Rowley, MA: Newbury House.

—— and KELLERMAN, ERIC (1986), 'Crosslinguistic Influence in Second Language Acquisition: An Introduction', in M. Sharwood Smith and E. Kellerman (eds.), *Crosslinguistic Influence in Second Language Acquisition*, 1–9. New York and Oxford: Pergamon Press.

SHERZER, JOEL (1976), *An Areal-Typological Study of American Indian Languages North of Mexico*. Amsterdam: North-Holland.

SIEGEL, JEFFREY (1999), 'Transfer Constraints and Substrate Influence in Melanesian Pidgin', *Journal of Pidgin and Creole Languages*, 14: 1–44.

——(2000), 'Substrate Influence in Hawai'i Creole English', *Language in Society*, 29: 197–236.

SILVA-CORVALÁN, CARMEN (1994*a*), *Language Contact and Change: Spanish in Los Angeles*. Oxford: Clarendon Press.

——(1994*b*), 'The Gradual Loss of Mood Distinctions in Los Angeles Spanish', *Language Variation and Change*, 6: 255–72.

SIMANGO, SYLVESTER RON (1995), Chicheŵa/English codeswitching corpus.

——(2000), '"My madam is fine": The Adaption of English Loans in Chicheŵa', *Journal of Multilingual and Multicultural Devleopment*, 21: 487–507.

SINGLER, JOHN (ed.) (1990), *Pidgin and Creole Tense–Mood–Aspect Systems*. Amsterdam: Benjamins.

——(1996), 'Theories of Creole Genesis, Sociohistorical Consideration, and the Evaluation of Evidence: The Case of Haitian Creole and the Relexification Hypothesis', *Journal of Pidgin and Creole Languages*, 11: 185–230.

SKAADEN, HANNE (1999), 'In Short Supply of Language: Signs of First Language Attrition in the Speech of Adult Migrants'. Ph.D., Oslo, Norway: Univ. of Oslo.

SLABBERT, SARAH, and MYERS-SCOTTON, CAROL (1997), 'The Structure of Tsotsitaal and Iscamtho: Code Switching and In-group Identity in South African Townships', *Linguistics*, 35: 317–42.

SLATER, KEITH W. (forthcoming), *Mangghuer: A Mongolic Language of China's Qinghai-Gansu Sprachbund.* London: Curzon.

SMOLICZ, JERZY J. (1981), 'Language as a Core Value of Culture', *RELC Journal*, 11: 1–13.

SORENSEN, A. P. (1972), 'Multilingualism in the Northwest Amazon', in John B. Pride, and Janet Holmes (eds.), *Sociolinguistics*, 78–93. Harmondsworth, Middlesex: Penguin Books.

SRIDHAR, S. N., and SRIDHAR, K. (1980), 'The Syntax and Psycholinguistics of Bilingual Code-Mixing', *Canadian Journal of Psychology*, 34: 407–16.

STEMBERGER, JOSEPH P. (1985*a*), *The Lexicon in a Model of Language Production.* New York: Garland.

——(1985*b*), 'An Interactive Activation Model of Language Production', in A. Ellis (ed.), *Progress in the Psychology of Language*, vol. I, 143–86. London: Erlbaum.

STENSON, NANCY (1990), 'Phrase Structure Congruence, Government, and Irish–English Code-Switching', in Randall Hendrick (ed.), *Syntax and Semantics: The Syntax of the Modern Celtic Languages* (Syntax and semantics series, vol. 23), 167–97. New York: Academic Press.

SWAMY, GOPAL (1985), *Growth of the World's Urban and Rural Population, 1920–2000.*

SWIGART, LEIGH (1992), 'Practice and Perception: Language Use and Attitudes in Dakar'. Ph.D., Seattle: University of Washington.

SYLVAIN, S. (1936), *Le Créole haïtien: morphologie et syntaxe.* Wetteren, Belgium: Imprimerie De Meester/Port-au-Prince: by the author.

TALMY, LEONARD (1985), 'Lexicalization Patterns: Semantic Structure in Lexical Forms', in Timothy Shopen (ed.), *Language Typology and Syntactic Description*, 57–149. Cambridge: Cambridge Univ. Press.

——(2000), *Toward a Cognitive Semantics*, vol I. Cambridge, MA: MIT Press.

TANDEFELT, MARIKA (1992), 'Some Linguistic Consequences of the Shift from Swedish to Finnish in Finland', in Willem Fase, Koen Jaspaert, and Sjaak Kroon (eds.), *Maintenance and Loss of Minority Languages*, 149–68. Amsterdam: Benjamins.

THOMASON, SARAH (1983), 'Genetic Relationship and the Case of Ma'a (Mbugu)', *Studies in African Linguistics*, 14/2: 195–231.

——(ed.) (1997*a*), *Contact Languages: A Wider Perspective.* Amsterdam: Benjamins.

——(1997*b*), 'Ma'a (Mbugu)', in Thomason (1997*a*), 468–87.

——(1997*c*), 'Mednyj Aleut', in Thomason (1997*a*), 449–68.

——(1997*d*), 'On Mechanisms of Interference', in Stig Eliasson and Ernst Håkon Jahr (eds.), *Language and Its Ecology*, 181–207. Berlin: Mouton de Gruyter.

——(2000), *Contact Languages: An Introduction.* Washington, DC: Georgetown University Press.

—— and KAUFMAN, TERRENCE (1988), *Language Contact, Creolization, and Genetic Linguistics.* Berkeley, CA: Univ. of California Press.

TIMM, LENORA (1975), 'Spanish–English Code-Switching: *El porque y how-not-to*', *Romance Philology*, 28: 473–82.

TORIBIO, ALMEDIA J., and RUBIN, EDWARD J. (1996), 'Code-Switching in Generative Grammar', in A. Roca and J. B. Jensen (eds.), *Spanish in Contact: Issues in Bilingualism*, 203–26. Somerville, MA: Cascadilla Press.

TREFFERS-DALLER, JEANINE (1994), *Mixing Two Languages: French–Dutch Contact in a Comparative Perspective.* Berlin: Mouton de Gruyter.

——(1999), 'Borrowing and Shift-Induced Interference: Contrasting Patterns in French–Germanic Contact in Brussels and Strasbourg', *Bilingualism, Language and Cognition*, 2: 1–22.

TÜRKER, EMEL (2000), 'Turkish–Norwegian Codeswitching: Evidence for Intermediate and Second Generation Turkish Immigrants in Norway'. Ph.D., Oslo: University of Oslo.

TURNER, LORENZO (1949[1969]), *Africanisms in the Gullah Dialect.* New York: Arno Press and the *New York Times.*

ULLMAN, MICHAEL T. (2001), 'The Neural Basis of Lexicon and Grammar in First and Second Language: The Declarative/Procedural Model'. *Bilingualism, Language and Cognition*, 4: 105–22.

VAKHTIN, NIKOLAI (1998), 'Copper Island Aleut: A Case of Language "Resurrection"', in Lenore A. Grenoble and Lindsay J. Whaley (eds.), *Endangered Languages*, 317–27. Cambridge: Cambridge Univ. Press.

VERHOEVEN, LUDO, and BOESCHOTEN, HENDRIK E. (1986), 'First Language Acquisition in a Second Language Submersion Environment', *Applied Psycholinguistics*, 7: 241–56.

WEI, LONGXING (1996), 'Variation in the Acquisition of Morpheme Types in the Interlanguage of Chinese and Japanese Learners of English as a Second Language'. Ph.D., Columbia, SC: Univ. of South Carolina.

——(1998), Chinese/English codeswitching corpus. Unpublished.

——(2000*a*), 'Unequal Election of Morphemes in Adult Second Language Acquisition', *Applied Linguistics*, 21/1: 106–40.

——(2000*b*), 'Types of Morphemes and Their Implications for Second Language Morpheme Acquisition', *International Journal of Bilingualism*, 4/1: 29–43.

WEINREICH, URIEL (1967), *Languages in Contact.* The Hague: Mouton. (Originally published in 1953, Publications of the Linguistic Circle of New York, 1.)

WEINSTEIN, BRIAN (1983), *The Civic Tongue: Political Consequences of Language Choices.* New York, London: Longman.

WELTENS, BERT, and COHEN, ANDREW (1989), 'Language Attrition Research: An Introduction', *Studies in Second Language Acquisition*, 11: 127–33.

——, DE BOT, KEES, and VAN ELS, THEO (eds.) (1986), *Language Attrition in Progress.* Dordrecht, Holland: Foris Publications.

WHITELEY, WILFRED (1960), 'Linguistic Hybrids', *African Studies*, 19: 95–7.

WILLIAMS, EDWIN (1994), *Thematic Structure in Syntax.* Cambridge, MA: MIT Press.

WILSON, DEIRDRE, and SPERBER, DAN (1993), 'Linguistic Form and Relevance', *Lingua*, 90: 1–25.

WINFORD, DONALD (1993), *Predication in Caribbean English Creoles.* Amsterdam: Benjamins.

WOOLFORD, ELLEN (1983), 'Bilingual Code-Switching and Syntactic Theory', *Linguistic Inquiry*, 14: 520–36.

ZENTELLA, ANA (1997), *Growing Up Bilingual.* Oxford: Blackwell.

ZHU, YONGZHONG, CHULUU, ÜJIYDIIN, SLATER, KEITH, and STUART, KEVIN (1997), 'Gangou Chinese Dialect', *Anthropos*, 92: 433–50.

Substantive Index

4-M model 16–18, 73–86, 168–9
  abstract oppositions 73–4
  defined 17–18, 73
  diagram of classification 73
  empirical distributions as motivation 74
  examples of morpheme type 18, 78–82
  explaining double morphology 91–2
  explaining speech errors 82
  hypotheses about production as motivation 76–8
  hypotheses depending on model 298–309
  lexicosyntactic properties as motivation 74–5
  morpheme types reviewed 194, 299–305
  non-finite forms in codeswitching 92–5
  related classification 86
  relation to activation levels 77
  summarized 106
  wide applications 85
  see also attrition; codeswitching; convergence; creoles; split languages
Abstract Level model 18–21, 168
  congruence checking, *see* asymmetry; congruence
  hierarchy model (implied) 196, 231, 307
  related to classic codeswitching 97
  related to convergence, composite codeswitching 99–100
  splitting and recombining levels 99
  summarized 106, 307
  three levels of abstract structure 96, 194
  value for predicting attrition 195, 205
  see also attrition
activation levels 155–6
  see also codeswitching; congruence; EL islands
Arabic articles and codeswitching 114–17, 119, 123–7
  French substitutes in Algerian Arabic/French codeswitching 115–16
  missing in Moroccan Arabic/Dutch codeswitching 113–15
asymmetry 15, 109, 164, 178, 296–7
  asymmetry principle 9
  role in convergence 101
  see also Differential Access Hypothesis; Matrix Language–Embedded language opposition; System Morpheme Principle
attrition 164, 172
  Anderson's hypotheses 189–90
  case in adults 217–22
  case in children 223–8
  compared with convergence 164, 179, 229–30
  content morphemes 206–7, 216–17, 219
  early system morphemes 207–11, 226–7
  English bare nouns and composite matrix language 227–8
  functional explanations 193
  hierarchies, summaries 231
  hierarchy of abstract levels 196
  hierarchy of morpheme types 206, 229
  hypotheses of hierarchies based on abstract levels 196–205
  hypotheses of hierarchies based on morpheme type 206–29
  individual attrition followed by group shift 179
  Jakobson and regression hypothesis 188
  late system morphemes 212, 214, 216, 217
  markedness 190–2
  pro-drop parameter 201
  reasons for loss in advanced attrition 184
  Regression Hypothesis 187–8, 189
  research emphasis on words 178
  retention of late system morphemes 186–7, 231, 301
  social and psychological factors 178–9, 192–3
  studies, adults:
    Croatian in Australia 217–19
    East Sutherland Gaelic 213–16
    German 211–12, 216–17, 219–21, 222
    Other 220, 221
    Pennsylvania German 201
    Polish 222
    Russian 221–2
  studies, children:
    Hungarian 198–9, 204, 208, 225–6
    Other 182–3, 250–2
    Russian 197–8, 200–1, 203–4, 224–5, 227–8
    Turkish 223–4
  trends in literature 186–7
  typology of types 185
  word order 202–3, 210
  see also 4-M model; Abstract Level model

Bantu languages:
  'do' construction 135–6
  double morphology 92
  see also bare forms

bare forms 67
  Bantu bare nouns 127–32
  defined 113
  Dutch bare nouns 116–17, 124–5
bare nouns and attrition 227–8
  relevance of Uniform Structure Principle 129–31, 161
  see also Arabic articles and codeswitching, Bantu bare nouns
bilingual CP:
  defined as basic unit of analysis 8, 54–6
  examples 56–7
  no change of matrix language 64–6
bilingualism:
  allocation to domains 40, 43
  bilingual competence 33
  bilingual speech defined 7
  contrast with contact linguistics as subject 4–5
  costs to businesses, nations 34
  covert and overt awareness 1–4
  ethnolinguistic vitality 50–1
  how allocation matters 49–50
  individual or societal 30
  as instrumental asset 36–8
  language contact cycle 30
  macro-factors promoting 31–3
  motivations to become bilingual 36–40
  as political capital 35
  self-perception as a factor 38–40
  as symbolic capital 33–4
borrowing (lexical) 41–3, 234–45
  asymmetrical 238–9
  borrowing and interference (Thomason and Kaufman) 235–7, 245
  contrast with codeswitching 41
  cultural or core as types 41–2, 239–40, 299–300
  distinguished from new grammatical outcomes 242–4
  mechanisms involved 242–3
  morphosyntactic integration 42–3
  motivations 238, 243
  nonce borrowings 138, 155
  status in the mental lexicon 41
  Strasbourg, Brussels 237–8
borrowing vs. codeswitching 153–9, 162
  activation at issue 155–6
bound vs. free morphemes 72
bridge late system morphemes 75, 78
  issue of counter examples 91, 305
Broca's aphasia 72

Canada (French–English contact) 51, 170, 239–40
classic codeswitching:
  combined with 4-M model 86
  congruence checking with Abstract Level model 97
  defined 8, 105, 297
  under stable bilingualism 111
  see also Matrix Language Frame (MLF) model
closed and open class as unit of analysis 71
code mixing 3
  mixed languages 3, 246
  see also split languages
codeswitching:
  activation level 67, 92, 131, 140–1, 163
  adjacency as triggering 142–5
  as a subject 10
  asymmetry 53
  contextualization cue 45
  conversation analysis 45, 47
  emphasis on grammatical structure 12–13
  emphasis on inferential messages 11
  generational differences in patterns 161
  government and binding models 157–8
  Markedness Model 47
  Minimalist Program 158–60
  MLF model approach 13–16
  MLF model explicated 54–69
  neutrality strategy 47
  negotiation strategy 45
  proficiency required 110–11
  rational choice model 46–7
  relation to language loss or shift 165, 298
  sentence as analytic unit 55
  social motivations 10–11, 43–8
  theoretical basis for different models 162–3
  triggering 142
  typology of types 161
  the unmarked choice 45
  with convergence, mechanisms in other contact phenomena 105, 298
  see also Matrix Language (ML)
competence and performance 26–8, 105
  relation of compromise strategies 21
complementizers as heads 211–12
composite codeswitching:
  defined 8, 105, 297
  relation to language shift 298
composite Matrix Language 22, 228, 242, 307
  convergence and composite Matrix Language 99–105, 165–8
  presence in attrition 194–232
  retention of morpheme types 303
  related to creole development 277
  related to shift 184
  related to 'structural borrowing' 101, 242–4
  split languages 246–7
compromise strategies 21
  see also bare forms; congruence; 'do' constructions

conceptual level 24
conceptually activated elements 73–6
  see also 4-M model
congruence:
  checking in codeswitching 19–21, 97–100, 154
  checking with EL islands 140, 145–8
  checking with ML Generalized Lexical Knowledge 69, 130
  congruent lexicalization 97 n.6, 100, 163
  insufficient, sufficient congruence 97–8, 124–5, 136–7, 306
constituent, defined 7
contact linguistics:
  contact phenomena considered 4, 295
  contrast with bilingualism as a subject 5
  focus in this volume 5
  requirements for theories 193
  term used in sociopolitical conflicts 4
content morphemes:
  as heads 163
  assign/receive thematic roles 69–70
  directly elected morphemes 77
Control Agreement Principle 121
convergence 101, 164
  both mechanism and outcome 164
  community phenomenon 172
  compared with attrition 164, 179, 229–30
  competing definitions 169–73, 178, 230
  creolization 176
  defined 169–70, 297–8
  examples 102–4, 166–8
    involving lexical-conceptual structure 102
    involving morphological realization patterns 103
    involving predicate-argument structure 104
  mechanism for structural changes, new system morphemes 243–4
  resulting in composite Matrix Language 100
  waxing and waning process 101
convergence areas (Sprachbunde) 173–9
  Arnhem Land 176
  Balkans 174, 178
  Kupwar 175–6
  mechanisms 177–8
  Meso America 174
  morpheme types 174–5, 179
  Northeast China 174, 178
  Pacific Northwest 174
  South Asia 174
CP (projection of complementizer) 7
  as a bilingual CP 8, 56
  bilingual CP as mixed constituent 58
    examples 56–7
  defined 54–5
  unit of analysis 54, 55–6
creoles:
  composite matrix language 277, 293
  content morphemes 281–3
    reconfiguring 283–5, 308
  definitions and background 271–2
  early system morphemes 286–7, 309
  hypotheses summarized 308
  late system morphemes 288–9
  relevance of 4-M model 276
  relevance of Abstract Level model 276, 283
  role of Differential Access Hypothesis 276
  scenario for development 291–2
  structural history 274–5
  as subject 273–4
  substrate frame 277, 281
  two targets 272–3, 293

Dakar, Senegal 65, 118
Danish/German border, attrition 111
determiner complex:
  Arabic requirements 114
  figure 123
  scenarios 125–7
dialect levelling 290
Differential Access Hypothesis 17, 78, 301
diglossia 49
discourse markers 70, 239, 240–1
  opposition with system morphemes 15, 69–73
  Shona forms 142
  support in lemmas 75
  see also conceptually activated elements
'do' constructions 134–7, 161–2
  explanations for Turkish 136
  serial verbs 137
double morphology 91–3, 301

Early System Morpheme Hypothesis 92
early system morphemes 75, 77, 300
  codeswitching 91–3
  examples 78–9
  indirectly elected morphemes 77
elite closure 35–6
Embedded Language:
  adjectives 132–3
  distributions 72
  islands, *see* EL islands
  verbs 133–9
Embedded Language (EL) islands 67, 139–53
  activation 149, 152–3, 162
  defined 54, 139–40
  examples 139
  formulaic nature 141
  grammatical motivations 146–8
  internal EL islands 68, 115, 122 n.6, 149–52
  IP islands in Arabic/English codeswitching 61, 146

Embedded Language (EL) islands (*cont.*):
  pragmatic motivations 145
  proficiency levels 148–9
  quantifier in initial position 147–8
  recognizing 54 n.1
English nouns with Finnish as Matrix Language 126
ethnolinguistic vitality 50–1

FOOT features 121
Formulator 17–18, 99, 105, 147, 194, 288, 301
  activating late system morphemes 77
  place in production figure 24
frame requirements, changes 242–4, 306
  see also composite Matrix Language; Matrix Language turnover
French determiners:
  codeswitching with Arabic 115–16, 123–7
  codeswitching with Lingala 119
  codeswitching with Wolof 118, 126
  in creoles 118
functional element as unit of analysis 71–2

Generalized Lexical Knowledge 68–9, 97, 130–1, 137, 144
Generalized Phrase Structure Grammar (GPSG) 120–1

HEAD features 121, 130, 152

interference 171, 235–6

language loss 164, 179
language production model 23–4, 76–7
  figure 24
  feedback or not 99
  flexibility 67
  production feedback 99
language shift 48–52, 164, 179
  contact phenomena favoring 298
  definitions 179
  domain allocation 49
  ethnic salience 184
  ethnolinguistic vitality 50–1
  hierarchy 299
  psychological factors 49–50
  see also bilingualism
language spread 31–3
late system morphemes 75–6, 301–5
  examples 79–80
  later activation 77
  see also 4-M model; outsider late system morphemes
lemmas 14, 19, 76–7
  abstract entries in mental lexicon 24–5
  production figure 24
lexical borrowing, *see* borrowing
lexical-conceptual structure, examples 102
  early loss in attrition 196–200
lingua franca 32

Ma'a (Mbugu):
  background 265–6
  matrix language turnover 268–70
  relexification 270
  structure 266
markedness 174, 219–20, 230–1
  definitions 192
  explanation in attrition 190–3
  regression hypothesis 187–8
Matrix Language:
  as abstract frame 68
  change in matrix language 64
  contrast with dominant language 62
  contrast with unmarked choice 62
  identification in bilingual speech 59, 61–2, 66–7
  identified by finite verb 61
  identified in urban 'street' varieties 62–3
  implied hypotheses/assumptions 112
  in monolingual speech 58
  quantitative evidence 66
  relation to source language 66–7
  stability of Matrix Language 112
  structural role 60
Matrix Language Frame model, *see* MLF model
Matrix Language Principle 8
Matrix Language turnover 247–52
  incursions of structurally assigned morphemes 242–4
  relation to split languages 249
  see also composite Matrix Language; convergence
Matrix Language–Embedded Language opposition:
  absence in monolingual speech 58–9
  defined 15, 58–9
  exemplified, explicated 56–7
  reviewed 109–10
  see also asymmetry, MLF model
Matrix Language–Embedded Language roles 15, 59
  see also Matrix Language–Embedded Language opposition
Morpheme Order Principle defined 59
maximal projection defined 7
Mednyj Aleut (Copper Island Aleut):
  background 258–9
  origin 259–60, 261–5
  role of Russian 261–3
  structure 260
  two turnovers? 261–2

mental lexicon 6
  contrast in its role with phrase structure rules 163
  figure 14
  lemmas in mental lexicon 14
Michif:
  background 254–5
  Embedded Language islands 257–8
  evidence for convergence 258
  head marking 255–6
  role of French determiners 255, 257–8
  verb phrases 255, 257
Minimalist Program 121, 137
mistiming, *see* double morphology
mixed languages, *see* split languages
MLF model 10:
  how it differs from other models 13–16, 162–3
  key oppositions 15
  lexically based 14–15
  mixed constituents defined 15
  revisions in Afterword 53
  three constituent types 57–8
  see also Embedded Language; Matrix Language; Morpheme Sorting Principle; System Morpheme Principle
morpheme counting in bilingual speech 61–2
Morpheme Sorting Principle 9
  morpheme types, lack of parity 297
morphological realization patterns 96, 200–3
multimorphemic elements 305

Nairobi, Kenya 2, 45, 56, 62
nonce borrowings 154–5
North African Arabic and codeswitching 113–17, 121–7
  diagrams 123–4

optimal codeswitching constituent 108
outsider late system morpheme 75–6, 78, 88
  signalling hierarchical relationships 78
  speech error accommodation 83–4
  see also 4-M model; System Morpheme Principle

Papua New Guinea 39
  New Ireland 44, 111
predicate-argument structure 96
  how affected in attrition 200, 203–4
prepositions, classifying 72
proficiency 25, 148–9
projection of complementizer, *see* CP
pull down principle 82, 305

quantifiers 70

restructuring in attrition 231–2

semantic/pragmatic feature bundle 76, 98
  place in production model 24
South Africa townships 63, 66, 148
speech errors and the 4-M model 82–3
  division between early and late system morphemes 85
  plural affixes as early system morphemes 82
split languages:
  defined 246, 249–50, 271, 307
  historical perspective 246
  motivations 252–3
  turnover process 248–9
  see also Ma'a; Mednyj Aleut; Michif
structurally assigned elements 77–8
  minus reading for conceptually activated 76–7
  see also late system morphemes
System Morpheme Principle 59
  capturing generalizations 61
  Embedded Language elements 72
  misunderstandings 87–8
  supporting examples 88–91
system morphemes:
  borrowed with heads 42, 241–2
  new structural morphemes in frame 242–5
  see also 4-M model; early system morphemes; outsider late system morphemes

Tree Adjacency model 160

Uniform Structure Principle 8, 120, 161, 178, 305
  addenda 127, 129, 131
  applying principle to Acholi/English constructions 131–2
  theoretical antecedents 120–1
universal bifurcation in language: lexicon vs. grammar 233

Western Kenya 37, 50
word order:
  as an early system morpheme 175, 202–3
  see also Morpheme Sorting Principle

Zimbabwe 128–9, 135

Index of Authors

Abdulaziz, Mohammed 62–3
Abney, Stephen 71, 75 n.
Al-Khatib, Mahmoud 124
Allard, Réal 50–1
Alleyne, Mervyn 275
Amuzu, Evershed 64, 89, 135, 138
Anderson, Roger 188–90, 215
Annamalai, E. 135
Arends, Jacques 273–4
Aronoff, Mark 15, 182–3, 251–2
Auer, Peter 45, 47
Azuma, Shoji 139

Backus, Ad 10, 64, 69, 93–4, 98, 112, 134, 135–7, 141–3, 149, 152–3, 161
Bailey, Beryl 281
Baker, Philip 273, 279, 283–4, 286–7, 291, 309
Bakker, Peter 247, 250, 253–8, 270–1, 283
Barkhuizen, Gary 38
Barth, Frederick 40
Bavin, Edith L. 186–7
Beck, David 174–5
Belazi, H. M. 157–8
Bell, Alan 23
Beniak, Edouard 169–70, 239–40
Bentahila, Addelâli 68, 90–1, 161
Berg, Thomas 84–5
Berko-Gleason, Jean 188
Bernsten, Janice 2, 69, 93–4, 128, 135–6, 161
Bhatia, Tej K. 14, 137
Bickerton, Derek 27, 273–5, 280, 284, 309
Bickmore, Lee S. 135
Blakemore, Diane 241
Blom, Jan-Peter 11
Bock, Kathryn 77
Boeschoten, Hendrik E. 136, 180–1, 196
Bokamba, Eyamba 93
Bolinger, Dwight 71
Bolonyai, Agnes 10, 23, 46–7, 49, 54, 80, 159, 165, 167, 196, 199, 201, 204, 207–9, 225–8, 231, 252, 268, 306
Booij, Geert 86
Boumans, Louis 2, 67, 90, 109 (note), 113–17, 123, 149, 150, 151 n., 153, 161
Bourdieu, Pierre 33
Bourhis, Richard 49–51
Boyd, Sally 92
Brendemoen, Bernt 248
Brenzinger, Matthias 187
Bruyn, Adrienne 273
Budzhak-Jones, Svitlana 155

Callahan, Laura 13
Calteaux, Karen 66, 148
Campbell, Lyle 103, 174–5, 221
Caubet, Dominique 113, 115–16
Chomsky, Noam 1, 26, 79, 158
Chuluu, Üjiydiin 178
Clyne, Michael 31, 61, 142, 182, 187–8, 192, 202
Corne, Chris 286–7
Coulmas, Florian 34
Crawhall, Nigel 93, 136, 300

D'Andrea, Daniel 181
Davies, Eirlys E. 68, 90–1, 161
Dawkins R. M. 245
de Bot, Kees 164, 168, 179, 182–4, 187–8, 206
de Klerk, Vivian 38
de Rooij, Vincent 305
DeGraff, Michel 27, 273–4, 277
Denison, Norman 185, 230
Dimmendaal, Gerrit 184, 246, 248, 254–8, 263, 265
DiSciullo, Anne-Marie 157–8
Dorian, Nancy C. 49, 183, 186, 187, 213–17, 223, 230
Dowty, David 70
Drewes, A. J. 250
Ďurovič, Ludmila 218
Dussias, Paola E. 158
Dutkova, Ludmila 166–7

Edwards, John 33, 36, 40, 48, 51
El Aissati, Abderrahman 165
Emeneau, Murray B. 174
Enninger, Werner 165, 206
Essien, Okon 35
Eze, Ejike 137–8

Faraclas, Nicolas G. 273, 283, 285
Fase, Willem 37, 49
Fay, David 83
Ferguson, Charles A. 49
Fernández, Mariela 196
Finlayson, Rosalie 66, 135, 148
Fishman, Joshua A. 31, 40, 49
Forson, Barnabas 138
Fredsted, Elin 221
Freed, Barbara 187
Fuller, Janet 3, 138, 201, 209–10, 300, 303

Gal, Susan 39
Garcia, Ofelia 196

Garrett, Merrill 82–3
Gazdar, Gerald 120
Genesee, Fred 62, 295
Giles, Howard 48–51
Golovko, Evgenij V. 253, 259–63, 265, 308
Gonzo, Susan 181
Goodman, Morris 246–7, 265, 267, 271, 279
Greenberg, Joseph 32, 121, 137, 202
Grosjean, Francois 31, 160
Gross, Steven 54, 159–60, 182, 188 n., 202–3, 211–12, 216, 219–20, 223, 232, 252, 303–4
Gumperz, John 11, 45, 175–7
Gupta, Anthea F. 38, 43
Gwara, Scott 172 n.

Hagège, Claude 281
Håkansson, Gisela 168
Hakuta, Kenji 181
Halmari, Helena 126, 133, 150, 153, 157, 228
Harwood, Jake 49
Hasselmo, Nils 11, 60
Haugen, Einar 3, 36, 42, 184, 206, 234–5, 240, 242
Heath, Jeffrey 116, 176
Hill, Jane 102, 197, 246, 250
Hill, Kenneth 102, 197, 246, 250
Hlavac, Jim 64, 89–90, 149, 153, 203, 207, 217–20, 223, 232, 298, 303–4
Hock, Hans Henrich 173–8
Hoekstra, Teun 15
Holm, John 274–5, 278–80, 285, 288–9
Horrocks, Geoffrey 121, 130
Huber, Magnus 273
Huls, Erica 181
Hulsen, Madeleine 183, 206
Hyltenstam, Kenneth 39, 50, 187
Hymes, Dell 11, 246

Jackendoff, Ray 15, 21, 24, 96, 310
Jake, Janice L. 4–5, 12, 16–21, 24, 27, 54, 55, 61, 65, 68–72, 82, 95, 97–8, 125–6, 130–2, 135, 137, 145–8, 160, 194–5, 205, 216, 241, 279, 296, 300, 306
Jake, Janice L. and Myers-Scotton, Carol 4, 12, 20, 61, 70, 98, 131 n., 132, 137, 146–8
Jakobson, Roman 184, 188
Jaspaert, Koen 37, 49
Jenkins, Rebecca Sue 44, 111, 280–1, 285, 309
Johanson, Lars 240–1, 243
Jones-Jackson, Patricia A. 282
Jordens, Peter 188
Joseph, Brian 173–7
Joshi, Aravind 60

Kamwangamalu, Nkonko 93, 119
Kaufman, Dorit 169, 171, 173–5, 182–3, 191, 193, 235–7, 241–5, 247, 251, 252, 259, 265, 272
Kellerman, Eric 171
Ketelsen, Eike 221
Klavans, Judith L. 60–1
Klein, Wolfgang 95, 120
Klintborg, Staffan 104, 186
Kravin, Hanne 168, 209
Kroon, Sjaak 37, 49
Kuhberg, Heinz 165, 168, 182, 250–1
Kulick, Don 37, 39, 50

Lahlou, Moncef 115
Lambert, William E. 48, 187
Landry, Rodrigue 50–1
Langacker, Ronald W. 141
Lanza, Elizabeth 62, 295
Lefebvre, Claire 273, 279, 283, 289–91
Lehnert, Heike 209, 210
LePage, Robert 273
Levelt, Willem, J. M. 14, 23, 25, 77, 83–4, 99
Levin, Beth 96
Li, Wei 12–13
Lieberson, Stanley 31
Lumsden, John 273, 283, 289–91

Maandi, Katrin 220
Mackey, William 30–1, 33
MacSwan, Jeff 14, 64, 157–9, 162
Mahootian, Shahrzad 160
Masica, Colin 174
Mather, Patrick-Andre 272
Matras, Yaron 246–7, 270
McWhorter, John H. 273–4, 280
Meechan, Marjory, 118 n., 133, 154–6, 162
Meillet, Antoine 236
Menovščikov, Georgij A. 259, 262
Milian, Silvia 166
Miller, J. L. 160, 240
Mithun, Marianne 186
Moortgat, Michael 15
Morais, Elaine 48
Morales, Amparao 103
Mougeon, Raymond 169–70, 239–40
Mous, Maarten 247, 250–2, 266–7, 269–70
Mufwene, Salikoko 275, 277, 291
Mühlhäusler, Peter 274
Muntzel, Martha C. 221
Mustafa, Zahra 124
Muysken, Pieter 54 n., 64, 68–9, 91, 97n., 100, 116–19, 122–4, 134, 137, 142–3, 156–8, 161–2, 254, 271–4, 290
Myers-Scotton, Carol M. 2, 4, 5, 8, 10–12, 14, 16–21, 23–7, 35, 41, 46–7, 54–8, 61–2, 64, 66–72, 82, 89–90, 93–4, 97 n., 98–100, 110–11, 119, 125–6, 128, 130, 133, 135–7, 142–9, 153–4, 158, 194–5, 205, 216, 239, 240–2, 249, 266, 268, 270, 273 n., 279, 290, 296, 300, 303, 306

Nartey, Jonas 138
Nelde, Peter 4
Nichols, Johanna 256
Nicoladis, Elena 62, 295
Noonan, Michael 95
Nortier, Jacomine 113–14, 116, 147

Obler, Loraine K. 187
Obondo, Margaret Akinyi 50
Okasha, Maha 124, 146–7, 161, 241
Olshtain, Elite 206, 210
Osinde, Ken 62–3
Otheguy, Ricardo 196
Owens, Jonathan 115

Pan, Junlin 166–7
Papen, Robert A. 254–5, 257–8, 271
Paradis, Johanne 62, 295
Park, K. S. 53, 161
Pfaff, Carol 146, 223
Pinker, Steven 96
Polinsky, Maria 185–6, 201, 205, 221–4, 232
Poplack, Shana 13, 80, 87, 110, 118 n., 133, 135–9, 154–7, 158 n., 162, 170–1, 193, 240
Preston, Dennis 187, 190, 222
Pullmun, Geoffrey 120
Py, Bernard 171

Raith, Joachim 206
Rappaport, Malka 96
Rayfield, Joan Rachel 216–17
Rhodes, Richard 254
Richardson, Irvine 284
Rickford, John R. 273
Ritchie, William C. 14, 137
Roberts, Murat H. 36, 60, 241, 270
Romaine, Suzzane 134–5, 158, 170, 274
Rosenthal, D. 51
Rowlands, E. C. 279
Rubin, E. J. 157–8
Ryan, Elen B. 48, 50

Sag, Ivan 120
Saltarelli, Mario 181
Sankoff, David 20, 135, 240
Santorini, Beatrice 160
Sarullo, Paola 168
Sasse, Hans-Jürgen 185
Savič, Jelena 104
Saville-Troike, Muriel 166–7
Schmid, Monika S. 220, 222
Schmitt, Elena 13, 22, 49, 132, 183, 197–8, 200–5, 210, 213, 223–8, 252, 304, 306
Sebba, Mark 273
Seliger, Herbert 165, 179, 187, 190–1, 195
Sharwood Smith, Michael 171, 187, 190
Sherzer, Joel 174
Siegel, Jeffrey 273, 288, 309
Silva-Corvalán, Carmen 192
Simango, Sylvester Ron 135, 151
Singh, Rajendra 157
Singler, John 273, 287
Skaaden, Hanne 231
Slabbert, Sarah 63
Slater, Keith W. 174, 178
Smith, Norval 271, 274, 283
Smith-Stark, Thomas C. 174–5
Smolicz, Jerzy J. 50
Sorensen, A. P. 31
Sridhar, K. 140 n.
Sridhar, S. N. 140 n.
Stemberger, Joseph 82–4
Stenson, Nancy 139
Stroud, Christopher 39, 50
Stuart, Kevin 178
Swamy, Gopal 38
Swigart, Leigh 65, 118
Sylvain, S. 279

Tabouret-Keller, Andrée 273–4
Talmy, Leonard 96, 233, 288, 310
Tandefelt, Marika 186
Taylor, Donald M. 50
Thomason, Sarah 6, 92, 169–70, 173–4, 191, 193, 235–7, 241–5, 247, 259–60, 262–7, 272
Timm, Lenora 13
Toribio, A. J. 157–8
Trapman, Henk 188
Treffers-Daller, Jeanine 3, 60, 110, 139, 141, 150, 237–40, 244
Türker, Emel 13, 64, 90, 111, 134–6, 153, 161, 199, 200
Turner, Lorenzo 222, 282, 287 n., 307 n.

Ullman, Michael T. 17
Ury, William 11

Vago, Robert M. 187, 190
Vakhtin, Nikolai 259–61
Valois, Daniel 169
van de Mond, Anneke 181
van der Hulst, Harry 15
van Els, Theo 187
Vanniarajan, S. 135
Veenstra, Tonjes 283
Verhoeven, Nikolai 181
Verrips, M. 273

Wei, Longxing 4, 9, 70, 302
Weinreich, Uriel 48, 234, 236
Weinstein, Brian 36
Weltens, Bert 168, 183–4, 187–8, 206

Whiteley, Wilfred 246
Wilson, Robert 175–7
Winford, Donald 273
Woolford, Ellen 157

Yeok, Siew Pui 38, 43

Zentella, Ana 11, 44
Zhu, Yongshong 178, 271

Index of Languages

Note that a listing with two languages separated by a forward slash indicates an example of codeswitching in those languages *or* a discussion of codeswitching between that pair of languages. A listing of the language name otherwise just indicates a mention of the language in the text.

Acholi 95, 132
Acholi/English 91, 93, 94, 132, 133, 145
Adaŋme Akuapem 138
Afrikaans 63
Albanian 174, 185
Aleut 262–3, 264, 265
see also Atkan Aleut
Aleut/Russian 261
Algerian Arabic 116
Algerian Arabic/French 113, 115–16
Alsatian 239, 244
American English 206–7
American Finnish 221
American Finnish/English 126, 150, 228
American Norwegian 184, 235, 242
American Russian 185–6, 201, 221
American Swedish 92, 104, 186
Arabic 42–3, 49
see also Algerian Arabic; Jordanian Arabic; Moroccan Arabic; Palestinian Arabic
Arvanitika 185
Asia Minor Greek 245
Atkan Aleut 261

Baluchi 40
Bavarian (German) 212
Bella Coola 175
Berbice Dutch 277
Breton 33
Brussels Dutch 239, 244
Brussels Dutch/French 3, 139, 150
Bulgarian 174

Cameroon Pidgin 275
Canadian French 239
Cantonese 43
Central Pomo 186–7
Chichewâ 44, 135, 151
Chichewâ/English 135, 140, 151–2
Chinese 9, 38, 136, 178
see also Cantonese; Guangou dialect; Mandarin; Shanghai dialect
Chinese/English 9, 70
Congo Swahili/French 93
Cree 118, 246, 254–8, 300
Croatian 89, 174, 203, 207, 217–19, 298–9, 303
Croatian/English 64, 90, 203, 218, 298, 304

Cushitic (group) 267–8
Czech 166

Dholuo 37, 50, 62
Dutch 2, 9, 50, 64, 67, 98, 100, 113–19, 123–7, 134, 140, 142, 151–2, 181–2, 192, 197, 202, 244
see also Brussels Dutch
Dutch/English 61

East Sutherland Gaelic 183, 213–16
Egyptian 31
English 1, 9, 22, 34, 36, 38, 42–3, 45–8, 56, 58, 60, 62, 66, 81, 82–4, 88–9, 104, 125, 131, 139, 142, 144–5, 147, 169, 180–1, 184–5, 192, 196–7, 201, 210–11, 216–17, 219–20, 227, 239, 250, 301, 306
English/Finnish 168
English/Japanese 139
Engsh (sic), 62–3
Ewe/English 64, 89

Finnish 186, 209
see also American Finnish
Flemish 35
Fongbe 156, 279, 290
Fongbe/French 133, 156, 279
French 13, 31–2, 35, 37–8, 41, 48–9, 65, 68–9, 80, 90–1, 111, 113–18, 122–4, 126–7, 133, 147, 156, 170–3, 207, 239, 244, 246, 252, 255, 257–8, 268, 283, 286, 290, 305, 309
French/English 139
French/Italian/Valle d'Aosta 167
Frisian 100

Gangou dialect (Chinese) 178, 271
Gaelic, *see* Breton; Irish; Welsh
German 3, 38, 48, 81–2, 84–5, 142, 160, 168, 182, 192, 201–2, 209, 211–12, 219–21, 222, 223–4, 234, 250–1, 252, 300, 303, 306
see also Schmiedschau German
German/English, 138, 201, 210, 212
see also Bavarian; Pennsylvania German
Greek 31, 38, 50, 245
Gullah 282, 287, 307

Haitian Creole 278–9, 283, 289, 290–1, 309
Hausa 134–5

Hawaiian Creole English 288, 309
Hebrew 182–3, 210, 251
Hebrew/English 251–2
Hindi/English 137
Hungarian 46–7, 49, 80, 166–7, 198–9, 204, 208, 225–7, 306
Hungarian/English 47, 159, 165, 167, 199, 208, 225

Ibibio 35
Igbo/English 137–8
Irish Gaelic 33
Irish/English 139
Iscamtho 63
Italian 38, 48, 167, 250

Jamaican Creole 281, 289
Japanese 135–7, 139, 302
Jordanian Arabic/English 124–6

Kannada 176–7
Kikuyu 62
Kiswahili, *see* Swahili
Kurdish 50

Lango 95, 135
Latin 31–2, 172
Latvian 50
Lingala 119, 122–3, 161
Lingala/French 93, 119, 126
Luo, *see* Dholuo

Ma'a (Mbugu) 246–7, 253, 265–70, 271, 308
Macedonian 174
Malay 47–8
Malinche Mexicano 102, 197
see also Nahuatl
Maltese 250
Mandarin 38
see also Chinese
Marathi 176–7
Masai 267
Mauritian Kreol 286, 309
Media Lengua 271, 290, 293
Megleno-Rumanian 92
Mendyj Aleut (Copper Island Aleut) 249, 253, 258–65, 308
Michif 118, 246, 253–8, 259, 300
Modern Greek 174
Moroccan Arabic 113–15, 124, 164
Moroccan Arabic/Dutch 2, 67, 114–15, 116, 123, 126, 150
Moroccan Arabic/French 115, 116, 123

Nahuatl (Mexicano) 250
see also Malinche Mexicano
Navaho 167
Nigerian Pidgin English 37, 272–3, 285
North African Arabic 113, 122, 250
North African Arabic/French 113, 116, 161
Norwegian 38, 89, 90, 111, 140, 184, 199
see also American Norwegian

Old English 172

Palestinian 126
Palestinian Arabic/English 61, 146, 147, 156
Palestinian/English 124
Panjabi/English 158
Papiamentu 281, 289
Pare 266, 267
Pashto 40
Pennsylvania German 3, 22, 201, 206, 207, 209, 235, 300, 303
Persian 240
Persian/English 160
Pipil 103, 221
Polish 222
Portuguese 49
Puerto Rican Spanish 103

Quechua 137, 271

Romani 271
Romanian 174
Romansh 48
Russian 22, 23, 31, 49, 183, 197, 198, 200, 201, 203, 204, 205, 210, 223, 227, 259, 261, 262, 263, 264, 306, 308
Russian/English 13, 132, 200–1, 252

Sango 272
Schmiedschau German 211
Scottish Gaelic 186
Serbian 104, 174
Seychelles, Creole 286
Shaba Swahili 305
Shaba Swahili/French 305
Shamba(1)a 266–7
Shanghai dialect (Chinese) 37
Sheng 62
Shona 1, 130, 135–66, 142
Shona/English 87, 93, 128–9, 135, 301
Sinhala 35
Sotho 38, 66, 146
Sotho/English 66
Spanish 11, 31, 34, 36, 103, 125, 139, 159, 166, 169, 171–2, 180–1, 192, 196, 271
Spanish/English 13, 111, 126, 138, 146, 158, 166
Sranan 100
Standard Nigerian English 37
Swahili 42–3, 45, 50, 56, 58, 62–3, 80, 88, 94, 97–8, 127–8, 130–1, 132, 144–5, 267, 305

Swahili (*cont.*):
  see also Congo Swahili/French; Shaba Swahili/French
Swahili/English 2, 46, 56–7, 89, 91, 94–5, 98–9, 111, 128, 133, 135, 138, 143, 149, 151, 160, 241, 303
Swedish 60, 186
  see also American Swedish
Swiss German/Italian 82

Taiap 38
Tamil 35
Tigak 44, 111, 279–81, 283
Tok Pisin 37–8, 50, 111, 272, 279–80, 284–5, 308–9
Tsotsitaal 63
Turkish 9, 64, 89–90, 98, 111, 135–7, 140, 152, 181–2, 197, 199–200, 223, 241, 245, 250–1
Turkish/Dutch 10, 93, 98, 134, 136, 149, 152
Turkish/German 251
Turkish/Norwegian 13, 64, 89, 90, 134, 136, 200
Twi 281

Ukrainian/English 155
Urdu 176–7

Vulgar Latin 36

Warlpiri 186–7
Welsh 33
Wolof 119, 122–3, 161
Wolof/French 65, 118, 126

Xhosa 38

Yiddish 216–17
Yoruba 37, 279, 281
Yupik/Russian 260

Zulu 63, 66, 148
Zulu/English 66